Carters Dictionary of Gardening

Camellia × williamsii 'Donation'

Carters
Dictionary of Gardening

Compiled by
OLIVER DAWSON

in collaboration with the technical staff of
CARTERS TESTED SEEDS LTD

Most of the illustrations were drawn by
LESLIE GREENWOOD

HEINEMANN : LONDON

BY THE SAME AUTHOR

Planning and Planting the Small Garden
Making the Most of Your Garden
Shrubs and How to Use Them
Plants for Small Gardens
Improving Your Garden
The Herbaceous Border

ALSO PUBLISHED BY HEINEMANN

Carters Book for Gardeners
A. G. L. Hellyer

Carters Book for the Casual Gardener
Jim Mather

William Heinemann Ltd
15 Queen St, Mayfair, London W1X 8BE

LONDON   MELBOURNE   TORONTO
JOHANNESBURG   AUCKLAND

© Carters Tested Seeds Ltd 1975

First published 1975

SBN 434 17931 0

Printed in Great Britain by
Jarrold & Sons Ltd, Norwich

Foreword

All gardeners, whether professional or merely enthusiastic amateurs, need a dictionary. We feel that this is one of the best of its kind, covering as it does not only flowers, trees, and vegetables, but also giving many helpful hints on gardening practice. As well as giving a general description of each plant, details regarding height, habit, cultural requirements, and methods of propagation are included. A selection of reliable varieties is suggested in each instance.

In addition it is very beautifully illustrated. The unique drawings are the product of Britain's leading horticultural artists. They depict the plants truly and with great sensitivity.

This remarkable and informative book is presented tastefully, simply, and above all accurately, and we are confident it will enhance the bookshelves of every gardener.

Upper Dee Mills,   CARTERS TESTED SEEDS LTD
Llangollen,
Clwyd.

Author's Note

The cultural instructions given in this work relate to a temperate climate without violent extremes of temperature. In milder areas and in Mediterranean-type climates, it will be possible to grow out of doors many of the plants recommended for greenhouse cultivation, especially those for which cool conditions under glass are recommended.

It will be noted that, for convenience sake, individual fruit and vegetable entries have been dealt with under the headings 'Fruit Garden' and 'Kitchen Garden' respectively. Cross-references will also be found in correct alphabetical order.

Dahlia Redskin

ABELIA
(Caprifoliaceae)

Sun-loving shrubs related to the honeysuckles. They are fairly tender but make excellent wall shrubs for a south or west aspect. The flowers are tubular, with reddish calyces and are followed by decorative coloured sepals. Abelias make good seaside shrubs. Plant late spring or early autumn.
Cultural requirements: Any good garden soil.
Propagation: Layers in late spring; cuttings in a cold frame around midsummer.

Best garden forms

A. chinensis 5 ft (1·5 m)   China
White scented flowers, tinged with pink. Late summer.

A. floribunda 6 ft (2 m)   Mexico
Semi-evergreen tender species needing greenhouse protection in all but the warmest districts. The rosy-purple flowers are borne in drooping clusters in great abundance. Midsummer.

A. × grandiflora (*A. chinensis* × *A. uniflora*)
6 ft (2 m)   Origin unknown
A compact semi-evergreen shrub needing wall protection in colder districts. Profusion of pink-tinged white flowers, borne over a long period. Late summer to autumn.

ABELIOPHYLLUM
(Oleaceae)

A deciduous winter flowering shrub with fragrant white, yellow-centred stellate flowers on the bare branches in winter.
Cultural requirements: Any ordinary well-drained garden soil and a sunny sheltered situation.

This is a monotypic genus, the only known species being *A. distichum*, from Korea, growing about 3 ft (1 m) tall with scented white pink-tinged flowers on the bare stems. Late winter.

ABIES
(Pinaceae) Silver Fir

Evergreen coniferous trees of pyramidal habit, some reaching great heights. Many species and varieties make handsome specimen trees. The foliage (needles) is flattened and linear. The trees bear erect cylindrical cones, bluish-purple when young in a number of species. Slow growing at first, but very vigorous once established.

Cultural requirements: Moist well-drained sandy soil and an open situation. Will not thrive on shallow chalky soils.
Propagation: From seed under glass in heat in early spring or outdoors later.

A. alba (syn. *A. pectinata*) 150 ft (45 m)
European Silver Fir   C. and S. Europe
Handsome tree, susceptible to late frosts and therefore unsuitable for colder districts.

A. amabilis
up to 250 ft (75 m)   Western N. America
Large tree with silvery-white bark and aromatic foliage.

A. balsamea up to 75 ft (22 m)
Balsam Fir or Balm of Gilead   N. America
Medium-sized tree with dark green aromatic foliage. 'Hudsonia' (syn. 'Nana') is an attractive dwarf cultivar.

A. cephalonica up to 120 ft (36 m)   Greece
This is one of the best firs for chalky soils. 'Nana' is an attractive dwarf cultivar.

A. concolor up to 150 ft (45 m)   S.W. U.S.A.
Shapely tree, slow growing at first. 'Candicans' is a form with attractively silvered foliage. 'Glauca Compacta', one of the finest dwarf firs, does not exceed 3 ft (1 m) in height and reaches this only after many years.

A. delavayi up to 70 ft (21 m)
Chinese Silver Fir   W. China
A tree with glaucous foliage and cinnamon-brown stems. 'Forrestii' is a cultivar of more modest dimensions; 'Nana' is a dwarf, slow growing form.

A. grandis up to 200 ft (60 m)   California
A fast growing tall species that needs moist, well-drained soil conditions. It is fairly lime-tolerant.

A. magnifica up to 120 ft (36 m)
Californian Red Fir   U.S.A.
A slender tree of conical habit with long grey-green needles. 'Glauca' has leaves of a deep blue-green; 'Nana' is an attractive dwarf form. This species is not suitable for chalky soils.

A. pinsapo up to 100 ft (30 m)
Spanish Fir   Spain
A medium to large conifer and one of the best firs for chalky soils. 'Aurea', a dwarf cultivar, and 'Glauca', a large tree, have golden-yellow and blue-grey foliage respectively.

ABUTILON
(Malvaceae)

The abutilons form a group of half-hardy herbaceous plants and shrubs, some of which can be grown outdoors in milder districts. The more tender forms are useful as 'dot' or focal plants in summer bedding schemes.

Cultural requirements: A rich medium loam and a south wall or sunny greenhouse with a minimum winter temperature of not less than 50 °F (10 °C). The plants require plenty of water in spring and summer but much less in autumn and winter.

Propagation: From seed under glass in spring. Seedlings should be potted on as the roots get overcrowded or until they are ready for planting out.

Good garden forms

A. megapotamicum up to 10 ft (3 m)　　　Brazil
A small to medium shrub, excellent for a south wall in favoured districts. It bears striking yellow and scarlet pendent flowers. 'Variegatum' has leaves conspicuously splashed with yellow and makes a good plant for summer bedding schemes. Summer and autumn.

A. vitifolium up to 10 ft (3 m)　　　Chile
A large shrub for a sheltered position or a warm wall. Handsome vine-like leaves and mauve or white mallow-type flowers.

A. vitifolium is fairly short lived, but replacements are easy to raise from seed. 'Veronica Tennant' is a good named form. Late spring.

ACACIA
(Leguminosae)

Evergreen flowering shrubs or small trees for the greenhouse. Some species are hardy outdoors in more favoured districts.

Cultural requirements: John Innes No. 2 or similar potting compost. Water freely in spring and summer, sparingly for rest of year. Minimum temperature 50 °F (10 °C).

Propagation: From seed under glass in heat in spring; by cuttings in heat in summer.

A. armata up to 10 ft (3 m)
Kangaroo Thorn　　　Australia
Small-leaved prickly bush of dense habit with masses of fluffy yellow globular flowers. This kind of flower is typical of the acacias. Winter.

A. baileyana up to 15 ft (4·5 m)　　　Australia
Glaucous foliage and yellow flowers. Late winter.

A. dealbata 10 ft (3 m)
Silver Wattle or Mimosa　　　Australia
One of the hardier species that can be grown outdoors in a sunny sheltered situation in more favoured districts, this is the florists' mimosa,
with its attractive fluffy yellow flowers. Early spring.

A. longifolia up to 15 ft (4·5 m)　　　Australia
This is another of the hardier species, with needle-like foliage and pale yellow flowers. Spring.

ACAENA
(Rosaceae)

Evergreen hardy perennials, useful in the rock garden, in crevices in paving and on the tops of dry walls. The small rose-like leaves and the crimson burrs that follow their somewhat uninteresting flowers constitute their main decorative appeal. They are dense carpeters, useful as ground cover.

Cultural requirements: Light well-drained soil and a sunny or partly shaded situation.

Propagation: From seed under glass in spring; by cuttings in a cold frame in summer; division in spring or autumn.

A. × Blue Haze 9 in. (22 cm)　　　Garden origin
Supposed hybrid form with low hummocks of blue-grey ferny foliage and red stems. Late summer.

A. buchananii 2 in. (5 cm)　　　New Zealand
Blue-grey leaves and attractive red spiny burrs. Late summer.

A. inermis 2 in. (5 cm)　　　New Zealand
Bronzy-green leaves and brown spineless burrs. Late summer.

A. microphylla 2 in. (5 cm)　　　New Zealand
Good carpeting plant, with bronzy foliage studded with masses of scarlet burrs. Late summer.

ACANTHUS
(Acanthaceae) Bear's Breeches

Hardy perennials with handsome semi-evergreen foliage. Plants of great architectural value in the garden.

Cultural requirements: *A. mollis*, any good garden soil and a sunny or partly shaded situation. *A. spinosus* needs a sunny situation in well-drained soil and a position sheltered from cold winds.

Propagation: From seed under glass in heat in spring; by root cuttings or division.

A. mollis 3 ft (1 m)　　　Italy
Leaves large and narrowly ovate, with fluted margins. Spikes of white or rosy-lilac flowers. Mid to late summer.

A. spinosus 3 ft (1 m)　　　S. Europe
Dark green, glossy leaves, deeply cut with spiny edges. Handsome spikes of white or purple flowers with attractive green bracts. Mid to late summer.

ACER
(Aceraceae) Maple

Extensive group of ornamental trees grown primarily for the beauty of their foliage. Some do not exceed shrub-like proportions. The lobed palmate leaves of many kinds provide striking autumn colour. All have winged fruits.

Cultural requirements: Well-drained loam. With the exception of the Japanese maples, whose lacy foliage needs protection from wind and strong sunlight, any open position will suit them.

Propagation: From seed sown in autumn; by layering, grafting, or budding according to species.

A. campestre up to 70 ft (21 m)
Field Maple   Europe and W. Asia
This tree, native to Britain, is widely used as a hedging plant. It clips well and the small lobed leaves turn a clear yellow in autumn.

A. ginnala up to 20 ft (6 m)   China and Japan
Large shrub or small tree of bushy habit. The leaves, which are three lobed, colour to brilliant shades of orange and crimson in autumn.

A. griseum up to 30 ft (9 m)
Paperbark Maple   China
Trifoliate leaves that colour brilliantly in autumn. Old bark peels to reveal polished trunk and stems of rich mahogany-red.

A. negundo up to 40 ft (12 m)
Box Elder   N. America
Makes an excellent specimen tree of medium size for smaller gardens. 'Elegans', with golden variegation and 'Variegatum', with distinctive white variegation are the two most outstanding forms.

A. palmatum up to 10 ft (3 m)
Japanese Maple   Japan
These are very small trees of shrub-like habit and dimensions grown for the beauty of their finely cut, lacy foliage. They need shelter from cold winds and prefer a lime-free soil. Most have striking autumn leaf tints.

Some of the best cultivars are found in the 'Dissectum' group whose leaves are even more finely divided into as many as nine lobes. These include 'Atropurpureum', 'Palmatifidum', 'Septemlobum', and what is probably the most brilliantly coloured of all in autumn, 'Heptalobum Osakazuki'.

A. platanoides up to 80 ft (24 m)
Norway Maple   Europe
Vigorous and rapid growing trees, suitable only for larger gardens. 'Crimson King' (syn. 'Goldsworth Purple') is a striking cultivar with deep wine-purple foliage.

A. pseudoplatanus up to 80 ft (24 m)
Sycamore   Europe and W. Asia
Mainly too large for garden planting but there are several cultivars suitable for this purpose including 'Brilliantissimum', with brilliant coral-pink spring foliage; 'Purpureum' and 'Spathii', both with deep purple leaves.

A. rubrum 80–100 ft (24–30 m)
Red Maple   N. America
Fine specimen tree with rounded head and brilliant flame-coloured autumn tints. 'Schlesingeri' is the best form

ACHILLEA
(Compositae) Yarrow or Milfoil

Hardy perennials of various heights suitable for border and rock gardens.

Cultural requirements: Any garden soil and a sunny situation.

Propagation: From seed outdoors in spring or early summer; by division in spring or autumn.

A. filipendulina 3 ft (1 m)   Caucasus
Greyish, feathery foliage and flat plate-like heads of flower. 'Coronation Gold', mustard-yellow; 'Gold Plate', golden-yellow; and 'Moonshine', sulphur-yellow are all good cultivars. Summer.

A. ptarmica 3 ft (1 m) Sneezewort   Europe
Clusters of small white button flowers. 'The Pearl' and 'Perry's White' are good forms. Summer.

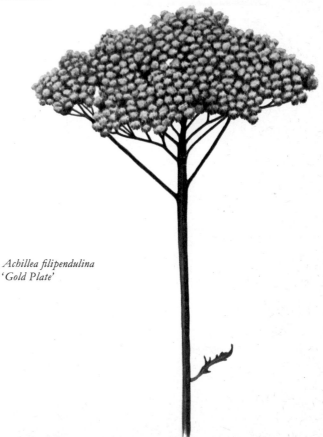

Achillea filipendulina
'Gold Plate'

ACIDANTHERA
(Iridaceae)

Tender autumn flowering bulbous plants with sweetly scented gladiolus-like flowers.

Cultural requirements: Light well-drained soil, rich in humus for outdoor cultivation. Bulbs should be lifted and stored for winter.

A. bicolor murielae (syn. *Gladiolus murielae*)
1½ ft (45 cm)   Ethiopia
Large white orchid-like flowers, 2 in. (5 cm) across, borne in spikes. They are very sweetly scented. Autumn.

ACONITUM
(Ranunculaceae) Monkshood

Handsome hardy perennials with attractive helmet-type flowers which are, however, very poisonous, which makes it a plant to be avoided where young children use the garden.

Cultural requirements: Cool moist soil and a partly shaded situation but can be grown in full sun provided the roots are not allowed to dry out in summer.

Propagation: From seed outdoors in spring; by division.

A. napellus up to 6 ft (2 m)   Europe and Asia
The most widely grown species, with deeply cut leaves that resemble those of a delphinium and blue or purple helmet flowers. Good forms include 'Barker's Variety', deep violet; 'Bressingham Spire', violet-blue; and 'Spark's Variety', deep violet-blue. 'Blue Sceptre' is an attractive blue and white bicolor. Late summer to autumn.

ACORUS
(Araceae)

Hardy aquatics for marginal planting.

Cultural requirements: Heavy soil and a situation at the edges of a pool or stream.

A. calamus 3 ft (1 m)
Sweet Flag   Europe and Asia
Leaves and yellow flowers like those of the flag irises. All parts of the plants are aromatic. Late spring.

A. gramineus 1 ft (30 cm)
Prostrate species with grassy leaves, suitable for a water feature in the rock garden. 'Variegatus' has leaves striped with white.

ACROCLINIUM – see *Helipterum*

ACTINIDIA
(Actinidiaceae)

Hardy climbing shrubs, deciduous, self-clinging. Not completely hardy in colder districts.

Cultural requirements: Well-drained soil and a sunny wall or border.

Propagation: By layers in autumn.

A. chinensis up to 30 ft (9 m)   China
A very vigorous climber with attractive foliage. The young leaves and stems are covered with a reddish down. Small cream flowers and cinnamon-brown fruits with green fleshy insides, marketed commercially as Chinese Gooseberries and Kiwi Fruit.

A. kolomikta up to 10 ft (3 m)   China and Japan
Grown primarily for its curiously marked foliage which is a medley of green and pink. The greenish-white scented flowers are comparatively insignificant.

ADIANTUM
(Polypodiaceae) Maidenhair Fern

A race of lovely ferns with finely cut foliage, mostly too tender for outdoor cultivation, requiring a heated greenhouse.

Cultural requirements: For greenhouse species, John Innes No. 2 or similar compost. Outdoor cultivation in pockets of equal parts of peat and good garden soil in a shady but sheltered situation.

Propagation: From spores under glass.

A. capillus-veneris
6 in. (15 cm)   Europe, including British Isles
This species is one of the hardiest and can be grown outside in mild districts. The variety *imbricatum* is particularly beautiful.

A. pedatum 1 ft (30 cm)   N. America
Another comparatively hardy species, with lacy fronds on long wiry stems.

A. venustum 6 in. (15 cm)   Himalayas
A more tender species with pale green lacy fronds. Unsuitable for outdoor cultivation in any but the most favoured districts.

ADONIS
(Ranunculaceae)

Hardy annual and perennial plants with feathery, fennel-like foliage and crimson, white or yellow flowers.

Cultural requirements: Any good garden soil in an open position in border or rock garden, according to species.

Propagation: Annuals from seed in spring; perennials from seed or by division in spring or autumn.

Perennial species

A. amurensis 1 ft (30 cm)   China
Yellow globular flowers 2–3 in. (5–8 cm) in diameter, feathery foliage. Early spring.

A. vernalis 1½ ft (45 cm)   S. Europe
Yellow flowers, feathery foliage. Spring.

Annual species

A. aestivalis 1 ft (30 cm)   S. Europe
Crimson cup-shaped flowers, feathery foliage. Mid to late summer.

A. autumnalis 2 ft (60 cm)
Pheasant's Eye   Europe, including British Isles
Scarlet flowers. Autumn.

AEONIUM
(Crassulaceae)

A genus of succulent plants related to the sempervivums, or house leeks, for greenhouse cultivation.
Cultural requirements: Greenhouse temperature of not less than 40 °F (4 °C) in winter. Plant in well-drained, gritty compost, grow in full sun, watering sparingly during winter.
Propagation: Seed sown under glass in heat during spring; leaf or shoot cuttings in summer; division in spring.

A. arboreum 3 ft (1 m)   Mediterranean
Rosettes of fleshy leaves 6 in. (15 cm) in diameter, yellow flowers. Winter.

A. tabulaeforme
1 ft (30 cm)   Madeira and Canary Islands
Large rosettes of fleshy foliage, pale yellow flowers. Late summer.

AESCULUS
(Hippocastanaceae)

Of this group, only the small pink- and red-flowered forms, together with the shrubby *A. parviflora*, are suitable for the medium-sized garden. The former make splendid ornamental trees, their candle-like flower spikes are a magnificent sight in late spring.
Cultural requirements: Any good garden soil, including heavy clay.
Propagation: Seed, cuttings, or grafting.

A. × carnea (*A. hippocastanum* × *A. pavia*)
up to 40 ft (12 m)   Garden origin
Hybrid form of the above with rose-pink flower spikes up to 8 in. (20 cm) in length. 'Briotii', more compact and with deeper coloured flowers, is the best garden form. Late spring.

A. hippocastanum up to 100 ft (30 m)
Horse Chestnut   S.E. Europe
A magnificent flowering tree for the really large garden with divided palmate leaves and masses of white flower spikes. These are followed by the polished mahogany nuts – i.e. conkers. Late spring.

A. parviflora 8 ft (2·5 m)   S.E. U.S.A.
Shrub of spreading habit, valuable for its late flowering period. Delicate spikes of white horse chestnut flowers 1 ft (30 cm) long. Late summer.

AETHIONEMA
(Cruciferae) Stone Cress

Free-flowering evergreen perennials of prostrate habit suitable for the rock garden or dry walls.
Cultural requirements: Light well-drained soil and a sunny situation.
Propagation: From cuttings in summer.

A. grandiflorum 1 ft (30 cm)
Persian Candytuft   Persia
Glaucous foliage, rosy-pink flowers. Mid to late summer.

A. pulchellum 6 in. (15 cm)   Armenia
Trailing species with blue-grey leaves and pink flowers. Spring.

A. × Warley Rose 6 in. (15 cm)   Garden origin
The best garden form, making dense cushions of glaucous foliage and clusters of vivid rose-pink blooms over a long period. Late spring to midsummer.

AFRICAN VIOLET – see Saintpaulia

AGAPANTHUS
(Liliaceae) African Lily

South African perennials suitable for tubs or other containers. In milder districts, they make excellent border plants.
Cultural requirements: For tub culture, a mixture of three parts loam, one part well-rotted manure or compost, one part leafmould or peat and half part of sand makes a suitable growing medium. Outdoors, a well-drained soil and a sunny situation. Water freely in summer, sparingly in winter.
Propagation: Division in spring.

A. africanus (syns. *A. orientalis*, *A. umbellatus*)
1½ ft (45 cm)   S. Africa
Strap-like leaves surmounted by handsome globular heads of deep blue flowers. Not completely hardy, except in milder districts and requires greenhouse protection in winter. Late summer.

A. campanulatus 1½ ft (45 cm)   S. Africa
Hardier than the above with sky-blue flowers. The white form 'Albus' is very attractive. Late summer.

A. Headbourne Hybrids
2–3 ft (60 cm–1 m)   Garden origin
A race of hardy hybrids raised in Hampshire by the Hon. Lewis Palmer from species native to South Africa. Colours range from palest blue to deep violet. Late summer.

AGAVE
(Amaryllidaceae)

Handsome greenhouse plants with fleshy, sometimes spiny foliage and spikes of greenish-yellow or scarlet tubular flowers. The hardier species, such as *A. americana*, make good tub plants for a summer display outdoors.

Cultural requirements: Planting medium of three parts loam to one part well-rotted manure or compost, one part peat or leafmould and quarter part sharp sand. Water freely in summer, but withhold supplies almost completely in winter.

Propagation: From suckers which form at base of plants, dibbed into pots containing equal parts peat and sand.

A. americana flower stems, up to 30 ft (9 m)
Century Plant   America
This plant gets its popular name from the belief that it flowered only once every 100 years. This is not true, although flowering is a rare occurrence in Britain. The cultivars 'Picta' and 'Variegata' have attractively variegated leaves up to 3 ft (1 m) long.

A. filamentosa 10 ft (3 m)   Mexico
A species whose leaf margins are furnished with long threads.

In addition to these there are many other species not in general garden cultivation.

AGERATUM
(Compositae)

Half-hardy annuals widely used for summer bedding and as edging plants. Very free flowering over a long period. Many new and improved hybrid forms including a number of outstanding F_1 hybrids.

Cultural requirements: Any well-drained open soil and a sunny situation suits them. They are not partial to stiff heavy clay soils.

Propagation: From seed sown in spring under glass in a warm greenhouse to provide plants that go out when danger of frost is past.

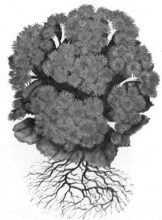

Ageratum 'Blue Mink'

Good garden forms

'Blue Blazer' F_1 hybrid 6 in. (15 cm), early with powder-blue flowers;
'Blue Ball' 8 in. (20 cm), a compact grower with rich blue flowers. First rate for edging;
'Blue Mink' 9 in. (22 cm), a popular form with delicate blue flowers in large clusters on compact plants;
'North Sea' F_1 hybrid 6 in. (15 cm), flowers an unusual shade of reddish-violet opening to a rosy-mauve;
'White Cushion' 6 in. (15 cm), compact hummocks covered in fluffy white flowers. Best of the whites. Summer.

AILANTHUS
(Simarubaceae)

Beautiful ornamental trees with pinnate ash-like foliage up to 3 ft (1 m) in length. Good specimen trees, especially valuable for town planting.

Cultural requirements: Soil rich in humus and a fairly sheltered position.

Propagation: By root cuttings or from suckers which appear around parent plant.

A. altissima 60 ft (18 m) Tree of Heaven   China
Large deciduous tree with handsome foliage suitable as a lawn specimen for larger gardens.

A. vilmoriniana 60 ft (18 m)   China
Very similar in appearance to *altissima*, but with hairier stems and leaves.

AJUGA
(Labiatae) Bugle

Creeping plants that make first rate ground cover in the border. Vigorous and rapid spreading. Can take over unless controlled.

Cultural requirements: Any ordinary garden soil.

Propagation: Division in spring or autumn.

A. reptans
6 in. (15 cm)   Europe, including British Isles
The type plant is a native of Britain growing in damp situations and on the margins of streams. Spikes of blue flowers are freely borne. There are several attractive cultivars: 'Atropurpurea', with bronzy-purple leaves; 'Multicolor' (syn. 'Rainbow'), whose leaves are a medley of green, bronze, yellow, and pink; and 'Variegata', with grey-green and cream foliage.

The hybrid, *genevensis × reptans* is equally useful as ground cover with downy leaves and pale blue flowers. Late spring to summer.

AKEBIA
(Lardizabalaceae)

Vigorous, self-clinging twining shrubs with handsome foliage and dull red-purple scented flowers

followed, in favourable seasons, by decorative purple sausage-shaped fruits.
Cultural requirements: Most garden soils and a position in sun or shade.
Propagation: From cuttings under glass in summer.

A. quinata up to 30 ft (9 m)   China and Japan
Leaves made up of five obovate leaflets, fragrant reddish-purple flowers, dark purple fruits. Spring.

A. trifoliata (syn. *A. lobata*)
up to 30 ft (9 m)   China and Japan
The leaves of this species are made up of three leaflets. Flowers are a darker purple, fruits pale mauve. Spring.

ALCHEMILLA
(Rosaceae)
Excellent ground cover plants for either sun or partial shade.
Cultural requirements: Any moist well-drained soil.
Propagation: Seed or division.

A. mollis 1½ ft (45 cm)
Lady's Mantle   S.E. Europe
Rounded grey-green silky leaves, dainty sprays of lime-green flowers, much sought after by flower arrangers. Seeds itself freely. Summer.

ALKANET – see *Anchusa*

ALLIUM
(Amaryllidaceae)
Decorative bulbous plants, members of the onion family grown for the beauty of their flowers. Their long lasting qualities make them useful for cutting.
Cultural requirements: Any ordinary well-drained soil and a sunny situation. Plant in late autumn.
Propagation: Seed or offsets.

A. albopilosum 2 ft (60 cm)   C. Asia
Large heads of lilac flowers, good for cutting. Midsummer.

A. azureum (syn. *A. caeruleum*)
2 ft (60 cm)   C. Asia
Globular heads of sky-blue flowers. Midsummer.

A. giganteum 4 ft (1·2 m)   C. Asia
Very tall and handsome species with large lilac flower heads. Summer.

A. moly 1 ft (30 cm)   S.W. Europe
Popular species with broad grey leaves and umbels of yellow flowers. Midsummer.

A. ostrowskianum 6 in. (15 cm)   S.E. U.S.A.
Dainty species for the rock garden with masses of carmine-pink flowers. Midsummer.

A. rosenbachianum 3 ft (1 m)   C. Asia
This taller species bears large heads of lilac-purple flowers on stout stems. Early summer.

ALNUS
(Betulaceae) Alder
The alders are a race of trees useful for their tolerance of really damp soils. The main garden forms are varieties of the common alder, *A. glutinosa* and the grey alder, *A. incana*.
Cultural requirements: Any type of soil except shallow over chalk. Damp situation.
Propagation: Seed, suckers, or hardwood cuttings

A. glutinosa up to 100 ft (30 m) Common Alder
Europe, including British Isles,
W. Asia, and N. Africa
Small to medium-sized trees with yellow catkins in spring. The golden-leaved form 'Aurea' makes an attractive garden specimen.

A. incana up to 80 ft (24 m)
Grey Alder   Europe and N. America
Tree or large shrub whose leaves are grey on reverse. 'Aurea' has soft grey-green foliage, orange twigs, and reddish catkins. Fairly upright in habit.

ALOE
(Liliaceae)
Tender evergreen succulents for the cool greenhouse or for outdoors in tubs and pots in a sheltered situation during summer, perennial.
Cultural requirements: John Innes No. 2 or similar potting compost. Water moderately during summer, very sparingly for rest of year. Minimum winter temperature 45 °F (7 °C).
Propagation: By division or offsets.

A. variegata 1 ft (30 cm)
Partridge-breasted Aloe   S. Africa
This is the best known species, with triangular leaves, banded with dark green and white. The leaves are prickly and the red flowers are borne in loose spikes. It makes a good house plant. Late spring.

ALONSOA
(Scrophulariaceae) Mask Flower
Beautiful half-hardy annuals, some greenhouse plants, others used for summer bedding. They also make good pot plants.
Cultural requirements: For pot culture: John Innes No. 2 or similar compost. Outdoors: Any good garden soil and a sunny sheltered situation.
Propagation: From seed under glass in heat in spring. The seed of the hardier species can be sown outdoors when danger of frost is past.

A. linifolia
2 ft (60 cm)   Peru
Sprays of scarlet flowers on dainty stems.
Summer.

A. warscewiczii
2 ft (60 cm)   Peru
Bright green leaves and orange-scarlet flowers.
Summer.

ALOPECURUS
(Gramineae)
Hardy perennial grasses of decorative value in the
garden and for drying for winter arrangements.
Cultural requirements: Light well-drained soil
and a sunny situation.
Propagation: From seed and by division, in
spring.

A. pratensis 3 ft (1 m)
Meadow Foxtail   Europe
'Aureo-variegatus' ('Foliis Variegatis'), a cultivar
whose narrow leaves are striped with yellow, is
the showiest form. Summer.

ALPINE PLANTS – see Rock Gardens

ALSTROEMERIA
(Amaryllidaceae)
Tuberous-rooted perennials with striking umbels
of striped and spotted lily-like flowers.
Cultural requirements: Moist rich soil and a
sunny well-drained situation. Can also be grown
in pots in a cool greenhouse.
Propagation: Seed under glass in spring; root
division in autumn. Protect young growths from
spring frosts.

A. aurantiaca
3 ft (1 m)   Chile
Orange flowers spotted with brown in loose
clusters. Narrow greyish leaves. Summer.

A. Ligtu Hybrids. Crosses of *A. ligtu* and *A.
haemantha* have produced this lovely hybrid strain
with flowers ranging in colour from cream
through pink to flame. Summer.

ALTHAEA
(Malvaceae) Hollyhock
A race of perennials that include the hollyhock,
A. rosea and the native marsh mallow, *A.
officinalis*. Hollyhocks are less widely grown today
owing to their susceptibility to hollyhock rust,
Puccinia malvacearum, but this can be kept under
control by fungicidal sprays, avoiding overcrowding of the plants, and treating as annuals.
Cultural requirements: A good rich soil, deeply
dug and rich in humus. Plenty of water in dry
weather. Cut down close to soil level after
flowering.

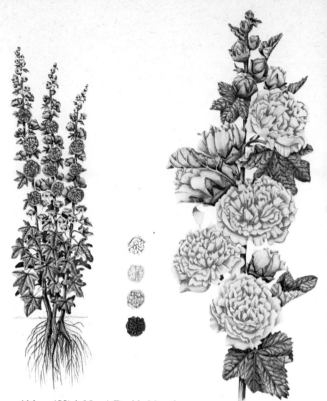

*Althaea 'High Noon' Double Mixed
(Hollyhock) showing colours available*

Propagation: From seed sown in late spring or
summer, divisions, or cuttings. Treated like half-
hardy annuals and sown under glass early in the
year, the resulting plants will produce flowers in
their first season.

Good cultivars
'Silver Puffs', double blush-pink flowers;
'Summer Carnival', a strain containing red, pink,
yellow, and white; and 'Triumph Supreme',
early flowering strain that contains a wide range
of coloured double fringed flowers and is very
rust resistant.

ALYSSUM
(Cruciferae) Madwort
Dwarf and compact hardy annual and perennial
plants widely used in summer bedding and the
rock garden.
Cultural requirements: Any soil provided it is
well-drained, and an open sunny position.
Propagation: Annual cultivars from seed; perennial kinds seed and cuttings.

A. maritimum (syn. *Lobularia maritima*)
Sweet Alyssum
One of the most popular summer bedding plants
used for edging, with massed clusters of fragrant
white flowers. 'Little Dorrit', 'Minimum', and
'Snow Carpet' are good white varieties; 'Rosie
O'Day' and 'Violet Queen' have lilac-pink and
violet flowers respectively. Summer.

A. saxatile 9 in. (22 cm)
Rock Madwort   C. and S. Europe
Shrubby plant ideally suited for the rock garden;
masses of golden-yellow flowers. Good named
cultivars include 'Citrinum', lemon-yellow and
'Flore Pleno', a handsome double yellow. Late
spring.

A. montanum 4 in. (10 cm)
Mountain Gold   Europe
This dwarf alpine species has grey foliage and
bright yellow flowers. Midsummer.

AMARANTHUS
(Amaranthaceae)
Hardy and half-hardy annuals. The former are
summer flowering, the latter handsome foliage
plants used in the greenhouse and for summer
bedding.
Cultural requirements: Any ordinary garden
soil and a sunny situation.
Propagation: Hardy forms: From seed sown
outdoors in spring. Half-hardy species: From
seed sown in heat in spring.

A. caudatus 3 ft (1 m)
Love-Lies-Bleeding   Tropics
The flowers of this hardy annual form are long,
drooping, and tassel-like, great favourites with
the flower arrangers. The type plant has crimson
flowers, there is also a form with lime-green
tassels. Midsummer.

A. hypochondriacus 3 ft (1 m)
Prince's Feather   Tropics
Good border plant with upright flower spikes of
a deep crimson. Hardy annual. Summer.

A. tricolor 2–3 ft (60 cm–1 m)   India
Half-hardy annual cultivated for the beauty of its
colourful foliage in striking shades of green,
scarlet, and yellow. The cultivar 'Illumination'
has bronzy leaves red and yellow at their centres.

AMARYLLIS
(Amaryllidaceae)
These bulbous plants are not completely hardy,
but can be grown outdoors at the foot of a warm
sunny wall. See also *Hippeastrum*.
Cultural requirements: Outdoors: Well-drained
soil at the foot of a south wall. Plant bulbs 9 in.
(22 cm) deep in autumn. For pot culture under
glass, equal parts loam, leafmould, and well-
rotted manure or compost.
Propagation: Offsets or seed. Plants from seed,
sown in heat under glass, should flower in their
third year from sowing.

A. belladonna 18 in. (45 cm)
Belladonna Lily   S. Africa
Large heads of pale pink trumpet flowers in loose
clusters appear before the new leaves. Autumn.

Alyssum 'Violet Queen'

Alyssum 'Snow Carpet'

Alyssum saxatile 'Gold Dust'

AMELANCHIER
(Rosaceae) Snowy Mespilus or June Berry
Hardy small trees or shrubs of great decorative value for their flowers in spring and leaf colouring in autumn.
Cultural requirements: Any well-drained lime-free soil and an open situation.
Propagation: Seed, layers, or rooted offsets.

A. canadensis up to 25 ft (8 m)
Shadbush   N. America
Medium-sized shrub with erect stems and suckering habit, often confused with *A. laevis* and with similar flowers and foliage. Spring.

A. laevis 20 ft (6 m)   N. America
A small and shapely tree with masses of white blossom in spring and vivid autumn leaf colour. Also obtainable in bush form. Spring.

AMPELOPSIS – see *Vitis*

AMYGDALUS – see *Prunus*

ANANAS
(Bromeliaceae) Pineapple
Evergreen perennial plants, with pineapple fruits for the warm greenhouse.
Cultural requirements: John Innes No. 2 or similar potting compost, with the addition of well-rotted manure, grit, and sterilized bonemeal. Minimum winter temperature 65 °F (18 °C). Water freely in summer, sparingly in winter. Withhold water while fruit is ripening.
Propagation: By suckers or fruit crowns under glass in heat in spring.

A. comosus 3 ft (1 m)   Brazil
In addition to the pineapple grown commercially for its fruit, this species includes cultivars such as 'Variegatus', with striped foliage and 'Porteanus', with leaves banded with yellow.

ANAPHALIS
(Compositae)
Hardy perennials with grey foliage and creamy-white papery 'everlasting' flowers that dry well for winter arrangements.
Cultural requirements: Any good garden soil and a sunny open situation.
Propagation: From seed outdoors in spring; by division in spring or autumn.

A. cinnamomea 2 ft (60 cm)   China and Japan
Long grey leaves, white on their undersides and clusters of pearly-white flowers. Sometimes incorrectly described as *A. yedoensis*. Summer.

A. triplinervis 1½ ft (45 cm)   Tibet
Similar to but shorter and more compact than the former species. The silvery leaves are prominently veined. Late summer.

ANCHOR PLANT – see *Colletia*

ANCHUSA
(Boraginaceae) Alkanet
Hardy perennials and biennials with hairy stems and intensely blue flowers.
Cultural requirements: Well-drained fertile soil and a sunny situation.
Propagation: Perennial kinds: From seed, by root cuttings or division. Biennials: From seed.

A. angustissima (syn. *A. caespitosa*)
1 ft (30 cm)   Crete
Dwarf compact species, suitable for edging, with masses of gentian-blue flowers. Perennial. Early summer.

A. azurea (syn. *A. italica*)
up to 5 ft (1·5 m)   Caucasus
The vivid blue flowers of this perennial species provide a striking effect when plants are massed in large groups. Good named cultivars include 'Little John', a dwarf form; 'Loddon Royalist', large gentian-blue flowers; 'Morning Glory', deep blue; and 'Opal', a paler sky-blue. Summer.

ANDROMEDA
(Ericaceae)
A genus of low growing twiggy shrubs with narrow leaves and pendent clusters of urn-shaped flowers.
Cultural requirements: Lime-free moist soil or damp acid peat. Shady situation.
Propagation: From seed sown in peat in a cold frame in spring; by layers in autumn.

A. polifolia 1 ft (30 cm) Bog Rosemary
              Europe, N. Asia, and N. America
Dwarf shrub, also native to some parts of Britain. Glaucous green leaves, clusters of pink flowers. There are some good cultivars, including 'Compacta', 'Major', and 'Minima', the last named a prostrate form with darker green leaves, useful in the rock garden. Early summer.

ANDROSACE
(Primulaceae) Rock Jessamine
An extensive group of choice alpine plants needing full sun and good drainage. All are hardy perennials.
Cultural requirements: Light sandy soil to which plenty of gritty material has been added to assist drainage. Some varieties, better suited to the alpine house, should be grown in a gritty compost.
Propagation: From seed under glass in spring; by cuttings or division in spring.

A. carnea 2 in. (5 cm)   Europe
Green rosettes of leaves, topped by pink flowers with a yellow eye.

A. lanuginosa 3 in. (8 cm) Himalayas
Silver rosettes with pale pink flowers borne in clusters and having a darker eye. Makes a useful carpeting plant. Summer.

A. sarmentosa 4 in. (10 cm) Himalayas
Silver hairy rosettes that form dense mats. Soft pink flowers in rounded clusters. Early summer.

A. villosa 3 in. (8 cm) Europe
Dense mats of hairy rosettes. The flowers are white with a golden eye. A good species for the alpine house. Outdoors, the plants need protection from an excess of moisture in winter. Early summer.

ANEMONE
(Ranunculaceae) Windflower
The genus contains hardy tuberous- and fibrous-rooted plants.
Cultural requirements: Any good garden soil rich in humus; sunny or partly shaded situation.
Propagation: Herbaceous species: Seed, division, or cuttings; tuberous-rooted kinds, from seed sown in early spring in cold frame.

A. blanda 6 in. (15 cm) Asia Minor
Delightful star flowers up to 2 in. (5 cm) across; white, shades of pink or blue. Good named forms include 'Blue Pearl', true blue; 'Charmer', silvery-pink; 'Radar', rosy-purple; and 'White Splendour'. Early spring.

A. coronaria up to 1 ft (30 cm)
Poppy Anemone E. Mediterranean
The popular winter cut flower of the florists in a wide range of colours including pinks, reds, blues, and purples. Tubers can be planted in autumn or early spring to give a long flowering season. 'St Brigid' and 'De Caen' are two popular strains and there are, as well, a number of good cultivars in single colours.

A. elegans (syn. *A.* × *hybrida*)
3–4 ft (1–1.2 m) Japanese Anemone
Valuable late flowering border plants with single or semi-double flowers on erect stems. 'Honorine Jobert', white, is the cultivar most widely grown, other good named forms include 'Lorelei', rose-pink; 'Louise Uhink', white semi-double; 'Mont Rose', large semi-double rose-pink flowers; and 'September Charm', lilac-pink. Late summer.

A. hupehensis japonica 3 ft (1 m)
Japanese Anemone China
Also known as Japanese anemones, this Chinese species contains white, pink, and mauve forms. The saucer-shaped flowers measure 2 in. (5 cm) or more across. Both this species and *A.* × *hybrida* resent disturbance and are best increased by root cuttings. Late summer to autumn.

Anemone
Giant Single Mixed

Anemone
St Brigid Mixed

A. nemerosa 6 in. (15 cm)
Wood Anemone   Europe, including British Isles
Dainty native woodland plants that will freely
naturalize in moist woodland soils. For garden
purposes, it is better to plant one of the named
forms such as 'Allenii', lavender-blue or 'Royal
Blue', a deep blue cultivar. Early spring.
A. pulsatilla – see *Pulsatilla vulgaris*

ANGELICA
(Umbelliferae)
Biennial herb whose green stems are candied and
used for cake decoration.
Cultural requirements: Rich moist soil and a
shady situation.
Propagation: Seed sown *in situ* in spring.

A. archangelica 5 ft (1·5 m)   Europe
Tall handsome foliage plant with large umbels of
greenish-white flowers much in demand by
flower arrangers. Midsummer.

ANNUALS
Annual plants are those which grow, flower, set
seed, and die, all in a single season. They are very
valuable in the garden, bringing, as they do,
colour and beauty to beds and borders in established gardens and, in new ones, providing a rapid
and colourful effect. Both hardy and half-hardy
annuals play an important role in our gardens.

The seed of hardy annuals is generally sown
outdoors in spring in the position in which the
plants are to flower. Some kinds can also be sown
in late summer, to overwinter and produce their
blooms earlier in the following season.

The seed of half-hardy annuals is sown under
glass in spring. The resulting seedlings are
pricked out into pots or boxes and are later
hardened off in a cold frame prior to planting
outdoors when all danger of frost is past. Many
kinds, however, can also be sown outdoors in
late spring in the positions in which they are to
flower. These will come into bloom a month to
six weeks later than those raised under glass.

Half-hardy annuals are widely used in summer
bedding schemes and as gap fillers in the shrub or

*When four leaves appear,
transplant seedlings into
boxes of potting compost.
To harden off, put boxes
in a frame or keep in a
sheltered part of the
garden by day, but take
them in at night in case of
frost*

mixed border. Hardy kinds are seen to better
advantage in beds or borders devoted to them
exclusively although they, too, can be used to
provide continuity of colour and interest in other
parts of the garden, including the rock garden.
Cultural requirements: The majority of hardy
and half-hardy annuals prefer a sunny open
situation and well-drained friable soil. Too rich
conditions tend to produce lush leaf growth at
the expense of blooms. Over generous applications of animal manure should, therefore, be
avoided. Sterilized bonemeal is one of the best
organic fertilizers for annuals and it can be forked
into the planting site at the rate of two to three
ounces to the square yard a few weeks before
sowing.
Propagation: Hardy annuals: The surface soil of
the planting site should be well raked over to
provide a fine and friable tilth for sowing. The
time of sowing will vary from early to mid-spring
according to district and prevailing weather
conditions. This operation should not be carried
out when the soil is wet and sticky; it is always
better to delay sowing until conditions improve.

Hardy annual seed should be sown fairly thinly.
This will prevent overcrowding of the seedlings
and simplify the task of thinning. Nowadays, the
seed of many kinds of annuals is obtainable in
pelleted form. This makes the job even more
simple as the pellets, which contain one seed each,
can be so spaced as to reduce thinning to a
minimum.

Thinning of the seedlings should commence as
soon as possible. Overcrowding at any stage is
the cause of weak spindly growth which renders
the plants susceptible to attacks of pests and
disease. The final thinning should leave the young
plants enough room to develop so that, at
maturity, the leaves of adjacent plants are just
touching.

Deadheading is a vitally important operation
where annuals are concerned if a long flowering
period is required. Once an annual is allowed to
set seed freely, its purpose in life is achieved and,
usually, no further flowers will be produced.
Regular and frequent removal of dead or faded
flowers is, therefore, essential.

List of worthwhile Hardy Annuals
(see also under individual entries for
descriptions, etc.)

Acroclinium	1½ ft (45 cm)
Agrostemma	up to 4 ft (1·2 m)
Alyssum	6 in. (15 cm)
Anchusa capensis	15 in. (38 cm)
Amaranthus caudatus	
(Love Lies Bleeding)	2½ ft (75 cm)
Bartonia aurea	2 ft (60 cm)
Calendula (Pot Marigold)	up to 2 ft (60 cm)

Calliopsis	
(Annual Coreopsis)	2 ft (60 cm)
Candytuft (Iberis)	up to 1 ft (30 cm)
Centaurea moschata imperialis	
(Sweet Sultan)	1½ ft (45 cm)
Chrysanthemum (Annual)	up to 4 ft (1·2 m)
Clarkia elegans	2 ft (60 cm)
Collinsia bicolor	1 ft (30 cm)
Convulvulus major	Climber
Convulvulus minor	1 ft (30 cm)
Coreopsis (Calliopsis)	up to 3 ft (1 m)
Cornflower (see under	
Centaurea)	up to 2 ft (60 cm)
Cosmos	up to 3 ft (1 m)
Cynoglossum nervosum	
(Hound's Tongue)	2 ft (60 cm)
Dimorphotheca	
(Star of the Veldt)	1 ft (30 cm)
Echium	1 ft (30 cm)
Eschscholzia	
(Californian Poppy)	1 ft (30 cm)
Godetia	up to 1½ ft (45 cm)
Grasses, ornamental	various
Gypsophila	1½ ft (45 cm)
Larkspur	
(Annual Delphinium)	4 ft (1·2 m)
Lavatera (Mallow)	4 ft (1·2 m)
Layia	1 ft (30 cm)
Leptosiphon	6 in. (15 cm)
Limnanthes douglasii	
(Poached Egg Plant)	6 in. (15 cm)
Linaria (Toadflax)	1 ft (30 cm)
Linum (Annual Flax)	2 ft (60 cm)
Matthiola bicornis	
(Night-scented Stock)	1 ft (30 cm)
Mignonette (Reseda)	1 ft (30 cm)
Nasturtium (Tropaeolum)	1 ft (30 cm) and
	Climbers
Nemophila insignis	
(Baby Blue Eyes)	6 in. (15 cm)
Nigella (Love-in-a-Mist)	1½ ft (45 cm)
Phacelia	up to 2 ft (60 cm)
Poppies	up to 2½ ft (75 cm)
Salvia horminum (Clary)	1½ ft (45 cm)
Saponaria (Soapwort)	2 ft (60 cm)
Silene	6 in. (15 cm)
Sunflower (Helianthus)	up to 8 ft (2·5 m)
Sweet Pea	Climber
Sweet William (annual form)	up to 1½ ft (45 cm)
Tropaeolum canariensis	
(Canary Creeper)	Climber
Virginian Stock	9 in. (22 cm)
Viscaria	15 in. (38 cm)

Half-hardy annuals: Seed of half-hardy annuals should be sown thinly in pans or boxes under glass in spring, using John Innes seed compost, or a soil-less seed compost. As soon as the seedlings are large enough to handle (usually when the first pair of true leaves develops) they should be pricked out into boxes about 2 in. (5 cm) apart each way. After this, they are grown on until they are ready for hardening off in a cold frame, preparatory to planting them out in their flowering positions, when danger of frost is past.

The use of a suitable fungicide during these preliminary stages will protect the seedlings from damping-off disease. Where facilities for raising them under glass are not available, many types of half-hardy annual can be sown outdoors in late spring in the positions in which the plants are to flower. Treatment is then similar to that advised for hardy annuals.

List of worthwhile Half-Hardy Annuals*
(see also under individual entries for descriptions, etc.)

Ageratum	up to 1½ ft (45 cm)
Amaranthus tricolor	
(Joseph's Coat)	3 ft (1 m)
Arctotis (African Daisy)	1½ ft (45 cm)
Aster	up to 2 ft (60 cm)
Begonia (Fibrous-rooted)	8 in. (20 cm)
Brachycome	
(Swan River Daisy)	9 in. (22 cm)
Cineraria maritima	1 ft (30 cm)
Cosmos	3 ft (1 m)
Dianthus	
(Annual Carnation)	up to 1 ft (30 cm)
Felicia bergeriana	
(Kingfisher Daisy)	6 in. (15 cm)
Gaillardia (Blanket Flower)	1½ ft (45 cm)
Gourds	Climbers,
	grown for their
	ornamental fruits
Helichrysum	up to 2½ ft (75 cm)
Heliotrope	up to 2 ft (60 cm)
Impatiens (Balsam)	1½ ft (45 cm)
Ipomoea (Morning Glory)	Climber
Kochia trichophylla	
(Burning Bush)	2 ft (60 cm)
Lobelia	6 in. (15 cm)
Marigold (African and	
French)	up to 3 ft (1 m)
Matricaria	1 ft (30 cm)
Mesembryanthemum criniflorum	
(Livingstone Daisy)	6 in. (15 cm)
Mimulus (Monkey Flower)	1 ft (30 cm)
Molucella laevis	
(Bells of Ireland)	2 ft (60 cm)
Nemesia	1 ft (30 cm)
Nicotiana (Sweet Tobacco)	up to 3 ft (1 m)
Penstemon	1½ ft (45 cm)
Petunia	up to 1½ ft (45 cm)
Phlox drummondii	up to 1 ft (30 cm)
Portulaca	6 in. (15 cm)
Rudbeckia (Gloriosa Daisy)	up to 3 ft (1 m)
Salpiglossis	2 ft (60 cm)

Salvia splendens	up to 2½ ft (75 cm)
Sanvitalia	6 in. (15 cm)
Scabious	2½ ft (75 cm)
Statice	1½ ft (45 cm)
Stock	up to 1½ ft (45 cm)
Tagetes	9 in. (22 cm)
Ursinia	1 ft (30 cm)
Venidium fastuosum	
(Monarch of the Veldt)	3 ft (1 m)
Verbena	15 in. (38 cm)
Zinnia	up to 2 ft (60 cm)

* List includes perennials treated as half-hardy annuals.

ANTENNARIA
(Compositae)

Carpeting perennials for the rock garden with silvery foliage and pink flowers.
Cultural requirements: Any ordinary garden soil and a sunny situation.
Propagation: By division in spring.

A. dioica 3 in. (8 cm)
Cat's Ear   Europe, including British Isles
Dense carpet of silvery-grey leaves, clusters of small pink 'everlasting' flowers. Midsummer.

ANTHEMIS
(Compositae) Chamomile

A group of hardy perennials with aromatic foliage and daisy-like flowers over a long period during summer.

Shirley Poppy Single Mixed

Cultural requirements: Any ordinary soil and a sunny situation.
Propagation: From seed, by division or cuttings, in spring.

A. cupaniana 6 in. (15 cm)   Mediterranean
Dense mats of silver-grey aromatic foliage and white flowers. Midsummer to autumn.

A. nobilis 1 ft (30 cm)
Common Chamomile   Europe
The white daisy flowers of this species, dried, are used to make camomile tea. The plants can also be used to make an unusual lawn, fragrant when clipped or walked on. Summer.

A. sancti-johannis 1½ ft (45 cm)   C. Europe
Grey ferny foliage and orange-yellow daisy flowers on wiry stems. Good for cutting. Summer.

A. tinctoria 2½ ft (75 cm)
Dyer's Greenweed   Europe
Finely cut feathery foliage, yellow daisy flowers up to 3 in. (8 cm) in diameter. Good forms include 'Beauty of Grallach', deep yellow; 'E. C. Buxton', lemon-yellow; 'Grallach Gold', deep golden-yellow; 'Perry's Variety', bright yellow; and 'Wargrave Variety', lemon-yellow. Summer to early autumn.

ANTHER

The part of the stamen (q.v.) which bears the pollen.

ANTHERICUM
(Liliaceae)

Hardy perennials of the lily family with tufts of narrow leaves and delicate spikes of flowers.
Cultural requirements: Rich well-drained soil, partly shaded situation.
Propagation: Seed in cold frame, spring or autumn. Division in autumn, after plants have flowered.

A. liliago 1½ ft (45 cm)
St Bernard Lily   S. Europe
Sprays of white flowers, up to 2 in. (5 cm) across, on slender stems. Early to midsummer.

A. ramosum 2 ft (60 cm)   S. Europe
Tufts of grassy foliage and sprays of small white flowers that cut well. Midsummer.

ANTHURIUM
(Araceae) Flamingo Plant

Handsome perennials for the warm greenhouse, with striking leaves and brightly coloured spathes in scarlet, pink, and white. The leathery, heart-shaped leaves measure up to 8 in. (20 cm) in length.
Cultural requirements: Warm humid conditions, with a minimum winter temperature of 60 °F (15 °C) and a well-drained compost contain-

ing chopped sphagnum moss. Water freely from spring to autumn, sparingly for rest of year.
Propagation: From seed under glass in heat; by root division in spring.

A. andreanum 3 ft (1 m)   Colombia
Unusual and interesting heart-shaped scarlet or white spathes. Spring to autumn.

A. scherzerianum 2½ ft (75 cm)   Guatemala
Scarlet spathes, smaller than those of the former species. Spring to autumn.

There are also several species grown for their decorative foliage, including *A. magnificum*, green and white and *A. veitchii*, green.

ANTIRRHINUM
(Scrophulariaceae) Snapdragon
Popular hardy perennials, mainly treated as half-hardy annuals for summer bedding. Plants are susceptible to the fungus disease antirrhinum rust but many rust resistant strains have been developed. Most garden forms are derived from *A. majus*, the common snapdragon. The dwarf forms are useful for walls and in the rock garden.

Cultural requirements: Any ordinary garden soil and a sunny situation.
Propagation: For summer bedding, seed is sown under glass in heat in late winter or early spring, treating the plants as half-hardy annuals. May also be sown *in situ* or in a nursery plot and transplanted later. Also, by cuttings of young shoots in a cold frame in late summer.

A. majus up to 3 ft (1 m)   Mediterranean
The species contains a very wide range of colours and there are also numerous strains, some of hybrid origin, ranging in height from 6 in. (15 cm) to 3 ft (1 m). Among the best of the latter kinds are 'Hybrid Coronette', uniform in height and with a large central flower spike surrounded by a cluster of up to a dozen equally large spikes, all in flower at the same time and 'Magic Carpet', a dwarf strain ideal for the rock garden. There are also some outstanding F_1 hybrid strains, including 'Bright Butterflies', with double flowers like miniature azalea blooms and 'Floral Carpet', an ideal strain for dwarf bedding, edging, or window-boxes. Summer to autumn.

Ornamental Gourds

As the plants grow, support them by tying them to canes, netting, or a trellis

Antirrhinum Bell Flowered

Antirrhinum 'Magic Carpet'

ANTS – see Pest Control

APHELANDRA
(Acanthaceae)

Evergreen shrubs for the warm greenhouse, with flowers that are distinguished for their brightly coloured bracts.

Cultural requirements: John Innes No. 2 or similar compost and a humid atmosphere. Minimum winter temperature 60 °F (15 °C).

Propagation: By cuttings under glass in heat in spring.

A. aurantiaca 3 ft (1 m)   Mexico
Orange flowers useful for their winter display. Winter.

A. squarrosa 1–2 ft (30–60 cm)   Brazil
Dark green leaves with white veins and bright yellow bracts. Summer to winter.

A. tetragona 3 ft (1 m)   W. Indies
A species with striking scarlet flowers. Autumn.

APHIDS – see Pest Control

APONOGETON
(Aponogetonaceae)

Aquatic plants with floating white flowers and leaves. Much too rampant for small garden pools.

Cultural requirements: Planting in bottom of pond or pool in tubs or baskets of good soil.

Aquilegia Long Spurred Mixed

Propagation: From seed, sown when ripe or by division of tubers.

A. distachyus 4 in. (10 cm)
Water Hawthorn   S. Africa
Bright green floating leaves; white hawthorn-scented flowers. Late spring to autumn.

APPLE OF PERU – see *Nicandra physalodes*

APPLES – see Fruit Garden

AQUILEGIA
(Ranunculaceae) Columbine
Hardy herbaceous perennials of delicate beauty, useful in the border for their early flowering season. The foliage is finely cut and fern-like and makes a perfect complement to the spurred bonnet-like flowers. Most garden forms are hybrids, of which there are many attractive named cultivars.
Cultural requirements: Any kind of garden soil, including chalk. Sunny or partly shaded situation.
Propagation: Mainly from seed sown in a cold frame in spring or outdoors in early summer. Cultivars can be increased by division in autumn.

A. alpina 1 ft (30 cm)   Europe
Good plant for rock garden with powder-blue flowers. Early summer.

A. glandulosa 1 ft (30 cm)   Siberia
Lovely but short lived species, blue and white. Early summer.

A. longissima 2 ft (60 cm)   U.S.A.
Yellow flowers with extra long spurs. Midsummer.

A. vulgaris 2 ft (60 cm)
Granny's Bonnet   Europe
The true columbine species with small single or double short-spurred flowers in blue and white. Early summer.

Hybrids: Among the best of the hybrids are 'Crimson Star', crimson and white long-spurred flowers; 'Dragonfly', a large flowered strain of medium height with colours ranging from bright red and wine shades to blue, yellow, and bronze; 'Spring Song', an F_1 hybrid strain with long-spurred blooms in a wide colour range; and 'Toy Town', a neat and compact miniature strain with double or single flowers in a variety of colours. Early to midsummer.

ARABIS
(Cruciferae) Rock Cress
A large group of plants of which the species below is the one normally used in the rock garden or on dry walls. Associates well with aubrieta and yellow alyssum.
Cultural requirements: Any ordinary garden soil; sunny situation.
Propagation: From seed in spring; cuttings in summer; division in autumn.

A. albida 9 in. (22 cm)   S.E. Europe
Vigorous and invasive plant forming mats of silver-grey foliage. Masses of white flowers make an effective contrast. Best form is double white 'Flore Pleno'. There is also an attractive pink-flowered cultivar, 'Rosea Grandiflora'.

ARALIA
(Araliaceae)
Trees or large shrubs of suckering habit grown for the architectural and decorative value of their handsome deeply dissected leaves.
Cultural requirements: Moist soil, rich in humus and a situation sheltered from cold winds in sun or part shade.
Propagation: Seed, suckers, or root cuttings.

A. chinensis 20 ft (6 m)
Chinese Angelica Tree   N.E. Asia
Small tree or large suckering shrub with stout and upright spiny stems, plumes of creamy-white blossom and ash-like foliage up to 4 ft (1·2 m) in length and 2 ft (60 cm) in width. Late summer.

A. elata up to 30 ft (9 m)
Japanese Angelica Tree   Japan
Large shrub similar in character to *A. chinensis* but with leaves restricted mainly to the ends of the

stems. There are two distinctive variegated forms 'Aureovariegata' and 'Variegata', whose leaves are edged with gold and creamy-white respectively. Late summer.

A. spinosa 20 ft (6 m)
Devil's Walking Stick   S.E. U.S.A.
Erect stems, bare of leaves except at tips, armed with vicious spines. Flowers greenish-white, less showy, but earlier than those of above mentioned species. Summer.

ARAUCARIA
(Araucariaceae)

Evergreen conifers from southern hemisphere with horizontal branches and leathery overlapping leaves arranged in spirals. Very resistant to winds.
Cultural requirements: Rich loamy soil and an open situation.
Propagation: Seed sown in heat in spring.

A. araucana (syn. *A. imbricata*) 70 ft or more (21 m)
Monkey Puzzle   Chile
An interesting and unusual conifer with wide spreading horizontal branches, but unsuitable for smaller gardens. Scaly leaves spirally overlapping on stems.

ARBUTUS
(Ericaceae) Strawberry Tree

Handsome evergreen shrubs or small trees that make superb specimens for the smaller garden. Good for seaside districts.
Cultural requirements: Deep well-drained soil and a sheltered position. Unlike most other ericaceous plants, arbutus do not object to lime.

A. × andrachnoides
up to 20 ft (6 m)   Garden origin
A beautiful hybrid between the Killarney strawberry tree, *A. unedo*, and a Greek species, *A. andrachne*. Striking cinnamon-red trunk and branches. White urn-shaped flowers at same time as strawberry-like fruits. Early to late winter.

A. unedo up to 30 ft (9 m)
                     Mediterranean and S.W. Ireland
Small tree or large shrub with dark green polished leaves and cream flowers produced at the same time as the fruits. Autumn.

ARCTOTIS
(Compositae) African Daisy

Half-hardy annuals of South African origin which thrive in hot dry soils and are good for cutting.
Cultural requirements: Any ordinary garden soil and a sunny situation.
Propagation: Seed under glass in spring.

A. breviscapa 6 in. (15 cm)   S. Africa
Brilliant orange daisy flowers with dark centres, leaves downy on reverse. Summer.

A. grandis 2 ft (60 cm)   S. Africa
White daisy flowers shaded with metallic blue on reverse of petals. Grey-green foliage. Summer.

There are also many hybrid forms, in colours ranging from white through yellow, red, and orange to carmine. The flowers of many are centrally banded with contrasting colours. Summer.

ARENARIA
(Caryophyllaceae)

Useful rock garden plants of creeping habit with masses of white flowers.
Cultural requirements: Any well-drained soil and a sunny situation in rock garden, paving, or wall.
Propagation: Seed in cold frame in spring; cuttings or root division.

A. balearica 1 in. (3 cm)   Balearic Isles
The most widely grown species with minute dark green leaves and glistening white flowers. Excellent carpeting plant for a shady rock garden. Early summer.

ARISTOLOCHIA
(Aristolochiaceae)

Large group of shrubs, climbers, and perennials, of which the hardy *A. macrophylla* is the most widely grown.
Cultural requirements: Fairly rich moist soil, sun or shade.

A. macrophylla (syn. *A. sipho*) up to 30 ft (9 m)
Dutchman's Pipe   E. U.S.A.
Vigorous climber with handsome heart-shaped foliage and tubular saxophone-shaped flowers sparsely borne. Self-clinging twiner. Summer.

ARMERIA
(Plumbaginaceae) Thrift

Plants with hummocks of grass-like foliage and heads of pink or white flowers. Long flowering and good for seaside districts.
Cultural requirements: Well-drained gritty soil and a sunny situation.
Propagation: Seed outdoors in spring or root division.

A. caespitosa 4 in. (10 cm)   Spain
Dense hummocks of short grass-like foliage with lilac-pink flowers. 'Beechwood', a deep pink large flowered cultivar and 'Bevan's Variety', deep rose, are both good. There is also a form, 'Alba', with white flowers. Late spring.

A. maritima 6 in. (15 cm) Sea Pink   British Isles
Grass-like foliage in dense tufts; heads of pink flowers lasting for many weeks. 'Alba' is a white form; 'Vindictive', bright crimson. Summer.

ARTEMISIA
(Compositae) Wormwood

Aromatic herbs and sub-shrubs displaying a wide variety of differing characteristics both in flower and leaf structure. The silver-leaved kinds, with their finely cut foliage are useful plants for the grey garden.

Cultural requirements: Any ordinary garden soil and a situation in full sun.

Propagation: Cuttings taken in summer for shrubby species; root division in spring for perennial kinds.

A. abrotanum 3 ft (1 m) Southernwood;
also Old Man, Lad's Love   Europe
Popular sub-shrub of cottage gardens. The aromatic foliage is said to act as a fly repellent indoors.

A. absinthium 2 ft (60 cm) Wormwood   Europe
Finely cut foliage covered with white silky down. 'Lambrook Silver' is a particularly fine form.

A. lactiflora 5 ft (1·5 m) White Mugwort   China
Perennial species ideal for back of herbaceous borders. Does not spread and needs no support. Milky-white plumes of blossom are delicately scented. Autumn.

ARUM
(Araceae)

A group of plants whose flowers are like those of an arum lily. Cultivated forms bear a resemblance to the native cuckoopint *A. maculatum*. The scarlet berries that follow the flowers are poisonous.

Cultural requirements: Any ordinary garden soil; partly shaded situation.

Propagation: Offsets in autumn.

A. italicum 1½ ft (45 cm)   S. Europe
Pale lime-green spathes with darker spadix. Leaves arrow-shaped and very decorative. Those of the cultivar 'Marmoratum', marbled with cream, are much used in flower arrangements. Spring.

A. maculatum 6 in. (15 cm) Lords and Ladies
or Cuckoo pint   British Isles
Green arrowhead leaves sometimes spotted with purple. Apple-green spathes followed by spikes of scarlet berries. Native wildling that well deserves a place in the garden.

ARUM LILY – see *Zantedeschia*

ARUNCUS
(Rosaceae) Goat's Beard

Hardy moisture loving perennials formerly included in genus *Spiraea*.

Cultural requirements: Moist, humus-rich soil and a shady situation.

Propagation: Seed or division in autumn.

A. sylvester (syn. *Spireae aruncus*)
4 ft (1·2 m)   N. Hemisphere
Attractive lacy foliage and large plumes of creamy-white flowers. 'Kneiffi' is a form with more finely cut foliage and a more compact habit. Midsummer.

ARUNDINARIA
(Gramineae)

Members of the bamboo family, mainly hardy.

Cultural requirements: Fairly rich moist soil and a sheltered situation.

Propagation: By division in spring.

A. anceps 10 ft (3 m)   Himalayas
Vigorous species, ideal for windbreaks and a useful source of supply of garden canes. Arching stems and glossy leaves.

A. gigantea 10 ft (3 m) Cane Reed   S.E. U.S.A.
Leaves up to 1 ft (30 cm) in length, strong and vigorous canes. Needs a sheltered situation.

A. japonica 10 ft (3 m) Metake   Japan
Extremely hardy species, inclined to be invasive, widely grown as windbreaks and for covert planting. Olive-green canes, arching at their tips and dark green leaves up to 1 ft (30 cm) long.

A. nitida 10 ft (3 m)   China
An attractive clump-forming species of elegant and graceful habit. Arching canes and narrow leaves. Does best in partial shade.

ASCLEPIAS
(Asclepiadaceae) Milkweed

Hardy and tender perennials that flower in late summer.

Cultural requirements: Hardy species: Moist soil and a sunny situation. Greenhouse species: John Innes No. 2 or similar compost. Minimum winter temperature 60 °F (15 °C).

Propagation: From seed under glass in heat in spring; by root division in spring or autumn.

A. curassavica 2 ft (60 cm)   Tropical America
Clusters of orange-red flowers on long stems. Seed sown in a heated greenhouse in early spring will produce plants that will flower in their first season. Late summer.

A. tuberosa 2 ft (60 cm)   N. America
Hardy perennials with clusters of orange flowers on erect stems. Late summer.

ASH – see *Fraxinus*

ASPARAGUS
(Liliaceae) – see also Kitchen Garden

Although the foliage of the culinary kinds of asparagus is often used in floral decoration, the ornamental kinds, grown specially for their decorative value, are much more attractive.

Cultural requirements: Warm greenhouse in a

compost of equal parts sand, loam, and leafmould or peat.
Propagation: Seed and root division.

A. asparagoides up to 10 ft (3 m) Smilax S. Africa
Vigorous climbing species.

A. myersii (*A. densiflorus* 'Myersii')
15 in. (38 cm)   S. Africa
Distinctive but easily grown species with narrowly pyramidal fronds of vivid green foliage.

A. plumosus up to 10 ft (3 m)
Asparagus Fern   S. Africa
Delicate feathery foliage, greatly valued for cutting. The variety *nanus* is more compact.

A. sprengeri (*A. densiflorus* 'Sprengeri')
3 ft (1 m)   S. Africa
Popular species, easy to grow and the best for hanging baskets.

ASPERULA
(Rubiaceae) Woodruff

Hardy perennials and annuals, useful as edging plants and in the rock garden.
Cultural requirements: Well-drained gritty loam and an open situation.
Propagation: Division of perennial species; hardy annuals from seed.

A. gussonii 2 in. (5 cm)   Italy
Small pink flowers on compact plants. Summer.

A. lilaciflora caespitosa
2 in. (5 cm)   E. Mediterranean
Mat-forming plant with carmine-pink flowers. Midsummer to early autumn.

A. orientalis (syn. *A. azurea setosa*)
9 in. (22 cm)   Syria
Annual species with sweetly scented lavender-blue flowers. It makes a useful edging plant. Summer.

ASPIDISTRA
(Liliaceae)

The much despised 'parlour palm' has come into its own again of recent years with a reputation as an almost indestructible house plant. It is grown primarily for its foliage but bears insignificant daisy-like flowers at the foot of its leaves, close to the soil surface. Perennial.
Cultural requirements: John Innes No. 2 or similar potting compost. Water freely in summer, more sparingly in winter. Minimum winter temperature: 45–50 °F (7–10 °C).
Propagation: By root division in spring.

A. elatior (syn. *A. lurida*) 2 ft (60 cm)   China
The best known form is the type plant, with large green leaves up to 2 ft (60 cm) long and nearly half as wide. 'Variegata' has leaves attractively striped with cream.

ASPLENIUM
(Polypodiaceae) Spleenwort

The hardy kinds of spleenwort are useful for cool shady parts of the garden. They are ferns with attractively divided fronds.
Cultural requirements: Moist soil, rich in humus, and a shady situation.
Propagation: From ripe spores under glass and from frond plantlets.

A. adiantum-nigrum 1 ft (30 cm) Black Spleenwort
                          Europe, including British Isles
Finely divided fronds with dark brown spores on their reverse.

A. ruta-muraria 3 in. (8 cm)
Wall Rue   Europe, including British Isles
Dwarf species, native to Britain with finely divided dark green fronds. Good for the rock garden or shady dry walls.

A. trichomanes 6 in. (15 cm) Maidenhair Spleenwort
                   North America, Asia, and Europe,
                              including British Isles
Wiry black stems with two rows of broadly oval leaflets. Likes similar conditions to the former species.

ASTER
(Compositae) Michaelmas Daisy
– see *Callistephus* for China Aster

Valuable race of hardy perennials for the late summer and early autumn display in herbaceous

Aster Single Mixed

Aster Ostrich Plume Mixed

A. ericoides 2½ ft (75 cm)   N. America
This species bears dense sprays of tiny flowers turning the plants into a mist of blue when in bloom. There are several named varieties, including 'Blue Star', pale-blue; 'Esther', delicate pink; and 'Ringdove', rosy-lilac. Autumn.

A. × frikartii (*A. amellus × A. thompsonii*)
2½ ft (75 cm)   Garden origin
Attractive hybrid form with large pale blue flowers with orange centres. Late summer to autumn.

A. novae-angliae up to 5 ft (1·5 m)   U.S.A.
Noteworthy mainly for the pink-flowered and rosy-red varieties: 'Barr's Pink', 'Crimson Beauty', 'September Ruby', and 'Harrington's Pink'. Late summer to mid-autumn.

A. novi-belgii up to 4 ft (1·2 m)   U.S.A.
The source of many of the most popular named hybrids grown. Among the many outstanding forms are those named after members of the Ballard family to whom the development and improvement of the michaelmas daisy owes so much. 'Ada Ballard', 'Ernest Ballard', and 'Marie Ballard' are all fine varieties; 'Winston S. Churchill' is an unusual shade of beetroot-red; 'Blandie' is a good white. There are many others equally good. Dwarf cultivars include 'Audrey', pale blue; 'Blue Bouquet', bright blue; 'Jenny', violet-purple; and 'Snowsprite', white. Autumn.

ASTILBE
(Saxifragaceae)
A race of moisture loving hardy perennials often incorrectly referred to as spiraeas (q.v.) and bearing similar dense plumes of blossom above fern-like foliage.
Cultural requirements: Cool moist loam, rich in humus. Ideal for a damp shady border or for the margins of streams or garden pools.
Propagation: Seed, division.

A. × arendsii up to 3 ft (1 m)   Garden origin
The vast majority of garden forms are drawn from this lovely race of hybrids between four different species. Some of the best known are 'Betsy Cuperus', white with pink centres; 'Bridal Veil', creamy-white; 'Fanal', deep garnet-red; 'White Queen', white; and 'William Reeves', crimson-scarlet.

ASTRANTIA
(Umbelliferae) Masterwort
Hardy perennials, whose flower heads, with their conspicuous ring of bracts, are much prized by flower arrangers.
Cultural requirements: Any ordinary garden soil. Cool situation, preferably in partial shade.
Propagation: From seed in cold frame in spring; division in spring or autumn.

or mixed borders. Various species provide excellent garden material but the majority of the more widely grown garden forms are derived from the *amellus*, *dumosus*, *novae-angliae*, and *novi-belgii* groups. The current trend is to grow those forms of low to medium height that need little or no staking and tying.
Cultural requirements: Any good garden soil that remains moist during the growing season and a sunny open situation. With the exception of *A. amellus*, clumps should be split up annually.
Propagation: Although some kinds are easily raised from seed, few come true to type. It is better, therefore, to increase stocks by division in spring or autumn or from cuttings.

A. acris 3 ft (1 m)   S. Europe
Lilac-purple flowers with golden centres. Late summer.

A. alpinus 6 in. (15 cm)   Europe
Useful rock garden plant with golden-centred purple flowers. 'Beechwood' and 'Roseus', rosy-purple, are both good cultivars. Late spring.

A. amellus 2½ ft (75 cm)   Europe
Large-flowered species flowering in advance of the main groups. Should be planted in spring. Good cultivars are 'King George', violet-blue; 'Lac de Genève', lavender-blue; 'Mauve Queen', soft mauve; and 'Rudolph Von Goethe', deep lavender.

A. carniolica 1 ft (30 cm)   Europe
Low growing species with white flowers. The variety 'Rubra' has purple-red flowers and bracts. Early summer.

A. major 2 ft (60 cm)   Europe
Palest green flowers tinged with red. Summer.

A. minor 6 in. (15 cm)   Europe
White flowers tinged with green. Useful for edge of border with taller species behind. Midsummer.

ATHYRIUM
(Polypodiaceae)

Hardy and greenhouse ferns, of which our native lady fern is the best known example. Similar in appearance to the male fern (*Dryopteris*).
Cultural requirements: Hardy kinds: Cool shady situation with soil rich in peat or leafmould.
Propagation: From spores or by division.

A. felix-femina 3 ft (1 m)
Lady Fern   Europe, Asia, and N. America
Large light green fronds with divided foliage. One of our loveliest native ferns.

ATRIPLEX
(Chenopodiaceae)

Hardy annuals, perennials, and shrubs, many of which are particularly suited to seaside districts.
Cultural requirements: Any ordinary garden soil provided it is well-drained.
Propagation: From cuttings in a cold frame in late summer.

A. halimus 4 ft (1·2 m)   S. Europe
Evergreen shrub with oval, metallic-grey leaves. Flowers insignificant.

Aubrieta 'Springtime' Mixed

A. hortensis 4½ ft (1·3 m)
Mountain Spinach   C. Asia
Annual species sometimes grown as a substitute for spinach. The cultivar 'Rubra', with striking beetroot-red leaves makes a useful and decorative plant for the annual border.

AUBRIETA
(Cruciferae) Rock Cress

Carpeting plants with long flowering season ideal for rock gardens, walls, banks, or as edging material. Cascades of bloom in a variety of lovely colours.
Cultural requirements: Any ordinary garden soil; they also like lime. Sunny border, wall, bank, or rock garden.
Propagation: Cuttings in sandy soil in summer; from seed or root division in spring. Seeds of named varieties do not come true.

A. deltoidea
2–3 in. (5–8 cm)   S. Europe and Asia Minor
Named varieties of this species provide the majority of garden forms. The following are all good: 'Carnival', deep violet; 'Crimson Queen', rich crimson; 'Dr Mules', rich purple; 'Maurice Prichard', pale rose-pink; and 'Magician', bright purple. Spring.

AUCUBA
(Cornaceae)

Evergreen shrubs, adaptable to any soil or situation, including town and industrial conditions. Shade loving. Decorative berries on female plants.
Cultural requirements: Any ordinary garden soil; sun or shade.
Propagation: From seed or cuttings in cold frame in autumn. Also from rooted layers.

A. japonica up to 10 ft (3 m)
Japanese or Spotted Laurel   Japan
The type plant has handsome dark green polished foliage with scarlet marble-sized berries on the female plants. There are also a number of cultivars with attractively variegated foliage, including: 'Crotonifolia', leaves mottled with gold; 'Gold Dust', gold speckled leaves; and 'Variegata', with yellow-mottled leaves, the plant first introduced from Japan nearly 200 years ago.

AURICULA – see *Primula auricula*

AUTUMN CROCUS – see *Colchicum*

AVENA (Gramineae) Oat Grass
– see Helictotrichon

AZALEA – see *Rhododendron*

AZARA
(Flacourtiaceae)

Evergreen shrubs bearing numerous small but intensely fragrant flowers in early spring.

Cultural requirements: Any ordinary soil; protection of south wall or sheltered border.

Propagation: Cuttings under glass in summer.

A. microphylla up to 15 ft (4·5 m)　　　Chile

The hardiest and most widely grown species, attaining the dimensions of a small tree. Fan-like growths of glossy green leaves. Small but intensely fragrant yellow flowers in axils of leaves. Early spring.

BABY BLUE EYES – see *Nemophila insignis*

BALLOON FLOWER – see *Platycodon*

BALLOTA
(Labiatae)

Sub-shrubs of great decorative and architectural value in the grey border.

Cultural requirements: Well-drained soil and a sunny open situation.

Propagation: By division or cuttings.

B. pseudodictamnus 2 ft (60 cm)

False Dittany　　　Crete

Evergreen perennial sub-shrub with heart-shaped leaves thickly felted with white. The flowers, white, spotted with purple are insignificant. This is a useful plant for the flower arranger.

BALM – see *Melissa officinalis*

BALSAM – see *Impatiens balsamina*

BAPTISIA
(Leguminosae) False Indigo

Attractive hardy perennials with indigo-blue pea flowers. A useful plant for the back of the herbaceous border.

Cultural requirements: Any well-drained soil and a sunny open situation.

Propagation: From seed in a cold frame in spring; by division in spring or autumn.

B. australis 5 ft (1·5 m)　　　U.S.A.

This is the species most commonly seen in gardens. The small indigo flowers are borne in terminal spikes. Summer.

BARBERRY – see *Berberis*

BARTONIA – see *Mentzelia*

BEANS – see Kitchen Garden

BEARDED IRIS – see *Iris germanica*

BEAUTY BUSH – see *Kolkwitzia amabalis*

BEDDING PLANTS

In the wide category of bedding plants, there are usually included all those bulbs, tubers, hardy and half-hardy annuals, and perennials that are used in spring and summer bedding schemes. The cult of bedding-out reached the zenith of its popularity between the late nineteenth century and first decade of the present one with the undoubtedly colourful but often tasteless displays that culminated in Victorian carpet bedding.

With the problems of finding help in the garden becoming increasingly difficult, this type of gardening has largely fallen into disfavour although there is still much to be said for bedding schemes where a striking effect is required in the shortest possible time; for example during the first few years in the life of a new garden.

The variety of geometrical shapes formerly employed in bedding-out schemes should be avoided, particularly in the small garden where lawn space is too valuable to be cut up in this manner. Avoid, therefore, the stars, crescents, and scrolls that were once so popular. Edge trimming creates unnecessary extra work and the lawn is broken up into a series of fussy little beds in which the beauty of the contents plays second fiddle to the ingenuity of the design.

Present-day bedding schemes should have simplicity as their keynote. Beds are best restricted to rectangles, circles, or ovals. Whenever practicable, rather than cutting into the lawn area, they should be restricted to its edges.

For spring bedding there are wallflowers, tulips, narcissi, hyacinths, and forget-me-nots. With this basic material, the changes can be rung to provide many lovely combinations of form and colour. For interplanting, or for carpeting effects, there are double daisies, polyanthus, auriculas,

When the flowers are over, cut the old flower stems away to let new ones grow

and primroses, together with the more compact strains of wallflowers and forget-me-nots, all of which can be used to good effect.

Summer brings an even wider choice of bedding material. For edging, there are fibrous-rooted begonias, sweet alyssum, lobelias, and thrift, while for the main planting use can be made of such varied subjects as scarlet salvias, zonal pelargoniums, commonly known as geraniums, bedding dahlias, China asters, African marigolds, petunias, and verbenas, to name only a few.

Provided that due attention is paid to the removal of spent flowers, most of these summer bedding plants will stage a display that will last from midsummer to early autumn.

BEETROOT – see Kitchen Garden

BEGONIA
(Begoniaceae)

A race of tender perennials that includes kinds with tuberous or fibrous roots and others grown solely for the beauty of their foliage. The two former kinds are widely used for summer bedding, the last named are much in demand as house plants.

Cultural requirements: Tuberous-rooted kinds: Start tubers into growth, flat or hollow side uppermost, in late winter or early spring, in boxes or trays of moist peat or leafmould in a temperature of 65 °F (18 °C), transferring to pots in John Innes No. 2 or a similar compost as soon as growth begins. Pot on as growth progresses and water moderately. Shade plants from direct sunlight. When flowering is finished, withhold water completely. When foliage has died down, tubers can be stored in a mixture of sand and peat in a frost-proof shed or garage.

For bedding purposes outdoors, plants should be raised in heat, hardened off in late spring and planted out when danger of frost is past.

Fibrous-rooted kinds: Seed of these, which is dust fine and needs careful handling, should be sown under glass at a temperature of 65–70 °F (18–21 °C). From then on, treatment is the same as for the tuberous species and hybrids.

The culture of the ornamental-leaved sorts is the same as for fibrous-rooted kinds.

Propagation: Fibrous- and tuberous-rooted kinds: From seed sown in spring in heat, or cuttings of young shoots in spring.

Ornamental-leaved kinds: From leaf or stem cuttings, in spring or summer.

Begonia 'Crown Jewels'

Begonia F₁ Hybrid
Semperflorens Colorita

Tuberous-rooted begonias

The present race of garden hybrids was obtained from crosses between *B. boliviensis* and other South American species. These have given rise to a wide variety of hybrid strains. They fall into several categories: Multiflora, compact plants bearing masses of small flowers, which are ideal for bedding; the large flowered kinds which in addition to being first class summer bedding plants are useful for pots and tubs; Pendula, with medium-sized single or double flowers on arching or pendulous stems. The last named are useful for hanging baskets, pots, or window-boxes.

Fibrous-rooted begonias

The hybrid strains of fibrous-rooted begonias make summer bedding plants *par excellence*. They have an exceptionally long flowering season, lasting from just after midsummer until cut down by frost. The named cultivars of these, like those of the tuberous-rooted species, are too numerous to mention and are constantly changing as new ones are introduced. A choice can be made from current seedsmens' or nursery catalogues. Those with dark bronzy foliage, which makes a striking foil for the flowers, are particularly effective.

Water the boxes from below by putting them in shallow water so that it soaks through gradually

Ornamental-leaved begonias

These begonias, once restricted to greenhouse cultivation, are now highly esteemed as house plants. They include *B. rex*, with metallic green foliage marked with red, purple, and silver; *B. metallica*, aptly named for the metallic sheen of its leaves; and *B. masoniana*, the Iron Cross begonia, whose pale green foliage is marked with a chocolate-brown cross at its centre.

BELLIS
(Compositae) Double Daisy

Hardy perennials with double daisy flowers, widely used in spring bedding.

Bellis 'Buttonball' Large
Double Flowered Mixed (Daisy)

Cultural requirements: Any ordinary garden soil; position in sun or part shade.
Propagation: From seed in cold frame in spring or outdoors in early summer; division in summer when plants have finished flowering.

B. perennis up to 6 in. (15 cm)
Daisy   Europe, including British Isles
The double 'Monstrosa' is the source of the large flowered garden cultivars. There are also many useful smaller strains, including the F_1 hybrid, 'Fairy Carpet', which produces compact plants that bear masses of double rose-pink and white flowers throughout spring and early summer.

'Dresden China', pink and 'Rob Roy', crimson are two cultivars of more compact habit (2 in. – 5 cm) that are particularly suitable for the rock garden. Spring to early summer.

BELLS OF IRELAND – see *Molucella laevis*

BELOPERONE
(Acanthaceae)
Evergreen flowering plants for a cool greenhouse or as house plants.
Cultural requirements: Minimum winter temperature of 45 °F (7 °C) and, when used as a house plant, a light position. John Innes No. 2 or similar rooting medium.
Propagation: From cuttings in heat in spring or summer.

B. guttata 1½ ft (45 cm) Shrimp Plant   Mexico
Small shrub, so called from the resemblance to shrimps of the pinkish-brown bracts that enclose the small white flowers. There is also a form with greenish-cream bracts. Spring to autumn.

BERBERIS
(Berberidaceae) Barberry
An extensive family of deciduous and evergreen shrubs, noteworthy for flowers, foliage, and fruit and a source of much valuable garden material.
Cultural requirements: Any ordinary garden soil provided it is not constantly wet. Sunny or partly shaded situation.
Propagation: From seed, hardwood cuttings, or layers in spring.

Deciduous species

B. aggregata 5 ft (1·5 m)   W. China
Dense upright habit, large clusters of coral-red berries profusely borne. July.

B. thunbergii 6 ft (2 m)   Japan
Delightful small shrub, noteworthy for the brilliant colouring of its autumn foliage and scarlet berries. 'Atropurpurea' and the dwarf 'Atropurpurea Nana', both with striking purple foliage, 'Red Pillar' and 'Rose Glow', are all out-standing forms. The last named cultivar has rosy-pink young growth flecked with silver.

B. wilsonae 3 ft (1 m)   W. China
Elegant shrub of semi-prostrate habit; yellow flowers followed by an abundance of coral-red berries. Soft green foliage turning purplish as it matures. July.

Evergreen species

B. darwinii 8 ft (2·5 m)   Chile
Both flowers and foliage are superb. The latter, which is dark green and glossy, is shield-shaped. The abundant blossom is orange-yellow and is followed by purple berries. Spring.

B. × *stenophylla* 8 ft (2·5 m)   Garden origin
This fine hybrid, ideal for hedging or as a specimen shrub, bears cascades of orange-yellow flowers against a background of dark green linear foliage. Among the many fine named forms are 'Coccinea', a small shrub with crimson buds opening to orange; 'Corallina' and 'Corallina Nana', both with coral-pink buds opening to yellow; and 'Pink Pearl', an unusual cultivar whose dark green leaves are streaked with pink and cream.

B. verruculosa 5 ft (1·5 m)   W. China
Compact and fairly slow growing barberry with arching dense habit. The dark green polished foliage is silvered on its reverse. The pendent flowers are golden-yellow. Early summer.

BERGAMOT – see *Monarda didyma* and Herb Garden

BERGENIA
(Saxifragaceae) Pigsqueak
Beautiful race of evergreen hardy perennials formerly known as 'Megasea', whose large polished leaves make a valuable contribution to the garden in winter. They make first rate cover- and smother plants and do well in tubs. The large heads of bloom are a welcome sight in late winter and spring.
Cultural requirements: Any ordinary garden soil; they do particularly well on chalk. Sunny or shady situation.
Propagation: From seed or division in spring or autumn.

B. beesiana 2 ft (60 cm)   Himalayas
'Ballawley Hybrid' (syn. 'Delbees'), a hybrid between this species and *B. delavayi*, is one of the finest examples. The handsome rounded dark green leaves turn crimson-purple in winter. Very large heads of rosy-crimson flowers. Late winter to early spring.

B. cordifolia 1½ ft (45 cm)   Siberia
The best known species; pink flowers on long stems. Early spring.

B. crassifolia 1 ft (30 cm)　　　　Siberia
Large rounded leaves tinged with red in winter. Cyclamen-pink flowers. Early spring.

Of the many fine hybrids 'Evening Glow' ('Abendglut'), crimson-purple; and 'Silver Light' ('Silberlicht'), white, are both well worth growing.

BETULA
(Betulaceae) Birch
Race of hardy trees of which the silver birches (*B. pendula*) are widely used as specimens or for grouping in the garden.
Cultural requirements: Any soil or situation.
Propagation: From seed when ripe in spring, and by grafting named varieties on to the common silver birch.
B. pendula (syn. *B. verrucosa*, *B. alba*)
50 ft (15 m) Silver Birch　Europe and Asia Minor
The silver birch, known as 'Lady of the Woods', is also native to the British Isles. Silver-grey to white bark. Various cultivars are obtainable, including 'Dalecarlica', the Swedish birch, tall and slender with deeply cut fern-like foliage and 'Youngii', the finest weeping birch, compact enough for the smaller garden.

BIENNIALS
Biennials are plants which produce leaves in their first year and flowers and seeds in their second season after which they die. They are widely used for spring and early summer bedding. Of these the three most widely grown are Wallflowers, Sweet Williams, and Canterbury Bells.

The majority of biennials are easy to raise from seed, sown out of doors in early summer, or in a cold frame a month or more earlier. The aim, in either case, is to obtain sturdy plants ready to go out into their flowering quarters in the autumn, or in the case of the later flowering kinds, in early spring.

Among other widely grown subjects that are either true biennials or treated as such are *Anchusa capensis, Cheiranthus allionii, Digitalis purpurea* and its hybrids, *Myosotis, Oenothera biennis, Papaver nudicaule, Matthiola incana,* and *Hesperis matronalis.*

BILLBERGIA
(Bromeliaceae)
Perennials for the warm greenhouse that also make good house plants. They are evergreen, with grey-green sword-shaped leaves, serrated at their edges. The pendent flower spikes have brightly coloured bracts.
Cultural requirements: John Innes No. 2 or similar potting compost and a minimum winter temperature of 45 °F (7 °C).
Propagation: By offshoots in spring.

B. nutans 1½ ft (45 cm)　　　　U.S.A.
Spikes of greenish bell-shaped flowers emerging from colourful cyclamen-pink bracts. Summer.

BINDWEED – see Weed Control

BIRCH – see *Betula*

BIRD OF PARADISE FLOWER
– see *Strelitzia reginae*

BIRDS
Birds can be a mixed blessing in the garden although, in the main, their activities are beneficial. They destroy enormous numbers of grubs, caterpillars, and other harmful insects. We should not, therefore, complain about the loss of a few soft fruits or the too rapid disappearance of decorative berries, particularly if we do not take the steps necessary to protect them.

Soft fruits such as raspberries, black and red currants, and gooseberries should have the protection of a fruit cage. Strawberries can be protected with netting, or cloches.

Sparrows sometimes wreak havoc among crocuses, primroses, and polyanthus, literally tearing every blossom to shreds. Black cotton, stretched between short twigs to cover the plants, is the best solution to this. The dormant flower buds of ornamental crab-apples and cherries, forsythias, pears, and plums are often attacked by bullfinches, which seem to delight in taking out every bud and dropping it on the ground underneath. With small trees, cottoning may afford some protection but for larger trees some form of bird scare or a repellent in spray form will have to be used. Where jays and pigeons cause damage among the peas and broad beans and brassicas, netting will have to be resorted to.

Birds can be attracted to the garden with feeding tables, nesting boxes, and pools or birdbaths.

BLACK CURRANT – see Fruit Garden

BLACK-EYED SUSAN – see *Thunbergia alata*

BLADDER SENNA – see *Colutea*

BLANKET FLOWER – see *Gaillardia*

BLAZING STAR – see *Liatris*

BLECHNUM
(Polypodiaceae)
Evergreen ferns, several hardy forms of which are useful in the garden.
Cultural requirements: Good garden soil not too heavy and a shaded situation.

Propagation: From spores sown in heat; division in spring or autumn.

B. spicant 1 ft (30 cm)
Hard Fern   Europe, including British Isles
A fern for dry shade with bright deep green fronds.

B. tabulare (*B. magellanicum*) 2 ft (60 cm)
          W. Indies, Falkland Islands, and S. Africa
Dark green leathery fronds, ladder-like in appearance.

BLEEDING HEART – see *Dicentra*

BLUEBERRY – see *Vaccinium corymbosum*

BORAGE – see Herb Garden

BOUGAINVILLEA
(Nyctaginaceae)

Dedicuous climbing plants for the warm greenhouse, whose attraction lies in their strikingly coloured bracts.

Cultural requirements: Well-drained loamy soil in the greenhouse border or in large pots or tubs. Keep dry after flowering and prune back shoots to old wood in winter.

Propagation: By cuttings under glass in late spring.

B. glabra up to 8 ft (2·5 m)   Brazil
A vigorous grower, with lilac-pink bracts in great profusion. 'Mrs Butt' is a handsome cultivar with crimson bracts. Summer.

BOUVARDIA
(Rubiaceae)

Late flowering evergreen shrubs for greenhouse cultivation. In more favoured districts, they can be grown against a sheltered south wall.

Cultural requirements: John Innes No. 2 or similar compost for pots or tubs in the greenhouse. The shoots of the current year's growth should be pruned back hard in late winter. Water sparingly in winter.

Propagation: By cuttings under glass in heat in spring; by root cuttings in late winter.

B. triphylla 2 ft (60 cm)   Mexico
Small shrub with brilliant orange-scarlet tubular flowers. Late summer to autumn.

Bougainvillea glabra

BRACHYCOME
(Compositae)
Half-hardy annuals with daisy-like flowers.
Cultural requirements: Any ordinary garden soil and a sunny situation.
Propagation: From seed under glass in early spring, or outdoors in late spring.

B. iberidifolia 1 ft (30 cm)
Swan River Daisy   Australia
Dwarf half-hardy annual with masses of daisy flowers. The type plant has purple flowers but there are various mixtures in a wide range of colours, including white. Summer.

BRACT
Bracts are small leaves surrounding flowers. Some are green but in many plants they serve a decorative purpose, e.g., the lime-green bracts of some euphorbias and hellebores, the scarlet bracts of poinsettias and the many colours of those of clary.

BRAMBLE – see *Rubus*

BRASSICAS – see Kitchen Garden

BRIZA
(Gramineae) Quaking Grass
Decorative annual and perennial grasses, useful for cutting. They dry well for winter arrangements.
Cultural requirements: Any ordinary garden soil and a sunny situation.
Propagation: From seed in spring where plants are to grow.

B. maxima 1½ ft (45 cm)   Mediterranean
Elegant drooping oat-like seedheads on slender stems. Annual. Summer.

B. media 1 ft (30 cm)   W. Europe
Similar to the above mentioned species but flowers purple tinged, smaller and daintier in appearance. Perennial. Summer.

BROOM – see *Cytisus*, *Genista*, and *Spartium*

BROWALLIA
(Solanaceae)
Long flowering greenhouse annuals with attractive blue or purple flowers similar to those of large violets.
Cultural requirements: John Innes No. 2 or similar potting compost.
Propagation: From seed sown in early spring for autumn flowering or in summer for winter and spring flowering.

B. speciosa 2 ft (60 cm)   Colombia
The large bright blue flowers make this a good winter plant for the greenhouse. *B. s. major* is the best form and there are also varieties with white and deep violet-blue flowers. Autumn or late winter.

BRUNNERA
(Boraginaceae)
Formerly part of the anchusa family and a hardy perennial useful in the border in late spring.
Cultural requirements: Moist, well-drained soil; sun or part shade.
Propagation: Division in autumn.

B. macrophylla 1½ ft (45 cm)
Giant Forget-me-Not   Caucasus
Formerly known as *Anchusa myosotidiflora*, this plant has large rough-textured heart-shaped leaves and sprays of blue flowers like those of a large forget-me-not. Early summer.

BUDDLEIA
(Loganiaceae)
A genus of shrubs, whose hardy forms are of great value in the garden.
Cultural requirements: Any ordinary garden soil and a sunny situation. *B. davidii* and *B. fallowiana* should be pruned back hard each spring; *B. alternifolia* and *B. globosa* are pruned after flowering.
Propagation: From cuttings in summer; seed under glass in spring.

B. alternifolia up to 10 ft (3 m)   China
A large shrub or small tree of weeping habit, ideal as a lawn specimen in the small garden. Elegant pendent branches wreathed in fragrant lilac-mauve flowers. Best effect is obtained when *B. alternifolia* is restricted to a single main stem. Summer.

B. davidii up to 15 ft (4·5 m)
Butterfly Bush   China
The most popular and widely grown species and a valuable shrub for the late summer display. The long, vanilla-scented flower spikes attract butterflies. Good named forms include 'Black Knight', deep violet; 'Fortune', lilac with orange eye; 'Royal Red', wine-red; and 'White Profusion', pure white with yellow eye. Late summer.

B. fallowiana 8 ft (2·5 m)   China
This more compact species is on the tender side and needs the protection of a warm wall in colder districts. Attractive silver-grey felted foliage and large trusses of lavender-blue flowers. 'Lochinch', a hybrid between *B. davidi* and *B. fallowiana* is more compact than either, with soft grey foliage and dainty pale lavender flower spikes. Late summer.

B. globosa 12 ft (4 m) Orange Ball Tree   Chile
This species is semi-evergreen, with clusters of orange ball-like flower heads. Early summer.

BULRUSH – see *Scirpus*

BUPHTHALMUM
(Compositae)

Hardy perennials with yellow daisy flowers, useful in the herbaceous border.

Cultural requirements: Any ordinary garden soil and a sunny open situation.

Propagation: Division in spring.

B. salicifolium 2 ft (60 cm)   S. Europe
Narrow leaves on erect stems, bright yellow daisies, 1½ in. (4 cm) across. Summer.

BUSY LIZZIE – see *Impatiens sultanii*

BUTCHER'S BROOM – see *Ruscus aculeatus*

BUTOMUS
(Butomaceae)

Aquatic plants for margins of pools and streams.

Cultural requirements: Any ordinary soil. Shallow water, up to 4 in. (10 cm) deep.

Propagation: Division in spring.

B. umbellatus 3 ft (1 m)
Flowering Rush   Europe, including British Isles
Rush-like leaves, bronzy when young, large heads of rose-pink flowers. Summer.

BUTTERFLY BUSH – see *Buddleia davidi*

BUXUS
(Buxaceae)

Hardy evergreen shrubs, widely used for edging, hedging, and topiary work. Clipped, makes an effective tub plant.

Cultural requirements: Any ordinary garden soil; position in sun or shade.

Propagation: Semi-hard stem cuttings in late summer, or layering in autumn.

B. sempervirens up to 15 ft (4·5 m)
Common Box
                S. Europe, W. Asia, and N. Africa
Dense mass of small dark green leaves. There are numerous forms and varieties, including 'Aureo-variegata', with gold-splashed foliage; 'Elegantis-sima', whose leaves are margined with silver; and 'Handsworthensis', one of the best forms for hedging. 'Suffruticosa', the form used for box edging is a dwarf cultivar sold by length by most nurseries. This is put in with each plant almost touching. It was widely used in the knot gardens of Tudor times and still makes one of the best permanent edgings for a formal or terrace garden.

CABBAGE – see Kitchen Garden

CACTI

The cultivation of cacti has always held a fascination for many people and with the growing popularity of house plants, this interest has greatly increased of recent years. Cacti make excellent indoor plants that are comparatively undemanding and that need only a minimum amount of attention. Being mainly desert plants, they can go without water for long periods, a useful characteristic for those who spend a good deal of time away from home and a solution to the problem of who is to do the watering during the holidays.

The flowers of many kinds are ephemeral – sometimes lasting only a matter of hours. They redeem this shortcoming, however, by their brilliant colouring and beauty of form, as well as by the interesting and attractive appearance of the plants at all times.

Not all types of cactus are easy to cultivate, particularly where bringing them to the flowering stage is concerned, but the following, which are described in the appropriate sections of the text, would make a good initial choice for the novice: Chamaecereus, Cereus, Echinopsis, Mammilaria, and Rebutia.

The best position for cacti is on a sunny window-ledge indoors or on a sunny shelf in the greenhouse. Without a reasonable quota of sunlight, few of the cactus species are likely to produce flowers.

Plants growing in a greenhouse must be kept frost-free in winter. For most kinds of cactus, a minimum temperature of 40 °C (4 °C) will be sufficient. Keeping the plants completely dry during winter will reduce their susceptibility to damage from cold. Plants growing indoors, however, may need watering occasionally during winter.

John Innes No. 2, with the addition of some

Cactus Choice Mixed

coarser material such as crushed brick rubble or coarse grit, makes a suitable compost in which to grow cacti. Propagation is from seed or by cuttings or offsets. Cuttings should be dried off for a few days prior to insertion in a rooting medium. This will seal the cuts and reduce the risk of rotting. The best times for such operations are in late spring and summer.

Seed sowing should be carried out in very early spring under glass in a temperature of not less than 65–70 °F (18–21 °C).

CALADIUM
(Araceae)

Tuberous-rooted perennials for the warm greenhouse, cultivated for their handsome and colourful arrow-head leaves. They are also popular house plants, although somewhat difficult to manage in the latter conditions.

Cultural requirements: A potting compost rich in humus, i.e., with the addition of well-rotted manure or garden compost. Pots should be in a shaded position in the greenhouse. Withhold water during winter.

Propagation: By division in early spring.

C. candidum 2 ft (60 cm)   S. America
This popular species has large to small and wide to narrow green and red leaves. There are many cultivars and hybrids with red, orange, green, and white patterned foliage.

CALANDRINIA
(Portulaceae) Rock Purslane

Hardy annuals and perennials, suitable for the rock garden or border.

Cultural requirements: Any well-drained garden soil and a sunny situation.

Propagation: Annual species from seed under glass in early spring or outdoors later; perennial species from seed or by root division in spring.

C. grandiflora 1½ ft (45 cm)   Chile
Hardy perennial, often treated as an annual, with rosy-purple flowers, and grey-green fleshy leaves, useful for sunny beds and borders. Summer.

C. umbellata 6 in. (15 cm)   Peru
Perennial of trailing habit, normally treated as a hardy annual. The leaves and stems are fleshy and it has bright magenta flowers. Early to late summer.

CALANTHE
(Orchidaceae)

An easily cultivated terrestrial orchid, noteworthy for the long lasting quality of its flowers. There are both evergreen and deciduous species.

Cultural requirements: Potting compost of fibrous loam, sand, leafmould, and chopped sphagnum moss. Water freely in summer, very sparingly during winter. Minimum winter temperature 60 °F (15 °C). Plants should be shaded from sun during summer.

Propagation: By division of pseudobulbs in spring.

C. furcata   Java
Evergreen species with long spikes of creamy-white flowers. Summer.

C. vestita   India
One of the most popular and widely grown orchids, with sprays of white flowers that last for an exceptionally long time. They are widely used for table decoration and as corsages. Deciduous. Winter.

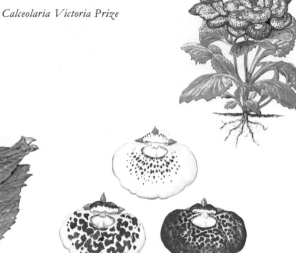

Calceolaria Victoria Prize

Calendula Pacific Beauty Mixed

CALCEOLARIA
(Scrophulariaceae)

Half-hardy herbaceous plants and sub-shrubs. The perennial kinds are usually treated as half-hardy annuals. In addition to their value as bedding plants, they make attractive pot plants for the cool greenhouse or a sunny window-ledge.

Cultural requirements: Shrubby forms: John Innes No. 2 or similar compost. Perennial kinds: Treatment as for half-hardy annuals.

Propagation: Outdoor bedding cultivars: From seed under glass in early spring to provide plants for summer bedding. Greenhouse varieties: From seed under glass in late spring or early summer. Minimum temperature of 45 °F (7 °C). Shrubby species and cultivars: By cuttings in a shady cold frame in early autumn.

Hardy species

C. biflora 9 in. (22 cm)   Peru
A dwarf form with yellow pouched flowers, suitable for the rock garden. Summer.

C. darwinii 4 in. (10 cm)   Patagonia
Orange-yellow pouched flowers, striped with white and spotted with brown. Summer.

C. polyrrhiza 6 in. (15 cm)   Argentine
Creeping species with yellow spotted flowers. Summer.

Bedding species and cultivars

These are mainly cultivars of *C. rugosa* (syn. *C. integrifolia*). F_1 hybrid forms such as 'Sunshine' are a great improvement on the older kinds and are invaluable for bedding, pots, or window-boxes. Summer.

Greenhouse species and cultivars

C. × multiflora, largely hybrids of *C. crenatiflora* and *C. purpurea* are deservedly popular as pot plants for house or greenhouse. There are some excellent strains with very large flower trusses in a wide range of colours. These include 'Victoria Prize', with an interesting colour range that rings the changes on orange, yellow, and scarlet. 'Grandiflora' is a strain noteworthy for the size of its flowers, 'Multiflora Mixed', produces plants of more compact habit that bear large trusses of smaller flowers. Late summer to autumn.

CALCIFUGE

A plant which cannot tolerate lime or alkaline soil conditions. Typical examples are rhododendrons, azaleas and many of the heather species. Other plants may be tolerant of lime in varying degrees.

CALENDULA

(Compositae) Pot Marigold

Popular and easy to grow hardy annuals with flowers in shades of orange and yellow.
Cultural requirements: Any ordinary garden soil and a sunny or partly shaded situation.
Propagation: From seed outdoors where plants are to flower. Seed can also be sown in late summer to provide plants to flower early the following season.

C. officinalis 1 ft (30 cm)
Common Marigold   S. Europe
There are numerous cultivars and hybrids of the common marigold in cultivation, all of them a great improvement on the type. They include such forms as 'Golden King', with very large golden-yellow flowers; 'Radio', orange flowers with quilled petals; 'Chrysantha', buttercup-yellow with chrysanthemum-like blooms; and 'Apricot Beauty', with flowers of an unusual shade of apricot-yellow. Summer.

CALICO BUSH – see *Kalmia latifolia*

CALIFORNIAN POPPY – see *Eschscholzia*

CALLA

(Araceae) Bog Arum

Aquatic plants, ideal for boggy soil or shallow pools. Perennial.
Cultural requirements: Rich waterlogged soil.
Propagation: By offshoots of rootstock.

C. palustris 6 in. (15 cm)
White arum-like spathes, freely produced. Not to be confused with *Caltha palustris*, the kingcup or marsh marigold. Summer.

CALLA LILY – see *Zantedeschia aethiopica*

CALLICARPA

(Verbenaceae)

Hardy shrubs grown primarily for the beauty of their purple berries. Their leaves also colour attractively in winter.
Cultural requirements: Well-drained soil and a sheltered situation, such as a south or west wall. To obtain good crops of berries, callicarpas should be planted in groups.
Propagation: From seed or by softwood cuttings, under glass in late summer.

C. bodinieri 10 ft (3 m)   China
Long leaves, lilac flowers, and violet fruits. The variety *giraldii*, sometimes still offered as *C. giraldiana*, is one of the hardiest forms, with masses of pale violet fruits.

CALLIOPSIS – see *Coreopsis*

CALLISTEMON

(Myrtaceae) Bottle Brush

Evergreen Australasian shrubs, suited only for more favoured districts outdoors. They also make good plants for the cool greenhouse. Their popular name is derived from their flower spikes which are cylindrical with long fluffy stamens.
Cultural requirements: Outdoors: Well-drained acid soil and a sunny sheltered situation. Greenhouse culture: John Innes No. 2 or similar compost. Prune lightly after flowering.
Propagation: By cuttings under glass in heat during summer.

C. citrinus (syn. *C. lanceolatus*)
8 ft (2·5 m)   Australia
This, the most widely grown species, has bottle brush flowers with crimson stamens. In the cultivar 'Splendens', these are a striking scarlet. Summer.

C. speciosus 8 ft (2·5 m)   Australia
A shrub of medium size with narrow pointed foliage and red flower spikes. Summer.

CALLISTEPHUS

(Compositae) China Aster

Half-hardy annuals, the many hybrid strains of which are widely used in summer bedding.
Cultural requirements: Rich soil and a sunny or lightly shaded situation.
Propagation: From seed sown under glass in heat in spring to produce plants for hardening off and planting out in early summer. Sowings can also be made outdoors in late spring in the positions in which the plants are to flower. Under glass, use Cheshunt Compound to prevent the damping-off disease to which Asters are particularly susceptible.

C. chinensis up to 3 ft (1 m) China
Various forms and strains of this species are available including dwarf, peony-flowered, ostrich plume, comet, and giant flowered. The 'Unicum' strain of the last named, with needle-thin petals like those of a rayonnante chrysanthemum, are particularly attractive. The large flowered singles with long stemmed flowers are useful for cutting. Colours range from white through various shades of pink and crimson to deepest purple. Summer.

CALLUNA
(Ericaceae) Heather or Ling
This is the common heather, native of the heaths and moors of Europe, including the British Isles.
Cultural requirements: Preference is for an acid peat soil, but will flourish in most garden soils provided they are lime-free. A sunny situation is best although they will thrive in light shade. Prune after flowering.
Propagation: From cuttings under glass in late summer or division in spring.

C. vulgaris
up to 2 ft (60 cm) Europe, including British Isles
This single *Calluna* species has given rise to many fine cultivars, of which some of the best are 'Alba Plena', double white; 'H. E. Beale', long rose-pink flowers; 'J. H. Hamilton', dwarf pink double; and 'Peter Sparkes', deep pink double. Midsummer to autumn.

CALTHA
(Ranunculaceae)
Hardy, moisture loving perennials, ideal for poolside planting or the bog garden.
Cultural requirements: Rich, moist, loamy soil at margins of pools or streams.
Propagation: Root division in spring.

C. palustris 1 ft (30 cm) Marsh Marigold
or Kingcup Europe, including British Isles
There are several attractive cultivars of the golden kingcup, with its large, buttercup-like flowers. 'Flore Pleno' is a double golden-yellow form; 'Alba' has attractive single white blooms. Spring.

CALYCANTHUS
(Calycanthaceae)
Hardy deciduous shrubs with fragrant flowers and aromatic leaves and stems.
Cultural requirements: Any good garden soil rich in humus and a fairly sheltered, sunny situation.
Propagation: From seed in a cold frame in spring; layers in summer.

C. fertilis 6 ft (2 m) N. America
Glossy foliage, small brownish-crimson metallic looking flowers. Summer.

C. floridus 6 ft (2 m) Carolina Allspice S. U.S.A.
Often confused with *C. fertilis*, this species has similar blooms but the leaves are downy on their underside. Summer.

CAMELLIA
(Theaceae)
Beautiful evergreen flowering shrubs most of which, contrary to former belief, are completely hardy although buds and flowers are susceptible to frost damage. They make ideal plants for tubs or the cool greenhouse.
Cultural requirements: Any good garden soil provided it is lime-free and a shady or sheltered situation. Where late spring frosts are prevalent plant on north or west to prevent early morning sun from thawing out the buds and flowers too rapidly.

C. japonica up to 30 ft (9 m) Japan
Large, but fairly slow growing evergreen shrub, with beautifully polished oval leaves. Of the numerous cultivars, many of which are outstanding, the following are particularly deserving of mention: 'Adolphe Audusson', deep red semi-double, with prominent central boss of golden stamens; 'Donckelarii', semi-double crimson-red, marbled with white; 'Elegans' (syn. 'Chandleri Elegans'), double pink flowers up to 5 in. (13 cm) across; and 'Tricolor', semi-double white, streaked with carmine. Late winter to spring.

C. reticulata up to 20 ft (6 m) China
A superb species, needing the protection of a cool greenhouse in all but the most favoured districts, where it can be grown against a sheltered south or west wall. The first plants were brought to Britain on the China tea clippers and are named after the masters of these vessels. 'Captain Rawes', with semi-double rose-pink flowers, up to 8 in. (20 cm) across, is one of these and was for long regarded as the type plant until the discovery of a single wild form in China in 1924. 'Mary Williams' is a hardy cultivar with large single deep pink flowers. Late winter to early spring.

C. × williamsii up to 15 ft (4·5 m)
(*C. japonica* × *C. saluensis*) Garden origin
These hybrids, the first of which were raised by Mr J. C. Williams of Caerhays Castle in Cornwall, are among the finest camellias for outdoor cultivation. They flower freely over a very long period from midwinter to late spring. They have the tidy habit, inherited from their japonica parent, of dropping their flowers as soon as they fade.

Good cultivars include 'Donation', pink, semi-double; 'J. C. Williams', pale blush-pink with prominent golden stamens; and 'Mary Christian' a small pink single. Midwinter to late spring.

Campanula Medium
(Canterbury Bells)

CAMPANULA
(Campanulaceae) Bellflower

A very large family of annuals, biennials, and perennials, and a source of valuable material for the border, rock garden, and greenhouse.

Cultural requirements: Any ordinary garden soil, rich in humus and a situation in sun or part shade.

Propagation: Annual kinds: From seed sown under glass in spring. Biennials: From seed outdoors in early summer to provide plants to go out in their flowering quarters in autumn. Perennial species: From seed or root division.

C. × burghaltii 2 ft (60 cm)   Garden origin
Long pendent bells of pale violet produced in axils of upper leaves. Hardy perennial. Summer.

C. carpatica 6 in. (15 cm)   E. Europe
Dwarf carpeting plants, useful in the rock garden, with very long flowering period. Good named forms include 'Ditton Blue', deep indigo, and 'White Star', a large flowered white. Hardy perennial.

C. glomerata up to 1½ ft (45 cm)
                    Europe, including British Isles
Clusters of violet-purple flowers, rather like those of a rhododendron on erect stems. 'Alba' is a good white form; 'Dahurica', deep violet; and 'Superba', a deep violet-blue. Hardy perennial.

C. lactiflora up to 5 ft (1·5 m)   Caucasus
The taller varieties of this species make excellent border plants with beautiful pale blue wide open bell flowers. 'Loddon Anna' has flowers of a soft lilac-pink; 'Prichard's Variety' is a striking violet-blue. Hardy perennial. Mid to late summer.

C. latifolia 4 ft (1·2 m) Giant Bellflower
          Europe, including British Isles, and Asia
Good plant for back of the border. Large pendulous flowers on erect stems. 'Alba' is a white form; 'Brantwood' is a rich violet-purple. Hardy perennial. Mid to late summer.

C. medium 3 ft (1 m) Canterbury Bell S. Europe
These are hardy biennials, easy to grow from seed and useful for late spring bedding; wide colour range, through pink, lavender, and blue and including white. In addition to the ordinary kinds, dwarf and double strains are obtainable as well as the popular cup and saucer form, *C. m. calycanthema*. Early summer.

C. persicifolia
3 ft (1 m)   Europe, including British Isles
One of the best of the border species. Single blue flowers. 'Snowdrift' is a good white; 'Telham Beauty' an attractive pale blue. Hardy perennial. Mid to late summer.

C. portenschlagiana 4 in. (10 cm)   S. Europe
Prostrate perennial and a useful, although some-
what invasive carpeting plant for the rock garden or on dry walls. Masses of light bluish-purple bells over a long period. Summer.

C. pyramidalis 5 ft (1·5 m)
Chimney Bellflower   Dalmatia
Tall spires of blue flowers. There is also a white form 'Alba'. Hardy perennial. Late summer.

CAMPION – see *Lychnis*

CAMPSIS
(Bignoniaceae) Trumpet Vine

Deciduous climbers with striking scarlet trumpet flowers, some of which are self-clinging by means of aerial roots.

Cultural requirements: Good loam, rich in humus and a sunny sheltered position against a south wall. Can be cut back hard in early spring.

Propagation: Hardwood cuttings in autumn, suckers, root cuttings, or seeds.

C. grandiflora (syn. *C. chinensis*)
up to 30 ft (9 m)   China
Vigorous climber with orange-scarlet funnel-shaped flowers. Late summer to early autumn.

C. radicans up to 25 ft (8 m)   S.E. U.S.A.
Self-clinging species with attractive pinnate foliage, coarsely toothed. Orange-scarlet trumpet flowers up to 4 in. (10 cm) long, borne in terminal clusters.

C. × tagliabuana is a striking hybrid between the two above mentioned species of which 'Madame Galen', with salmon-red flowers, is the best form.

CANDYTUFT – see *Iberis*

CANNA
(Cannaceae) Indian Shot

Greenhouse perennials, also widely used for focal planting in summer bedding schemes.

Cultural requirements: In pots in rich growing medium in a sunny greenhouse. Outdoors, in a sunny sheltered situation during summer. Roots can be stored in winter in dry soil or sand in a frost-proof shed or garage.

Propagation: From seed under glass in heat in early spring; by root division in spring. Seed should be chipped or soaked before sowing.

The garden cultivars are hybrids between a number of different Central and South American species. The spikes of scarlet or yellow flowers range from 2 to 4 ft (60 cm to 1·2 m) and are extremely decorative and are set off perfectly by the bright green or crimson-purple flushed leaves. Summer to autumn.

CANTERBURY BELL
– see *Campanula medium*

CAPE FIGWORT – *Phygelius capensis*

CAPE GOOSEBERRY – see *Physalis*

CAPSICUM
(Solanaceae) Red Pepper

Greenhouse sub-shrubs grown for their decorative fruits and also (chilis and cayenne) commercially for their use as spices. They are normally treated as annuals and raised from seed.
Cultural requirements: John Innes No. 2 or similar potting compost or outdoors in rich sandy soil against a sheltered south wall.
Propagation: From seed under glass in heat in early spring.

C. annuum up to 2 ft (60 cm)   Tropics
This species contains cultivars with widely differing types of fruit – red, black, round or pointed.

CARDIOCRINUM
(Liliaceae) Giant Lily

Hardy bulbous plants, formerly members of the lily genus.
Cultural requirements: Well-drained soil rich in humus. Bulbs will benefit by feeding with a liquid fertilizer during the growing period. A partly shaded situation suits them best.
Propagation: From bulb offsets in autumn or from seed in a mixture of peat and sand in a cold frame in autumn. The resulting plants will take six or seven years to come into flower.

C. giganteum up to 8 ft (2·5 m)   Himalayas
Numerous white trumpet flowers, red at their base, 6 in. (15 cm) or more long, borne on tall stems, followed by decorative seedheads. The basal leaves are heart-shaped. Summer.

CARDOON – see *Cynara cardunculus*

CARNATION – see *Dianthus*

CARPINUS
(Betulaceae) Hornbeam

Hardy deciduous trees, many forms of which are too large for the small to medium-sized garden. The American species *C. caroliniana* and the Japanese *C. japonica* are, however, both useful small trees.
Cultural requirements: Medium to heavy soils for preference.
Propagation: From seed outdoors in autumn.

C. betulus up to 70 ft (21 m) Common Hornbeam
 Europe, including British Isles, and Asia Minor
Useful either as specimen trees for large gardens, or for hedging. Like beech, a hornbeam hedge retains its dead foliage in winter and is a good substitute for the former in heavy clay soils.

'Columnaris' and 'Fastigiata' are both smaller trees of upright habit; 'Pendula' is an attractive weeping form of compact habit.

CARROT – see Kitchen Garden

CARTWHEEL FLOWER
– see *Heracleum mantegazzianum*

CARYOPTERIS
(Verbenaceae)

A race of useful late flowering deciduous shrubs of compact habit, with aromatic foliage and blue flowers.
Cultural requirements: Well-drained soil and a sunny situation.
Propagation: From cuttings in a frame in autumn.

C. × *clandonensis* (*C. incana* × *C. mongolica*)
3 ft (1 m)   Garden origin
There are several selected forms of this attractive hybrid. 'Arthur Simmonds', named for the secretary of the Royal Horticultural Society, who first raised it, has bright blue flowers and grey-green foliage. 'Ferndown' has flowers of a deeper blue-violet; 'Heavenly Blue', an American introduction, is more compact than the original with flowers slightly deeper in colour. Late summer to autumn.

CASTOR OIL PLANT – see *Ricinus*

CATALPA
(Bignoniaceae) Indian Bean

Hardy deciduous trees, low and spreading with ornamental leaves.
Cultural requirements: Any well-drained soil and a sheltered situation.
Propagation: From seed in spring, layers in autumn or cuttings under glass in summer.

C. bignonioides up to 30 ft (9 m)   E. U.S.A.
Medium-sized tree with decorative heart-shaped leaves, up to 9 in. (22 cm) in length. The flower clusters, rather like those of a foxglove, are white, with yellow and purple markings. 'Aurea' is a striking form with leaves of clear golden-yellow. Late summer.

CATANANCHE
(Compositae)

Hardy perennials with cornflower-like flowers, borne in great profusion.
Cultural requirements: Any well-drained garden soil and a sunny situation.
Propagation: From seed under glass in spring; root cuttings in autumn.

C. coerulea 2 ft (60 cm) Cupid's Dart   S. Europe
Deep mauve or white semi-double flowers with

papery bracts silvered on their reverse. The flowers dry well for winter arrangements. Summer to early autumn.

CATERPILLARS – see Pest Control

CATMINT – see *Nepeta*

CAULIFLOWER – see Kitchen Garden

CEANOTHUS
(Rhamnaceae) Californian Lilac
An extensive group of evergreen and deciduous shrubs, best grown as wall shrubs in colder districts.
Cultural requirements: Light well-drained soil and a sunny situation against a south or west wall. Prune deciduous kinds by cutting back in spring, laterals to within about 4 in. (10 cm) of the base of the previous year's growth. Evergreen kinds need only occasional light pruning to keep them within bounds.
Propagation: From layers or from semi-hard stem cuttings under glass in late summer.

Evergreen kinds

C. × Autumnal Blue 8 ft (2·5 m)   Garden origin
One of the hardiest of the evergreen ceanothuses with small glossy leaves and masses of soft blue flowers. Late summer to autumn.

C. × Burkwoodii up to 20 ft (6 m) Garden origin
A shrub of medium size, growing taller against a wall. Small flowers of a rich deep blue, delicately fragrant. Late summer to autumn.

C. Cascade up to 20 ft (6 m)   Garden origin
One of the loveliest spring flowering hybrids. Long sprays of intensely blue flowers on arching stems. Early summer.

C. × Delight 10 ft (3 m)   Garden origin
Another of the hardiest evergreen kinds with dark green polished foliage and rich blue flowers. Late spring.

C. × Gloire de Versailles
10 ft (3 m)   Garden origin
The most widely grown deciduous ceanothus. Soft powder-blue flowers in profusion. Early summer.

C. thyrsiflorus 15 ft (4·5 m)   California
One of the hardier evergreen species, with bright blue flowers. *C. t. repens*, with a prostrate habit of growth is ideal for a low wall or a position under a window. Early summer.

C. × Topaz 8 ft (2·5 m)   Garden origin
This is another delightful deciduous hybrid with flowers of a light indigo-blue. Summer to early autumn.

CEDAR – see *Cedrus*

CEDRUS
(Pinaceae) Cedar
A small group of noble hardy evergreen conifers, of immense architectural value with their wide spreading horizontal branch structure but unfortunately, too big and extensive for any but the larger gardens.
Cultural requirements: Deep, rich, sandy soil, either acid or alkaline.
Propagation: From seed in a cold frame or open ground in spring. Cultivars by grafting on to species or by cuttings in late summer.

C. atlantica 120 ft (36 m) Atlas Cedar   N. Africa
Magnificent and stately fast growing tree with green or grey-green needle-like foliage and barrel-shaped cones. *C. a. glauca*, the most widely grown variety, has striking silvery-blue foliage.

C. deodara 100 ft (30 m) Deodar   Himalayas
The branches of this species are more pendulous than those of *atlantica* or *libani*. The dwarf forms 'Pendula' and 'Pygmaea' make ideal specimens for the large rock garden.

C. libani 120 ft (36 m)
Cedar of Lebanon   Asia Minor
Large and wide spreading trees with grey-green foliage. There are several interesting dwarf cultivars, including 'Aurea Prostrata', a horizontal, bush-like form with golden foliage; 'Nana', dense and conical in habit; and 'Sargentii', a blue-green weeping pygmy cedar. All of these make good specimen plants for the rock garden.

CELASTRUS
(Celastraceae)
Self-clinging twining shrubs, of which there are numerous species but only one, *C. orbiculatus*, in general garden cultivation. Their berries have great decorative value in winter.
Cultural requirements: Any ordinary garden soil, in sun or part shade.
Propagation: From seed, by layers, or softwood cuttings in autumn.

C. orbiculata (syn. *C. articulata*)
up to 40 ft (12 m)   S.E. Asia
Vigorous deciduous self-clinging climber grown for the beauty of its brownish seed capsules which split open at maturity to reveal scarlet seeds. The yellow autumn foliage makes a perfect setting for these.

CELOSIA
(Amaranthaceae)
Half-hardy annuals for the greenhouse and for use as summer bedding plants. Crested or plumed flower heads in shades of crimson, scarlet, and orange.

Cultural requirements: Greenhouse cultivation: John Innes No. 2 or similar compost.

Outdoors: A fairly light soil and a sunny situation.

Propagation: From seed under glass in heat in spring.

C. argentea up to 3 ft (1 m) Cockscomb China
The two most popular kinds are 'Cristata', with crested flower heads in various colours and 'Plumosa', with a more feathery type of blossom. 'Jewel Box' is an excellent strain of the former kind, with large cockscomb flowers in a wide range of colours, from yellow, through apricot, pink, salmon, and bronze to deep crimson. The 'Lilliput' mixture of 'Plumosa' produces attractive dwarf plants of pyramidal habit in shades of yellow, crimson, and scarlet. Summer.

CELSIA
(Scrophulariaceae)

Half-hardy annuals and perennials that make useful greenhouse pot plants.

Cultural requirements: John Innes No. 2 or similar compost. Position in full sun. The pots can also stand outdoors in summer in a sunny sheltered situation.

Propagation: From seed sown in heat in spring or late summer. Perennial species: From cuttings under glass in a cool greenhouse spring or autumn.

C. arcturus 2 ft (60 cm) Crete
Half-hardy shrubby perennial bearing long spikes of golden-yellow flowers with violet-purple anthers. Late summer.

CENTAUREA
(Compositae) Knapweed

Hardy and half-hardy annuals and perennials which include the annual cornflower and others with similar cornflower-type blooms.

Cultural requirements and propagation: Annuals: From seed sown outdoors in autumn or spring where plants are to flower. They like fairly rich soil and a sunny situation.

Perennials: Any good ordinary garden soil and a sunny situation.

Half-hardy species: From seed sown in heat in spring, plants grown on in pots for greenhouse decoration or planted outdoors in late spring for summer bedding.

C. cyanus up to 3 ft (1 m)
Cornflower Europe, including the British Isles
Popular hardy annuals with flowers in shades of blue, mauve, crimson, pink, and white. Good cutting material. Good strains include 'Blue Diadem', with larger flowers of a deeper blue than those of the ordinary kind; 'Polka Dot', a decorative dwarf mixture with a wide colour range; and 'Snowball', a form with fully double

Centaurea cyanus
'Polka Dot' (Cornflower)

white flowers carried well above the leaves. Summer.

C. dealbata 2 ft (60 cm)   Caucasus
Pinkish-purple, thistle-like flower buds. The variety 'Sternbergii' has rosy-crimson flowers. Perennial. Late summer to autumn.

C. macrocephala 3 ft (1 m)   Caucasus
Useful back of the border perennial plant with large yellow cornflowers having brown scaly bracts. Late summer to autumn.

C. montana 2 ft (60 cm)   Caucasus
Grey-green foliage and masses of large blue cornflowers. There are also forms with white, pink, or rosy-red flowers. Perennial. Late spring to summer.

C. moschata 2 ft (60 cm)
Sweet Sultan   E. Mediterranean
Hardy annuals with fragrant thistle-like flowers in shades of lilac-purple, pink, yellow, and white. Summer.

CENTRANTHUS
(syn. *Kentranthus*) (Valerianaceae)
Useful perennial for walls and banks.
Cultural requirements: Any ordinary garden soil and a sunny situation.
Propagation: From seed under glass in spring or by division in spring or autumn.

C. ruber 2 ft (60 cm)
Red Valerian   Europe, including British Isles
Clusters of crimson flowers profusely borne. There is an attractive white form 'Alba'. Summer to autumn.

CEPHALARIA
(Dipsaceae) Giant Scabious
Only one species of this race of hardy perennials is of particular use in the garden, *C. gigantea*.
Cultural requirements: Any garden soil, sunny or partly shaded situation.
Propagation: From seed outdoors in spring.

C. gigantea (syn. *C. tatarica*) 5 ft (1·5 m)   Siberia
A vigorous perennial, useful at the back of the border. Large heads of creamy-yellow, scabious-like flowers. Summer.

CERASTIUM
(Caryophyllaceae)
Useful but very invasive silvery-grey-leaved carpeting perennial. Can be used in the larger rock garden where it has sufficient room to spread, but is best relegated to dry walls and banks.
Cultural requirements: Any ordinary garden soil.
Propagation: From seed outdoors or division in spring; from cuttings in a shady border in summer.

C. tomentosum 6 in. (15 cm)
Snow-in-Summer   Europe
Silvery foliage and masses of white flowers. Rampant and invasive. Summer.

CERATOSTIGMA
(Plumbaginaceae) Leadwort
Hardy perennials or sub-shrubs with slate-blue, plumbago-like flowers.
Cultural requirements: Light sandy soil and a sunny situation.
Propagation: From rooted suckers or division in spring; or semi-hard stem cuttings in late summer.

C. plumbaginoides 1 ft (30 cm)   China
Dwarf sub-shrub with clusters of deep blue flowers. The leaves provide good autumn colour. Late summer to autumn.

C. willmottianum 3 ft (1 m)   W. China
Small shrubby plant with rich blue flowers and reddish-tinted autumn foliage. Late summer to autumn.

CERCIS
(Leguminosae)
Small trees with attractive rounded foliage and clusters of pea flowers.

Centaurea moschata
(Sweet Sultan)

Cultural requirements: Deep light rich soil and a sunny sheltered situation.
Propagation: From seed under glass in warmth in spring; by layers in spring or autumn.

C. siliquastrum 40 ft (12 m)
Judas Tree S. Europe
Masses of rosy-purple pea flowers in advance of the attractive foliage. Low and bushy habit when young. Early summer.

CEREUS
(Cactaceae)
Greenhouse succulents with spiny stems and no leaves.
Cultural requirements: John Innes No. 2 or similar compost, with the addition of crushed brick, mortar rubble, or grit. They do best on a sunny shelf in the greenhouse or on window-sills indoors. Water sparingly at all times.
Propagation: From seed or by stem cuttings in moist sand. The best known species include *C. aethiops* (syn. *C. caerulescens*), with white or pink flowers; the pink and white hybrid, *kewensis*; *C. peruvianus*, red and *C. tetragonus*, white. All of them flower in summer and can reach heights of 4 ft (1·2 m) or more. Summer.

CHAENOMELES
(Rosaceae)
Deciduous shrubs, still often referred to as 'Japonicas' or 'Cydonias', their former generic names. They are usually grown as wall shrubs; their apple-blossom-type flowers are followed by yellow fruits that make a good quince jelly.
Cultural requirements: Any type of garden soil. Prune summer and autumn as for apples and pears.
Propagation: From layers, grafts, or seed.

C. speciosa up to 10 ft (3 m) China
The species from which most garden forms are obtained. Most have red flowers. Some of the best are 'Atrococcinea', deep crimson; 'Moerloosii', pink and white; 'Simonii', blood-red; and 'Spitfire', deep crimson-red. Spring to early summer.

C. × *superba* (*C. japonica* × *C. speciosa*) 5 ft (1·5 m)
Small to medium-sized shrubs, vigorous and free flowering. 'Knap Hill Scarlet', orange-scarlet, and 'Rowallane', blood-red, both with a profusion of large flowers, are the two most widely grown forms. Spring to early summer.

CHALK PLANT – see *Gypsophila*

CHAMAECYPARIS
(Pinaceae) False Cypress
A genus of evergreen conifers which, in spite of containing few species, has given rise to countless cultivars of varying forms and sizes, with a wide range of coloured foliage. They have a variety of uses in the garden – as lawn specimens, for shelter and hedging and, in the case of the pygmy forms, in the rock garden. Formerly included with the true cypresses, they differ from these in having flattened branchlets and smaller cones.
Cultural requirements: Moist, well-drained soil, preferably slightly acid.
Propagation: From seed in spring; cuttings in late summer or autumn.

C. lawsoniana Lawson's Cypress California
This species contains many of the most popular garden forms, both large and small. Of the former, 'Columnaris' (30 ft – 9 m) is one of the finest, making a slender column of dense blue foliage. 'Fletcheri' and 'Ellwoodii' are two good grey-green cultivars of medium height; 'Lanei' and 'Lutea' are two of the most widely grown golden forms.

There is a wide choice of dwarf and miniature forms, including 'Chilworth Silver', a dwarf replica of 'Ellwoodii' not exceeding 4 ft (1·2 m) in height; 'Minima Aurea', a lovely golden pygmy of attractive conical outline; and 'Gimbornii' (2 ft – 60 cm), an exceptionally compact grey-green conifer of globular shape.

C. lawsoniana itself is a fine hedging variety, but less striking than the newer 'Green Hedger' which is fast growing with bright green foliage.

C. obtusa Japan
Some of the loveliest conifers are found in this species ranging from large trees to midgets, only 1 ft (30 cm) tall.

The best known of the taller kinds is 'Crippsii', a beautiful golden conifer not exceeding 30 ft (9 m) at maturity.

There are numerous dwarfs, including some attractive Japanese cultivars. 'Intermedia' (1 ft – 30 cm) makes a dense bush, closely packed with rich green foliage; 'Juniperoides', even smaller at about 4 in. (10 cm) makes an attractive specimen for a trough or sink garden; 'Kosteri' (6 ft – 2 m) is a useful conifer for the rock garden with bright green foliage that bronzes in winter.

C. pisifera
The best known cultivar of this species is the widely grown medium-sized 'Boulevard', with blue-grey sprays of feathery foliage and a loose, conical habit. 'Plumosa Aurescens' is a taller form with golden foliage; 'Filifera' is a tree of medium size with pendent branches and thread-like foliage.

CHEIRANTHUS
(Cruciferae) Wallflower
Hardy perennials, normally treated as hardy biennials and invaluable for spring bedding.

Cheiranthus cheiri (Common Wallflower)

Cultural requirements: Any ordinary well-drained garden soil and a sunny situation. Too rich a soil produces excessive leaf growth at the expense of flowers.

Propagation: From seed in early summer. Transplant seedlings to nursery beds when 2–3 in. (5–8 cm) high and plant out in flowering positions in autumn.

C. Allioni up to $1\frac{1}{2}$ ft (45 cm)
Siberian Wallflower
Bright orange flowers and a long flowering season make the Siberian wallflowers ideal bedding plants for bridging the gap between the spring and early summer displays. Cultivars include 'Apricot Delight', soft apricot; 'Golden Bedder', deep yellow; and 'Lemon Delight', lemon-yellow. Mid to late spring.

C. cheiri up to $1\frac{1}{2}$ ft (45 cm) Common Wallflower
One of our loveliest spring bedding plants noteworthy for its colour and delicious fragrance.

Taller cultivars: 'Blood Red', velvety-crimson; 'Cloth of Gold', golden-yellow; 'Eastern Queen', apricot-pink; 'Fire King', orange-red; and 'Scarlet Emperor', orange-scarlet.

Dwarf bedding cultivars: 'Golden Bedder', golden-yellow; 'Orange Bedder', rich orange; 'Vulcan', velvety-crimson; and 'Tom Thumb' strain, crimson, golden-yellow or mixed. Very dwarf and good for edging. Early to late spring.

CHELONE
(Scrophulariaceae) Turtlehead
Hardy perennials, useful in the herbaceous or mixed border.
Cultural requirements: Deep rich soil and an open situation.
Propagation: From seed under glass in heat in early spring; by division in early autumn.

C. glabra 3 ft (1 m)   N. America
Pink or white flowers on tall spikes. Late summer.

C. obliqua 3 ft (1 m)   N. America
Rosy-purple penstemon-like flowers in clusters on 2 ft (60 cm) stems. Late summer.

CHERRIES – see *Prunus*

CHERRY PIE – see *Heliotropium*

CHICORY – see Kitchen Garden

CHILEAN FIREBUSH – see *Embothrium*

CHIMONANTHUS
(Calycanthaceae) Wintersweet
Monotypic genus of hardy deciduous shrubs noteworthy for their winter flowering.
Cultural requirements: Any well-drained soil and a sunny sheltered situation which will encourage earlier flowering.

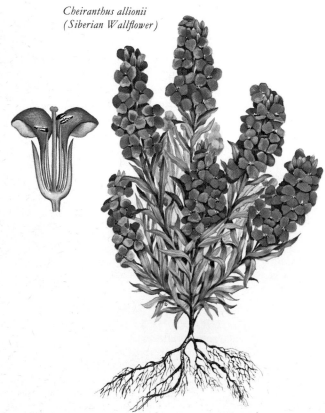

*Cheiranthus allionii
(Siberian Wallflower)*

Propagation: From seed in spring; by layers in spring or late autumn.

C. praecox 8 ft (2·5 m)
The waxy-textured yellow flowers, blotched with purple at their centres, are intensely fragrant. The variety 'Luteus', which flowers a little later than the type, has larger flowers of a uniform primrose-yellow that are not so strongly scented. Winter.

CHINESE BELLFLOWER – see *Platycodon*

CHIONODOXA
(Liliaceae) Glory of the Snow
Delightful early spring flowering bulbs with a profusion of small flowers that are mainly blue and white. They make good subjects for the rock garden or for planting in drifts in the border.
Cultural requirements: Light soil and a sunny situation. Plant bulbs in autumn.
Propagation: From seed in cold frame in late summer; from offset bulbs in autumn.

C. luciliae 6 in. (15 cm)   Turkey
Pale blue flowers with white centres up to ten a stem. Left undisturbed will naturalize freely. Early spring.
C. sardensis 6 in. (15 cm)   Turkey
Flowers of a deeper blue with less white at centre make this a more colourful species. *C. sardensis* spreads freely to make carpets of blue when established. Early spring.

CHLOROPHYTUM
(Liliaceae) Spider Plant
An attractive easily grown foliage plant for the house or cold greenhouse. Also used for hanging baskets and as a summer bedding plant.
Cultural requirements: John Innes No. 2 or similar compost for pot culture. A winter temperature of 45 °F (7 °C).
Propagation: From offshoots or root division.

C. capense (syn. *C. elatum*) 1 ft (30 cm)   S. Africa
The form most commonly seen is 'Variegatum', whose narrow green leaves are centrally striped with creamy-white. The small white flowers are insignificant. Young plantlets form on ends of flower stems and these can be pegged down into pots and grown on.

CHOISYA
(Rutaceae) Mexican Orange Blossom
Handsome evergreen shrubs with trifoliate leaves and sweetly scented creamy-white blossom.
Cultural requirements: Any good loam enriched with peat or leafmould. In colder districts the shelter of a south wall is advisable. Not averse to chalky soils and good for seaside districts.

Propagation: Cuttings under glass in heat in spring to early summer; or in a cold frame in early autumn.

C. ternata 5 ft (1·5 m)   Mexico
The foliage is aromatic when crushed; the creamy-white blossoms are intensely fragrant. Spring to early summer.

CHRISTMAS CACTUS – see *Zygocactus*

CHRISTMAS ROSE – see *Helleborus niger*

CHRYSANTHEMUM
(Compositae)
Chrysanthemums comprise a large group of hardy and greenhouse perennials as well as hardy annuals. The culture of the greenhouse varieties is a specialist job and competition is keen. The hardy perennial and annual varieties, however, are much easier to grow and make excellent subjects for the herbaceous or mixed border.
Cultural requirements: Annual and hardy perennial varieties: Any good garden soil and an open sunny situation.
Propagation: Annual varieties: From seed sown under glass in early spring or outdoors later in year. Hardy perennial varieties: From seed under glass in spring or division in spring.

Florists' Chrysanthemums: the Florists' or Japanese Chrysanthemums are mainly hybrids of

Chrysanthemum 'Sundance'
Annual Mixed

obscure parentage. Both the early flowering outdoor and the later indoor kinds are extremely popular with amateur gardeners and exhibitors. They include many different name forms divided into a number of classes for exhibition purposes. These include those with reflex and incurved petals, singles, sprays, and *rayonnante* or spider-flowered types. New stocks are raised annually from cuttings taken from the previous year's plants, in gentle heat under glass in late winter. These are potted on and in the case of early flowering kinds planted out in late spring or, for the late varieties, are stood outside in pots till early autumn when they are taken into a cool greenhouse to flower.

Hardy Annuals

C. carinatum up to 3 ft (1 m)   N. Africa
This chrysanthemum bears single flowers, banded with contrasting colours. It is a useful annual that will come into flower within a few weeks of an outdoor sowing. Dobies 'Rainbow Mixture' with flowers 2½ in. (6 cm) across have a colour range in combinations of yellow, scarlet, orange, bronze, and white. Summer.

C. coronarium 3 ft (1 m)   S. Europe
Semi-double button flowers, yellow and white. Very free flowering. Summer.

C. parthenium – see *Matricaria eximea*

C. × spectabile up to 3 ft (1 m)   Garden origin
A cross between the two species mentioned above, these hybrids produce long-stemmed

Chrysanthemum coccineum Single Mixed (Pyrethrum)

flowers excellent for cutting. 'Cecilia' has pure white blooms (4 in. – 10 cm) across; 'Sunray' has flowers of a vivid canary-yellow. Summer.

Hardy Perennials

C. coccineum (syn. *Pyrethrum roseum*)
up to 2½ ft (75 cm)   Caucasus
Valuable early summer flowering perennials with colourful daisy flowers that cut and last well. The single and double forms have a wide colour range that includes white, pink, salmon, scarlet, and crimson. There are many good named cultivars, including 'Brenda', cerise; 'Kelway's Glorious', scarlet; and 'Eileen May Robinson', salmon-pink. Early summer.

C. densum amanum (syn. *C. haradjanii*)
6 in. (15 cm)   Asia Minor
Dwarf plants, suitable for rock gardens, with finely cut silvery-white foliage and yellow flowers. Summer.

C. maximum 3 ft (1 m) Shasta Daisy   Pyrenees
Large flowered daisies, both single and double, that make good border plants, and a valuable source of flowers for cutting.

Some of the best cultivars are 'Esther Read', double white; 'Everest', large flowers, good for cutting; 'Wirral Pride', large double white flowers centrally tinged with yellow; and 'Wirral Supreme', another large flowered white double. Summer.

C. rubellum 2½ ft (75 cm)   China
Pink or lilac-pink daisy flowers. 'Clara Curtis' is a good form. Autumn.

C. uliginosum 5 ft (1·5 m)
Moon Daisy   E. Europe
Useful tall late flowering plant for back of border. White daisy flowers with yellow centres. Autumn.

CIMICIFUGA
(Ranunculaceae) Bugbane
Tall hardy perennials useful in the herbaceous border with decorative spikes of feathery white blossom.
Cultural requirements: Moist soil and, for preference, a shady situation.
Propagation: From seed under glass in autumn; division in spring.

C. americana (syn. *C. cordifolia*)
3 ft (1 m)   N. America
Creamy-white flower spikes on tall stems. Summer.

C. dahurica 6 ft (2 m)   China
White flower spikes tinged with pale mauve before opening. Summer.

C. racemosa 5 ft (1·5 m) Snake-root   N. America
Feathery plumes of creamy-white borne above finely cut polished green foliage. Summer.

Cineraria Brilliant Mixed

CINERARIA
(Compositae)

Half-hardy annuals and perennials of which the former are popular greenhouse or indoor pot plants with showy and colourful flowers.

Cultural requirements: see below.

Propagation: From seed under glass in gentle heat in early spring for *C. maritima* and late spring for *C. multiflora*. A temperature of 50 °F (10 °C) is sufficient and plants should be shaded from direct sunlight.

C. maritima see *Senecio maritima*

C. cruenta up to 2½ ft (75 cm)   Canary Islands
The correct name for this plant is *Senecio cruentus*. Although perennial, it is always treated as a half-hardy annual. Modern cultivars provide an exceptionally wide range of colours and flower form and are usually sold as *C. hybrida grandiflora*. Seed is sown from mid to late summer to provide a succession of flowers. Moist cool conditions suit cinerarias best. John Innes No. 2 or similar compost is used for final potting.

The plants produce large clusters of broad-petalled daisy-like blooms in brilliant colours. The taller stellata group, with delicate star-like flowers, is particularly attractive. Early to late winter.

CINQUEFOIL – see *Potentilla*

CISSUS
(Vitaceae)

A race of tender evergreen climbers suitable for the cool greenhouse and very popular as house plants.

Cultural requirements: In pots of John Innes No. 2 or similar compost in a cool greenhouse or on a light window-sill.

Propagation: From stem cuttings under glass in heat.

C. antarctica Kangaroo Vine   Australia
This popular climbing house plant will stand room temperatures as low as 40 °F (4 °C). It requires some form of support. The dark green glossy toothed foliage is very decorative. The kangaroo vine will thrive in partial shade.

CISTUS
(Cistaceae) Sun Rose

Sun-loving compact evergreen shrubs, useful in the rock garden, on dry banks etc. The flowers resemble those of a miniature wild rose. Not all species are completely hardy in colder districts.

Cultural requirements: Any good garden soil, including chalk, provided that drainage is good.

Propagation: From seed under glass in spring; by cuttings in a cold frame in late summer.

C. × corbariensis 3 ft (1 m)   Garden origin
This hybrid is one of the hardiest of the cistuses. The buds, tinged with crimson, open to pure white. Summer.

C. ladaniferus up to 5 ft (1·5 m)
Gum Cistus   S.W. Europe
Tall erect species with sticky lanceolate foliage.

White flowers up to 4 in. (10 cm) in diameter, blotched at their centres with crimson. Summer.

C. laurifolius up to 6 ft (2 m)   S.W. Europe
Another hardy species with leathery, dark blue-green leaves and white flowers with yellow centres. Summer.

C. salvifolius 2 ft (60 cm)   S. Europe
This species is commonly found in the wild in Mediterranean regions. The flowers are white, with yellow blotches at the base of the petals. Summer.

In addition to the above, there are many named cultivars and hybrids of garden origin, all of which make ideal plants for warm sheltered gardens in more favoured districts.

CITRUS
(Cistaceae)
Sub-tropical evergreen shrubs whose main horticultural use is for greenhouse decoration. They are also of great industrial importance for their fruits – orange, lemon, grapefruit, lime, etc.
Cultural requirements: A warm greenhouse or conservatory, with a minimum winter temperature of 45–50 °F (7–10 °C). In exceptionally favoured districts, some species, such as *C. ichangense*, can be grown outdoors against a sunny sheltered wall. All the greenhouse species can stand outside in summer.
Propagation: By cuttings in heat under glass in summer or by layers in autumn.

C. ichangense up to 5 ft (1·5 m)
Ichang Lemon   China
A shrub of medium size with oval leaves and white scented flowers followed by edible, lemon-shaped fruits.

C. mitis 2 ft (60 cm)
Calamondin Orange   Philippines
A small shrub with fragrant white waxen-textured star-shaped flowers followed by orange fruits about 2 in. (5 cm) in diameter.

CLADANTHUS
(Compositae)
Hardy annuals with finely cut feathery foliage and yellow daisy flowers.
Cultural requirements: Any ordinary garden soil and a sunny open situation.
Propagation: From seed sown outdoors in spring where plants are to flower.

C. arabicus 2½ ft (75 cm)
Palm Springs Daisy   S.E. Europe
Hardy annuals with sweetly scented yellow flowers and a long season of bloom. Sometimes listed as *Anthemis arabica*. Summer.

CLARKIA
(Onagraceae)
Popular hardy annuals of which the present-day garden strains are forms of *C. elegans* and *C. pulchella*. Their colour range is extensive.
Cultural requirements: Rich light soil and a sunny situation.
Propagation: From seed sown in autumn, spring, or in early summer where plants are to flower.

C. elegans up to 2 ft (60 cm)   California
Seedsmen offer numerous strains of these easily grown annuals with tall sprays of fully double flowers in colours ranging from white through various pinks and reds to deep purple. Summer.

CLARY – see *Salvia horminum*

CLEMATIS
(Ranunculaceae) Virgin's Bower
Evergreen and deciduous climbing plants and border perennials of outstanding beauty. The latter kind are less widely grown than the climbers, which are among the most popular of all climbing plants, supporting themselves by their twining stems.
Cultural requirements: A rich well-drained loam to which, if possible, old mortar rubble (not cement) and plenty of well-rotted manure or

Clarkia Double Mixed

garden compost has been added. The climbing forms need their roots in the shade and their heads in the sun. Such conditions can be provided either by protecting the roots with a suitable low growing shrub or by planting on the north and allowing the clematis to climb round into a sunny position.

Pruning: Clematis are divided into a number of different groups and pruning is carried out according to the group to which they belong. All newly planted clematis, however, should be pruned back to a pair of buds 6–12 in. (15–30 cm) from the ground.

Alpina and Montana Groups and most of the species: Once established these will need only sufficient pruning to keep them tidy and within bounds. For this purpose they can be cut back practically to the old wood after flowering.

Florida, Lanuginosa, and Patens Groups: These flower early on the previous year's wood. All that is needed is to cut back growths that have flowered as soon as the flowers have faded.

Jackmanii and Viticella Groups: These flower during late summer and autumn on the current season's growths. They should be pruned back hard in late winter.

Clematis is subject to a disease, clematis wilt, for which, at the time of writing, no cure has been found. This mainly affects young plants which suddenly collapse for no apparent reason. Plants sometimes recover, even after twelve months, so that it pays to leave them in until it is absolutely certain they are dead.

Perennial border clematis: These are treated in a similar manner to other hardy perennials. They will succeed in any fairly rich soil in a sunny open situation.

Propagation: From seed in a cold frame; the large flowered kinds from grafts or layers. Border species can be increased by cuttings in spring or division of the plants in autumn.

Climbing species and cultivars

C. armandii China
Vigorous evergreen clematis with dark green polished trifoliate leaves. Creamy-white flowers 2–2½ in. (5–6·5 cm) across. 'Apple Blossom', a form with white flowers, shaded with pink on their reverse, is finer than the type. Late spring.

C. flammula S. Europe
Very strong grower, noteworthy for the intense fragrance of its clusters of small white flowers. An ideal species for scrambling into old trees or for covering unsightly sheds or outbuildings.

C. ×*jackmanii* (*C. lanuginosa* ×
C. viticella) Garden origin
A large flowered hybrid clematis, probably the best known of all. Flowers of a rich violet-purple,

velvety in texture and profusely borne. There are many superb garden sorts including 'Hagley Hybrid', shell-pink; 'Jackmanii Superba', an improved form of the original; 'Madame Edouard André', rich crimson; and 'Perle d'Azur', pale blue. Late summer to autumn.

C. ×*jouiniana* (*C. heracleifolia* ×
C. vitalba) Garden origin
Vigorous climber, with a profusion of lilac-tinted white flowers in autumn. The foliage is coarsely toothed and its habit somewhat shrubby.

C. macropetala N. China
Useful spring flowering species with semi-double violet-blue flowers, followed by decorative silky seedheads. 'Markham's Pink', with flowers of a striking crushed strawberry shade, is an outstanding form. Spring.

C. montana Himalayas
The most popular and widely grown of the clematis species. Plants are a sheet of blossom over a long period in spring. Extremely vigorous, *C. montana* is equally successful on walls, fences, pergolas, or scrambling through the branches of old fruit trees.

In addition to the type, with white flowers, there are a number of valuable forms. *C. m. rubens* is the best known of these, 'Elizabeth' and 'Tetrarose' are two newer introductions, with larger pink flowers than the former. Early summer.

Some suitable flowers for children to grow: Godetia, Cornflower, Calendula, Candytuft, Virginian Stock, Clarkia, and Chrysanthemum

Clematis Barbara Jackman

C. orientalis Orange Peel Clematis   N. Asia
This species gets its popular name from its curiously thick yellow sepals which bear a resemblance to segments of orange peel. The bell-shaped flowers are followed by decorative silken seedheads. Late summer.

C. tangutica   China
This species is grown as much for its masses of silky seedheads which remain decorative throughout the autumn as for the unusual beauty of its yellow Chinese lantern flowers. Autumn.

Large flowered hybrids

Jackmanii Group: Summer to early autumn.
'Comtesse de Bouchaud', cyclamen-pink with golden stamens;
'Gipsy Queen', violet-purple with velvet sheen;
'Hagley Hybrid', shell-pink flowers with brown anthers;
'Jackmanii', free flowering and vigorous, with violet-blue flowers;
'Madame Edouard André', deep red flowers with yellow stamens;
'Perle d'Azur', pale blue counterpart of 'Comtesse de Bouchaud'.

Viticella Group: Summer to early autumn.
'Ascotiensis', sky-blue pointed sepals, very free flowering;
'Ernest Markham', petunia-red, velvety texture yellow stamens. Free flowering;
'Lady Betty Balfour', rich violet-blue, yellow stamens;
'Ville de Lyon', popular variety with carmine-red flowers whose colour is enhanced by the golden stamens.

Lanuginosa Group: Early to midsummer.
'Lady Northcliffe', deep lavender tinged with bright blue, white stamens;
'Marie Boisselot' (syn. 'Mme Lecoultre'), probably the finest white clematis with creamy stamens and overlapping sepals that produce a semi-double appearance;
'Mrs Cholmondeley', intense sky-blue; long and narrow sepals;
'W. E. Gladstone', large lavender flowers with a paler central band to the sepals. White stamens and black anthers.

Florida and Patens Groups: Early summer with repeat flowering in early autumn in some varieties.
'Duchess of Edinburgh', the finest pure white double;
'Vyvyan Pennell', violet-blue double flowers, single at repeat autumn flowering;
'Barbara Dibley', violet sepals barred with petunia-purple. Free flowering;
'Lasurstern', extra large deep blue flowers with yellow stamens;

'Nelly Moser', rivals 'Jackmanii' in popularity; pale mauve-pink flowers with carmine bar to petals. Very free flowering.

Herbaceous Perennial Clematis

C. heracleifolia 4 ft (1·2 m)   China
Vigorous border plant producing clusters of blue hyacinth-like blooms. Late summer to autumn.

C. integrifolia 4 ft (1·2 m)   S. Europe
Hanging violet-blue bell-shaped flowers. Summer to early autumn.

CLEOME
(Capparidaceae)

Half-hardy annuals useful in bold bedding schemes or as pot plants for the cool greenhouse.
Cultural requirements: For pot culture, John Innes No. 2 or similar compost; any good garden soil and a sunny situation outdoors.
Propagation: From seed sown in heat in spring.

C. spinosa 3 ft (1 m) Spider Flower
Spiny leaves and stems and large heads of pinkish-purple or white spidery flowers. 'Rose Queen' is an attractive form with paler pink flowers.

CLERODENDRUM
(Verbenaceae)

Deciduous flowering shrubs, the hardy species of which are useful for their late flowering character.
Cultural requirements: Any good garden soil and a sheltered situation.
Propagation: From seed or cuttings under glass in heat in early spring or half-ripe stem cuttings in late summer.

C. bungei (syn. *C. foetidum*) 4 ft (1·2 m)   China
A small shrub with large heart-shaped leaves and terminal clusters of rosy-pink flowers. The leaves have an unpleasant odour when crushed. Early autumn.

C. trichotomum 10 ft (3 m)   China and Japan
Clusters of white scented flowers followed by decorative turquoise-blue berries framed in a deep crimson calyx. Early autumn.

CLIANTHUS
(Leguminosae)

Semi-evergreen half-hardy climbing shrubs too tender for outdoor cultivation except in warmer districts. Good cool greenhouse climbers.
Cultural requirements: Sunny greenhouse border or sheltered south or west wall outdoors.
Propagation: From seed or cuttings in heat under glass in spring.

C. puniceus up to 12 ft (4 m)
Lobster Claw or Parrot's Bill   New Zealand
Attractive semi-evergreen pinnate foliage and

striking scarlet pea flowers whose keels are enlarged and so shaped as to warrant the two popular names of this plant. Early summer.

CLIMBING PLANTS

Climbing plants, as opposed to wall shrubs, which are not actually climbing in habit, can be divided into two categories, clingers and twiners. The former cling to the surface on which they are growing by means of adventitious (aerial) roots on their stems, e.g., ivies; the latter, which include many popular wall plants such as clematis, honeysuckles, and vines, support themselves by means of tendrils or twining leafstalks. Climbers are useful for walls, fences, pillars, and pergolas. The clingers may need a little help at first; after a season they become self-supporting. Twiners will need something to cling to in the shape of wires, wire or plastic netting, trellis, or a host plant through which they can scramble.

There are climbers suitable for every aspect, including the normally inhospitable north wall. Here, many of the clematises, all the ivies, and the climbing hydrangea, *H. petiolaris*, will flourish. South walls will be ideal for partly tender climbers like the passion flower, *Passiflora coerulea*, and the so-called climbing potato, *Solanum crispum*.

As the soil at the foot of a wall is generally exceptionally dry, climbers should be planted as far away from the base as possible, afterwards being trained in to the wall surface. The planting holes should be enriched with well-rotted manure or compost and attention should be given to watering during dry spells until the plants are properly established.

CLIMBING POTATO – see *Solanum*

CLIVIA

(Amaryllidaceae) Kaffir Lily
Evergreen fleshy-rooted flowering plants for the warm greenhouse or for use as house plants.
Cultural requirements: John Innes No. 2 or similar compost and a sunny greenhouse shelf or window-sill indoors. Water copiously during the growing season, sparingly while the plants are dormant.
Propagation: From seed or by offsets.

C. miniata 1½ ft (45 cm)
This species, with its cultivars and hybrids, is the one most widely grown for greenhouse or indoor decoration. The leaves of the plants are strap-like and the flowers of the type are borne on erect stems in clusters, scarlet or yellow. Spring.

CLONE

Clones are plants originating from one individual plant that are kept in cultivation by vegetative propagation. Each clone is identical in character with the original plant.

COBAEA

(Polemoniaceae)
Tender climbing perennials, generally treated as half-hardy annuals outdoors. Only one species is normally found in garden cultivation – *C. scandens*.
Cultural requirements: Fairly rich soil and a sunny south wall or a cool greenhouse.
Propagation: From seed under glass in gentle heat in spring.

C. scandens up to 30 ft (9 m)
Cathedral Bells   C. America
A very fast growing half-hardy climber that will reach roof level in a single season. The large bell-shaped flowers are an interesting greenish-purple with pale green bracts that remain decorative after the flowers have faded. Summer.

COCKSCOMB – see *Celosia*

COIX

(Gramineae)
Half-hardy annual grasses grown for their decorative seedheads.
Cultural requirements: Light soil, rich in humus and a sunny open situation.
Propagation: From seed under glass in heat in spring or outdoors later where the plants are to remain.

C. lachryma-jobi up to 3 ft (1 m)   Job's Tears
The grey-green pearl-like seedheads, dried and used in winter arrangements, are very attractive. Summer.

COLCHICUM

(Liliaceae)
Corms often incorrectly called autumn crocus. The crocus-like flowers of all but a few species appear in autumn, before the leaves.
Cultural requirements: The tubers should be planted in late summer. They will come into flower within the next two months. A light rich soil suits them best. Colchicums do well in grass and do not mind partial shade. Deep planting is advisable.
Propagation: From seed sown outdoors when ripe or by division of offset corms in late summer. Plants from seed take four or five years to flower.

C. autumnale 8 in. (20 cm)
Naked Ladies   Europe, including British Isles
Rosy-lilac crocus-like flowers 6 in. (15 cm) tall, rise direct from the soil. Autumn.

C. cilicium 6 in. (15 cm)   Turkey
Dark rosy-purple goblet-shaped blooms. The large leaves appear after flowers have faded. This species has a preference for full sun.

When plants are 6 in. (15 cm) tall pinch out the growing tips to help them grow bushy

Coleus Rainbow Mixed

C. speciosum 10 in. (25 cm)　　Asia Minor
The best garden species, with pale rosy-lilac flowers up to 10 in. (25 cm) tall. There are several good named cultivars, including 'Album', white; 'Disraeli', deep mauve; and 'The Giant', an extra large form with pinkish-mauve blooms marked with white at their throats.

COLEUS
(Labiatae)
Half-hardy shrubby perennials grown for the exceptional brilliance of their leaf colouring. They are useful both as pot plants for the greenhouse or indoors and as a colourful component of summer bedding schemes in sheltered areas.
Cultural requirements: John Innes No. 2 or similar compost for final potting and a sunny shelf in the greenhouse.
Propagation: From seed under glass in spring and summer. Growing point should be pinched out when plants are about 6 in. (15 cm) high. This will induce bushy growth. To perpetuate any particular colour combination, fresh stocks can be obtained from cuttings.

C. blumei 1½ ft (45 cm) Fire Nettle　　Java
This species, with its cultivars, is the source of plants with richly coloured, beautifully marked foliage. Strains such as 'Rainbow Strain', 'Kimono Colours', and 'Old Lace' produce plants with leaves in infinite permutations of pink, red, copper, apricot, salmon, and bronze. The leaves of the last named kinds are fringed, fluted, and laced. Summer.

COLLETIA
(Rhamnaceae)
Half-hardy evergreen shrubs whose stems and branches are armed with sharp spines.
Cultural requirements: Well-drained rich loamy soil. Sunny sheltered situation – not suitable for cold districts.
Propagation: From hardwood cuttings in a cold frame in autumn.

C. armata 10 ft (3 m)　　Chile
Compact shrub with long needle-like spines. The small white flowers are delicately fragrant. 'Rosea' has flowers that are pink in bud. Late summer to autumn.

C. cruciata up to 8 ft (2·5 m)
Anchor Plant　　Uruguay
In this species the formidable spines are flattened and triangular and are responsible for the popular name. Flowers are similar to those of *C. armata* – small, scented, and pitcher-shaped. Late summer to autumn.

COLLINSIA
(Scrophulariaceae)

Useful race of hardy annuals of which the most important species is *C. bicolor*.

Cultural requirements: Any good fertile garden soil, open or partly shaded situation.

Propagation: From seed outdoors in early autumn or spring where plants are to flower.

C. bicolor 1 ft (30 cm) California
Easily grown annual with lavender and white flowers. Makes a useful edging plant in summer bedding schemes. Summer.

COLUMBINE – See *Aquilegia*

COLUTEA
(Leguminosae) Bladder Senna

Hardy deciduous flowering shrubs with pinnate foliage and small yellow pea flowers. Excellent for poor soils and dry banks.

Cultural requirements: Any ordinary garden soil, open or partially shaded situation.

Propagation: From seed sown outdoors in spring or from hardwood cuttings in autumn.

C. arborescens up to 12 ft (4 m) Mediterranean
Yellow flowers followed by bladder-like greyish-brown seed pods. Very vigorous but can be pruned back hard in spring. 'Bullata' is a slower growing and more compact form. Late summer.

COMFREY – see *Symphytum*

COMPOST MAKING

Any type of soil will benefit from the addition of as much humus-rich material as possible. One valuable source of humus, especially when animal manure is so difficult to obtain nowadays, is the compost heap. By making use of all available organic waste material from house and garden we can help to maintain and even increase the level of humus in the soil, as well as improving its texture and growing potential.

There are many different ways of making compost although basically, they all follow a similar course. A compost heap should always be constructed on the soil to allow free access to earthworms and other organisms and bacteria, which do such valuable work in assisting in the rotting down of the raw materials.

Almost anything of organic origin is suitable for rotting down – garden refuse, kitchen waste, lawn mowings (but not immediately after applications of hormone weedkillers), weeds, hedge clippings, old woollen garments, and the contents of the vacuum cleaner dust bag. Woollens should preferably be cut into strips before being added to the heap.

For the garden of medium size the optimum dimensions of the heap will be in the region of 6 ft (2 m) by 4 ft (1·2 m). It should be about 5 ft (1·5 m) high on completion and will sink by about one-third as the contents decompose.

The very small garden will not provide enough material for a heap of this size and it may be necessary to construct some type of slatted bin or similar container to retain the heat generated by decomposition.

A compost heap is built up as a repetition of three layers or stages. These consist of (1) a 6 in. (15 cm) layer of any of the materials mentioned above trodden down lightly, (2) a sprinkling of lime sufficient to whiten the surface, and (3) a topping up with a 1 in. (3 cm) layer of good soil.

When the heap reaches the required height, it should be cased in on all sides with a thin layer of soil. If accelerators are used, they are added to or watered into the heap in accordance with the makers' instructions.

In dry weather, compost heaps may need watering with a fine spray from a rosed watering can. They must, however, not be allowed to become sodden and should be protected from heavy rain with polythene sheeting or a few old sacks or sheets of polythene laid across the top of the heap.

CONE FLOWER – see *Rudbeckia*

CONIFERS

An extensive group of trees, of varying size and predominantly evergreen that are of great value in the garden. They range in size from majestic trees 100 ft (30 m) in height to pygmy forms small enough for the rock garden. They are typified by narrow or needle-like leaves and cones, which are composed of woody scales and bracts protecting the seeds. On yews and junipers these take the form of fleshy fruits.

Forms for garden decoration are drawn mainly from the cypresses (*Cupressus* and *Chamaecyparis*), firs (*Abies*), junipers (*Juniperus*), spruces (*Picea*), pines (*Pinus*), and yews (*Taxus*), but there are many other sorts that make a valuable contribution and it could safely be claimed that suitable kinds can be found for every type of soil or situation.

CONVALLARIA
(Liliaceae) Lily-of-the-Valley

Hardy herbaceous perennials much valued for their sweetly scented flowers. The dense foliage makes useful ground cover for shady borders or in the wild garden.

Cultural requirements: Soil rich in humus and a moist shady situation. Can also be forced into bloom early in a cool greenhouse.

Propagation: From seed outdoors in spring; division of crowns in autumn.

C. majalis
9 in. (22 cm)   Europe, including British Isles
Spikes of pure white, very fragrant, waxy pendent bell flowers and attractive pale green foliage deepening with age. 'Fortin's Giant' has larger flowers than the type; those of 'Rosea' are a soft pink in colour. Spring.

CONVOLVULUS
(Convolvulaceae)

Hardy annuals and perennials, the majority of which are of climbing or trailing habit.
Cultural requirements: Any ordinary garden soil and a sunny situation.
Propagation: From seed outdoors or root division in spring.

C. althaeoides 2 ft (60 cm)   Mediterranean
Hardy perennial with pink flowers, elegant lobed leaves and a trailing or climbing habit. Summer.
C. cneorum 1½ ft (45 cm)   S. Europe
A shrubby species with attractive silvery foliage and small white and pink trumpet flowers, ideal in a grey garden. Late spring to midsummer.
C. tricolor (syn. *C. minor*) 1 ft (30 cm) S. Europe
Dwarf annual species that makes a striking bedding or border plant. The large funnel-shaped flowers are in a wide range of colours and there are some good named forms, including 'Crimson Monarch', cherry-red and 'Royal Ensign', dark blue with a golden centre. Summer.

CORDATE
Heart-shaped, applied to leaves.

CORDYLINE
(Liliaceae)

Half-hardy trees from Australasia, the Pacific, and South Asia. The species most commonly seen is *C. australis*, the New Zealand cabbage tree.
Cultural requirements: In favoured districts, *C. australis* can be grown outdoors in a sunny sheltered situation; elsewhere this, and other species will need the protection of a greenhouse.
Propagation: From seed sown under glass in heat in spring; by offshoots.

C. australis up to 20 ft (6 m)   New Zealand
Small evergreen trees whose branches are topped with rosettes of sword-like foliage. The clusters of creamy-white flowers are very striking. Summer.
C. indivisa up to 10 ft (3 m)   New Zealand
This species is more tender than the former. The sword-blade leaves are broader and grey-green in colour, springing from the top of an unbranched stem. Early summer.

COREOPSIS
(Compositae) Tickseed

Hardy annuals and perennials that make useful border plants. The annual kinds are generally known as 'Calliopsis'.
Cultural requirements: Any ordinary garden soil and a sunny situation.
Propagation: From seed outdoors in spring and also, for the perennial species, by division in spring or by cuttings in a cold frame in summer.

There are several different annual species cultivated under the name of 'Calliopsis', including *C. coronata* and *C. tinctoria*, both with yellow and maroon flowers. Seedsmen offer special mixtures containing a wider range of colours.

C. grandiflora 3 ft (1 m)   S. U.S.A.
This perennial species contains several cultivars that are invaluable in the herbaceous or mixed border. They include 'Badengold', with large long-stemmed golden-yellow flowers, excellent for cutting; 'Mayfield Giant', with large bright orange-yellow flowers, and 'Sunburst', a double yellow form. Summer.
C. verticillata 2 ft (60 cm)   E. U.S.A.
The finely divided, asparagus-like foliage of this species makes a perfect foil for the small but profusely borne yellow flowers. Summer.

CORM
A corm is a fleshy underground stem, adapted as a food storage vessel for the following year's bud. It differs from a bulb in lacking fleshy scales and leaves and in forming its new corm above the old one. Examples of corms are gladiolus, crocus, and cyclamen.

CORNELIAN CHERRY – see *Cornus mas*

CORNFLOWER – see *Centaurea*

CORNUS
(Cornaceae) Dogwood

An extensive genus of shrubs and small trees, noteworthy for the decorative effect of flowers, foliage, bracts, and in the case of some species, the colourful effect of their bare stems in winter.

C. canadensis is an exception in being a prostrate perennial species useful in the larger rock garden or as ground cover.
Cultural requirements: Any garden soil provided it is not too dry. The coloured-stemmed species, *C. alba* and *C. stolonifera* will thrive even in waterlogged soils.
Propagation: From hardwood stem cuttings of ripened wood in autumn, softwood stem cuttings in a cold frame in summer; also, with most kinds, from layers.

C. alba up to 10 ft (3 m)
Scarlet-stemmed Dogwood   China and Japan
Grown for the striking effect of its scarlet stems in winter. Should be cut back hard to base each spring as the most intense colouring is in the young growths. *C. a.* 'Sibirica', better known as the 'Westonbirt Dogwood' has the most brilliant bark colouring.

C. canadensis 4 in. (10 cm)
Creeping Dogwood   N. America
A good ground cover plant for moist shady conditions with pure white flowers followed by scarlet berries. Needs a lime-free soil. Summer.

C. florida 10 ft (3 m)
Flowering Dogwood   N. America
Large shrub with flower heads consisting of four white petal-like bracts. Noteworthy for brilliant autumn leaf colour. The variety *rubra* has rosy-pink bracts. Early summer.

C. kousa 20 ft (6 m)   Japan
Small shrubby tree with large creamy-white bracts, profusely borne. Rich autumn leaf colour. Midsummer.

C. mas 15 ft (4·5 m)
Cornelian Cherry   C. and S. Europe
Spreading shrubby tree producing masses of small yellow flowers on the bare branches in winter. Late winter.

C. stolonifera 6 ft (2 m)   N. America
Vigorous suckering shrub of which the yellow-barked variety, 'Flaviramea', is grown for the beauty of its bright greenish-yellow winter stems and branches. Should be cut back hard each spring in a similar manner to *C. alba*.

COROKIA
(Coriaceae)
New Zealand shrubs, of which *C. cotoneaster* is the species most commonly seen in gardens.
Cultural requirements: Fertile, moist, well-drained soil and sheltered situation, preferably a south or west wall.
Propagation: From cuttings under glass in summer or from layers in autumn.

C. cotoneaster 8 ft (2·5 m)
Wire Netting Bush   New Zealand
Slow growing shrub with wiry zigzag twigs and branches, tiny leaves, yellow star-shaped flowers followed by orange berries. Early summer.

CORTADERIA
(Gramineae) Pampas Grass
Hardy ornamental grasses of great beauty and of outstanding architectural value in the garden.
Cultural requirements: Rich light soil and a fairly sheltered situation.
Propagation: From seed under glass in spring.

C. fulvida 6 ft (2 m)   New Zealand
This New Zealand species has large clumps of narrow sword-like foliage and large plumes of buff flowers. It makes an excellent lawn specimen and flowers two months earlier than the better known *C. selloana*. Midsummer.

C. selloana (syn. *C. argentea*)
8 ft (2·5 m)   Argentine
The loveliest and most striking of all the hardy grasses with silvery plumes of blossom that cut well for winter decoration indoors. 'Pumila' (4 ft – 1·2 m) is a more compact form; 'Rendatleri' has plumes with a pinkish tinge. Late summer.

CORTEX
The outer tissue of trees or shrubs which later becomes the bark.

CORYDALIS
(Papaveraceae) Fumitory
Hardy annuals and perennials with attractive ferny foliage. They make useful rock or wall plants.
Cultural requirements: Any ordinary garden soil and a sunny situation.
Propagation: From seed sown in spring where plants are to flower. The following species can also be divided after flowering.

C. cheilanthifolia 9 in. (22 cm)   China
Tufts of finely divided ferny foliage, spikes of yellow flowers. Spring to summer.

C. lutea 1 ft (30 cm)   Europe
A useful wall plant, provided it is not allowed to get out of hand when it can sometimes become a troublesome weed. Early summer to autumn.

C. wilsonii 9 in. (22 cm)   China
Grey-green tufted finely cut foliage. Deep yellow flowers. Late spring.

CORYLOPSIS
(Hamamelidaceae)
Hardy deciduous shrubs, relations of the witch hazels, that flower in early spring.
Cultural requirements: Moderately rich soil and a situation protected from cold winds. Sun or part shade. Corylopsis do not thrive in very limy soils.
Propagation: From layers in autumn.

C. pauciflora 4 ft (1·2 m)   Japan
Usually the first species to open its clusters of primrose-yellow flowers in very early spring. Late winter to early spring.

C. spicata 6 ft (2 m)   Japan
A shrub of medium size with hazel-like foliage and racemes of bright yellow flowers up to 6 in. (15 cm) in length, followed by dark purple fruits. Early spring.

Cosmos Giant Early Flowering Mixed

CORYLUS

(Betulaceae) Cob Nut or Filbert
Group of hardy deciduous shrubs or small trees grown mainly for their nuts but containing also, some decorative garden species and varieties.
Cultural requirements: Rich loamy soil and a sunny open situation.
Propagation: From seed outdoors in autumn; suckers or layers in autumn.

C. avellana up to 10 ft (3 m) Common Hazel
W. Asia, Europe, including British Isles
Native hazel nut whose yellow catkins do so much to brighten our hedgerows in late winter. 'Contorta' is an unusual cultivar, with curiously twisted branches. Sometimes known as the 'Corkscrew Hazel' or 'Harry Lauder's Walkingstick'.

C. maxima 10 ft (3 m) Filbert   Balkans
This species has larger and longer nuts than the hazel and also includes a striking purple-leaved form 'Purpurea', which forms a large shrub whose leaves have a similar colouring to those of the copper beeches.

CORYMB

A flat or dome-shaped head of flowers of which the inner stems are shorter and bring all the flowers to approximately the same level.

COSMOS or COSMEA

(Compositae)
Hardy and half-hardy annuals, useful in the border and as a source of cut flowers. Most garden forms are cultivars of either *C. bipinnatus* or *C. diversifolius*.
Cultural requirements: Any ordinary soil and a sunny situation.
Propagation: From seed sown in gentle heat in spring.

C. bipinnatus 3 ft (1 m)   Mexico
The type plant has rosy-purple flowers. Seed is obtainable, however, of rose, crimson, white, and double strains. Midsummer to autumn.

C. diversifolius 3 ft (1 m)   Mexico
This species bears lilac flowers but there is an interesting cultivar, 'Goldilocks', whose flowers are a striking golden-yellow. Autumn.

COTINUS

(Anacardiaceae)
Large deciduous summer flowering shrubs formerly included in the genus *Rhus*. Noteworthy for the beauty of their coloured autumn foliage.
Cultural requirements: Any ordinary well-drained soil and a sunny situation.
Propagation: From seed, layers or root cuttings.

C. americanus (syn. *Rhus cotinoides*)
up to 20 ft (6 m)   S. U.S.A.
A shrub that is distinguished by its brilliant autumn leaf tints.

C. coggygria (syn. *Rhus cotinus*) up to 10 ft (3 m)
Smoke Bush   C. and S. Europe
The feathery, plume-like greyish inflorescences of this species are responsible for its popular name. The rounded green leaves colour strikingly in autumn. There are various cultivars of distinctive character, including 'Flame', the best for autumn leaf colour; 'Foliis Purpureus', with rich purple foliage that turns a clearer red in autumn; and 'Royal Purple', with translucent wine-purple leaves. Summer.

COTONEASTER

(Rosaceae)
A very useful group of evergreen and deciduous hardy shrubs that also includes several species and hybrids of tree-like habit. Most kinds are grown primarily for the decorative qualities of their berries. The small white flowers appear in early summer.
Cultural requirements: Any ordinary garden soil and a sunny or partly shaded situation. Many species make good subjects for the tops of walls or for covering banks.
Propagation: From seed outdoors in spring; by cuttings or layers in autumn and spring respectively.

C. congestus up to 1 ft (30 cm)   Himalayas
Dense and compact prostrate evergreen shrub
that forms a hummock of tiny blue-green leaves.

C. conspicuus up to 5 ft (1·5 m)   Tibet
Evergreen shrub of medium size with widely
spreading branches and an arching habit of
growth. The white flowers are followed by
brilliant red berries that last for a long time.
'Decorus', a low growing form, makes ideal
ground cover.

C. × Cornubia up to 20 ft (6 m)   Garden origin
A vigorous and striking semi-evergreen hybrid
with large clusters of scarlet berries freely borne.
This is a first-rate shrub for the larger shrub
border.

C. dammeri (syn. *C. humifusa*) Prostrate   China
This is one of the best of the prostrate species,
good for covering banks, for planting in paving
or as ground cover. The long trailing shoots are
massed with sealing wax red berries in autumn
and early winter.

C. franchetii up to 10 ft (3 m)   China
A popular semi-evergreen species, with oval
sage-green leaves and large crops of orange-
scarlet berries, which remain for several months.

C. horizontalis up to 5 ft (1·5 m)   China
This is the well known and deservedly popular
'fishbone' cotoneaster, which, with its herring-
bone branch structure, makes a good shrub for
walls or banks. It grows and fruits well even on a
north wall. The scarlet bootbutton berries are
perfectly set off by the fishbone pattern of the
bare branches in winter.

C. × Hybridus Pendulus
up to 10 ft (3 m)   Garden origin
Grown on a single stem, this lovely hybrid will
make an attractive small weeping tree. It is evergreen and bears its scarlet fruits in great profusion.

C. lacteus 10 ft (3 m)   China
Another vigorous and popular species, with
attractive foliage silvered on its reverse. The
fruits, which are borne in large clusters, are
long lasting.

C. microphyllus 2 ft (60 cm)   Himalayas
An evergreen trailing shrub, useful for clothing
low walls and banks. It bears large crops of red
berries.

C. salicifolius up to 15 ft (4·5 m)   W. China
A vigorous, fast growing, and graceful species,
with willow-like evergreen foliage and large
crops of small scarlet fruits in autumn. The named
form, 'Autumn Fire', is exceptionally fine. It is
smaller than the type with orange berries and a
semi-weeping habit.

C. simonsii up to 10 ft (3 m)   Himalayas
Although this species has less than most others to
recommend it as a specimen shrub, it makes a good
hedging plant that will stand up well to clipping
and that is a cheerful sight in winter when the
upright branches are densely clothed with large
scarlet berries.

COTTON LAVENDER – see *Santolina*

COTYLEDON
(Crassulaceae)

Evergreen succulent plants of shrubby or prostrate habit.
Cultural requirements: Cotyledons do best in a
cool greenhouse although in more favoured
districts, some kinds can be planted outside in a
sunny sheltered situation. They also make good
house plants for a sunny window-sill.
Propagation: By division in spring.

C. oppositifolia (syn. *C. simplifolia*)
6 in. (15 cm)   S. Europe
Hardy creeping succulent species with clusters of
yellow flowers on red stems. The grey-green
foliage turns a pale crimson as it matures. Now
known as *Chiastophyllum oppositifolium*. Summer.

C. paniculata 4 ft (1·2 m)   S. Africa
Stout fleshy stems topped with rosettes of
glaucous foliage and red flowers edged with
green. Summer.

CRAB-APPLE – see *Malus*

CRANE FLY – see Pest Control

CRANESBILL – see *Geranium*

CRASSULA
(Crassulaceae)

Greenhouse evergreen succulent plants, some of
which can be grown outside in milder districts.
Cultural requirements: Under glass; John
Innes No. 2 or a similar compost.
Propagation: From seed under glass in spring;
by cuttings under glass in summer.

C. arborescens up to 5 ft (1·5 m)   S. Africa
Small round grey-green leaves, edged and spotted
with red. Pink flowers. Early summer.

C. sarcocaulis 1 ft (30 cm)   S. Africa
Small pointed green leaves and clusters of pink
flowers. This species succeeds outside in mild
districts. Late summer.

CRATAEGUS
(Rosaceae) Hawthorn

Small trees or large shrubs of great decorative
value adaptable to all kinds of soils and situations
including industrial districts and exposed coastal
areas. Attractive flowers and fruits and in some
kinds, good autumn leaf colour.

C. crus-galli 20 ft (6 m)
Cockspur Thorn   N. America
Small tree with wide spreading habit, white
flowers and attractive scarlet haws that last well.
The long sharp thorns, up to 3 in. (8 cm) long,
are a distinctive feature of this species.
C. × lavallei a hybrid thorn of which *C. crus-galli*
is a parent, is one of the best fruiting forms with
large orange-red fruits and handsome glossy
dark green foliage, which remains on the tree
well into the winter.
C. monogyna 25 ft (8 m) Common Hawthorn
or May   Europe, including British Isles
Our native quickthorn which is widely used for
hedging. Fragrant white may blossom is followed
by scarlet haws. Early summer.
C. oxyacantha
15 ft (4·5 m)   Europe, including British Isles
Another native thorn, less commonly seen, however, than *C. monogyna*. It is among the cultivars
of this species that the most popular ornamental
garden forms are found. Good named kinds
include 'Paul's Scarlet', an old favourite with
double scarlet flowers; 'Plena', a double white
'may'; and 'Rosea Flore Pleno', an attractive
double pink. Early summer.
C. prunifolia 15 ft (4·5 m) Possible garden origin
An attractive large-leaved form, possibly a hybrid
with a rounded spreading head. A good all-
rounder with masses of white blossom, striking
red fruits and brilliant autumn leaf colour. Early
summer.

CREEPING JENNY
– see *Lysimachia nummularia*

CREPIS
(Compositae) Hawkbit
Hardy annuals and perennials, related to the yellow
hawkbit which is sometimes a troublesome lawn
weed.
Cultural requirements: Any ordinary garden
soil and an open sunny situation.
Propagation: From seed outdoors in spring.

C. rubra 1 ft (30 cm) Hawk's Beard   S. Europe
A hardy annual species with pale pink dandelion-
like flowers, freely produced. Autumn.

CRESS – see Kitchen Garden

CRINODENDRON
(Elaeocarpaceae)
South American evergreen trees, suitable only
for milder areas.
Cultural requirements: Moist but well-drained
lime-free soil and a sheltered partly shaded
situation, in sun or partial shade.

Propagation: From cuttings of partly ripened
wood under glass in gentle heat in summer.

C. hookerianum (syn. *Tricuspidaria lanceolata*)
30 ft (9 m) Chilean Lantern Tree   Chile
A handsome evergreen tree or large shrub with
pendent crimson lantern-like flowers of distinctive
beauty. Early summer.

CRINUM
(Amaryllidaceae)
Greenhouse and outdoor bulbous plants with
clusters of large lily like pink or white trumpet
flowers.
Cultural requirements: Rich, deep, well-drained
soil and a position at the foot of a sunny south
or west wall for the outdoor kinds. Cover with
ashes or bracken to protect bulbs in winter.
Propagation: From seed or offsets under glass
in spring.

C. × powellii 3 ft (1 m)   Garden origin
Magnificent bulbous plants with clusters of six to
eight trumpet flowers, 3–4 in. (8–10 cm) long,
pink or white and handsome strap-like foliage.
Late summer.

CROCOSMIA
(Iridaceae) Montbretia
Hardy and half-hardy corms, of which the popular
and tough montbretia is the best known.
Cultural requirements: Light sandy soil and a
sunny or partly shaded open situation. Half-hardy
kinds in pots, in John Innes No. 2 or similar
compost in a cool greenhouse.
Propagation: From seed or offsets.

C. × crocosmiiflora 2 ft (60 cm)
Montbretia   Garden origin
This hybrid is the common montbretia, with
orange flowers, that has naturalized itself in many
parts of the British Isles. Selected forms with
larger flowers are not as hardy and the corms may
need lifting and storing in winter like those of
the gladioli. Late summer to autumn.
C. masonorum 2–2½ ft (60–75 cm)   S. Africa
A hardy plant, similar to the above mentioned
hybrid but with larger, more brilliant orange
flowers and distinctive pleated leaves. Late
summer to autumn.

CROCUS
(Iridaceae)
Popular early flowering corms which by a choice
of species and varieties will provide garden colour
from autumn until late spring. They can also be
grown in pots or bowls for indoor or greenhouse
decoration.
Cultural requirements: Sunny open situation
and a light, rich, well-drained soil. When crocuses

are planted in lawns, the grass should not be cut until the foliage has yellowed.

Propagation: From seed in a cold frame in autumn; from offsets of old corms removed and planted in summer or early autumn.

C. chrysanthus   S.E. Europe
Among the many good named forms are 'Blue Pearl', pale blue with orange centre; 'Cream Beauty', pale creamy-yellow with orange centre; 'E. A. Bowles', butter-yellow and bronze; and 'Warley', pale cream marked with blue. Early spring.

C. imperati   Mediterranean
Deep satin-mauve flowers, buff-yellow on the outside. Needs well-drained soil and a sunny situation. Winter.

C. laevigatus   Greece
Pale lilac flowers, striped with deep mauve. Midwinter.

C. tomasinianus   S. Italy
Pale blue-mauve flowers, lilac-purple on inside. There are several good selected forms, including 'Barr's Purple', pale greyish-mauve flowers, rich lilac-purple inside; 'Taplow Ruby', reddish-purple; and 'Whitewell Purple', purplish-mauve. Midwinter.

C. vernus   C. Europe
The wild species of the Alps from which the popular Dutch crocuses have been derived. These include a variety of colours and named forms such as 'Haarlem Gem', pale lilac-mauve; 'Kathleen Parlow', white; 'The Bishop', reddish-purple; and 'Striped Beauty', white striped violet. Late winter.

Autumn flowering

C. sativus Saffron Crocus   S. Europe
The true 'Meadow Saffron' or autumn crocus with lilac-purple flowers. Saffron dye is obtained from the stigmas of this species. Autumn.

C. speciosus   S. Europe
Large pale bluish-mauve flowers with darker veins. *C. speciosus* will quickly naturalize itself from self-sown seeds and cormlets and makes a useful subject for the wild or partly wild garden. Autumn.

C. zonatus (syn. *C. kotschyanus*)   S. Europe
Pale lilac flowers marked with yellow at the base. Early autumn.

CROWN IMPERIAL
– see *Fritillaria imperialis*

CRYPTOMERIA
(Pinaceae)
Monotypic genus of conifers, of which there are numerous cultivars of varying sizes and forms.

Cultural requirements: Deep, rich, moist loam and a situation sheltered from cold winds.

Propagation: From seed under glass or outdoors in spring; from stem cuttings with a heel in a cold frame in early autumn.

C. japonica up to 100 ft (30 m)   Japan and China
The type is a fast growing evergreen conifer. 'Elegans' (20 ft – 6 m) is the most widely grown cultivar, with glaucous green foliage that turns a striking bronze-purple in autumn. 'Pygmaea' (2½ ft – 75 cm) is a dwarf form in appearance rather like a Japanese Bonsai tree. 'Vilmoriniana' (2 ft – 60 cm) is another delightful dwarf, dense and globular in appearance and very slow growing.

CULTIVAR
Short for cultivated variety and referring to a distinct variant, usually of a species or hybrid that is maintained in cultivation. Such a plant might be purposely bred by man or arise spontaneously by mutation in gardens or in the wild, e.g., a sport (mutant) with double flowers or variegated leaves.

CUPHEA
(Lythraceae)
Half-hardy annuals, useful for summer bedding or as pot plants in the cool greenhouse.

Cultural requirements: Sunny sheltered border and fairly rich well-drained soil.

Propagation: From seed under glass in heat in spring.

C. miniata 1 ft (30 cm)   Mexico
Masses of tubular red flowers. The cultivar 'Firefly' is an improvement on the type. Summer.

CUPRESSOCYPARIS × *leylandii*
(Pinaceae)
A bigeneric hybrid between *Cupressus macrocarpa* and *Chamaecyparis nootkatensis*, this is fast becoming one of the most useful and widely grown of conifers. It is the fastest growing of all conifers and makes an excellent screen or hedge that, once established, will increase by up to 3 ft (1 m) in height annually.

CUPRESSUS
(Pinaceae)
Evergreen conifers, mainly of pyramidal habit. Generally less hardy than *Chamaecyparis*. They make attractive lawn specimens.

Cultural requirements: Deep rich loam and a situation protected from cold winds.

Propagation: From seed in spring; from cuttings in a cold frame in autumn.

C. macrocarpa 80 ft (24 m)
Monterey Cypress   California
A fast growing evergreen, useful for providing a

shelter belt in milder districts. Also used for hedging, but not so good as *Cupressocyparis × leylandii* or Lawson's cypress on account of the tendency for individual plants to die off. 'Goldcrest' makes a slender golden pillar, ideal as a lawn specimen.

C. sempervirens 30 ft (9 m)
Italian Cypress   Mediterranean
A dark slender columnar tree, widely grown throughout the Mediterranean region. *C. sempervirens* is intolerant of lime. 'Gracilis' and 'Swaine's Gold', two attractive cultivars raised in New Zealand and Australia respectively, are both good specimen forms, the latter with gold-tinged foliage.

CURRANTS – see Fruit Garden

CURTONUS
(Iridaceae)
Hardy corms, similar in appearance to montbretia and formerly included in genus *Antholyza*.
Cultural requirements: Light sandy soil and a sunny situation.
Propagation: From seed in gentle heat in spring or from division of corm clusters in autumn.

C. paniculatus (syn. *Antholyza paniculata*)
4 ft (1·2 m)   S. Africa
Handsome sword-like foliage and spikes of brilliant orange-red, montbretia-like flowers. Summer.

CUTTINGS – see Propagation

CYCLAMEN
(Primulaceae) Sowbread
Hardy and greenhouse tuberous-rooted perennials, the latter widely grown in commerce as pot plants for winter.
Cultural requirements: Greenhouse kinds: In pots in John Innes No. 2 or similar compost; water freely when plants are flowering and withhold water during dormant period in summer.
Propagation: From seed sown in heat 60–65 °F (15–18 °C) in spring or autumn.
Cultural requirements: Hardy kinds: Medium soil, rich in humus. Shady situation; hardy cyclamen will thrive under trees.
Propagation: Hardy kinds: From seed in a cold frame in autumn.
C. coum 3–6 in. (8–15 cm)   Turkey
This name embraces several spring flowering hardy cyclamens, formerly given specific rank

Cyclamen Superb Mixed

Cymbidium 'Leslie Greenwood'

such as _vernum, ibericum, atkinsii_. The flowers are pink or magenta-pink and the leaves are rounded, plain green or marbled. They thrive in sun or partial shade and are also useful plants for the cold greenhouse. Midwinter to spring.

C. europaeum 6 in. (15 cm)   C. Europe
A species with deep pink or carmine flowers. Late summer to early autumn.

C. neapolitanum 3 in. (8 cm)   Mediterranean
Leaves of variable shape, green, marbled with silvery white. Dainty rose-pink shuttlecock flowers, white in the cultivar 'Album'. Autumn.

C. persicum 6–8 in. (15–20 cm)
          E. Mediterranean and Asia Minor
This species is the parent of the florist's strains of greenhouse cyclamen, of which there are various named forms, including 'Cardinal', cerise-scarlet; 'Puck', a new race of miniatures; and the 'Rex' strain, with deep green leaves margined with silvery-white, all of which are easily raised from seed.

C. repandum 3 in. (8 cm)   Italy
A species not totally hardy outdoors except in sheltered areas. The scented flowers are white, pink, or crimson. An excellent plant for the alpine house. Spring to early summer.

CYDONIA – see _Chaenomeles_

CYMBIDIUM
(Orchidaceae)
One of the largest and loveliest of the orchid genera with tall arching sprays of waxen-textured flowers in a wide range of colours. The grassy foliage is attractive when the plants are not in flower. Both the species and the many hybrids that have appeared in recent years are easy to grow.
Cultural requirements: Potting compost of coarse loam and osmunda fibre or sphagnum moss with peat and broken crocks. Water freely on hot dry summer days and syringe plants overhead in the evenings. Plenty of ventilation should be given at all times during the day. Minimum winter temperature 45 °F (7 °C).
Propagation: By division, after the plants have finished flowering.

C. eburneum 2 ft (60 cm)   N. India and Burma
Less widely grown than formerly, this species has contributed much to the parentage of some of the loveliest hybrids. The flowers are rosy-white or pure white, blotched with purple. Spring.

C. giganteum 3 ft (1 m)   N. India
Yellowish-green flowers, striped with brown. A parent of many outstanding hybrids. Autumn.

C. lowianum 3 ft (1 m)   Burma
Gracefully arching flower spikes, with exceptionally long keeping qualities, flowers up to thirty-

six on a spike, greenish-yellow with reddish-brown veining. Spring to early summer.

C. tracyanum 3 ft (1 m) Burma
Vigorous species with yellowish-green scented flowers, veined with brown; up to twenty-five on a spike. Autumn.

CYME
Flat or dome-shaped head of flowers of which the inner flowers open first.

CYNARA
(Compositae)
Hardy dual purpose perennials that make attractive border plants, and also have culinary uses.
Cultural requirements: Deep, rich, moist soil and a sunny open situation.
Propagation: From suckers or offshoots.

C. cardunculus 6 ft (2 m) Cardoon S. Europe
A plant of great architectural value with large, thistle-like flowers. The blanched stems and leaf midribs are used as a vegetable. Late summer.

C. scolymus 6 ft (2 m) Globe Artichoke Europe
A foliage plant of great architectural value with large blue thistle-like flowers that are delicious cooked at the bud stage and served with a vinaigrette sauce. Late summer.

CYNOGLOSSUM
(Boraginaceae)
Hardy biennials and perennials, of which the species most commonly seen is the perennial *C. nervosum*, normally treated as a hardy biennial.
Cultural requirements: Fairly rich well-drained soil and a sunny situation.
Propagation: From seed under glass in early spring, outdoors later.

C. nervosum 1 ft (30 cm)
Hound's Tongue Himalayas
Gentian-blue flowers in forget-me-not-like sprays. Summer.

CYPERUS
(Cyperaceae)
Grass-like greenhouse perennials, also useful as house plants.
Cultural requirements: John Innes No. 2 or similar potting compost. The plants need copious watering at all times. They are suitable for a cool greenhouse.
Propagation: From seed under glass in heat in spring or by division.

C. alternifolius 2½ ft (75 cm)
Umbrella Plant Madagascar
The slender stems are topped with circular clusters of narrow grassy leaves.

C. papyrus up to 10 ft (3 m) Egypt
The grass-like leaves are borne in umbels at the tops of the tall stems. The papyrus of the ancient Egyptians was made from this plant.

CYPRESS – see *Chamaecyparis* and *Cupressus*

CYPRIPEDIUM
(Orchidaceae) Lady's Slipper Orchid
This name is applied to several different orchid groups but is most commonly used for the hardy North American lady's slipper orchid which should be correctly called *Paphiopedilum*.
Cultural requirements: Potting compost of peat, loam, leafmould, and chopped sphagnum moss. They need a frost-proof frame or greenhouse in winter, well ventilated to give free circulation of air. The plants, in their pots, should stand outside in a shady situation during the summer.
Propagation: By division.

C. acaule 1½ ft (45 cm) N. America
Pale pink slipper flowers with a veining of deeper pink. Early summer.

C. californicum 1–2 ft (30–60 cm) California
Small greenish flowers, up to twelve to a stem. Early summer.

C. candidum 1 ft (30 cm) U.S.A.
Green flowers, striped with purple on their insides. Early summer.

C. parviflorum 1 ft (30 cm) U.S.A.
One of the loveliest species, very easy to cultivate. Yellow flowers with waved petals. Early summer.

C. reginae (syn. *C. spectabile*)
1½ ft (45 cm) U.S.A. and Canada
Large white and purple flowers, flushed with pale pink. Summer.

CYTISUS
(Leguminosae) Broom
Useful garden shrubs, fast growing and ideal for in-filling. Almost all are hardy.
Cultural requirements: Brooms thrive in even the poorest and lightest of soils but they require an open sunny situation.
Propagation: From seed outdoors or by grafts in spring; by cuttings in sandy soil in late summer.

C. ardoinii 6 in. (15 cm) Mediterranean
A mat-forming species with bright yellow flowers. Suitable for the rock garden. Late spring.

C. battandieri 12 ft (3·6 m)
Pineapple Broom Morocco
Vigorous shrub with erect stems and silken-silver trifoliate leaves. The terminal spikes of yellow flowers have a pineapple scent. Mid-summer.

C. × beanii (*C. ardoinii × C. purgans*)
1 ft (30 cm)   Garden origin
A delightful dwarf broom useful in the rock
garden. The bright yellow flowers smother the
slender stems. Early summer.

C. scoparius up to 10 ft (3 m) Common Broom
                    Europe, including British Isles
A native shrub of heaths and moorlands with rich

butter-yellow flowers. It is a parent of many good
named garden forms such as 'Cornish Cream',
pale yellow; 'Firefly', yellow and bronze; and
'Golden Sunlight', orange-yellow.

In addition to these, there are numerous
excellent named hybrids in a wide variety of self
and bi-colours. Early summer.

DABOECIA
(Ericaceae)

A small genus of evergreen lime-hating heaths,
related to the ericas.
Cultural requirements: Peaty soil and a situation in sun or part shade.
Propagation: From cuttings under glass in
summer; layers in autumn.

D. cantabrica (syn. *Menziesia polifolia*)
1½ ft (45 cm) St Dabeoc's Heath
                    W. Europe, including Ireland
A useful plant for the heath or rock garden
bearing an abundance of purple pitcher-shaped
flowers over a very long period. In addition to the

type, there are several attractive named forms,
including 'Alba', white; 'Bicolor', with white and
purple flowers on the same plant; and 'Pragerae',
a dwarf spreading form with pink flowers.
Midsummer to early winter.

DAFFODIL – see *Narcissus*

DAHLIA
(Compositae)

Half-hardy tuberous-rooted perennials. One of
the most popular of plants both for garden
decoration and exhibition for which latter purpose,
the flowers have been divided into a number of
different classes. The plants, according to type,
range in height from around 18 in. (45 cm) to
6 ft (2 m). The former kinds make useful summer
bedding plants. Dahlias can be treated as half-
hardy annuals, and raised from seed, but the
resulting plants will not breed true to type.
Cultural requirements: Rich, fertile, moist soil
and an open sunny situation. Dahlia tubers can be
planted outdoors in late spring or can be started
off in heat under glass and hardened off for
planting out in early summer. When frost
blackens the foliage in autumn, tubers can be
lifted and stored in peat or dry sifted soil, in a
frost-proof place for the winter.
Propagation: From seed, cuttings from shoots
on tubers, or division of tubers under glass in heat
in spring.

The dahlias cultivated in our gardens are
hybrids and are divided into ten classes, for
exhibition purposes as follows:

(1) Single flowered.
(2) Anemone flowered: One or more outer
    rings of florets surrounding a cluster of
    tubular florets.
(3) Collarette: Central ring of small florets
    surrounded by a single outer ring of florets.

Dahlia Single Bedding Mixed

DECAISNEA

(4) Peony flowered.
(5) Decorative, sub-classified under giant, large, medium, small and miniature flowered.
(6) Miniature Ball.
(7) Pompon.
(8) Cactus, sub-classified under giant, large, medium and small flowered.
(9) Semi-cactus, sub-classified as for cactus.
(10) Miscellaneous.

Coltness hybrids, which are easily raised from seed produce plants about 1½ ft (45 cm) tall with large single flowers in a wide range of colours. Summer to late autumn.

DAISY – see *Bellis*

DAISY BUSH – see *Olearia*

DAPHNE
(Thymelaeaceae)
Group of evergreen and deciduous shrubs of compact habit, mostly with very fragrant flowers, borne in late winter or early spring.
Cultural requirements: Well-drained moist loamy soil. Sun or part shade.
Propagation: *D. mezereum* is easily raised from seed sown as soon as it is ripe, other species from stem cuttings in late summer, layers in autumn or by grafting on to *D. laureola*.

D. blagayana 1 ft (30 cm)　　　　S. Europe
Evergreen shrub of creeping habit suitable for the rock garden. The creamy-white flowers are sweetly scented. Succeeds best in part shade. Early spring.

D. × burkwoodii (*D. cneorum* × *D. caucasica*)
3 ft (1 m)　　　　Garden origin
Vigorous semi-evergreen shrub with intensely fragrant pale pink flowers in terminal clusters. Late spring.

D. cneorum 1 ft (30 cm)
Garland Flower　　　　C. and S. Europe
Dwarf semi-prostrate evergreen shrub very useful for the rock garden. Clusters of pink flowers, up to 1½ in. (4 cm) across, are very fragrant. Early summer.

D. collina 1½ ft (45 cm)　　　　S. Europe
Slow growing evergreen shrub for rock garden. Very fragrant pink or pale lilac-purple flowers. Late spring.

D. mezereum 4 ft (1·2 m) Mezereon
Europe, including British Isles, and Asia Minor
Short lived deciduous shrubs with rosy-purple clusters of sweetly scented flowers on bare stems in winter, followed by scarlet berries, which are poisonous.
There is a white form 'Alba', with yellow fruits. Winter.

D. odora 3 ft (1 m)　　　　China and Japan
Partially tender evergreen shrub of spreading habit with intensely fragrant flowers. Needs a situation sheltered from north and east. The cultivar 'Aureomarginata', with gold-edged leaves, is hardier and more vigorous than the type. Midwinter to early spring.

D. retusa 3 ft (1 m)　　　　W. China
Slow growing evergreen species of bushy and compact habit. White or pale pink scented flowers in clusters. Early summer.

DATURA
(Solanaceae) Trumpet Flower
Greenhouse annuals and half-hardy annuals, all of which are poisonous.
Cultural requirements: John Innes No. 2 compost or a well-drained greenhouse border with soil rich in humus. Water plants under glass freely in summer, sparingly in winter.
Propagation: Annual kinds from seed under glass in heat; other kinds by cuttings under glass in heat in spring.

D. stramonium 2 ft (60 cm) Thorn Apple Britain
An annual species with white flowers, followed by large spiny poisonous fruits. Late summer.

D. suaveolens up to 10 ft (3 m)
Angels' Trumpets　　　　Mexico
Large white trumpet flowers that are very fragrant. Semi-evergreen in greenhouse cultivation. Summer.

DAVIDIA
(Cornaceae)
Medium-sized deciduous trees, suitable as specimens in the larger garden.
Cultural requirements: Any ordinary soil and, in cold districts, a fairly sheltered situation.
Propagation: From seed in a cold frame in autumn (germination can take up to two years) or cuttings of ripe wood in autumn.

D. involucrata 30 ft or more (9 m)
Handkerchief Tree　　　　China
In addition to its popular name of 'Handkerchief Tree' *D. involucrata* is also known as the 'Ghost' or 'Dove' tree, from the creamy-white bracts, up to 5 in. (13 cm) long, pairs of which enclose the clusters of insignificant flowers and persist on the trees for some weeks. Early summer.

DAY LILY – see *Hemerocallis*

DEADNETTLE – see *Lamium*

DECAISNEA
(Lardizabalaceae)
Deciduous shrubs with large pinnate leaves and

63

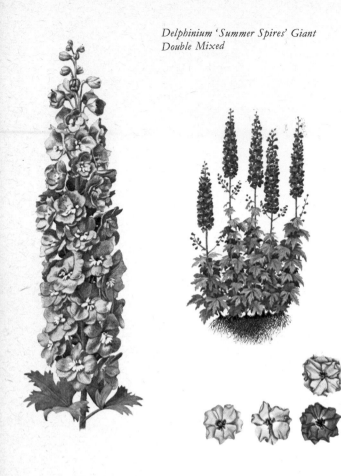

*Delphinium 'Summer Spires' Giant
Double Mixed*

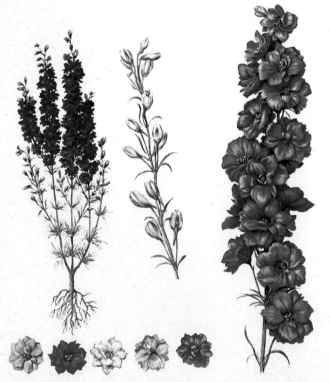

Larkspur Tall Double-Branching Mixed

distinctive fruits. Normally represented in our gardens by the species *fargesii*.

Cultural requirements: Moist, well-drained soil and a sunny or partly shaded situation.

Propagation: From seed under glass in early spring.

D. *fargesii* 8 ft (2·5 m)   W. China
A shrub of upright habit with pinnate leaves up to 3 ft (1 m) long. The greenish-yellow flowers are followed by clusters of cylindrical, fleshy blue seedpods, like those of the broad bean.

DELPHINIUM
(Ranunculaceae)

A large genus of annual and perennial plants of great value to gardeners. The tall hybrid strains, with flower spikes 5 ft (1·5 m) or more in height are most striking, and valuable for garden decoration, for cutting and for exhibition.

Cultural requirements: The annual delphiniums or larkspurs will succeed in any good garden soil but the perennial kinds need a deep rich soil with plenty of humus in the shape of well-rotted manure or compost. The dormant crowns should have protection from slugs in winter. The taller kinds will need secure staking.

Propagation: From seed in a cool greenhouse from spring to midsummer. Early sowings may produce plants that will flower in the same season. From cuttings in a cold frame in spring and by division in autumn.

Although there are several attractive species such as *D. grandiflorum* 'Blue Butterfly', with brilliant blue flowers, it is the perennial hybrid strains, known as elatum and belladonna, that are most widely grown. Good named forms of the taller kinds are numerous and it is best to consult a current catalogue. There are fewer of the daintier 'Belladonna Hybrids' which contain such tried and true favourites as 'Bees Blue', a clear light blue; 'Lamartine', violet-blue; 'Pink Sensation', clear pink; and 'Wendy', gentian-blue.

Seeds of both kinds are obtainable and the best of these produce plants with flowers possessing the same striking characteristics as those of the named varieties. Good strains of seed include Blackmore and Langdons' Prize strain, Giant-flowered mixed, and the Pacific Giant strains with huge spikes of very large individual blooms. Summer.

The annual delphiniums, or larkspurs, can be sown outdoors either in spring or early autumn. The latter sowings will produce extra strong and vigorous plants that will flower early the following summer. There are also some delightful hardy perennial species of outstanding grace and beauty, which are best treated as half-hardy annuals.

These include 'Azure Fairy' (1 ft – 30 cm), with lovely sky-blue flowers and 'Tom Thumb', a compact variety with gentian-blue flowers. Summer.

DERRIS – see Pest Control

DESFONTAINEA
(Loganiaceae)
Somewhat tender evergreen flowering shrubs, not suitable for very cold districts.
Cultural requirements: Rich well-drained acid soil and a sheltered situation – a useful shrub for a south wall.
Propagation: Cuttings under glass in heat in spring.

D. spinosa 6 ft (2 m)   Chile
Slow growing evergreen shrub with small holly-like leaves and waxen tubular flowers scarlet and yellow, 2 in. (5 cm) in length. Late summer.

DEUTZIA
(Saxifragaceae)
Deciduous hardy flowering shrubs, easy to grow and extremely decorative.
Cultural requirements: Any ordinary well-drained soil and a sunny situation. Prune after flowering.
Propagation: Softwood cuttings in a cold frame in summer; from hardwood cuttings in winter.

D. × elegantissima (*D. purpurascens × D. sieboldiana*) 5 ft (1·5 m)   Garden origin
Arching sprays of rosy-purple star-shaped flowers on elegant arching stems. Early summer.

D. × rosea (*D. gracilis × D. purpurascens*) 4 ft (1·2 m)   Garden origin
An attractive hybrid from which some of the most popular garden forms are drawn. These include 'Campanulata', white with a purple calyx and 'Carminea', with flowers tinged with rosy-crimson. Early summer.

D. scabra 8 ft (2·5 m)   Japan and China
A tall shrub of erect habit with clusters of white flowers. Named forms include 'Candidissima', double white; 'Plena', double flowers, suffused with rosy-purple; and 'Watereri', with single white flowers, tinged with carmine. Midsummer.

DIANTHUS
(Caryophyllaceae)
A valuable race of hardy annuals, biennials, and perennials, with a variety of uses in the garden. Most are delicately fragrant and have grey-green, narrow leaves. They include alpine and rock garden pinks, annual and biennial kinds such as sweet williams, border carnations, and perpetual carnations for the greenhouse.

Dianthus Annual Pink 'Baby Doll'

Cultural requirements: All types of dianthus have a preference for light well-drained soils and do well on chalk in a sunny situation.
Propagation: Annual and biennial kinds from seed in gentle heat in spring or outdoors later in the year for flowering the following season. Sweet williams, although actually perennials are usually treated as biennials. Also carnations and pinks from cuttings or layers.

D. × allwoodii 6–9 in. (15–22 cm)   Garden origin
This hybrid provides a race of hardy, perpetual flowering pinks. It was obtained by crossing *D. plumarius* with perpetual flowering carnations. There are many fine named forms and seed is also obtainable of strains giving a wide range of colours. Summer to autumn.

D. alpinus 3 in. (8 cm)   E. Alps
Tufts of dark green foliage and large red flowers make this dainty dwarf pink a useful perennial plant for the rock garden or for crevices in walls or paving. Summer.

D. barbatus 1–2 ft (30–60 cm)
Sweet William   S. Europe
The sweet williams are popular bedding or border plants for early summer. They associate well with Russell lupins. There is a wide range of colours and forms, including auricula – eyed and doubles.
'Sweet Wivelsfield' (1½ ft – 45 cm), a hybrid between sweet william and *D. × allwoodii* has similar but larger flowers in loose clusters. It is normally treated as a half-hardy annual.

Carnation Giant Annual Mixed

*Dianthus barbatus 'Indian Carpet'
(Sweet William)*

D. caryophyllus 1–2 ft (30–60 cm)
Clove Carnation   Europe
The clove carnations are hardy or half-hardy
perennials that are normally treated as half-hardy
annuals and sown under glass in early spring to
flower the same season. There are various strains
and named forms, most of which are deliciously
fragrant.

D. deltoides 6 in. (15 cm)
Maiden Pink   Europe, including British Isles
This is a dwarf perennial species with short green
leaves and freely borne small bright pink flowers
that makes a good rock garden subject. Midsummer to autumn.

D. gratianopolitanus (syn. *D. caesius*) 6 in. (15 cm)
Cheddar Pink   Europe, including British Isles
This is another dwarf pink, native to Britain with
sweetly scented pink flowers. Early summer.

Border Pinks and Carnations

These include many species, cultivars, and
hybrids as well as many named forms. Good
strains of seed are also obtainable.

Perpetual Carnations

These are raised and grown under glass in a
minimum temperature of 45–50 °F (7–10 °C) to
provide flowers over a long period.

DICENTRA
(Papaveraceae)
Hardy perennials with attractive lacy foliage and
curious, locket-like flowers.

Cultural requirements: Rich sandy or loamy soils and a sunny situation.
Propagation: By division of roots or root cuttings in spring.

D. eximia 1½ ft (45 cm) E. U.S.A.
Rosy-purple flowers on drooping stems. Attractive foliage. Early to late summer.

D. formosa 1 ft (30 cm) U.S.A.
The tufted glaucous foliage makes an attractive setting for the panicles of pink locket-like flowers. Spring to midsummer.

D. spectabilis 2 ft (60 cm) Bleeding Heart Japan
Also known as 'Dutchman's Breeches' and 'Our Lady in a Boat' because of its curiously shaped pink and white flowers, this popular cottage garden plant is attractive in or out of bloom, with smooth, grey-green dissected foliage. There is a white-flowered form 'Alba'. Early summer.

DICTAMNUS
(Rutaceae)
Hardy perennials with aromatic foliage.
Cultural requirements: Any ordinary garden soil and a sunny situation.
Propagation: From seed outdoors in late summer; root division in late autumn or early spring.

D. albus (syn. *D. fraxinella*) 3 ft (1 m)
Burning Bush E. Europe and Asia
This plant gets its popular name from the volatile oil, exuded by the flower stalks. This vaporizes and can be ignited on a still hot day. It is also known as 'Dittany'. The flowers are white. Summer.

DIDISCUS
(syn. *Trachymene*) (Umbelliferae)
Tender Australian annuals with blue flowers that make good greenhouse plants. They can also be treated as half-hardy annuals and grown outdoors in a warm and sheltered situation.
Cultural requirements: Under glass, in John Innes No. 2 or similar compost; outdoors in light sandy soil and a warm sunny situation.
Propagation: From seed under glass in spring.

D. caeruleus (syn. *Trachymene caerulea*) 2 ft (60 cm)
Blue Lace Flower W. Australia
Heads of lavender-blue lacy flowers on long stems that cut well. Midsummer to autumn.

DIEFFENBACHIA
(Araceae)
Evergreen perennials for the warm greenhouse or for use as house plants. Grown for the beauty of their foliage.
Cultural requirements: John Innes No. 2 or similar potting compost and a moist atmosphere.

Water freely during spring and summer, sparingly for rest of year.
Propagation: By stem cuttings under glass in heat in spring.

D. amoena 1 ft (30 cm) S. America
Dark green leaves, 1 ft (30 cm) long, strikingly marked with cream and yellow.

D. chelsonii 1 ft (30 cm) Colombia
This species has leaves mottled with green and yellow.

D. picta 3 ft (1 m) Colombia
The leaves, up to 12 in. (30 cm) in length, are green, with cream and silver markings.

DIELYTRA – see *Dicentra*

DIERAMA
(Iridaceae)
Hardy bulbous-rooted plants with sword-like foliage and long arching stems, bearing bell-shaped flowers, in mauve, pink, or white.
Cultural requirements: Light, sandy, well-drained soil and a sheltered southern aspect. Established plants resent disturbance.
Propagation: From offsets.

D. pulcherrimum 4 ft (1·2 m)
Wand Flower S. Africa
In addition to the type plants, described above, there is a graceful dwarf form 2½ ft (75 cm) tall.

DIERVILLA
(Caprifoliaceae)
Deciduous low growing suckering shrubs, related to the honeysuckles.
Cultural requirements: Any ordinary garden soil and a sunny or partly shaded situation.
Propagation: From rooted suckers or cuttings under glass in spring.

D. lonicera 4 ft (1·2 m) N. America
Small suckering shrub, with yellow tubular flowers. Summer.

D. rivularis 6 ft (2 m) S.E. U.S.A.
Similar to above, with lemon-yellow flowers and good autumn leaf colour. Late summer.

D. sessifolia 3 ft (1 m) S.E. U.S.A.
Compact shrub, useful for the large rock garden or banks, with sulphur-yellow flowers. Summer.

DIGGING – for various methods of digging, see Kitchen Garden

DIGITALIS
(Scrophulariaceae) Foxglove
Hardy biennials and perennials useful for shady borders and the wild garden.
Cultural requirements: Any ordinary garden soil and a sunny or shady situation.

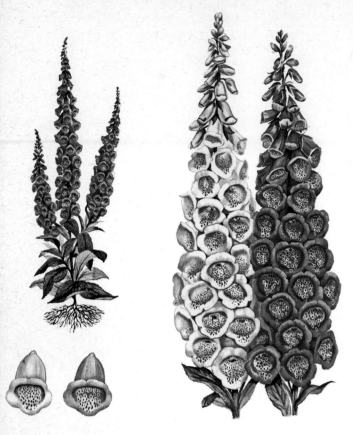

Digitalis Excelsior Hybrids (Foxglove)

Propagation: Biennial species from seed outdoors in early summer; perennial kinds by seed in same manner or by division in spring.

D. grandiflora (syn. *D. ambigua*)
2 ft (60 cm)   Europe
A perennial species with sulphur-yellow flowers.

D. purpurea
3 ft (1 m)   Europe, including British Isles
The common foxglove, a biennial species native to Britain with purple, spotted tubular flowers on tall spikes. There are some excellent hybrid strains, of which 'Excelsior Hybrids', with a wide range of colours and flowers produced all round the stems, is one of the most outstanding. Another good hybrid type is 'Foxy', a more compact form with flowers in shades of carmine, pink, cream, and white. Summer.

DIMORPHOTHECA
(Compositae)

Hardy, sun-loving annuals, perennials and sub-shrubs, easy to grow and producing showy daisy-like flowers.
Cultural requirements: Light sandy soil and a sunny warm situation.

Propagation: From seed under glass in early spring, outdoors later.

D. aurantiaca 1 ft (30 cm)   S. Africa
This species with its allied hybrids, is the most popular and widely grown. The large flower heads are a brilliant orange while the hybrid strains produce flowers ranging in colour from silvery-white through yellows to orange and apricot. Summer.

DISEASES OF PLANTS

Plant diseases fall into three main categories, those due to the activities of (*a*) viruses, (*b*) fungi, (*c*) bacteria. The best way of preventing any or all of these is to keep the soil in good heart and to practise good garden husbandry.

Healthy and vigorous plants can withstand attacks of disease that would prove fatal to others suffering on account of poor soil conditions, overcrowding or insufficient plant foods.

Virus diseases

These are the most serious of the plant diseases since for many, there is no effective cure. Many are introduced into the systems of the plants by sap-sucking insects, such as aphids, which act as hosts to the diseases.

Examples of virus diseases are the mosaics to which potatoes, tomatoes, raspberries, and strawberries are all susceptible, as well as the reversion of black currants. Such diseases do not always kill, but render the plants weak and unhealthy, valueless for cropping purposes, and fit only for the bonfire.

The best course open is the prevention of infection by destroying the pests that act as vectors, or carriers of the diseases. Such preventitive measures are dealt with in greater detail under Pests.

Fungus diseases

These are responsible for many of the commoner plant ailments, such as mildews, rusts, blight, canker, black spot, and others. Many can be prevented, cured, or rendered comparatively harmless by the appropriate treatment.

There are various sprays and dusts for this purpose, including the new systemic fungicides that penetrate the plants' circulatory systems through the leaves and stems and remain effective in the sap for several weeks.

Older remedies are copper or sulphur fungicides in the form of Bordeaux or Burgundy mixtures or lime sulphur. Such remedies, however, have been largely superseded by numerous proprietary fungicides, that are easier to use and which do the job a good deal more effectively.

Diseases and their cures

American Gooseberry Mildew: Lime sulphur, except for sulphur-shy cultivars such as 'Leveller' or 'Golden Drop'; systemic fungicides or dusts.

Apple Canker: Colloidal copper spray during leaf fall.

Black Spot – Roses: Systemic fungicide, rose fungicide, or Orthocide spray or dust after spring pruning and again in summer at fortnightly intervals if disease reappears.

Blight – Potatoes and Tomatoes: Copper fungicide spray; Bordeaux mixture or dust, at fortnightly intervals after midsummer.

Botrytis (Grey Mould): Systemic fungicide; Orthocide spray or dust.

Club Root – Brassicas: Calomel dust and rotation of crops so that brassicas do not occupy the same ground for two successive seasons.

Damping Off – seedlings: Proprietary seed dressing; ample ventilation and avoidance of overcrowding by sowing thinly. Watering with Cheshunt Compound.

Leaf Spot – Celery: Copper fungicide spray; Bordeaux mixture or dust.

Mildew – Roses: Colloidal sulphur spray or systemic fungicide.

Mildew – Tomato: Sulphur fungicide and adequate ventilation under glass.

Mildew – general: Systemic fungicide; sulphur fungicides or dusts.

Peach Leaf Curl: Lime sulphur or copper fungicide just before bud burst.

Rust – Roses, Antirrhinums, Chrysanthemums: Liquid copper fungicide.

DITTANY – see *Dictamnus*

DOG'S TOOTH VIOLET – see *Erythronium*

DOGWOOD – see *Cornus*

DORONICUM
(Compositae) Leopardsbane

Hardy perennials particularly useful for providing colour in the herbaceous border in spring.
Cultural requirements: Any good garden soil and a sunny or partly shaded situation.
Propagation: By root division in spring or autumn.

D. caucasicum 1½ ft (45 cm)   Europe
Deep yellow daisy flowers, 2 in. (5 cm) across. There are several good cultivars, including 'Magnificum', with flowers up to 3½ in. (9 cm) across and a striking double form 'Spring Beauty'. Spring.

D. cordatum 6 in. (15 cm)   S.E. Europe
A dwarf species with golden-yellow daisies. Mid spring to early summer.

D. plantagineum 3 ft (1 m)   W. Europe
The most widely grown species with long-stemmed golden-yellow daisy flowers, useful for cutting. Worth-while cultivars include the popular 'Harper Crewe' (syn. 'Excelsum'), an early tall variety and 'Miss Mason', free flowering, with bright yellow daisies. Mid spring to early summer.

DOUGLAS FIR – see *Pseudotsuga*

DRACAENA
(Liliaceae)

Evergreen shrubs or small trees for the warm greenhouse, grown for the decorative effect of their foliage. They also make good house plants.
Cultural requirements: John Innes No. 2 or similar potting compost. Water freely in spring and summer, more sparingly for rest of year.
Propagation: By stem cuttings under glass in heat in spring.

D. deremensis 3 ft (1 m)   Tropical Africa
Broadsword leaves 1½ ft (45 cm) long; dark green striped with silvery-white.

D. fragrans 3 ft (1 m)   Tropical Africa
Golden strap-shaped leaves, edged with gold.

D. sanderiana up to 5 ft (1·5 m)   Tropical Africa
Narrow, sword-like leaves up to 1 ft (30 cm) in length, striped with white and green.

DRAINAGE

The importance of well-drained soil for the successful cultivation of the majority of garden plants is something that cannot be too strongly emphasized. There are, of course, certain trees and shrubs, together with other plants, that actually thrive better in soil that is permanently damp or even waterlogged, but these are in the minority. Where lawns are concerned, good drainage is essential.

A good test of whether a plot is properly drained is to dig, during the winter, holes 2½ ft (75 cm) deep in various parts of the garden to get an idea of the general level of the water table. If water is still standing in the holes several days after a spell of rain, this is a sign that the drainage needs attention.

In small gardens, it is not always necessary to lay an elaborate system of land drains. Channels filled with large stones, or even with lengths of brushwood are often sufficient to lead the excess water away without the necessity for pipes. If there is a ditch or pond at the lowest part of the garden into which surplus water can drain, so much the better. Normally, however, it will be necessary to construct a soakaway for this purpose.

This is a pit, 3–4 ft (1–1·2 m) wide and deep, filled with large stones, broken bricks, or clinker, into which the drainage trenches or pipes are directed. The stones should be covered with tiles or turves laid grass side downwards to prevent the soil used to fill in the top of the soakaway from washing into it.

The slope of the drainage trenches should be about 1 in 20. If land drains are used, the pipes at the shallow end should be at least 15 in. (38 cm) deep, sloping evenly down to the soakaway and just touching one another. They should be bedded in sand or sifted soil to prevent movement.

In a small garden, a single row of pipes will usually provide adequate drainage. With larger areas, a more comprehensive system may be needed, with subsidiary drains running herring-bone fashion to a main drain which, in its turn, is led to a ditch or soakaway.

The drainpipes should be packed and covered with coarse gravel or small stones. The trenches are then filled with a finer gravel to within 1 ft (30 cm) of the surface before being filled in with soil.

DRIMYS
(Magnoliaceae)

Tender evergreen shrubs or small trees suitable only for milder districts.

Cultural requirements: Rich soil and a sheltered position in warm districts only.

Propagation: From cuttings of ripened wood in a cold frame in autumn; layers in spring.

D. winteri up to 20 ft (6 m)

Winter's Bark   S. America

A tall shrub or small tree with handsome leathery glaucous foliage and flat-topped loose clusters of ivory flowers. Early summer.

DRYAS
(Rosaceae)

Small evergreen creeping sub-shrubs, useful in the rock garden or as wall plants.

Cultural requirements: Any good garden soil but preferably a peaty one, a sunny situation in the rock garden, on walls, or banks.

Propagation: From seed in a cold frame in late spring; cuttings in a cold frame in autumn; division in autumn or spring.

D. octopetala 3 in. (8 cm)

Mountain Avens   Europe, including British Isles

Creeping plant with yellow-centred white flowers like small single roses followed by decorative silky seedheads. 'Minor' is a dwarf replica of the type plant. Early summer.

DRYOPTERIS
(Polypodiaceae) Buckler Fern

A race of greenhouse and hardy ferns to which the male fern, native to Britain, belongs.

Cultural requirements: Hardy species: Light soil rich in peat or leafmould and a shady situation.

Propagation: From spores in sandy soil in a cold frame, by division in late spring.

D. filix-mas 3 ft (1 m)

Male Fern   Europe, including British Isles

The male fern, with its handsome fronds, is a well known occupant of the woods and hedgerows. It makes an attractive plant for a shady bank or border or for the wild garden. There are several good named forms more suited to garden cultivation. These include 'Crispa' and 'Grandiceps'.

DUTCHMAN'S PIPE
– see *Aristolochia macrophylla*

EARWIGS – see Pest Control

ECCREMOCARPUS
(Bignoniaceae)

Half-hardy perennial climbers which, treated as half-hardy annuals, will come into flower in their first season.

Cultural requirements: Light rich soil and the protection of a sheltered south or west wall. The

soil round the roots should be covered with bracken or ashes in winter.

Propagation: From seed under glass in heat in spring.

E. scaber up to 20 ft (6 m)

Chilean Glory Flower   Chile

An exotic looking climber that clings by means of tendrils. The leaves are pinnate, the tubular scarlet flowers very showy. In milder districts it will survive the winter but may be cut down to ground level by frost. Summer to late autumn.

ECHEVERIA
(Crassulaceae)
Greenhouse or half-hardy succulent plants, formerly widely used in summer bedding schemes.
Cultural requirements: John Innes No. 2 or similar potting compost, with the addition of sharp sand or crushed brick rubble.
Outdoor cultivation: Any ordinary garden soil, provided it is well-drained, will suit them.
Propagation: By division in spring or by leaf cuttings under glass in heat in summer.

E. derenbergii 3 in. (8 cm) Mexico
House leek-like rosettes of bluish-white surfaced leaves and tubular, orange flowers. Summer.

E. gibbiflora 2 ft (60 cm) Mexico
Oval glaucous-blue leaves, in rosettes at the end of stems; red flowers. Autumn.

ECHINACEA
(Compositae)
Hardy perennials with a long flowering season. Useful as border plants and for cutting.
Cultural requirements: Any well-drained garden soil and a sunny situation.
Propagation: From seed under glass in spring, outdoors later; by division in spring or autumn.

E. purpurea (syn. *Rudbeckia purpurea*)
up to 5 ft (1·5 m) N. America
Pale rosy-purple cone flowers. 'The King' is a popular cultivar, taller and with larger flowers than the type. Summer to autumn.

ECHINOCACTUS
(Cactaceae)
Greenhouse succulents, cylindrical in shape, deeply ribbed and with vicious spines. The flowers seldom appear in cultivation.
Cultural requirements: Potting compost, John Innes No. 2 or similar with the addition of crushed brick or mortar rubble. Plants should be grown on a sunny greenhouse shelf or window-ledge indoors. Water sparingly during winter.
Propagation: From seed under glass in heat in spring; by stem cuttings in summer or by grafts.

E. grusonii 3 ft (1 m) Mexico
A species with yellow spines and red and yellow flowers.

ECHINOCEREUS
(Cactaceae)
Greenhouse succulents with ribbed and cylindrical spiny stems.
Cultural requirements: John Innes No. 2 or similar compost with the addition of crushed brick, mortar rubble, or grit. Water sparingly during winter.
Propagation: From seed under glass in heat in spring; by stem cuttings in summer or by grafts.

E. blanckii
A species with purplish-pink flowers. Summer.

E. scheeri Mexico and S. U.S.A.
Deeply ribbed spiny stems and cyclamen-pink flowers. Summer.

ECHINOPS
(Compositae)
Hardy perennials and biennials with thistle-like leaves and tall heads of globular flowers.
Cultural requirements: Any well-drained soil and a sunny situation.
Propagation: From seed outdoors in spring; by root division in spring or autumn.

E. ritro 4 ft (1·2 m) Globe Thistle S. Europe
Handsome border plants with metallic-blue flower heads that are useful in flower arrangements and also dry well. 'Veitch's Blue' and 'Taplow Blue' are two good cultivars. Summer.

ECHINOPSIS
(Cactaceae) Hedgehog Cactus
Succulents for the cool greenhouse forming low spiny cushions which also make good house plants.
Cultural requirements: John Innes No. 2 or similar compost with the addition of crushed brick, mortar rubble, or grit. Water very sparingly during winter, moderately for rest of year.
Propagation: From seed under glass in heat in spring; by cuttings in summer.

E. campylacantha (syn. *E. leucantha*)
1 ft (30 cm) Chile
Spiny hummocks and rose-pink flowers. Summer.

E. cristata (syn. *E. obrepanda*) 1 ft (30 cm)
Similar to former species but with creamy-white flowers. Summer.

E. multiplex 6 in. (15 cm) Brazil
A slightly more compact species with pink flowers. Summer.

ECHIUM
(Boraginaceae) Bugloss
Hardy annuals, biennials, and perennials of which the annuals are the most widely cultivated.
Cultural requirements: Any well-drained soil and a sunny situation.
Propagation: From seed outdoors in spring or in late summer to produce plants to flower the following season.

E. plantagineum 1 ft (30 cm) S. Europe
Hardy annuals with long flowering season. Very

free flowering. 'Blue Bedder' has deep blue flowers; 'Dwarf Hybrids' are a mixture of blue, lavender, rose, and white. Summer.

E. vulgare 3 ft (1 m)
Viper's Bugloss   Europe, including British Isles
This biennial species, with purple-violet flowers, is often found wild on the seashore. Summer.

EDELWEISS – see *Leontopodium alpinum*

ELAEAGNUS
(Elaeagnaceae)
Handsome shrubs, several species of which are evergreen. The variegated kinds bring colour to the shrub border in winter. The foliage is in great demand by flower arrangers. The silvery-white flowers are small, but very fragrant.
Cultural requirements: Any ordinary garden soil and an open but sheltered situation. They make good subjects for a south or west wall. Not suitable for shallow chalk soils unless enriched with plenty of compost or leafmould.
Propagation: From seed under glass in spring; from cuttings in cold frame in late summer or from layers in spring.

E. angustifolia 15 ft (4·5 m)
Oleaster   Europe and W. Asia
Deciduous species with yellow flowers followed by yellow fruits. The willow-like foliage is silver-grey. Summer.

E. × ebbingei (*E. macrophylla* × *E. pungens*)
8 ft (2·5 m)   Garden origin
Handsome, fast growing evergreen shrubs, ideal as windbreaks. The large grey-green leaves are silvered on their reverse. The fragrant flowers are followed by small dull orange fruits. Autumn.

E. macrophylla 8 ft (2·5 m)   China and Japan
A large spreading evergreen shrub with silvery leaves that become green on their upper surfaces as they mature. The flowers are fragrant. Autumn.

E. pungens up to 10 ft (3 m)   Japan
Evergreen species that contains several attractive variegated forms, including 'Dicksonii', with leaves broadly margined with gold; 'Maculata', leaves centrally blotched with gold; and 'Variegata', a vigorous cultivar with leaves that have a narrow margin of creamy-yellow.

ELDER – see *Sambucus*

ELM – see *Ulmus*

EMBOTHRIUM
(Protaceae)
Somewhat tender evergreen shrubs or small trees, very fast growing with striking flowers but suitable only for more favoured districts.

Cultural requirements: A lime-free peaty soil and a sheltered southerly situation.
Propagation: From seed under glass in heat in spring; by cuttings under glass in spring.

E. coccineum up to 30 ft (9 m)
Chilean Fire Bush   Chile
Large shrub or small tree with clusters of brilliant scarlet flowers. *E. c. lanceolatum* is a form with narrower foliage, while the 'Norquinco Valley' form is the hardiest embothrium in cultivation. Both have similar scarlet flowers, completely clothing the branches. Summer.

ENDYMION – see *Scilla*

ENKIANTHUS
(Ericaceae)
Ericaceous deciduous shrubs needing acid, lime-free soil. The flowers are urn-shaped and the leaves have exceptionally brilliant autumn colouring.
Cultural requirements: Any good garden soil, rich in humus and preferably peaty. It must be lime-free. A sheltered border and a sunny or partly shaded situation.
Propagation: By cuttings in heat under glass in spring.

E. campanulatus up to 8 ft (2·5 m)   Japan
This is the easiest species to grow, of erect habit, with cream and purple urn-shaped flowers in clusters and scarlet and gold autumn foliage. Late spring.

E. cernuus up to 5 ft (1·5 m)   Japan
Medium-sized shrub with brilliant autumn leaf colour. In *rubens* the flowers are edged with red. Late spring.

E. chinensis up to 15 ft (4·5 m)   China
Vigorous and tall growing shrub or small tree with larger leaves and flowers than those of other species. Good autumn leaf colour. Late spring.

E. perulatus (syn. *E. japonicus*)
up to 6 ft (2 m)   Japan
Slow growing and compact leafy shrub with white flowers and leaves that colour brilliantly in autumn. Late spring.

EPIMEDIUM
(Berberidaceae)
Hardy perennials, with attractive dissected foliage, useful both as edging plants and in the rock garden. All grow well in partial shade or a sunny situation.
Cultural requirements: Moist but well-drained soil rich in humus.
Propagation: By division in autumn.

E. grandiflorum 1 ft (30 cm)   Japan
The leaves, on wiry stalks, colour attractively in

autumn. The flowers are pale lilac and white. 'Rose Queen' has dainty spikes of rose-pink flowers. Spring.

E. × versicolor 1 ft (30 cm)   Garden origin
This hybrid form, with pale yellow spurred flowers like those of a miniature columbine, is particularly attractive in the woodland garden. Spring to midsummer.

E. × warleyense 9 in. (22 cm)   Garden origin
Another fine hybrid, with bronzy foliage and dainty spikes of orange-red flowers. Spring to midsummer.

EPIPHYLLUM
(Cactaceae)

Popular and widely grown group of succulent greenhouse and house plants with flattened stems sparsely covered with spines. The flowers, freely borne, are very colourful.
Cultural requirements: John Innes No. 2 or similar potting compost with the addition of crushed brick or mortar rubble. Water plants very sparingly during winter. Minimum winter temperature 50 °F (10 °C).
Propagation: From seed under glass or by stem cuttings.

E. ackermanii 2 ft (60 cm)   Mexico
Thin flat stems with few spines; crimson flowers. Late summer.

E. anguliger 2 ft (60 cm)   Mexico
Similar to the former species, but with white flowers. There are many named hybrids. Late summer.

ERANTHIS
(Ranunculaceae) Winter Aconite

Hardy tuberous-rooted perennials related to the buttercups and one of the first plants to bloom in midwinter.
Cultural requirements: Any ordinary garden soil that remains moist during growing period and a shady situation. Winter aconites look attractive under trees where, if left undisturbed, they will become naturalized.
Propagation: By division of tubers in autumn.

E. hyemalis
3 in. (8 cm)   Europe, including British Isles
The golden-yellow, buttercup-like flowers are surrounded by a ruff of green bracts. Midwinter.

E. cilicica 3 in. (8 cm)   Cilicia
Very similar to *hyemalis*, but with more finely divided bronze-green bracts.

E. × tubergenii 4 in. (10 cm)   Garden origin
A hybrid between the two species already mentioned, it has larger and more conspicuous golden-yellow flowers. 'Guinea Gold' is a good named form.

EREMURUS
(Liliaceae) Foxtail Lily

Handsome hardy perennials with tall spikes closely packed with flowers in a variety of pastel colours.
Cultural requirements: Rich, light, loamy soil and a sunny situation.
Propagation: By root division in spring or autumn; from seed sown in heat, with the seedlings being wintered in a cold frame for the first few seasons.

E. bungei (syn. *E. stenophyllus bungei*)
5 ft (1·5 m)   Persia
Narrow tapering leaves and close-packed bright yellow flower spikes make this a first class curtain-raiser in the border. Early summer.

E. robustus 8 ft (2·5 m)   Turkestan
A handsome species, with narrower leaves than *E. bungei* and with flower spikes of flesh pink or white. Early summer.

E. Highdown Hybrids 6 ft (2 m) Garden origin
This lovely race of hybrids was raised in the Sussex garden of the late Sir Frederick Stern. It contains plants with flowers in many attractive colours, including pink, amber, orange, and bronze. Early summer.

ERICA
(Ericaceae) Heath or Heather

Evergreen shrubs of great value in the garden for colour and ground cover. The more tender kinds make excellent greenhouse plants. *E. carnea* is particularly valuable as a source of winter colour.
Cultural requirements: Hardy species: Light well-drained soil, lime-free for all species except *E. carnea*, *E. mediterranea*, and *E. darleyensis* which will tolerate a certain amount of lime, and an open sunny situation.

Greenhouse species: Potting compost, two parts of peat to one of silver sand in a cool greenhouse. Use rainwater for watering.
Propagation: Greenhouse species: From cuttings in sandy peat, in gentle heat under glass in spring.

Hardy species: From semi-hard stem cuttings under glass in late summer; layering in spring.

The greenhouse species include *E. subdivaricata*, white and *E. ventricosa*, flesh-pink, both flowering in early summer, the summer flowering *E. cavendishiana* and *E. gracilis*, purplish-red, which blooms in late winter.

Hardy species

E. arborea 8 ft (2·5 m)
Tree Heath   S. Europe and Caucasus
A shrub of medium size with scented white flowers in great profusion. The cultivar 'Alpina' is much hardier than the type. Early spring.

Erica carnea 'Springwood Pink'

E. *australis* 4 ft (1·2 m)
Spanish Heath   Spain and Portugal
A shrub of small to medium size, unsuitable for cold districts. Very striking, with rosy-purple flowers in profusion. There is an attractive white form, 'Mr Robert'. Late spring to early summer.

E. *carnea* up to 1 ft (30 cm)   C. Europe
Dwarf carpeting evergreen shrubs, supremely useful as carpeting and ground cover plants. They flower between late autumn and late spring according to cultivars, of which there are very many. *E. carnea* is lime-tolerant but will not succeed in shallow chalky soils unless they are enriched with peat or leafmould. It does not object to light shade, but an open site is required to develop to the full the leaf colouring of those cultivars grown specially for this characteristic.

Among the best and most widely grown cultivars are the following:

'Atrorubra', deep rose-pink, late flowering;
'Cecilia M. Beale', white, mid-season flowering;
'C. J. Backhouse', pale pink, late flowering;
'Eileen Porter', carmine-red, early flowering;
'Queen Mary', deep rosy-red, early flowering;
'Ruby Glow', deep reddish-crimson, late flowering;
'Springwood Pink', rose-pink, mid-season flowering;
'Springwood White', white with spreading prostrate habit, mid-season flowering;
'Vivelli', deep carmine-red, mid-season flowering;
'Winter Beauty', clear rose-pink, mid-season flowering.

Cultivars with coloured foliage:

'Aurea', deep pink flowers, bright golden foliage, mid-season flowering;

'Ruby Glow', dark red flowers, bronzy foliage, late flowering;
'Vivelli', deep carmine-red flowers, striking bronzy-red tinted winter foliage, mid-season flowering.

                    Late autumn to early spring

E. *ciliaris* 1 ft (30 cm) Dorset Heath
          S.W. Europe, including British Isles
A low growing mat-forming species with rose-red flowers in summer. Among the few cultivars, 'Stoborough' is a good white form. Late summer to autumn.

E. *cinerea* up to 1½ ft (45 cm) Bell Heather
          W. Europe, including British Isles
The bell heather, native to the heaths and moorlands of Britain, makes a low growing, widely spreading shrub with a dense mat of wiry stems. The flowers of the type are a pinkish-purple. 'Alba Major' is a good white form and there are various cultivars with brighter colours than the type, including 'C. D. Eason', bright pink; 'C. G. Best', salmon-pink; 'P. S. Patrick', deep purple; and 'Velvet Night', an exceptionally deep purple. 'Golden Drop' and 'Golden Hue' are grown for their golden foliage which turns a coppery-red in winter. Midsummer to early autumn.

E. × *darleyensis* (*E. carnea* × *E. mediterranea*)
1½ ft (45 cm)   Garden origin
This hybrid and its cultivars are, like *E. carnea*, lime-tolerant. They flower in winter. 'Arthur Johnson' is an attractive form with magenta flowers; 'George Rendall' has flowers of a rich pink; 'Silberschmelze' is a fine white, with scented flowers. Winter to early spring.

E. lusitanica up to 10 ft (3 m)
Portugal Heath   Portugal
Tall erect shrub with scented white flowers, tender, but a useful winter flowering subject for milder districts. Late winter to spring.

E. mediterranea (syn. *E. erigena*)
up to 10 ft (3 m)   Mediterranean
This is the hardiest of the tree heaths, fairly tolerant of lime but unsuitable for very shallow chalky soils. The rosy-purple flowers are sweetly scented. There is a good white cultivar 'Alba', and an attractive compact form, 'Brightness', with bronzy-red flower buds opening to pink. 'W. T. Rackliff' is another fine cultivar dense and compact with attractive foliage and white flowers. Spring to early summer.

E. terminalis (syn. *E. stricta*) 6 ft (2 m)
Corsican Heath   W. Mediterranean
Late flowering tree heath with rosy-pink flowers and attractive dark green foliage. The faded blooms, russet in colour, are decorative in winter. Midsummer to early autumn.

E. tetralix 1½ ft (45 cm) Cross-leaved Heath
        N. and W. Europe, including British Isles
Lime-hating species, native to Britain. Named forms include 'Alba', white; 'Con Underwood', crimson with grey foliage; 'Pink Glow', pink with grey foliage; and 'Rosea', deep rose-pink. Summer to late autumn.

E. vagans up to 2 ft (60 cm) Cornish Heath
        S.W. Europe, including British Isles
Compact and spreading species with long spikes of rosy-pink or white flowers. Good named cultivars include 'Alba', white; 'Diana Hornibrook', rich red; 'Holden's Pink', mauve-pink; 'Mrs D. F. Maxwell', deep cerise-pink; and 'St Keverne', pale rosy-pink. Summer to mid-autumn.

ERIGERON
(Compositae) Fleabane
Hardy perennials, useful as summer border plants, with daisy flowers similar to those of the Michaelmas daisies. The dwarf species make useful plants for the rock garden.
Cultural requirements: Any ordinary garden soil and a sunny situation.
Propagation: From seed outdoors in spring; root division in spring or autumn.

E. aurantiacus 1 ft (30 cm)   Turkestan
Compact species, suitable for the rock garden, with orange flowers. Late summer to early autumn.

E. mucronatus 9 in. (22 cm)   Mexico
White and pink tiny daisy-like flowers in great profusion. Excellent for crevices in walls, or at sides of paths or steps. Summer.

The garden hybrids ranging from 1½ to 2 ft (45 to 60 cm) in height are useful in the herbaceous or mixed border. They include 'Charity', pale pink; 'Dignity', violet-mauve; 'Serenity', deep mauve; and 'Sincerity', bluish-mauve with a yellow centre.

ERINUS
(Scrophulariaceae)
Small hardy perennials, suitable for rock garden, dry walls, etc.
Cultural requirements: Well drained soil and a sunny sheltered situation.
Propagation: From seed outdoors in spring where plants are to grow; by division.

E. alpinus 4 in. (10 cm)   Pyrenees
Small tufted plants, useful in the rock garden or in crevices in paving. Rosy-purple flowers. Spring to early summer.

ERYNGIUM
(Umbelliferae)
Handsome and distinctive hardy perennials and biennials, noteworthy for their foliage and their flowers, the latter being a metallic-blue in some species. The flower heads cut and dry well for winter arrangements.
Cultural requirements: Any ordinary garden soil and a sunny open situation.
Propagation: From seed in a cold frame in late spring; by division in spring or autumn; from root cuttings.

E. alpinum 1½–2 ft (45–60 cm)   Europe
Pale green leaves, deeply cut and toothed, metallic-blue teazle-like flowers. Late summer to autumn.

E. giganteum 4 ft (1·2 m)   Caucasus
Biennial or short-lived perennial species, with large blue bracts and silvery foliage. If left undisturbed, will increase from self-sown seedlings. Summer.

E. planum 2 ft (60 cm)   Europe
Smaller deep blue flowers on candelabra-like stems. Late summer.

E. tripartitum
3 ft (1 m)   Of possible garden origin
Widely branching species with candelabra heads of small violet-blue flowers with narrow bracts. Late summer.

E. variifolium 2 ft (60 cm)   Europe
Silver-veined leaves and bracts make this a particularly attractive foliage plant. The flowers are blue. Summer.

ERYSIMUM – see *Cheiranthus*

ERYTHRONIUM
(Liliaceae)

Bulbous spring flowering plants with unusual and attractive small turkscap lily-like flowers and handsome marbled or mottled foliage, suitable for planting on shady banks or in light woodland conditions.

Cultural requirements: Any good garden soil and a shady sheltered situation. Plant corms in late summer or early autumn.

Propagation: From offsets or seeds sown when ripe.

E. americanum 6 in. (15 cm)　　　　N. America
Golden-yellow and purple flowers. Early summer.

E. dens-canis 6 in. (15 cm)
Dog's Tooth Violet　　　　　　　　Europe
This plant gets its popular name from the curious shape of the corms. The flowers are lilac in colour and the leaves are attractively marbled with dark and light green. There are several good named forms, including 'Lilac Wonder', lilac-pink with black anthers; 'Purple King', deep purple, blotched with brown; and 'Rose Queen', a delightful pink.

There are also a number of outstanding cultivars, larger and taller than the above mentioned species: 'Kondo', primrose-yellow with cinnamon markings; 'Pagoda', with reflexed canary-yellow petals; and 'White Beauty', are good examples of these.

*Eschscholzia New Hybrids
(Californian Poppy)*

ESCALLONIA
(Escalloniaceae)

Slightly tender evergreen shrubs or small trees, invaluable for seaside planting. Several species and cultivars make delightful flowering hedges.

Cultural requirements: Any well-drained soil rich in humus. Escallonias require shelter of a south or west wall in colder inland districts. Prune as soon as flowers have faded.

Propagation: From seed, cuttings in late summer, layers or offshoots.

E. macrantha 10 ft (3 m)　　　　　　Chile
This species, with glossy dark green foliage and carmine-pink flowers, is the one most widely used for hedging and windbreaks in seaside districts. Summer.

Hybrids

Most of the escallonias in general garden cultivation are hybrids, many with more distinctive and colourful flowers than those of the species. They range in height from 5 to 8 ft (1·5 to 2·5 m) in height. Among the smaller-leaved kinds, 'Donard Beauty', deep rose-pink; 'Donard Seedling', shell-pink; 'Glory of Donard', crimson-scarlet; and 'Langleyensis', rose-red, are all good. Other Donard hybrids with larger leaves are 'Apple Blossom', whose name is an apt description of its flower colour; 'Donard Radiance', rose-pink and very free flowering; and 'Pride of Donard', rosy-scarlet.

All of these make useful hedging material.

For use as wall shrubs in colder districts, all the following are excellent: 'C. F. Ball', scarlet; 'Crimson Spire', red; 'Ingramii', rosy-red; and 'Iveyi', pure white. Summer.

ESCHSCHOLZIA
(Papaveraceae) Californian Poppy

Popular hardy annuals with a long flowering season and elegant, finely cut grey foliage. Most garden forms have originated from the orange-yellow *E. californica*.

Cultural requirements: Any good garden soil and a sunny open situation.

Propagation: From seed outdoors in spring or late summer.

E. californica 1 ft (30 cm)　　　　California
Grey-green, finely divided leaves and vivid orange flowers. The various hybrids and hybrid strains have colours ranging from white through yellow, pink, orange, and red. There are also strains, such as 'Harlequin Hybrids', that are a brilliant mixture of double flowers. Dwarf forms such as 'Miniature Primrose' (6 in. – 15 cm), are useful in providing summer colour in the rock garden. Summer.

ESPALIER – see Fruit Garden

EUCALYPTUS
(Myrtaceae)

A family of evergreen trees of rapid growth, mainly from Australia. Some species are practically hardy, especially those selected from higher altitudes such as the Tasmanian mountains. The juvenile foliage often differs considerably from that of mature trees and is much sought after by flower arrangers for its form and colouring.

Cultural requirements: Almost any type of garden soil, with the exception of thin chalky ones and a sunny, sheltered situation. Avoid positions exposed to cold winds.

Propagation: From seed in heat during spring.

E. coccifera 30 ft (9 m)   Tasmania
Rounded glaucous foliage, narrower in adult trees. Clusters of white, urn-shaped flowers. One of the hardier species. Early summer.

E. gunnii up to 50 ft (15 m) Blue Gum Tasmania
The hardiest of the eucalyptus species with silver-blue disc-like, stalkless juvenile foliage, becoming green and narrow in adult specimens. Flowers creamy-white. Late summer.

E. niphophila 30 ft (9 m) Snow Gum   Australia
One of the hardiest and loveliest of the eucalyptus species. It is a small, slow growing tree with large glaucous leaves, up to 4 in. (10 cm) long and attractive peeling bark. Flowers white. Summer.

E. perriniana 30 ft (9 m)   Australia
Small silver-leaved tree with white stems and rounded juvenile foliage. Flowers white. Summer.

EUCRYPHIA
(Eucryphiaceae)

Hardy and partly tender evergreen flowering trees of outstanding beauty whose flowers, in summer, are of great value in the garden.

Cultural requirements: Sandy to medium soil, rich in peat or leafmould and preferably lime-free. Sheltered position in colder districts.

Propagation: From softwood cuttings under glass in summer or by layering.

E. cordifolia 15–20 ft (4·5–6 m)   Chile
A large evergreen shrub or small tree. The white flowers, with their central boss of stamens, resemble those of a single rose. The leaves are heart-shaped. *E. cordifolia* is the most lime-tolerant species. Late summer.

E. glutinosa (syn. *E. pinnatifolia*)
15 ft (4·5 m)   Chile
A deciduous or partly evergreen species and one of the loveliest of summer flowering trees. The leaves are pinnate, colouring attractively in autumn and there is a profusion of white flowers

with a striking central boss of golden stamens. Will not tolerate lime. Late summer.

E. × nymansensis (*E. cordifolia × E. glutinosa*)
up to 30 ft (9 m)   Garden origin
A lovely hybrid between the two foregoing species, *E. × nymansensis* is hardier than either and fairly lime-tolerant. The cup-shaped white flowers are honey scented with pinkish stamens and contrast well with the olive-green foliage. Late summer.

EUONYMUS
(Celastraceae)

This genus contains a wide variety of deciduous and evergreen shrubs which make particularly good subjects for town or seaside planting. Many have attractive winged fruits and the foliage of the deciduous kinds colours well in autumn.

Cultural requirements: Any ordinary garden soil including chalk.

Propagation: From semi-hard stem cuttings taken with a heel under glass in late summer or from seed in the autumn. Seed may not germinate until the second year.

E. alatus 8 ft (2·5 m)   China
A shrub of wide spreading habit with narrow leaves, up to 3 in. (7 cm) long that turn a fiery crimson-scarlet in autumn. In winter the curious corky 'wings' on the stems are a decorative feature.

E. europaeus 20 ft (6 m)
Spindle Tree   Europe, including British Isles
A deciduous shrub or small tree whose attraction lies in its scarlet winged seed capsules which open to reveal orange-scarlet seeds. 'Red Cascade' is the best named form.

E. fortunei (syn. *E. radicans*) 3 ft (1 m)   China
Evergreen creeping or self-clinging climbing shrubs, grown primarily for the beauty of their foliage. There are several good named cultivars some of which have attractively variegated leaves. 'Gracilis' (syn. 'Variegata') has grey-green leaves edged with white to which a pinkish tinge is added in winter.

E. japonicus 6 ft (2 m)   China and Japan
Evergreen shrubs, very useful for hedging especially in seaside districts. They thrive equally well in sun or partial shade. There are various named forms including several, such as 'Macrophyllus Albus', whose leaves are strikingly variegated with white or cream.

EUPATORIUM
(Compositae) Hemp Agrimony

Hardy and partially tender shrubs and herbaceous perennials, the hardy border species making handsome border plants.

Cultural requirements: Any ordinary garden soil and an open situation.
Propagation: Division in spring or autumn.

E. purpureum 6 ft (2 m)
A handsome plant for the back of the herbaceous border, with rounded heads of rosy-purple flowers on tall upright stems. Late summer.

EUPHORBIA
(Euphorbiaceae) Spurge

A large and varied group of annuals, biennials, perennials, and sub-shrubs each with a milky juice, or latex which in many is poisonous. The bracts are the showy part of the inflorescences. Most kinds are hardy but the poinsettia, *E. pulcherrima*, is a plant for the heated greenhouse and is popular as a Christmas house plant.
Cultural requirements: Any ordinary garden soil and a sunny or partly shaded situation. Poinsettias should have John Innes No. 2 or similar potting mixture and a winter temperature of 60 °F (15 °C).
Propagation: The hardy species can be raised from seed sown outdoors in spring. The herbaceous and shrubby species can also be increased by division in spring or autumn. Poinsettias are propagated from cuttings of young shoots under glass in late spring.

E. biglandulosa 1 ft (30 cm)   S. Europe
One of the handsomest of the hardy spurges, with blue-grey foliage borne spirally on long stems and flat golden heads of bloom. It needs well-drained soil and a position in full sun. Early spring.

E. characias 3 ft (1 m)   Europe
One of the shrubby species, very similar to the better known *E. wulfenii*. Large bottle-brush flower heads of pale green with a maroon eye to each floret. Early spring.

E. epithymoides (syn. *E. polychroma*)
1½ ft (45 cm)   S. Europe
A valuable species for the spring border when its bright lime-green bracts first appear, remaining decorative almost until midsummer. Fast growing and easily increased by division. Early spring.

E. griffithii 3 ft (1 m)   Himalayas
A striking species with large heads of orange-scarlet bracts like small poinsettias. Prefers moist soils and partial shade. Early summer.

E. lathyrus 4 ft (1·2 m) Caper Spurge   Europe
A biennial species which, once established, seeds freely and becomes naturalized. Handsome sculptured sea-green foliage. It is claimed that this plant will discourage moles.

E. myrsinites 6 in. (15 cm)   S. Europe
A prostrate spurge with long snaking stems covered in intense blue-grey scaly leaves. The yellow heads of blooms are very attractive. *E. myrsinites* makes a good subject for a dry sunny wall or the southern slopes of a rock garden. Spring.

E. robbiae 1½ ft (45 cm)   Asia Minor
An evergreen suckering species with a rhododendron-like foliage that provides good ground cover. Rapid increase from underground runners. The yellow bracts are striking. Early summer.

E. sikkimensis 3 ft (1 m)   Himalayas
A deciduous species with young ruby-red shoots in spring and attractive pale green foliage veined with red. The bracts are a pale greenish-gold. Summer.

E. wulfenii (syn. *E. veneta*) 4 ft (1·2 m)   Europe
The best known of all the spurges with large flue-brush heads of lime-green bracts and greyish evergreen foliage. Spring.

EURYOPS
(Compositae)

Silver-leaved sub-shrubs useful in a grey and silver garden, or in the rock garden.
Cultural requirements: Well-drained soil and a sunny situation.
Propagation: From cuttings or suckers in late summer.

E. acraeus (syn. *E. evansii*) 1 ft (30 cm)   S. Africa
A dense and compact silvery shrublet of great charm. Yellow daisy flowers. Summer.

EVENING PRIMROSE – see *Oenothera*

EVERGREENS

Evergreen plants are those which retain their leaves throughout the year. Although we tend to think mainly of shrubs in this connection, there are also evergreen trees – most conifers for example – and other trees such as arbutus, eucalyptus, and holm oak – perennials, such as bergenias, acanthus, and many of the spurges. The value of evergreen subjects in providing winter interest in the garden needs no stressing. Evergreen hedging shrubs, too, such as yew, holly, box, and laurel are additionally useful for the shelter and privacy that they provide at all times of the year.

EVERLASTING FLOWERS

The French call them *immortelles* and the term generally applies to those flowers with papery or straw-like petals which, gathered and dried just before they reach maturity, retain their form and colour and provide valuable material for use in winter arrangements. Among the best known of these, all easy to raise from seed, are hardy and half-hardy annuals such as acroclinium, helichrysum, rhodanthe, statice, and xeranthemum.

The flowers should be hung in bunches, head downwards, in a dry garage or shed for a few weeks after gathering.

EVERLASTING PEA – see *Lathyrus latifolius*

EXACUM
(Gentianaceae)

Tender biennials and perennials that make good pot plants for the warm greenhouse.

Cultural requirements: John Innes No. 2 or similar compost and plenty of light and water.

Propagation: From seed under glass in heat in spring; by cuttings of perennial species.

E. affine 9 in. (22 cm)   Socotra

This is the most widely grown species and is biennial, with mauve, violet-like flowers with a scent of lily-of-the-valley. Spring.

EXOCHORDA
(Rosaceae) Pearl Bush

Beautiful hardy deciduous shrubs with an elegant arching habit and pure white flowers.

Cultural requirements: Any ordinary garden soil that is fertile, moist and well-drained, and a sunny situation.

Propagation: From seed in a cold frame in spring or autumn; semi-hard stem cuttings under glass in late summer, taken with a heel.

E. giraldii 10 ft (3 m)   N.W. China

Free flowering shrub of arching habit with white flowers. The variety *wilsonii* has larger flowers than those of the type. Early summer.

E. racemosa 12 ft (4 m)   China

A delightful shrub whose arching branches are festooned with short spikes of white blossom. The best known species, of somewhat spreading habit. Early summer.

FABIANA
(Solanaceae)

A genus of a single species of heath-like evergreen shrubs bearing small scaly leaves.

Cultural requirements: Any well-drained neutral or acid soil and a fairly sheltered situation.

Propagation: From cuttings of young shoots in a cold greenhouse or frame in spring.

F. imbricata up to 8 ft (2·5 m)   Chile

The upright stems of this attractive shrub are smothered in white tubular flowers in early summer. 'Prostrata' is a form of arching or prostrate habit, hardier than the type; 'Violacea' is a cultivar with lavender flowers. Early summer.

FAGUS
(Fagaceae) Beech

Hardy deciduous trees, up to 80 ft (24 m) in height and of a broad and spreading habit. *F. sylvaticus*, the species native to the British Isles, makes an excellent hedging subject since under these conditions, provided it is clipped regularly, it retains its dead russet foliage throughout the winter.

Cultural requirements: Sandy or chalk soils and well-drained loam.

Propagation: From seed sown outdoors in autumn, transplanting the seedlings at the end of their second season.

F. sylvaticus up to
100 ft (30 m)   Europe, including British Isles

Handsome spreading trees which as specimens, are too large for the small to medium-sized garden. There are numerous cultivars, of which the most striking are the several kinds of copper beech with coppery-bronze foliage, translucent when young. These are well represented by 'Riversii' and 'Purpurea Pendula', the latter an outstandingly lovely weeping form. Other fine cultivars include 'Aurea Pendula', a weeping beech with golden foliage; *F. s.* 'Heterophylla', the fern-leaved beech, with finely cut and lobed leaves; and 'Luteovariegata', a cultivar whose foliage is attractively variegated with yellow.

FALSE ACACIA – see *Robinia pseudoacacia*

FAN-TRAINED TREES – see Fruit Garden

FASTIGIATE

Trees or shrubs of erect columnar habit such as the Lombardy poplar, Dawyck beech or the flagpole cherry, *Prunus* 'Amanogawa'.

FATSIA
(Araliaceae)

Slightly tender evergreen shrubs that also make good house plants.

Cultural requirements: Any well-drained garden soil and a partly shaded situation.
Propagation: By root cuttings under glass in spring.

F. japonica (syn. *Aralia sieboldii*)
10 ft (3 m)   Japan
Medium-sized shrub with dark green polished palmate leaves, often exceeding 1 ft (30 cm) across. The large panicles of ivory-white drumstick flowers are very striking. Early winter.

A cross between this species and the Irish ivy, *Hedera helix hibernica*, has produced an interesting bigeneric hybrid, × *Fatshedera lizei*, which makes a good ground cover plant for shady beds and borders as well as being an extremely handsome indoor foliage plant.

FELICIA
(Compositae)

South Africa genus of half-hardy annuals, biennials, and sub-shrubs with blue daisy-like flowers, most of which are normally treated as annuals.
Cultural requirements: Any ordinary garden soil and a sunny situation or as greenhouse pot plants.
Propagation: From seed under glass in gentle heat in spring; shrubby kinds by softwood cuttings under glass in spring or late summer.

F. amelloides 1½ ft (45 cm)   S. Africa
Tender half-hardy perennials or sub-shrubs with attractive sky-blue daisy flowers. Summer.

F. bergeriana 6 in. (15 cm)
Kingfisher Daisy   S. Africa
A dwarf shrub-like half-hardy annual, useful in the rock garden or as an edging plant. The daisy flowers are an intense shade of blue with yellow central discs. Summer.

FENCING

Although there is much to be said for the open plan garden, especially with the present-day trend towards smaller plots and with a view to creating a feeling of greater space, most people still feel the need for privacy that only an enclosed garden can give.

The best kind of screen is a living hedge but this is a long-term process and during the first few years in a new garden, the erection of some kind of artificial screen or fence will be necessary. One of the best ways of doing this is to use interwoven fencing panels. They are relatively inexpensive and blend well with garden surroundings. Looked after, such fencing will last for many years and is, therefore, ideal for providing shelter and privacy until a living hedge has had time to become established.

More permanent types of fencing include the close-boarded kinds in oak or softwoods, but with the present high price of timber combined with the cost of erection, the outlay on these is high. Ranch style fencing, constructed of horizontal planking, is also very popular and where saving of cost is concerned, there are few types of fencing better than the agricultural post-and-rail type.

The cheapest of all is chain-link or netting, strained between posts set at intervals of about 6 ft (2 m). This is essential to keep dogs from straying into or out of the garden, or where a garden abuts on to farmland, to keep out larger animals, in which case a top strand of barbed wire may be necessary. In such circumstances, too, the wire netting should be buried in the ground to a depth of 18 in. (45 cm) to keep out rabbits.

Brick or stone walls, with their potential for supporting climbing plants and wall fruits make the most attractive dividers of all. Their cost today, however, is so prohibitive that they are seldom found as a feature of new houses.

FENNEL – see Herb Garden

FERTILIZERS

Garden fertilizers are generally divided into two categories – organic and inorganic. In most instances, the former, as well as providing plant foods in an easily available form, contain bulk materials that help to improve the texture of the soil and give an additional boost to its fertility. This is particularly true of animal manures.

All plants need certain elements for healthy growth of which three – carbon, oxygen, and hydrogen – come from air or water. They are synthesized by the plants into sugars, starches, proteins. In addition to these, plants require nitrogen, phosphorus, and potassium together with smaller amounts of calcium, iron, and magnesium and a few other trace elements, such as boron, zinc, etc.

Most animal manures contain all of these, with the possible exception of calcium, in quantities sufficient for the needs of the plants. Nitrogen can also be supplied by sulphate of ammonia or nitrate of soda; phosphorus by superphosphate of lime and potash by sulphate of potash. These are obtainable in a suitably balanced mixture in commercial fertilizers, although some gardeners still prefer to mix their own.

Nitrogen promotes leaf growth, phosphorus is essential to seedlings and young plants as well as to root development in general. Potash assists in the ripening of fruits and new growth and promotes satisfactory flower and leaf formation.

Organic fertilizers which supply nitrogen are hoof and horn meal and dried blood. Bones are an organic source of phosphorus, which is released fastest from steamed bone flour, more slowly from bonemeal.

Wood ashes are rich in potash, but this is rapidly leached from the soil by rain. Bonfire ash, therefore, should be collected and stored under cover until required for use.

There are various commercial fertilizers designed for specific purposes – for fruit, vegetables, roses, chrysanthemums, etc. These should be applied strictly in accordance with the manufacturers' instructions.

Well made garden compost is rich in the elements necessary for healthy plant growth. Its humus content, too, can greatly improve the texture of all types of soil. Leafmould and peat fulfil a similar function in improving soil texture, but both are low in plant foods, with less than 1% nitrogen and less potash and phosphorus.

FESCUE – see *Festuca*

FESTUCA
(Gramineae)
Hardy perennial grasses with tufted inflorescences.
Cultural requirements: Any ordinary garden soil and a sunny situation.
Propagation: From seed outdoors or by division in spring.

F. ovina 9 in. (22 cm) Sheep's Fescue   Britain
Dense tufts of grey-green foliage with purplish feathery inflorescences. The best garden form is 'Glauca', with bluer leaves than those of the type. An excellent plant for edging or for the 'grey' garden. Summer.

FICUS
(Moraceae)
A genus containing numerous species, including the common fig. Only a few of these are hardy outdoors in temperate regions. It also includes the popular house plant, *Ficus elastica*, the indiarubber plant.
Cultural requirements: For figs, see Fruit Garden.
F. elastica: John Innes No. 2 or similar compost. Water sparingly during dormant period.
Propagation: By cuttings in sandy peat in heat in spring or summer.

F. elastica up to 10 ft (3 m)
Indiarubber Plant   India
The popular house plant with large polished leaves. In the tropics it makes a large tree, up to 50 ft (15 m) and more in height.

FIG – see *Ficus* and Fruit Garden

FILBERT – see *Corylus maxima*

FILIPENDULA
(Rosaceae)
Hardy perennials, formerly grouped with spiraeas, that make useful plants for the herbaceous border or wild garden.
Cultural requirements: Any good garden soil and a sunny open situation.
Propagation: By division in spring.

F. hexapetala (syn. *F. vulgaris*) 1½ ft (45 cm)
Dropwort   Europe, including British Isles
Fern-like foliage and creamy-white flowers on slim, erect stems. The double form, 'Flore Pleno', is showier than the type. Summer.

F. ulmaria up to 5 ft (1·5 m)
Meadowsweet   Europe, including British Isles
Our native meadowsweet with its delicate foliage and plumes of creamy-white flowers likes a moist situation. The best garden forms are the double 'Flore Pleno' and 'Variegata', with leaves that are marbled with gold. Summer.

FIR – see *Abies*

FIRETHORN – see *Pyracantha*

FLAG – see *Iris germanica*

FLAX – see *Linum*

FLEABANE – see *Erigeron*

FLOWERING CURRANT – see *Ribes*

FLOWERING NUTMEG
– see *Leycesteria formosa*

FOAM FLOWER – see *Tiarella cordifolia*

FORGET-ME-NOT – see *Myosotis*

FORSYTHIA
(Oleaceae) Golden Bells
Deciduous hardy flowering shrubs valuable for their early flowering season.
Cultural requirements: Any ordinary garden soil and an open sunny situation. They will flower earlier if grown against a south or west wall. Cut out flowering shoots as soon as blossom has faded.
Propagation: From hardwood cuttings in autumn.

F. × intermedia (*F. suspensa* × *F. viridissima*)
up to 9 ft (2·7 m)   Garden origin
Vigorous and fast growing hybrid with deep yellow flowers profusely borne along bare stems and branches. There are several good named forms

Forsythia × intermedia 'Spectabilis'

Cultural requirements: Rich loamy or peaty soil, neutral or acid in character.
Propagation: From layers or suckers in autumn.

F. gardenii (syn. *F. alnifolia*)
3 ft (1 m)   S.E. U.S.A.
The flower spikes, petal-less and made up of white stamens, are very fragrant. Late spring.
F. monticola 6 ft (2 m)   U.S.A.
The most widely grown species, with showy spikes of yellow and white florets. Late spring.

FOXGLOVE – see *Digitalis*

FOXTAIL LILY – see *Eremurus*

FRAXINUS
(Oleaceae) Ash
Deciduous trees with handsome pinnate foliage. The common ash, *F. excelsior* is a valuable timber tree, too big for the small to medium-sized garden.
Cultural requirements: Any ordinary well-drained garden soil.
Propagation: From stratified seed sown the following year. Ornamental cultivars by grafting on common ash.

F. excelsior 100 ft (30 m)
Common Ash   Europe, including British Isles
A large tree with handsome foliage and attractive black winter buds. The weeping form 'Pendula', makes a highly decorative specimen tree where sufficient space is available.
F. ornus 50 ft (15 m) Manna Ash   S. Europe
A decorative tree of medium size, with attractive frothy cream flower heads borne in clusters. Early summer.

FREESIA
(Iridaceae)
Greenhouse bulbous plants noteworthy for their delicious fragrance. They can be grown outdoors in very mild districts.
Cultural requirements: John Innes No. 2 or

including 'Lynwood', rich yellow flowers with broad petals and 'Spectabilis', one of the most profusely flowering forms. Spring.
F. suspensa 10 ft (3 m)   China
A species with a loose and rambling habit, useful as wall shrubs on any aspect. The variety *atrocaulis* has blackish-purple stems and large lemon-yellow flowers; *fortunei*, is the largest and most vigorous. Spring.

FOTHERGILLA
(Hamamelidaceae)
Small deciduous shrubs with white and yellow bottle brush spikes of blossom consisting of stamens and anthers only. Good autumn leaf colour.

Sow Freesia seeds thinly in boxes of compost from March to June at 60–65 °F (15–18 °C). When seedlings have four leaves, plant them six to a 5- or 6-in. (13–15 cm) pot of potting compost. Put a few 6–9 in. (15–22 cm) split bamboos round the pot to support the plants later on

Freesia Choice Hybrids

similar compost. Pot up corms in late summer or autumn to flower the following spring. Water freely during growing season.

Propagation: From seed in a cool greenhouse or frame in spring; outdoors summer to mid-autumn; they will flower in just over a year from sowing. The many hybrids and cultivars offer a wide range of colours and there are various named cultivars and worth-while strains of seed.

FREMONTIA
(Sterculiaceae)

Semi-evergreen flowering shrubs for mild districts.

Cultural requirements: Moist sandy soil and a sheltered situation. A south wall suits them well and they do not object to alkaline soils.

Propagation: From seed in a cold frame in spring.

F. californica up to 10 ft (3 m)　　　California
This makes a handsome wall shrub. The leaves are lobed and the large yellow chalice flowers are borne over a long period. Late spring to midsummer.

FRENCH MARIGOLD – see *Tagetes*

FRITILLARIA
(Liliaceae)

Hardy bulbous plants, the species described being of outstanding beauty.

Cultural requirements: Any ordinary rich garden soil and a shady situation.

Propagation: From seed in a cold frame in spring; from offsets in autumn.

F. imperialis 3 ft (1 m)
Crown Imperial　　　　　　　　W. Himalayas
A majestic plant, with a crown of glossy green foliage, subtended by a ring of pendent bell flowers. The type plant is orange-red, but there are also some attractive cultivars, including 'Aurora', coppery-red; 'Lutea Maxima', lemon-yellow; 'Rubra Maxima', bronzy-red; and 'Orange Brilliant', rusty-red. Spring.

F. meleagris 1–1½ ft (30–45 cm) Snake's Head Fritillary　　　　Europe, including British Isles
Delightful bulbous plants, magnificent when naturalized, with lantern-like flowers on slender stems, slaty-purple, chequered with white. There are also some good cultivars, including 'Aphrodite', white; 'Purple King', wine-purple; and 'Saturnus', reddish-purple. Spring.

FRUIT GARDEN

Fruit growing can be a rewarding garden operation in every sense of the word. The price of fruit becomes increasingly high and apart from the added flavour and freshness of home-grown fruit, it pays to grow one's own. Today, too, any gluts or surpluses can be stored in the deep freeze.

With the development of dwarfing rootstocks for tree fruits, even the smaller garden should be able to provide enough space for a selection of apples, pears, and stone fruits. Larger plots should find room for a miniature orchard and sufficient soft fruits for all domestic needs.

Preparation of the Site

The soil for a fruit garden should be well-drained, rich in humus, and in good condition. Apples and plums will succeed in a wide range of soil conditions but pears are intolerant of hot, dry, sandy soils. Shallow chalky soils will need to have plentiful supplies of humus incorporated before successful cultivation of any types of fruit can be carried out.

Most kinds of fruit blossom are highly susceptible to frost damage. Some gardens are located in low lying positions which act as frost pockets, with cold air running down into them. These are unsuitable for fruit growing; crops are likely to be sparse or a complete failure in most seasons.

In such areas, planting should be restricted to espaliers, cordons, or wall fruits which can be protected by netting or polythene sheeting. Cordon trees are grown on a single main stem, espaliers on a central stem with branches on either side of it in a flat horizontal plane. Fan-trained trees, as the name implies, have all their branches radiating from a short central stem in the shape of a fan.

The site for fruit trees should be deeply dug prior to planting since it would be injurious to their roots to cultivate the ground in their vicinity to any depth once the trees are established.

Double digging should be practised, breaking up the subsoil thoroughly with a fork as work progresses (see Kitchen Garden for digging procedures). If the soil is badly drained and waterlogged, surplus water should be led to a sump or should be carried away by land drains.

Trees can be manured in late autumn, using well-rotted animal manure or mature compost. It should be spread round the trees to the full extent of the branches, a rough indication of the spread of the root system.

Inorganic fertilizers should be applied with caution, especially to soft fruits, which can react unfavourably to some, particularly those containing sodium chloride or muriate of potash. Apart from this, the nutritional requirements of both bush and tree fruits are more or less the same as for most other types of tree or shrub.

APPLES

There are various forms in which apple trees can be grown. These include standard, half-standard, bush, and pyramid as well as espalier, fan, or cordon where support can be given.

The choice of trees on a suitable rootstock is important. There are various types, classified according to their dwarfing effect. A fairly dwarfing rootstock is needed for the small to medium-sized garden. This will give reduced yield but the trees will come into full bearing much more rapidly.

When choosing cultivars, consideration must be given to their mutual compatibility for cross-fertilization. Lists of these are given in the catalogues of fruit growers and nurserymen selling fruit trees.

Pruning of fruit trees is a complicated subject that is learned, to a large extent, by practice. Broadly speaking the principles are as follows:

Young trees: These are pruned in winter to produce a well shaped and balanced tree, open in the centre to admit light and air. Leading shoots should be shortened by about one-third, cutting them to an outward pointing bud. Lateral shoots should be left unpruned to encourage the development of fruit buds.

Mature trees: Winter pruning: Vigorous leading shoots should be shortened by about one-third, weak ones by up to two-thirds. Any dead, damaged or diseased wood should be cut out, together with inward growing and crossing shoots. The object of the operation is to create and maintain a shapely tree with an open centre.

Summer pruning: This is not necessary in the case of young trees, apart from those grown as espaliers and cordons. The procedure for these and for established trees of standard or bush form is to shorten all lateral growths of the current season to within 5–6 in. (12–15 cm), of their point of origin. This operation should be carried out progressively over several weeks during late summer. Leading shoots should be left alone to be shortened, if necessary, in winter.

Varieties

Dessert (Early): Beauty of Bath, Ellison's Orange, James Grieve, Lady Sudeley, Laxton's Epicure, and Laxton's Fortune.
Dessert (Keepers): Charles Ross, Cox's Orange Pippin, Laxton's Superb, Lord Lambourne, Sturmer Pippin, and Sunset.
Culinary (Early): Grenadier, Rev. W. Wilkes, and Peasgood Nonsuch.
Culinary (Keepers): Annie Elizabeth, Bramley Seedling, and Newton Wonder.

CHERRIES

Sweet cherries, as well as being extremely difficult to protect from birds, are not really suitable for the garden of small to medium size. They are not obtainable on dwarfing stocks and the large trees which they make are difficult for harvesting crops.

Where there is a considerable expanse of wall space, sweet cherries can be grown as fan-trained

Ficus carica (Fig)

wall specimens, but training and pruning can create a number of problems.

Morello, or so-called acid cherries are far more suitable for garden cultivation. They can be grown successfully in the fan-trained form and are especially satisfactory on a north facing wall.

The fruit has a sharp and distinctive almondy flavour and is ready for stewing or preserving when at the dark red stage. It later turns black and at this stage will require netting against birds. This fully ripe fruit is excellent for cherry jam.

Morello cherries are self-fertile, unlike the sweet kinds, which need a partner for cross-pollination. The morellos, too, bear their fruit only on one-year-old shoots. Old wood should, therefore, be cut out as soon as the trees have finished fruiting, once the basic fan structure of the trees has been obtained.

Cultivars

Sweet Cherries

Early Rivers }
Merton Heart }   Governor Wood }
                  Kent Bigarreau }

Napoleon Bigarreau }
Merton Bigarreau   }

Brackets indicate compatible partners for cross-fertilization.

Acid Cherries: Morello.

FIGS

Figs need plenty of sun and warmth and a position on a south or west wall suits them best. In this situation, they are normally grown in fan-trained form.

Since figs tend to grow too rampantly unless their root run is restricted, making too much leaf growth at the expense of fruit production, the roots should be boxed in by planting them in a hole about 4 ft × 4 ft (1·2 m × 1·2 m) and 2 ft (60 cm) deep. This hole should be lined with concrete or with broken bricks, well rammed down.

Cultivar: Brown Turkey.

PEACHES AND NECTARINES

These are normally grown in fan-trained form on a south or west wall but successful results can also be obtained in favoured districts from standard or bush forms in the open garden.

Well-drained soil is essential, with a light mulch of animal manure or compost in autumn and late spring.

The fruit is borne on wood of the previous year's growth. The dormant buds are of two kinds – single leaf buds, that are pointed and triple buds consisting of two rounded fruit buds on each side of a leaf bud. Pruning cuts should be made to an outward pointing single leaf bud.

Fan-trained kinds should have any shoots growing towards or away from the wall removed. One or two of the wood buds at the base of the previous year's growths should be allowed to grow on to act as replacement shoots. Terminal buds are pinched back to four leaves when they have made about 6 in. (15 cm) of growth, unless it is desired to extend them, when they can be grown on to the required length. Any side shoots should be pinched back to two leaves, spreading the entire operation over a period of several weeks.

Cutting out of dead and diseased wood should be postponed until after the fruit has been gathered. This will lessen the risk of infection by diseases such as Peach Leaf Curl and Dieback.

Cultivars

Peaches: Hale's Early, Peregrine, Royal George, and Waterloo.

Nectarines: Early Rivers and Lord Napier.

PEARS

Most of the remarks concerning apples also apply to pears, although the latter are somewhat more difficult to cultivate. They flower earlier than apples, which makes them more susceptible to frost. For this reason, a warm sheltered position should be chosen. Some of the finest dessert pears are grown against south or west walls.

Pears will not tolerate very dry soils. Like apples, they can be obtained on different types of dwarfing rootstock which accelerate fruit bearing. More pears than apples are self-sterile so that the choice of mutually compatible cultivars is important.

Pears, like apples, are obtainable as standards, half-standards, bush, pyramids, fans, cordons, and espaliers. The same general principles of pruning apply.

Cultivars

Early: Beurre Bedford, Jargonelle, and Laxton's Early Market.

Mid-season and Late: Dr Jules Guyot, Fondant d'Automne, William's Bon Chrétien, Doyenne du Comice, and Conference.

PLUMS, GAGES, AND DAMSONS

Plums will flourish in most kinds of soil except those that are very acid. These can be treated by the addition of lime or mortar rubble. On account of their early flowering, it is inadvisable to plant plums in gardens susceptible to late spring frosts. They will require liberal quantities of nitrogenous manures as well as an annual mulch of well-rotted manure or compost.

Plums and gages produce fruits of exceptionally fine flavour when grown on walls. Fan-trained trees are generally used for this purpose. Many cultivars are self-sterile and will need a different one to cross-pollinate them. There are two kinds of dwarfing stock available – Common Plum and Common Mussel. The latter are widely used for such cultivars as are incompatible with common plum stocks.

Trees are normally supplied as standards, half-standards, bush, or fan-trained. The last named kinds are used on walls.

Pruning: After the basic framework of the trees has been established, it will be necessary only to cut out any dead, damaged, or diseased wood together with inward growing branches that are robbing the centre of the tree of light and air.

Fan-trained plums are trained in a similar manner to fan-trained peaches and nectarines.

Cultivars

Dessert: Denniston's Superb, Early Transparent Gage, Mirabelle Petite, and Victoria.

Culinary: Belle de Louvain and Monarch.

All the above mentioned varieties are self-fertile.

Damsons: Bradley's King, Merryweather, and Quetsche.

SOFT FRUITS

Black and Red Currants and Gooseberries respond well to generous manuring – stable or farmyard manure if possible – failing this well-rotted compost, fortified with dressings of a general fertilizer.

BLACK CURRANTS

Newly planted bushes should have all shoots cut back to within 2–3 in. (5–8 cm) of soil level. This will enable them to perform the important task of building up strong new shoots on which the following year's crops will be borne. Subsequent pruning will consist of cutting out old wood and encouraging the development of new shoots. Pruning should ideally be carried out as soon as the fruit has been harvested but bushes can be pruned in autumn.

Cultivars

Boskoop Giant, Mendip Cross, Wellington XXX, and Baldwin.

RED AND WHITE CURRANTS

Pruning procedures for these differ from those employed for black currants. After the initial pruning, which consists of shortening all growths by one-half, the leading shoots are only tipped. The laterals, on which the bulk of the fruit is borne, are summer pruned to five leaves and cut back even further in winter.

Cultivars

Laxton's No. 1, Red Lake, and White Dutch.

GOOSEBERRIES

Gooseberries are pruned in a similar manner to red currants. It is important to keep the centre of the bush open in order to facilitate the gathering of the fruit.

Cultivars

Careless, Lancer, Langley Gage, Leveller, and Whinham's Industry.

RASPBERRIES

Raspberries root very near to the surface and do best on moist light soils, deeply dug, and well furnished with humus. Newly planted stools should be cut back to about 1 ft (30 cm) in spring to encourage the development of new shoots from the base. Subsequent procedure consists of cutting out all canes that have fruited and tying in the new growths as replacements. The latter should be restricted to about six to eight to each plant. Digging or forking in the vicinity of the plants should be avoided. Weeds can be kept down with summer mulches which are lightly forked in the following autumn.

Cultivars

Malling Exploit, Malling Jewel, Malling Promise, Norfolk Giant, and September (autumn fruiting).

STRAWBERRIES

Like other soft fruits, strawberries need a soil rich in humus. Deep digging and the incorporation of well-rotted manure or compost should precede planting. The best time for planting is in late summer but strawberries can go in at any time between autumn and early spring. It is inadvisable, however, to allow these late plantings to set crops of fruit in their first season unless they are well-rooted, pot-grown plants.

When the fruits start to develop, the beds should be strawed down to prevent the fruit being earth-splashed in wet weather. The plants will also require netting against birds, a precaution common to all soft fruits, which are best grown in a permanent fruit cage.

After the plants have fruited, the beds should be tidied up and all runners should be removed unless any are required as replacement stocks. A good way of tidying is to set fire to the straw on a dry day. This will burn off the old leaves and get rid of insect pests and disease spores in the process.

Cultivars

Cambridge Rival, Royal Sovereign, Grandee, Remontants (perpetual fruiting), Sans Rivale, Hampshire Maid, and Gento.

FUCHSIA
(Onagraceae)

Partly tender flowering shrubs many of which, although cut to ground level by frost in winter, spring up again from the base. Many species and cultivars are much hardier than is generally thought and make ideal shrubs for late summer and autumn thanks to their exceptionally long flowering season. The more tender kinds make excellent greenhouse pot plants and are also useful in hanging baskets and summer bedding schemes.

Cultural requirements: Greenhouse kinds: John Innes No. 2 or similar compost and a partially shaded part of the greenhouse. Pots can stand outdoors in a sunny position during summer and should never be allowed to go short of water.

Hardier outdoor kinds: Any ordinary garden soil, rich in humus. Sheltered borders or at foot of south or west wall.

Propagation: From seed in heat during spring; stem cuttings under glass from late winter to early spring.

F. magellanica up to 15 ft (4·5 m)   S. America
Some of the hardiest fuchsias are found in this species including 'Riccartonii', widely used as a hedging plant in milder districts of Britain. *F. gracilis* 'Versicolor', is a popular form whose leaves are a medley of grey-green, crimson, and creamy-white.

Larger flowered hybrid forms, many with *F. magellanica* as a parent include 'Madame Cornelissen', red calyx and white petals; 'Mrs Popple' with similar colouring and larger flowers; and 'Margaret' with flowers of purple and crimson. Midsummer to autumn.

The more tender species and hybrids make excellent plants for the cool greenhouse and can also be cultivated indoors if they can be given sufficient ventilation. They make good pot plants and are ideal for hanging baskets. In summer, the less hardy kinds can be used to give emphasis in bedding schemes. Plants under glass should be kept fairly dry in winter. They need a minimum temperature of around 40 °F (4 °C).

A good selection for greenhouse cultivation would include 'Heinrich Heinkel', purple and red; 'Molesworth', white and red; and 'Television', purple and white.

FUMITORY – see *Corydalis*

FUNGICIDES – see Diseases

FUNKIA – see *Hosta*

FURZE – see *Ulex*

Fuchsia 'Party Frock'

GAILLARDIA
(Compositae) Blanket Flower
Hardy but short lived perennials, valuable in the border and for cutting, with an exceptionally long flowering period.
Cultural requirements: Light well-drained soil and a sunny situation. Spring planting is best. Gaillardias do not thrive in heavy clay soils.
Propagation: From seed sown under glass in late winter or early spring, outdoors later. Treated like half-hardy annuals, perennial kinds will flower in the same season. The latter can also be propagated from stem cuttings in autumn, root cuttings in spring.

G. aristata 3 ft (1 m)   N. America
Most garden forms of gaillardias are hybrids or cultivars of *G. aristata*, and include 'Goblin', cardinal-red and lemon-yellow; 'Mandarin', deep red and bright yellow; 'Wirral Flame', deep orange-red; and the newer 'Dazzler', orange-yellow with a dark red centre. All have daisy-like flowers with prominent central discs. Summer to autumn.

G. pulchella 2 ft (60 cm)   N. America
This is a slightly tender species sometimes grown as an annual of which 'Picta' is the cultivar most commonly offered by seedsmen. The seed is best sown under glass in late spring, but sowings can be made outdoors later.

Good named forms and strains include 'Indian Chief', deep orange-scarlet; 'Lollipops', a strain with double flowers in a wide range of colours; and 'Blood-red Giants' with large, long-stemmed flowers, ideal for cutting. Summer.

GALANTHUS
(Amaryllidaceae) Snowdrop
Hardy winter flowering bulbous plants with pendent, pure white and green bell-shaped flowers.
Cultural requirements: Any ordinary garden soil and a situation in sun or partial shade. Snowdrops are seen at their loveliest when naturalized.
Propagation: From seed sown outdoors in boxes in a north facing situation; from offsets planted out before the foliage dies down in spring.

G. elwesii up to 1 ft (30 cm)
Giant Snowdrop   Turkey
This is one of the largest species with broad green markings at the base of the petals. Late winter.

G. nivalis 6 in. (15 cm) Common Snowdrop
Europe, including British Isles
This is the common species, vigorous and naturalizing well when given conditions to its liking. There are several large flowered forms and hybrids, including 'Atkinsii' and 'S. Arnott'. Winter.

G. plicatus 1 ft (30 cm)
Crimean Snowdrop   Caucasus
A distinctive species, with leaves folded at their edges. 'Warham' is the best named form. Spring.

GALEGA
(Leguminosae) Goat's Rue
Hardy perennials with attractive pea flowers. Very vigorous and long lived.
Cultural requirements: Any type of garden soil and an open situation.
Propagation: From seed outdoors or root division in spring.

G. officinalis 5 ft (1·5 m)   S. Europe and Asia
Handsome pinnate foliage and spikes of purple, lilac, or white pea flowers. Good named forms include 'Alba', white; 'Her Majesty', lilac-blue; and 'Lady Wilson', lilac.

GALEOBDOLON LUTEUM
– see *Lamium galeobdolon* 'Variegatum'

GALTONIA
(Liliaceae) (syn. *Hyacinthus candicans*)
Summer Hyacinth
Handsome bulbous plants, valuable in the borders in summer.
Cultural requirements: Any good garden soil, rich in humus and a sunny situation.
Propagation: By offsets.

G. candicans 4 ft (1·2 m)   S. Africa
Spikes of white bell flowers borne on tall stout stems. Leaves are strap-shaped and decorative when bulbs are not in flower.

GARDENER'S GARTERS
– see *Phalaris arundinacea*

GARDENIA
(Rubiaceae)
Evergreen flowering shrubs for the warm greenhouse, whose richly scented flowers have always

been traditionally used for buttonholes and corsages.

Cultural requirements: John Innes No. 2 or similar compost, with plenty of drainage material in the bottom of the pots. Minimum winter temperature 55 °F (12 °C). Water sparingly during the winter, freely for remainder of year.

Propagation: By cuttings under glass in heat in spring.

G. jasminoides up to 10 ft (3 m)
Cape Jasmine China and Japan
Both single and double forms have intensely fragrant white blossoms. They include *flore pleno*, double white and *radicans*, white. Summer.

GARRYA
(Garryaceae)

Evergreen shrubs, noteworthy for their conspicuous winter catkins and handsome dark green foliage.

Cultural requirements: Any type of garden soil, provided it is well-drained. Best grown as a wall shrub in colder districts. Garryas hate being moved and should be planted when young, ex pots or containers.

Propagation: From cuttings of partly ripened shoots under glass in late summer; from layers in autumn.

G. elliptica up to 12 ft (4 m) U.S.A.
The male forms bear jade-green catkins, up to 1 ft (30 cm) long, in great profusion. Those of the female plants are shorter and are followed by purplish fruits. 'James Roof' is a vigorous male form with extra long catkins. Winter.

GAULTHERIA
(Ericaceae)

A family of ericaceous, lime-hating shrubs with leathery evergreen foliage and small waxy bell flowers. Some are of vigorous spreading habit.

Cultural requirements: Lime-free peaty soil and for preference, a shady situation.

Propagation: From semi-hard stem cuttings in late summer; from seed sown outdoors in peaty soil in autumn; from rooted suckers and layering in spring.

G. forrestii 3 ft (1 m) China
Spreading evergreen shrub with white scented flowers followed by blue berries. Midsummer.

G. hookeri 3 ft (1 m) E. Himalayas
Dwarf spreading shrub with dense clusters of white flowers. Berries blue-black. Spring.

G. nummularioides 1 ft (30 cm) Himalayas
Small creeping shrub with white flowers and blue-black fruits. Summer.

G. procumbens 6 in. (15 cm)
Creeping Wintergreen N. America
A dwarf creeping shrub, thriving in dense shade right up to the base of large trees. Good carpeting plant with small polished green leaves, white urn-shaped flowers, and an abundance of scarlet berries in autumn. Midsummer.

G. shallon up to 6 ft (2 m) N. America
Vigorous species rapidly forming dense clumps and an ideal subject for covert planting. Broad leathery leaves, pink flowers, deep purple fruits. Early summer.

GAY FEATHER – see *Liatris spicata*

GAZANIA
(Compositae) Treasure Flower

South African half-hardy perennials useful for in-filling beds and borders in summer.

Cultural requirements: Light sandy soil and a sunny open situation.

Propagation: From seed sown in heat under glass in spring to provide plants to go out in early summer; from cuttings of side shoots in a frame in summer.

G. × hybrida 1 ft (30 cm) Garden origin
Bright orange flowers with a black centre. 'Longiscapa Treasure Chest' is an outstanding strain with a wide colour range. 'Sunshine' strain has larger flowers but blooms later. Colours include scarlet, orange, carmine-pink, and bronze. Summer to autumn.

GENISTA
(Leguminosae)

Evergreen members of the broom family, closely related to *Cytisus*, q.v. The dwarf kinds make good rock garden plants, the taller ones associate well with heathers. They also do well on hot dry banks.

Cultural requirements: An acid or neutral soil suits them best, but they are also fairly tolerant of lime. Their preference is for an open sunny situation.

Propagation: From seed outdoors in spring; by stem cuttings with a heel in late summer; by grafting or budding on laburnum stock.

G. aethnensis 10 ft (3 m) Mt Etna Broom Sicily
A shrub of loose habit and elegant appearance, with masses of golden flowers, very freely borne. Summer.

G. hispanica 3 ft (1 m)
Spanish Gorse S.W. Europe
Dense spiny hummocks up to 5 ft (1.5 m) in diameter, completely covered in yellow blossom at their flowering season. An ideal plant for hot dry banks.

G. lydia 2½ ft (75 cm)   Balkans
Another delightful dwarf with sickle-shaped
green shoots covered in golden flowers. A good
rock garden subject. Early summer.

G. tinctoria up to 2½ ft (75 cm) Dyer's Greenweed
                    Europe, including British Isles
Late and long flowering species with bright
yellow flower spikes. 'Plena' is a dwarf, semi-
prostrate form with double flowers; 'Royal Gold',
an excellent shrub for the smaller garden,
flowering throughout the summer. Summer to
early autumn

GENTIAN – see *Gentiana*

GENTIANA
(Gentianaceae)

Hardy perennials, the smaller of which are
excellent rock garden plants, the taller kinds
useful in the border.

Cultural requirements: A soil rich in humus,
with annual mulches of peat or leafmould.
Gentians should always be moist in summer and
dry in winter.

Propagation: Most species are best grown from
seed sown in a cold frame in spring. Some such
as *G. sino-ornata* and *G. acaulis* are easily increased
by division, but the majority dislike root
disturbance.

G. acaulis 4 in. (10 cm)   Europe
The most widely grown of the gentians, with
large trumpets of an intense blue. Spring.

G. asclepiadea 2 ft (60 cm)
Willow Gentian   Europe
A useful late flowering perennial for border or
poolside planting. Deep blue tubular flowers on
arching stems. There is also a white form, 'Alba'.
Late summer.

G. septemfida 6 in. (15 cm)   Asia Minor
Useful rock garden species with trailing stems
and deep blue trumpet flowers. The variety
lagodechiana is similar to the type but hugs the
ground more closely. Late summer.

G. sino ornata 4 in. (10 cm)   China
This highly attractive gentian species is sometimes difficult to establish but well worth the
effort. It needs a moist acid soil rich in peat or
leafmould. Forms mats of grassy foliage with
large vivid blue trumpet flowers. Autumn.

GENUS

The name given to a division of a family of plants.
E.g., *Rosa* is a genus of the family *Rosaceae*.

GERANIUM
(Geraniaceae) Cranesbill

A large group of hardy perennials not to be
confused with the tender zonal and regal pelargoniums, often referred to as geraniums.

Cultural requirements: Any ordinary well-
drained garden soil and a sunny situation. Many
make useful rock garden plants.

Propagation: From seed outdoors in spring;
root division in autumn or spring.

Geranium Florists' Strain

G. cinereum 6 in. (15 cm) Pyrenees
Grey-green deeply lobed foliage sets off the pale
pink, saucer-shaped flowers. 'Ballerina' has lilac
flowers, veined with red. Mid to late summer.

G. endressii 1½–2 ft (45–60 cm) Pyrenees
Long flowering species of semi-prostrate habit
which makes good ground cover. There are
several good cultivars such as 'A. T. Johnson',
silvery-pink; 'Rose Clair', white, veined purple;
and 'Wargrave', a deep rose-pink. Summer.

G. ibericum 2 ft (60 cm) Caucasus
Rich violet-blue flowers and rounded lobed
woolly leaves that colour brilliantly in autumn.
Summer.

G. pratense 2–3 ft (60 cm–1 m) Meadow Cranesbill
N. Europe, including British Isles
Garden forms of Britain's native meadow cranesbill include 'Album', white; 'Flore Pleno', double
blue; 'Roseum', rose-pink. Spring to early autumn.

G. sanguineum 6 in. (15 cm) Bloody Cranesbill
Europe, including British Isles
There are several attractive forms of this native
species, including 'Album', white and '*lancas-
triense*', clear pink. Summer.

GERBERA
(Compositae) Transvaal Daisy
Tender perennials for the cool greenhouse,
suitable for growing outdoors only in the most
favoured districts.
Cultural requirements: John Innes No. 2 or
similar potting compost. Winter and spring
temperature not less than 45 °F (7 °C), no artificial
heat in summer and autumn.
Propagation: From seed sown in gentle heat or
cuttings of side shoots in spring.

G. jamesonii 2 ft (60 cm)
Barberton Daisy S. Africa
Elegant daisy-like orange-scarlet flowers with
narrow petals. Several cultivars and hybrids are
known with a wide and brilliant colour range,
from pale primrose-yellow through shades of
rose, coral, and apricot to scarlet, in single and
double-flowered kinds. Midsummer to autumn.

GEUM
(Rosaceae)
Hardy perennials, with a long flowering period
from spring to early summer.
Cultural requirements: Any garden soil in
good heart and a sunny situation.
Propagation: From seed in a cold frame in
spring; by division of plants in autumn.

G. × borisii (*G. bulgaricum* × *G. reptans*)
1 ft (30 cm) Garden origin
Coarsely toothed dark green foliage and buttercup-
like flowers of a vivid scarlet. Early to late summer.

G. chiloense 2 ft (60 cm) Chile
This species contains most of the popular garden
forms, such as 'Lady Stratheden', a semi-double
yellow; 'Mrs Bradshaw', semi-double crimson;
and 'Prince of Orange', an orange-yellow double.
Summer.

GIANT FORGET-ME-NOT
– see *Brunnera macrophylla*

GIANT SAXIFRAGE – see *Bergenia*

GILIA
(Polemoniaceae)
Hardy and half-hardy annuals and biennials
normally treated as half-hardy annuals for summer
bedding.
Cultural requirements: Any ordinary garden
soil and a sunny situation.
Propagation: Hardy annuals: From seed sown
outdoors in spring where plants are to flower.
Half-hardy kinds: From seed under glass in heat
in late winter to produce plants to go out later.

G. tricolor 1 ft (30 cm) California
Hardy annuals with orange and purple flowers.
Summer.

G. rubra (syn. *G. coronopifolia*)
up to 4 ft (1·2 m) California
Biennial species, generally treated as a half-hardy
annual. Spires of tubular scarlet flowers. Summer.

GINKGO
(Ginkgoaceae) Maidenhair Tree
A distinctive monotypic genus of conifers, noteworthy as being the sole survivor of a group that
was distributed over many parts of the world in
prehistoric times. It is deciduous and its pyramidal
habit makes it a delightful lawn specimen for the
small garden.
Cultural requirements: Any well-drained fertile
soil and a sheltered south or west aspect.
Propagation: From seed in a cold frame, late
autumn to spring.

G. biloba 50 ft (15 m) China
A deciduous conifer with fan-shaped leaves
reminiscent of the foliage of an outsize maidenhair fern. The leaves turn a striking golden-yellow
in autumn. There are several interesting cultivars;
'Fastigiata' is a semi-erect form; 'Pendula' is
weeping in habit.

GLADIOLUS
(Iridaceae)
A popular family of half-hardy bulbous plants,
widely grown for garden decoration and cutting.
There are a large number of species, but it is the
more attractive hybrids that are commonly seen,

divided into large flowered, primulinus, and butterfly types. All have an extremely wide range of colours and are good for in-filling in the borders.

Cultural requirements: Deep, rich, well-manured soil and a sunny open situation. Gladioli normally need staking against summer gales. Corms are lifted in late autumn and stored in a frost-proof shed or garage.

Propagation: From seed under glass in early spring; from offset corms or cormlets surrounding the main corm, planted outdoors in spring.

The main species in cultivation are: *G. byzantinus*, with magenta flowers, that will quickly become naturalized in a warm border; *G. primulinus*, golden-yellow; *G. segetum*, rosy-purple; and *G. tristis*, red and yellow. The named cultivars of hybrids and hybrid strains are numerous and constantly changing. Any good bulb catalogue should offer a representative selection.

GLAUCOUS

Blue-green in colour as applied to the foliage of plants and often represented as a varietal name by *glauca*, e.g., *Hosta sieboldiana glauca*.

GLOBE ARTICHOKE – see *Cynara*

GLOBE FLOWER – see *Trollius*

GLOBE THISTLE – see *Echinops*

GLORIOSA
(Liliaceae) Glory Lily

Tuberous-rooted climbers for the warm greenhouse.

Cultural requirements: John Innes No. 2 or similar potting compost. Water freely during growing period and rest the tubers in a dry condition during winter. Minimum winter temperature 55 °F (12 °C).

Propagation: From seed or by offsets in early spring.

G. rothschildiana up to 8 ft (2·5 m)   Uganda
Exotic looking climbing plants with tubular flowers of a brilliant crimson and yellow like those of a turkscap lily. Summer.

G. superba up to 10 ft (3 m)   E. Africa
Similar in appearance to the former species but with orange and red trumpet flowers. Summer.

GLORY OF THE SNOW – see *Chionodoxa*

GLOXINIA – see *Sinningia*

GOAT'S BEARD – see *Aruncus*

GOAT'S RUE – see *Galega*

GODETIA
(Onagraceae)

Hardy annuals, formerly included in the genus *Oenothera*.

Cultural requirements: Any ordinary garden soil and a sunny situation.

Propagation: From seed outdoors in spring where plants are to flower.

G. grandiflora
up to 1½ ft (45 cm)   Western N. America
Most of the garden hybrids offered by seedsmen originate with this species. They include azalea-flowered mixtures, dwarf bedding kinds, and named forms such as 'Kelvedon Glory', salmon-orange; 'Blue Peter', lavender-blue; 'Sybil Sherwood', salmon-pink and many others. Summer.

GOMPHRENA
(Amaranthaceae) Globe Amaranth

Half-hardy annuals for the cool greenhouse.

Cultural requirements: John Innes No. 2 or similar potting compost.

Propagation: From seed under glass in heat in spring.

G. globosa 1½ ft (45 cm)   India
Oblong hairy leaves and small globular 'everlasting' flowers of pink, white, red, or yellow. There are several attractive cultivars, including dwarf forms 'Nana' and 'Buddy'. Summer.

Godetia 'Bush of Beauty' Dwarf Finest Mixed

GOOSEBERRY – see Fruit Garden

GORSE – see *Ulex*

GRAPE HYACINTH – see *Muscari*

GRASS – see Lawns

GREENHOUSES

After the acquisition of the necessary garden tools and equipment, one of the most pleasurable and profitable investments is a greenhouse. A greenhouse not only saves its owner money by enabling him to raise his own bedding plants cheaply, but also provides interest throughout those months of the year when outside garden attractions are at a minimum.

The choice of a suitable model is important. Before buying one, it is essential to decide the purposes for which it is to be used. There are different types of greenhouses to suit a wide variety of garden purposes and it is not always realized that even a completely unheated greenhouse will grow many interesting plants that would not stand outdoor conditions in winter.

Some of the choicest alpine plants, for example, have all the charm of exotics when raised under these conditions. And in summer, an unheated house can be used for growing tomatoes and other similar crops.

To keep a greenhouse frost-free and, by so doing, considerably extending its scope, some form of heating will be required. In a small greenhouse, a paraffin heater will be sufficient for this purpose. Larger ones will need something more elaborate. For these the simplest and most trouble-free is a form of electric heating controlled by a thermostat. It must be borne in mind, however, that for every extra 10 °F (5 °C) required, the cost of electricity will be practically doubled.

The so-called 'cold' house, with sufficient heat to exclude frost, needs a minimum temperature of 35–40 °F (1–4 °C). It can be used for over-wintering geraniums, fuchsias, and other tender garden subjects, as well as for growing primulas and bringing on hardy spring flowering plants in pots for indoor decoration.

Next up the heating scale comes the cool house. This must have its temperature kept to a minimum of 45–50 °F (7–10 °C). In this type of house, a much wider range of tender plants can be grown.

Among those that will flourish in cool house conditions are such attractive plants as begonias, cyclamens, the hardier orchids and that exotic looking climber, bougainvillea, which brings a breath of the sunny south to colder climates.

To grow successfully sub-tropical plants such as poinsettias and anthuriums, minimum temperatures of 55–60 °F (12–15 °C) plus a good deal of expert knowledge are needed while a stove house for tropical plants costs a small fortune to heat.

As far as different types of greenhouse are concerned, there is a choice between wood, metal, and even concrete for the basic materials of construction. Cedarwood houses need no painting and their colouring blends harmoniously into the garden background. The same goes for those constructed of oak. Softwood, white painted, looks attractive and business-like, but needs a lot of maintenance.

Aluminium greenhouses are completely trouble-free and will last for years without attention, but can look somewhat out of place in some gardens.

Most types of greenhouse are obtainable in the glass-to-ground or partly walled variety. The former admit a great deal more light and are ideal for tomatoes or for early salad or vegetable crops, grown in beds. But what is gained in light is lost in heat and a house on a partly boarded or brick base is more suitable for raising plants from seed and for growing pot plants on the staging.

It is possible, however, to have the best of both worlds. Many greenhouse firms offer models that are half boarded on one side with glass-to-ground on the other. There are even dual purpose models that double up as potting-shed and greenhouse.

Most greenhouse owners will quickly find an urge to extend their sphere of interest. There is a wide choice of accessories for this purpose, among them electrically heated soil warming cables and propagating frames, with mist propagation for the easier rooting of difficult cuttings and fully automated watering and ventilation systems.

GREVILLEA
(Protaceae)
Evergreen shrubs and trees for the cool greenhouse, some of which are hardy outdoors in mild districts.
Cultural requirements: Under glass: John Innes No. 2 or similar compost.
Outdoors: Peaty soil and a sheltered south or west wall.
Propagation: From seed under glass in heat in spring; by cuttings under glass in spring or early summer.

G. alpina 3 ft (1 m)   S. Australia
A low growing shrub of compact habit with needle-like foliage and red and cream flowers. Summer.

G. rosmarinifolia 6 ft (2 m)   Australia
A species with narrow linear foliage and vivid crimson flowers in clusters. Summer.

G. robusta 3 ft (1 m) Australia
A handsome foliage plant with ferny foliage, useful as a house plant and for summer bedding schemes.

G. sulphurea 10 ft (3 m) Australia
A shrub of medium size with needle-like leaves and terminal clusters of yellow flowers. Summer.

GRISELINIA
(Cornaceae)

Fast growing evergreen shrubs, very good in mild seaside districts.
Cultural requirements: Any fertile garden soil. Not suitable for cold inland areas. Spring planting.
Propagation: From layers in late summer.

G. littoralis up to 20 ft (6 m) New Zealand
Large evergreen shrub, of tree-like proportions in milder districts, with handsome leathery pale green foliage. 'Variegata' is a form whose leaves are strikingly variegated with white. Spring.

G. lucida 10 ft (3 m) New Zealand
Tender species whose larger leaves have a highly polished surface, shining in the sunlight. Spring.

GROMWELL – see *Lithospermum*

GROUND COVER PLANTS

In recent years, increasing use has been made of ground cover plants. This is largely due to the difficulty in obtaining help in the garden and the many conflicting demands on the leisure time of the average week-end gardener, so that his object is to cut down routine maintenance tasks to a minimum.

Ground cover plants are drawn mainly from the ranks of hardy evergreen perennials and prostrate mat-forming shrubs. By inhibiting weed growth they cut down the maintenance work of hoeing and weeding. At the same time, they serve a more decorative purpose by filling in bare patches with a continuous carpet of attractive foliage and/or flowers.

Before planting, it is important to ensure that the area to be covered is as free of weeds as possible. The cover-and-smother plants are not miracle workers and until they mature and grow together, weeding between them will be necessary. After the second or third season, however, the more vigorous kinds will suppress practically all weeds while the less rampant will keep all but the most invasive types down to a level that is easily coped with by occasional hand weeding.

The subjects listed below are described in greater detail in the appropriate alphabetical notings.

Vigorous ground cover
to suppress the majority of weeds
Ajuga reptans (Bugle);
Convallaria majalis (Lily-of-the-Valley);
Cornus canadensis (Creeping Dogwood);
Gunnera manicata (Giant Rhubarb);
Hedera helix and cultivars (Common Ivy);
Hypericum calycinum (St John's Wort);
Lamiastrum galeobdolon 'Variegatum' (Variegated Deadnettle);
Luzula sylvatica (Wood Rush);
Pachysandra terminalis (Japanese Spurge);
Vinca major (Periwinkle).

Less rampant cover plants
Alchemilla mollis (Lady's Mantle);
Bergenia species and cultivars (Giant Saxifrage);
Calluna species and cultivars (Heather);
Epimedium species and hybrids (Barrenwort);
Erica species and cultivars (Heather);
Euphorbia robbiae (Spurge);
Hosta species and cultivars (Plantain Lily);
Lamium maculatum;
Pulmonaria (Lungwort);
Stachys lanata (Lamb's Ears);
Tiarella cordifolia (Foam Flower).

Many other perennials and shrubs of prostrate habit serve a useful purpose as ground cover and this characteristic is referred to under their descriptions.

GUNNERA
(Gunneraceae) Giant Rhubarb

Hardy perennials noteworthy for the striking effect of their bold and massive foliage.
Cultural requirements: Rich, boggy soil at pool or stream side. Cover with bracken or dead foliage to protect crowns in winter.
Propagation: From seed in heat under glass or by division in spring.

G. chilensis up to 10 ft (3 m) Chile Rhubarb Chile
Large hairy rhubarb-like leaves up to 6 ft (2 m) across.

G. manicata up to 10 ft (3 m) Brazil
An even more striking plant of tropical appearance with prickly stems and leaves, the latter up to 10 ft (3 m) across. Good ground cover.

GYNURA
(Compositae)

Perennials for the warm greenhouse, grown for their decorative foliage.
Cultural requirements: John Innes No. 2 or similar potting compost. Water freely in spring and summer, sparingly for rest of year. Minimum winter temperature 55 °F (12 °C).
Propagation: By cuttings under glass in heat in summer.

G. aurantiaca 2 ft (60 cm)   E. Indies
Orange flowers and purplish stems and leaves. Summer.

G. sarmentosa 1½ ft (45 cm)   India
Twining species with small orange flowers and bluish-purple toothed leaves. Summer.

GYPSOPHILA
(Caryophyllaceae) Chalk Plant
Hardy annuals and perennials whose flowers are useful for cutting.

Cultural requirements: Any ordinary garden soil, with a preference for chalk.

Propagation: Annual species: From seed sown in autumn for following season, or from spring to early summer to provide a succession of flowers.
Perennial species: From basal stem cuttings or by division in spring.

G. elegans 1½ ft (45 cm)   Caucasus
Attractive hardy annual species with white or pink flowers that cut and associate well with roses or sweet peas. The cultivar 'Covent Garden' is particularly fine; 'Rosea' is an attractive pink form. Late spring to early autumn.

G. paniculata 3 ft (1 m) Baby's Breath   Europe
Clouds of tiny flowers on tall wiry stems that are excellent for cutting. 'Bristol Fairy' is the best double white; 'Rosy Veil' is a lovely pale pink cultivar. Perennial. Summer.

Gypsophila elegans 'Misty Morn'

G. repens 6 in. (15 cm)   Alps
A prostrate carpeting perennial with short, narrow greyish foliage and a profusion of white or pale pink flowers. A good plant for the rock garden. Summer.

HAEMANTHUS
(Amaryllidaceae) Blood Lily
Bulbous plants for the warm greenhouse with umbels of scarlet or white flowers like those of an agapanthus.

Cultural requirements: John Innes No. 2 or similar compost and a sunny position in the greenhouse. Water sparingly while growth is active, withhold water when bulbs are dormant.

Propagation: By offset bulbs.

H. coccineus 1 ft (30 cm)   S. Africa
Vivid scarlet flowers and bracts on short mottled stems, appearing in advance of the wide, flat leaves. Late summer.

H. katherinae 1 ft (30 cm)   S. Africa
Globular scarlet flower clusters on 1 ft (30 cm)

stems. Requires less heat than the former species. Spring.

HALESIA
(Styraceae) Snowdrop Tree
A small group of shrubs or small trees of North American origin with snowdrop-like flowers on their bare branches in spring. The flowers are followed by unusual winged fruits.

Cultural requirements: Light, moist but well-drained soil, free from lime. A sheltered sunny or partly shaded situation.

Propagation: From seed or root cuttings in spring; by layers in autumn.

H. carolina (syn. *H. tetraptera*)
up to 30 ft (9 m)   S.E. U.S.A.
A large shrub or small tree of spreading habit. It

Hamamelis mollis (Witch Hazel)

bears white pendent flowers in clusters. The winged fruits that follow are narrowly pear-shaped. Spring.

H. monticola up to 50 ft (15 m)   S.E. U.S.A.
Similar to the former species but more vigorous and tree-like in habit. The flowers and fruits are larger than those of *H. carolina*. The cultivar 'Rosea' has pink flowers. Spring.

HALIMIUM
(Cistaceae)
Compact evergreen shrubs, similar to the helianthemums and formerly included in that genus.
Cultural requirements: Light sandy soil and a sunny situation. They are not completely hardy in colder districts.
Propagation: From seed under glass in heat in spring; by semi-hard stem cuttings with a heel, in a cold frame in late summer.

H. lasianthum 3 ft (1 m)   Portugal
Low and spreading shrubs with silver-grey foliage and bright yellow flowers blotched with maroon at their centres. The cultivar 'Concolor' has petals unmarked with blotches. Summer.

H. libanotis 2 ft (60 cm)   S.W. Europe
Yellow flowers and very narrow grey foliage. Summer.

H. ocymoides 3 ft (1 m)   Portugal
Compact shrubs with grey leaves and yellow flowers, marked with maroon at the base of their petals. Early summer.

HAMAMELIS
(Hamamelidaceae) Witch Hazel
A genus of deciduous winter flowering shrubs or small trees. The hazel-like leaves are responsible for their popular name.
Cultural requirements: Moist well-drained soil, preferably lime-free. Open or partly shaded situation.
Propagation: By layering in autumn.

H. japonica up to 20 ft (6 m)
Japanese Witch Hazel   Japan
Broad hazel-like foliage that turns yellow in autumn. Yellow flowers with twisted strap-like petals and red calyx. Winter.

H. mollis 15 ft (4·5 m)
Chinese Witch Hazel   China
The most widely grown species with dense clusters of spidery yellow fragrant flowers and large softly hairy hazel-like leaves. There are several good cultivars, including 'Brevipetala', whose shorter-petalled flowers are orange in colour; 'Goldcrest', with golden-yellow flowers

suffused with red at their base; and 'Pallida', with sulphur-yellow blooms. Winter.

HANDKERCHIEF TREE – see *Davidia*

HARDENING OFF

This is the process of acclimatizing seedling plants, raised under glass in heat, to the temperatures in the open garden before they are planted out. This is achieved by transfer to a cold frame or suitable situation out-of-doors and increasing exposure to outside temperatures until the plants are sufficiently hardened to plant out.

HARDY PERENNIAL

A hardy perennial is a plant whose leaves and stems die off at the end of their growing season and are renewed from the base the following season. There are exceptions, such as bergenias and acanthus, both of which are evergreen and the various shrubby perennials, half-way between shrubs and perennials, which do not die completely down to ground level in winter.

HART'S TONGUE FERN – see *Phyllitis*

HAWKBIT – see *Crepis*

HAWTHORN – see *Crataegus*

HAZEL – see *Corylus*

HEATH, HEATHER
see *Calluna*, *Daboecia*, *Erica*

HEBE
(Scrophulariaceae)

A large genus of hardy and partly tender evergreen flowering shrubs, formerly classed under *Veronica*, ideal for seaside and industrial districts. They stand up well to maritime exposure.
Cultural requirements: Any ordinary well-drained garden soil and a sunny situation. In colder districts a position sheltered from north and east winds is essential.
Propagation: From cuttings in a cold frame in summer or autumn.

H. albicans 2 ft (60 cm)   New Zealand
Dense rounded shrub with spikes of pearly-white flowers and greyish foliage. Hardy. Summer.

H. anomala 3 ft (1 m)   New Zealand
A small-leafed compact and bushy shrub with white or pale pink flowers. Hardy. Summer.

H. armstrongii 3 ft (1 m)   New Zealand
An interesting species with olive-green cypress-like scaly leaves and white flowers. Hardy. Late summer.

H. brachysiphon 5 ft (1·5 m)   New Zealand
A popular species with a profusion of lilac-mauve flower spikes. There is an attractive white form, 'White Gem'. Hardy. Summer.

H. hulkeana 5 ft (1·5 m)   New Zealand
One of the loveliest of the hebes whose somewhat tender constitution makes it suitable only for a warm sheltered situation, preferably on a south or west wall. The pale lilac-blue flowers are borne in long panicles.

H. pinguifolia 1 ft (30 cm)   New Zealand
A delightful dwarf shrub with small pearly-grey rounded foliage and small glistening white flowers. Excellent for the rock garden. 'Pagei' is a compact prostrate form with glaucous foliage. Early summer.

H. speciosa up to 5 ft (1·5 m)   New Zealand
This is the species from which most of the larger flowered and more brightly coloured hybrids and cultivars have originated. The majority of these are tender and suited only to gardens in milder maritime districts. Good named kinds include 'Alicia Amherst', deep purple-blue; 'Midsummer Beauty', lavender-purple; 'La Séduisante', crimson; 'Mrs Winder', blue with purple foliage, moderately hardy.

HEDERA
(Araliaceae) Ivy

This group of evergreen climbing shrubs is of the greatest value in our gardens, thriving as they do in any type of soil and conditions. Ivies are self-clinging, attaching themselves to their hosts by aerial roots. At ground level they make excellent cover plants.
Cultural requirements: Any type of garden soil and any situation, even under shade of large trees.
Propagation: From cuttings or offshoots outdoors in early winter.

H. canariensis   Canary Islands
A vigorous species with leaves up to 8 in. (20 cm) across. Bright green in summer, bronze-tinged in winter. 'Variegata' (syn. 'Gloire de Marengo') is a handsome form with leaves edged with silvery-white.

H. colchica Persian Ivy   Caucasus
A vigorous, fast growing species with leaves 10 in. (25 cm) or more in length. The variegated forms, such as 'Dentata Variegata' with bright green leaves margined with creamy-yellow and 'Paddy's Pride', in which the former variegation is reversed, are particularly showy.

H. helix Common Ivy   Europe and Asia Minor
This species contains some of the most valuable and easily grown climbers obtainable, including numerous attractive cultivars, many of which

make excellent house plants. There is a lovely golden form 'Buttercup', known also as 'Russell's Gold' and various gold and silver-variegated forms of which 'Goldheart' and 'Glacier' are among the most striking. 'Tricolor' is an especially fine small-leaved cultivar whose leaves, as the name implies, are a medley of grey-green, white, and carmine-pink.

HEDGES

Hedges fulfil two important functions in the garden – the provision of shelter and privacy. They also form a framework for the overall garden picture and a background for other plantings.

For providing both shelter and privacy, no better subjects could be found than the many types of conifer suitable for hedging. Cypresses, yews, and thuya all make dense hedges to please the eye and act as a decorative backcloth for other garden features.

Many evergreen shrubs, too, are useful for hedging purposes. Among these are laurel, holly, and evergreen species of berberis and cotoneaster.

One of the best forms of cypress for hedging, rapidly surpassing all others on account of its exceptionally rapid rate of growth is *Cupressocyparis × leylandii*, a bigeneric hybrid between *Cupressus macrocarpa* and *Chamaecyparis nootkatensis*. Others that make good hedges are Lawson's cypress, *Chamaecyparis lawsoniana*, particularly the form known as 'Green Hedger'.

The following is a short list of shrubs and conifers suitable for hedging purposes:

Formal Hedges	Flowering and Berrying Hedges
Beech	Chaenomeles
Berberis stenophylla	*Cornus mas*
Buxus sempervirens (Box)	Forsythia
Cotoneaster simonsii	Lilac
Cypress	Philadelphus
Holly	Ribes
Hornbeam	Roses (Various)
Laurel	
Lonicera nitida	Seaside Hedges
Privet	Escallonias
Quickthorn	Euonymus
Thuya plicata	Hebe
Yew	Hydrangea
	Olearia
	Senecio

HEELING-IN

Is the term used for the process of protecting the roots of trees and shrubs while waiting for favourable planting conditions. A shallow trench is taken out, into which the roots of the plants are inserted and covered with soil.

HELENIUM
(Compositae)

Popular hardy perennials whose daisy flowers are decorative in the border and useful for cutting.

Cultural requirements: Any good garden soil, rich in humus, and a sunny situation.

Propagation: From seed outdoors in spring; by division in autumn or spring.

H. autumnale 2½ ft (75 cm)   Canada and U.S.A. It is from this attractive species, with golden-yellow flowers, that many of the finest garden hybrids are derived. These include 'Bruno', mahogany-red; 'Butterpat', rich yellow; 'July Sun', yellow with a brown disc; 'Moerheim Beauty', crimson with a brown centre; and 'Wyndley', bronzy-yellow. Summer to autumn (according to variety).

HELIANTHEMUM
(Cistaceae) Rock Rose or Sun Rose

Dwarf evergreen shrubs of great beauty flowering freely throughout the summer.

Cultural requirements: Light sandy soil and a sunny situation. Suitable for the rock garden.

Propagation: From seed outdoors in spring; from stem cuttings in a cold frame in late summer; by division in spring or autumn.

H. nummularium (syn. *H. chamaecistus*) 6–9 in. (15–22 cm)
                    N. Europe, including British Isles
Dwarf spreading sub-shrubs, forming dense mats of foliage that makes useful ground cover. The type plant has yellow flowers and there are numerous single and double varieties in a wide range of colourings. The following are all worth while: 'Amy Baring', buttercup-yellow; 'Ben Afflick', orange-yellow; 'Ben Nevis', yellow, with a bronzy centre; 'The Bride', creamy-white; and 'Wisley Pink', clear pink. Summer.

HELIANTHUS
(Compositae) Sunflower

Hardy annuals and perennials, vigorous and easy to grow. Useful plants for the herbaceous, mixed or annual border.

Cultural requirements: Any fertile well-drained soil and a sunny open situation.

Propagation: Annual species: From seed outdoors in spring where plants are to flower.

Perennial species: From seed outdoors in early summer; by division of roots in spring or autumn.

H. annuus up to 10 ft (3 m)
Common Sunflower   N. America
This annual species has large single yellow flowers up to 1 ft (30 cm) and more across, with a brown central disc. There are various hybrid forms both

Helianthus Tall Single (Sunflower)

Support Sunflowers by tying them to canes or strong sticks

Helichrysum Mixed (Strawflower)

single and double, ranging from 3 to 8 ft (1 to 2·4 m) with flowers of chestnut-brown, shades of yellow and creamy-white. Summer to autumn.

H. decapetalus 5 ft (1·5 m)　　　　　　Canada
Perennial species with golden-yellow flowers. There are both single and double forms of which 'Maximus' and 'Loddon Gold' are good examples. Late summer to autumn.

H. laetiflorus 6 ft (2 m)　　　　N. America
A vigorous perennial species with large orange-yellow flowers. Late summer to autumn.

HELICHRYSUM
(Compositae) Everlasting Flower
A varied genus of half-hardy annuals, hardy perennials, and evergreen shrubs, mostly with silver or grey foliage.
Cultural requirements: Any good garden soil and a sunny sheltered situation.
Propagation: Annual species: From seed in gentle heat in spring for planting out in early summer.
　　Perennial and shrubby species: By cuttings under glass in spring and late summer respectively.

H. angustifolium 1½ ft (45 cm)
Curry Plant　　　　　　　　　　S. Europe
Dwarf grey-leaved shrub with narrow leaves with the characteristic aroma of curry when crushed. Small yellow flowers in terminal clusters. Summer.

H. bracteatum 1½–2½ ft (45–75 cm)
Strawflower　　　　　　　　　　Australia
An annual species, widely grown for the colourful everlasting flowers which dry well for winter arrangements. The flower heads should be cut and dried before they are fully open. Summer.

HELICTOTRICHON
(Gramineae) Oat Grass
Hardy perennial grasses, of which the species, *H. sempervirens*, is used for decorative purposes.
Cultural requirements: Any ordinary garden soil.
Propagation: By division in spring.

H. sempervirens (syn. *Avena sempervirens*, *Avena candida*) up to 4 ft (1·2 m)　Mediterranean
Dense clumps of elegant blue-grey leaves and oat-like flower heads that dry well for winter arrangements. Late summer.

HELIOPSIS
(Compositae)
Hardy perennials very similar to sunflowers.
Cultural requirements: Any ordinary garden soil and a sunny situation.
Propagation: By division of plants in spring or autumn.

Helianthus 'Loddon Gold' (Sunflower)

H. scabra up to 5 ft (1·5 m)   U.S.A.
This species contains the most widely grown
garden cultivars all with yellow single, or double
flowers, including 'Golden Plume' and 'Incom-
parabilis', both with double yellow zinnia-like
blooms and 'Orange King', a deep yellow
semi-double. Late summer to autumn.

HELIOTROPE – see *Heliotropium*

HELIOTROPIUM
(Boraginaceae)
Half-hardy perennials, normally treated as half-
hardy annuals, whose flowers have an exceptionally rich perfume. They make excellent summer
bedding plants or pot plants for the cool
greenhouse.
Cultural requirements: John Innes No. 2 or
similar compost for potting; any good garden
soil and a sunny situation when planted outdoors.
Propagation: From seed under glass in heat in
spring; by cuttings in a frame in spring or early
autumn.

H. peruvianum 1½–3 ft (45 cm–1 m)
Cherry Pie   Peru
Sweetly scented half-hardy perennials with clusters
of lilac flowers. There are various hybrids and
cultivars, including 'Royal Marine' with flowers
ranging in colour from pale lavender to deep
violet. In the greenhouse, plants can be trained
as standards. Summer.

HELIPTERUM
(Compositae) (syn. Acroclinium)
Hardy annuals with showy everlasting flowers
that dry well for winter arrangements.

Cultural requirements: Light well-drained soil and a sunny situation.
Propagation: From seed under glass in spring or outdoors later where plants are to flower.

H. humboldtianum 1 ft (30 cm)   Australia
Plants of dwarf branched habit with bright yellow flowers. Parent of the seedsmens' hybrid strains. Summer.

H. manglesii 1½ ft (45 cm)   Australia
Pendent heads of white or rosy-pink flowers. Sometimes found listed as *Rhodanthe manglesii.* Summer.

H. roseum (syn. *Acroclinium roseum*)
2 ft (60 cm)   Australia
A showy everlasting with semi-double rosy-pink blooms. Summer.

HELLEBORE – see *Helleborus*

HELLEBORUS
(Ranunculaceae)
Hardy perennials, some of which are evergreen, flowering in winter or early spring.
Cultural requirements: Any good garden soil and preferably, a shady situation. An annual autumn dressing of compost and bonemeal. Hellebores should not be disturbed.
Propagation: From seed sown as soon as ripe in a cold frame. Some species, such as *H. orientalis,* can be divided successfully after flowering.

H. foetidus 2 ft (60 cm)
Stinking Hellebore   British Isles
Deeply divided dark evergreen foliage sets off to perfection the nodding apple-green bowl-shaped flowers, edged with purple. Late winter.

H. lividus corsicus (syn. *H. argutifolius, H. corsicus*)
2 ft (60 cm)   Corsica
Handsome, glossy toothed evergreen foliage and huge clusters of pale green, cup-shaped pendent blooms which last over an exceptionally long period. Winter to early summer.

H. niger 1 ft (30 cm) Christmas Rose   Europe
An attractive winter flowering plant, with pure white flowers and polished leathery foliage. 'Altifolius' and 'Potter's Wheel' are both improvements on the type; the former has petals tinted with pinkish-purple on their reverse. Winter.

H. orientalis 1½ ft (45 cm)   Greece
The handsome foliage of this species and its numerous hybrid strains makes good ground cover. The bowl-shaped flowers are held well above the leaves on stout stems. They vary in colour from white through pink and crimson, to slaty-purple. Winter to early spring.

H. viridis
1½ ft (45 cm)   Europe, including British Isles
This species has jade-green nodding cup-shaped flowers on tall stems. Winter.

HELXINE
(Urticaceae) Mind-your-own-Business
Dwarf carpeting plant with small bright green leaves. A rapid spreader that can become invasive especially in lawns.
Cultural requirements: Any ordinary soil. Sunny or shady situation.
Propagation: By division in spring.

H. solierolii 3 in. (8 cm)   Corsica
Green foliage and creeping stems, useful in the rock garden, in pots or hanging baskets, but must be kept severely in check.

HEMEROCALLIS
(Liliaceae) Day Lilies
Hardy perennials with arching strap-like foliage and a succession of short lived lily-like flowers. They have been the subject of intensive breeding in recent years and this has produced many striking new forms.
Cultural requirements: Any ordinary garden soil rich in humus. Moist soil conditions and an open or partly shaded situation.
Propagation: By root division in spring or autumn.

H. aurantiaca 3 ft (1 m)   Japan
A species with apricot-orange flowers. Summer.

H. dumortieri 2 ft (60 cm)   Japan
Orange-yellow flowers. Summer.

H. fulva 3 ft (1 m)   Europe and Japan
A larger species, with orange flowers. Midsummer.

Most garden forms today come from the ranks of the many splendid hybrids, available in an exceptionally wide range of colours. They can be found in the specialist catalogues.

HEMLOCK – see *Tsuga*

HEPATICA
(Ranunculaceae)
Formerly listed as 'Anemones', the hepaticas are hardy perennials with anemone-like flowers, and make superb plants for the wild garden.
Cultural requirements: Rich well-drained soil in shady situation, preferably open woodland.
Propagation: From seed outdoors in early summer; by root division in autumn.

H. nobilis 6 in. (15 cm)   Europe and N. America
The dark green, three-lobed leaves make a perfect setting for the blue flowers with yellow anthers. There is also a white form 'Alba'. Early to late spring.

H. transsilvanica 6 in. (15 cm)   E. Europe
A species with larger blue flowers than the above.
Spring.

HEPS

Sometimes referred to as hips, they are the fruits
of the various types of rose, varying in shape and
normally scarlet in colour. They provide a
decorative autumn bonus in many types of old
shrub rose.

HERACLEUM
(Umbelliferae) Giant Hogweed

Hardy perennials with coarsely toothed divided
foliage and outsize flattened heads of bloom.
Cultural requirements: Any ordinary garden
soil. They are very suitable for the wild garden.
Propagation: From seed outdoors in spring, by
root division in spring or autumn.

H. mantegazzianum 8–12 ft (2·5–4 m)
Cartwheel Flower   Caucasus
A bold and handsome plant for the wild garden
with huge rounded plate-like heads of white
flower. It should be noted that the plant can
cause a troublesome rash when handled by those
allergic to it.

HERB GARDEN

Herbs add savour and piquancy to many dishes
and are especially good picked fresh from the
garden. Everyone should find room for a few of
the better known kinds, such as mint, parsley,
chives, rosemary, and thyme. Where space
permits a herb garden can make an attractive
feature, with a carpet of chamomile and with
various other herbs planted in groups.

With the exception of mint, herbs need a position in full sun to develop their characteristic
flavours to the full. Mint needs a moist shady
situation and, since it is very invasive, plenty of
room to spread. It is advisable to dig up patches
of mint and replant, every second or third season.

Although many herbs are easy to raise from
seed, so few plants are normally needed that it is
often more convenient to buy roots. Perennial
and hardy annual herbs can be sown outdoors in
spring. Half-hardy kinds are sown under glass
for planting out in early summer.

Herbs for storing should be gathered on a dry
day, just before they come into flower. They are
tied in small bunches and hung up to dry in an
airy, well-ventilated room or shed. When completely dry, they can be stored in airtight jars.

*Some easy herbs to grow: Basil, Dill, Marjoram, Thyme,
Sage, and Savoury*

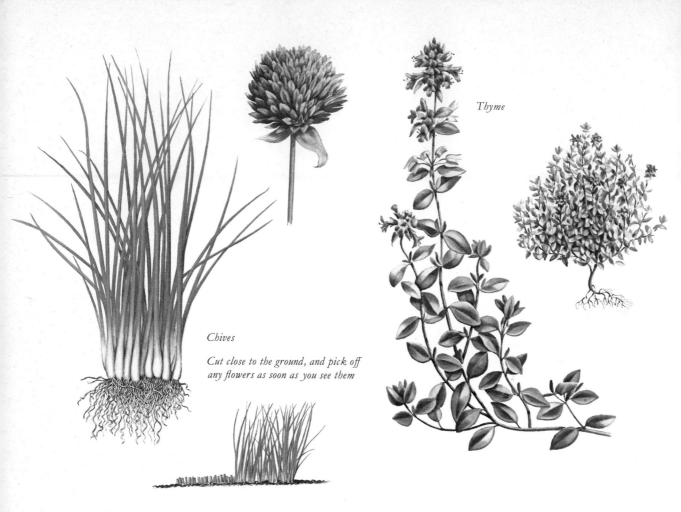

Thyme

Chives

*Cut close to the ground, and pick off
any flowers as soon as you see them*

Perennial Herbs

Balm: The refreshing lemon fragrance of balm
adds zest to iced drinks.

Bergamot: Aromatic foliage used to give the
distinctive flavour to 'Earl Grey' tea.

Chives: The mild onion flavour of the leaves
adds a pleasant flavour to salads or sandwich
spreads.

Fennel: The feathery foliage, with its aniseed
flavour, makes a useful garnish for fish.

Lavender: The dried flowers are used for making
sachets for the linen cupboard or for pot-pourri.

Lovage: The foliage has a celery flavour and is
used in soups, stews, or salads.

Marjoram: Half-hardy perennials with pink
flowers and aromatic foliage used in *bouquet-garni*.

Rosemary: The leaves are used for flavouring
soups, stews, and poultry, often as an ingredient
of a *bouquet-garni*.

Sage: Used for stuffing, especially for pork.

Tarragon: Used for salads and for flavouring
vinegar.

Thyme: Its many uses include the *bouquet-garni*
and as a seasoning for a variety of meat, egg,
poultry, and fish dishes.

Annual and Biennial Herbs

Angelica: A biennial herb that makes a handsome
border plant. The stems are candied and used
as a cake and confectionery decoration.

Basil: Sweet basil is a half-hardy annual with a
tangy flavour, interesting in salads or cooked
dishes.

Borage: Hardy annual herb with hairy leaves and
bright blue flowers, used for flavouring drinks.

Caraway: The seeds of this biennial are used for
flavouring bread and cakes.

Chervil: The leaves of this annual have a mildly
aniseed flavour. It is used in salads, egg dishes,
and fish sauces.

Dill: Annual herb whose seeds are used in pickles.
The leaves are good for flavouring salads.

Parsley: The attractively curled foliage of this
biennial herb has a host of culinary uses,
including the purely decorative, whole or
finely chopped; and as a flavouring for soups,
sauces, and other dishes.

HERBACEOUS BORDERS

The herbaceous border proper was a garden
feature introduced by Gertrude Jekyll and William

Robinson at the turn of the century in an effort to get away from the stiff formalism of Victorian bedding schemes. This was a revolution that was badly needed; there were far too many regimented schemes of brightly coloured bedding plants that reached their lowest point in gaudy ill-planned carpet bedding.

The influence of Miss Jekyll, Robinson, and others was towards a return to 'natural' gardening. There is, however, little that is really natural about a herbaceous border; just as much selection and planning has to go into its design as was necessary for the formal beds of the previous generation.

Today, owing to the general tendency to cut down on garden maintenance, the herbaceous border has taken on a new look. Nowadays, shrubs are incorporated in the planning and much is made of ground cover plants. The pleasing result is a mixed border in which herbaceous perennials predominate, but in which shrubs play their part in saving labour and providing greater continuity of interest.

As far as possible, the choice of hardy perennials should be made from among those needing a minimum of tying and staking. There are, in fact, many that need no such attention, including border plants both short and tall. Colour grouping is very much a matter of individual preference. Plants should go in in groups of three to a dozen, according to size and spread. This will avoid a spotty appearance.

Suitable material for planting, with approximate heights and flowering times will be found under the individual perennial species. By choosing carefully, it should be possible to have a really colourful display from early summer to mid-autumn, with shrubs providing interest during the remaining months of the year.

HESPERIS
(Cruciferae)

Hardy biennials and perennials with sweetly scented flowers. A great favourite in old cottage gardens.

Cultural requirements: Any type of soil, including chalk, and a sunny situation.

Propagation: Perennial species: From seed sown outdoors in spring; stem cuttings outdoors in summer; division of roots in spring or autumn.

Biennial species: From seed sown in spring where plants are to flower.

H. matronalis 1½–3 ft (45 cm–1 m) Sweet Rocket or Dame's Violet   S. Europe
Perennial species with purple-violet flowers. There are double and single forms, including 'Candidissima' a dwarf white and 'Purpurea' the best known purple variety. Early summer.

HEUCHERA
(Saxifragaceae) Alum Root

Hardy perennials, useful at the edge of the border or in the rock garden.

Cultural requirements: Light soil rich in humus and a sunny situation.

Propagation: From seed sown in a cold frame in spring; by division in spring.

H. sanguinea 1½ ft (45 cm)   Mexico
The elegant narrow clusters of deep pink bells are freely borne on wiry stems. Good named cultivars of hybrid origin include 'Red Spangles', crimson scarlet; 'Scintillation', reddish-purple; and 'Sparkler', carmine and scarlet.

There is an interesting bigeneric hybrid between a species of heuchera and the foam flower, *Tiarella wherryi*, known as *Heucherella*. This bears masses of rose-pink flowers over a very long period. 'Bridget Bloom', the best known form, has basal clusters of bronzy-green foliage from which elegant sprays of pale pink flowers emerge. If planted in part shade, the flowering period is greatly extended. Early summer to autumn.

HIBISCUS
(Malvaceae) Rose Mallow

Greenhouse and half-hardy annuals, evergreen, and deciduous tender and hardy shrubs.

Parsley Finest Double Curled

Cover with glass framelight or cloches for fresh parsley all winter

Cultural requirements: Greenhouse species: John Innes No. 2 or similar potting compost; temperature in winter must not fall below 45 °F (7 °C).

Annual and perennial species: Any ordinary garden soil and a sunny situation.

Shrubs: Light loamy soil, rich in humus; sunny sheltered situation.

Propagation: Greenhouse and hardy shrubs: From seed under glass in heat in spring; from cuttings in heat in spring or late summer.

Greenhouse annual species: From seed under glass in heat in spring.

Hardy annual species: From seed outdoors in spring where plants are to flower.

H. rosa-sinensis 5 ft (1·5 m)   China
Greenhouse shrub with mallow-type single or double blooms in pink, orange, yellow, or crimson. Summer.

H. syriacus 8 ft (2·5 m) Tree Hollyhock
A valuable race of late flowering deciduous shrubs with single or double mallow flowers. The named cultivars display a wide colour range and include 'Blue Bird', single blue; 'Hamabo', pale blush-pink and crimson; 'Duc de Brabant', double rosy-purple; 'William R. Smith', a pure white single; and 'Woodbridge', rose-pink and carmine. Late summer to autumn.

H. trionum 15 in. (38 cm)
Flower-of-an-Hour   N. America and Africa
Useful late flowering annual, with primrose-yellow flowers with a maroon centre. Late summer to autumn.

The new F_1 hybrid, 'Southern Belle' is a striking addition to the ranks of the hardy perennial hibiscus. The exotic flowers are almost 1 ft (30 cm) across and if seed is sown in heat in late winter, the plants should flower the same year. They can then be overwintered in a well-drained situation outdoors. Late summer to autumn.

HIPPEASTRUM

(Amaryllidaceae) Amaryllis
Greenhouse bulbous plants or house plants with handsome strap-like leaves and large satin-textured trumpet flowers in white, pink, or orange.

Cultural requirements: John Innes No. 2 or similar potting compost enriched with well-rotted manure or compost. Water freely during growing and flowering period, but withhold water when the bulbs are dormant.

Propagation: From seed in heat under glass in spring. Seedlings are potted into 2 in. (5 cm) pots and will flower in their third or fourth season. By offset bulbs – this is the only method of propagating hybrid forms.

H. aulicum 2 ft (60 cm)   Brazil
The large trumpet flowers, crimson and orange are 6 in. (15 cm) long. Winter.

H. pratense 2 ft (60 cm)   Chile
A spring flowering species with scarlet flowers. Spring.

H. vittatum 2 ft (60 cm)   Peru
Crimson and white flowers in spring. Spring.

These, together with other species have produced the many hybrids obtainable today in commerce. They include such lovely cultivars as 'Apple Blossom', white, flushed pale pink; 'Beautiful Lady' with enormous flowers, almost 1 ft (30 cm) in diameter of vivid salmon-orange; and 'United Nations', white striped with vermilion. Spring.

HIPPOPHAË

(Eleagnaceae)
A small genus of shrubs which make first class seaside plants.

Cultural requirements: Any ordinary garden soil, including light sand. Open or shady situation. Male and female flowers are borne on separate plants so that group planting is essential to obtain berries.

Propagation: From seed outdoors in early winter; from cuttings in spring or layers in autumn.

H. rhamnoides up to 20 ft (6 m)
Sea Buckthorn   Europe, including British Isles
This is the species most commonly cultivated. The leaves are narrow, silver-grey and willow-like; the berries, which remain on the plants for a very long period, are orange-scarlet.

HOHERIA

(Malvaceae)
Partially tender evergreen and deciduous shrubs with striking white flowers.

Cultural requirements: Deep, rich, loamy soil and a sunny sheltered situation such as a south or west wall.

Propagation: From cuttings under glass in summer.

H. glabrata (syn. *Plagianthus lyallii*)
25 ft (8 m)   New Zealand
Small upright branching shrub or small tree with clusters of white honey-scented blossom. Midsummer.

H. sexstylosa up to 20 ft (6 m)   New Zealand
This species, one of the hardiest, is evergreen, with narrow adult leaves and a profusion of white flowers.

HOLLY – see *Ilex*

HOLLYHOCK – see *Althaea rosea*

HOLM OAK – see *Quercus ilex*

HONESTY – see *Lunaria annua*

HONEYSUCKLE – see *Lonicera*

HOP – see *Humulus*

HORDEUM
(Gramineae)

Annual and perennial grasses, some of which are ornamental.
Cultural requirements: Any ordinary soil and an open situation.
Propagation: From seed sown outdoors in spring.

H. jubatum 2 ft (60 cm)
Squirrel's Tail   N. America
A hardy annual species, bearing silky, long-haired barley-like tassels that cut and dry well. Summer.

HORNBEAM – see *Carpinus*

HORSE CHESTNUT – see *Aesculus*

HOSTA
(Liliaceae) Plantain Lily

Hostas are hardy perennials, grown mainly for their boldly handsome plantain-like foliage although the spikes of lilac, violet, or white flowers offer a decorative bonus. They were formerly known as 'Funkias'.
Cultural requirements: Moist soil and partial shade.
Propagation: By division in spring or autumn.

H. albomarginata 1½ ft (45 cm)   Japan
Lanceolate pale green leaves with a narrow margin of cream; flowers mauve. Late summer.

H. crispula 1½ ft (45 cm)   Japan
Fluted leaves with a broad edging of cream-lavender flowers. Summer.

H. decorata 2 ft (60 cm)   Japan
A taller and larger replica of *H. albomarginata* with violet flowers. Often listed as 'Thomas Hogg'. Summer.

H. elata 4 ft (1·2 m)   Japan
Soft green leaves with fluted edges; flowers bluish-mauve. Summer.

H. fortunei up to 3 ft (1 m)   Japan
A popular species, with several attractive named cultivars including 'Albopicta', with broad foliage, butter-yellow, edged with green when it first unfurls, becoming a uniform green as it matures and 'Aurea', with yellow leaves. Flowers lilac-mauve. Mid to late summer.

H. plantaginea 2 ft (60 cm)   China and Japan
Large polished yellow-green foliage and large pure white scented flowers in bold spikes. Early autumn.

H. sieboldiana (syn. *H. glauca*) 2 ft (60 cm)   Japan
Huge grey-green leaves, heart-shaped and deeply etched with veins. Flowers white, barely tinged with lilac. Summer.

H. undulata 2½ ft (75 cm)   Japan
Large oval green leaves strikingly marbled with white. Flowers pale lilac. Late summer.

HOUND'S TONGUE – see *Cynoglossum*

HOUSELEEK – see *Sempervivum*

HOUSE PLANTS

It is a far cry from the aspidistras and ribbon ferns of our grandparents to the wide and varied choice of plants available today for culture indoors. This choice ranges from popular flowering shrubs such as azaleas, hydrangeas, etc., to others like cyclamen, primulas, cacti and other succulents together with the many subjects grown solely for the beauty of their foliage.

In the last named group are many that seem almost to thrive on neglect, such as 'Wandering Jew' (*Zebrina pendula*), 'Mother of Thousands' (*Saxifraga stolonifera sarmentosa*), and the 'Kangaroo Vine', *Rhoicissus rhomboidea*.

Other more exotic types of house plant need more careful handling and the newcomer to this fascinating branch of horticulture might be well advised to confine his choice to those tried and true favourites that will tolerate wide variations in light, heat, and atmospheric conditions.

Three factors vital to success with house plants are water, light, and air. Over-watering probably kills more indoor plants than anything else, particularly during the period when the plants are dormant or resting. Regular watering should be restricted to those times when growth is vigorous and should be sparing when it stops or slows down. This is usually, but not necessarily, during the winter months.

Where light is concerned, some plants thrive best on a sunny window-ledge, others are happiest in indirect light or partial shade. Plants with coloured or variegated foliage, however, usually need a full quota of light – but not necessarily direct sunlight – to develop this characteristic to the full.

Fresh air is good for house plants but not many will tolerate draughts. To many, fumes from gas or coal fires can be fatal. Two positions to be avoided are the close vicinity of radiators or a window-sill where curtains are closed at night, since this leads to a risk of excessively low or

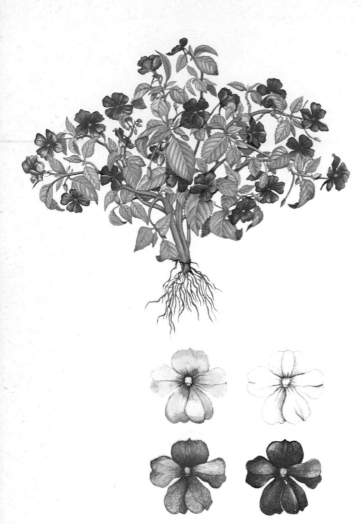

Impatiens Dwarf Mixed (Busy Lizzie)

extremes of temperatures. Always bring plants into the room at night.

Correct ways of feeding are important and the first step to this end is the provision of a suitable compost containing all the plants' nutritional requirements. For the majority of house plants, John Innes No. 2 potting compost is satisfactory and any variations from this have been noted under the individual subjects.

Plants should be re-potted as soon as they become potbound. Roots appearing through the drainage holes are normally an indication of this condition. Regular feeding should be carried out with a liquid fertilizer such as 'Baby Bio' or a soluble one such as 'Phostrogen', also obtainable in tabloid form as 'Phostrotabs'.

House plant specialists often help purchasers by providing cultural instructions on the plant labels and also by indicating, by colour coding or otherwise, the degree of difficulty of cultivation to be expected.

Twenty good **Foliage House Plants**

(For full description see under individual subjects)

Adiantum venustum	Maidenhair Fern
Asparagus sprengeri	Ornamental Asparagus Fern
Begonia masonorum	Iron Cross Begonia
Coleus	Multi-coloured foliage plants
Dracaena sanderiana	Striking foliage plant striped green and white
Fatshedera × lizei	Climbing foliage plant
Fatsia japonica	False Castor-Oil Plant
Ficus elastica	Indiarubber Plant
Hedera helix	Common Ivy with many attractive forms
Kalanchoë	Small succulent foliage plants
Maranta leuconeura	Pale green leaves, purple markings
Monstera deliciosa	Swiss Cheese Plant
Peperomia hederaefolia	Deeply veined blue-green leaves
Pilea cadieri	Aluminium Plant
Philodendron scandens	Climbing foliage plant
Rhoicissus rhomboidea	Kangaroo Vine
Sanseveria trifasciata	Mother-in-Law's Tongue
Saxifraga stolonifera sarmentosa	Mother of Thousands
Zebrina pendula	Wandering Jew
Zygocactus truncatus	Christmas Cactus

Twenty good **Flowering House Plants**

Achimenes	Hot Water Plant
Aphelandra tetragona	
Anthurium scherzerianum	Flamingo Flower
Beloperone guttata	Shrimp Plant
Billbergia nutans	
Bougainvillea	
Browallia	
Euphorbia pulcherrima	Poinsettia
Exacum affine	
Hippeastrum hybrids	
Hoya carnosa	Wax Plant
Impatiens sultani	Busy Lizzie
Passiflora coerulea	Passion Flower
Primula obconica	
Primula malacoides	Fairy Primula
Rhododendron indica	Azalea
Sinningia	Gloxinia
Stephanotis	Madagascar Jasmine
Streptocarpus	Cape Primrose
Thunbergia alata	Black-eyed Susan

HOYA

(Asclepiadaceae) Wax Flower
Evergreen greenhouse climbers with flowers of a waxy texture.
Cultural requirements: John Innes No. 2 or similar compost, or a position in well-drained soil in the greenhouse border. Water freely during growing period, very sparingly while plants are dormant.
Propagation: By stem cuttings under glass in heat in summer.

H. carnosa up to 12 ft (4 m)　　　　　　China
This is the most widely grown species. Flowers are pink or white and there is a form with variegated leaves. Summer.

HUMULUS

(Cannabidaceae) Hop
Annual and perennial climbing plants that cling by twining and are useful for pillars, pergolas, etc.
Cultural requirements: Any ordinary garden soil, rich in humus and a sunny or partly shaded situation. The perennial species need the protection of a sunny wall or fence.
Propagation: Annual species: From seed outdoors in spring where plants are to grow.
　Perennial species: From seed outdoors or by division, in spring.

H. japonicus (syn. *H. scandens*)
up to 10 ft (3 m)　　　　　　　　　Japan
This annual species provides rapid coverage and is useful for camouflaging unsightly garden objects. 'Variegatus' has leaves marked with silver and white.

H. lupulus up to 20 ft (6 m)　　　　　Europe
This is the commercial hop, used in the brewing of beer. The golden-leaved cultivar 'Aureus' makes a decorative climber for the garden.

HYACINTH　see *Hyacinthus*

HYACINTHUS

(Liliaceae)
Hardy bulbous plants, useful for spring bedding and for greenhouse or indoor culture in pots and other containers.
Cultural requirements: Pot culture: John Innes No. 2 or similar compost; bulb fibre for bowls lacking drainage. The bulbs are planted in early autumn, the containers then being plunged into ashes outdoors or placed in a dark cool cupboard for two to three months before being brought out to flower indoors.
　Outdoor culture: Any good garden soil.
Propagation: From seed in a cold frame; by offsets from mature bulbs.

H. amethystinus 1 ft (30 cm)
Spanish Hyacinth　　　　　　　　Pyrenees
Dainty pendent spikes of pale blue tubular flowers. There is also a white cultivar, *H. a.* 'Albus'. Spring.

H. azureus (syn. *H. ciliatus*)
6 in. (15 cm)　　　　　　　　　Asia Minor
Dense spikes of deep blue flowers, similar to those of a grape hyacinth. Spring.

H. orientalis up to 1 ft (30 cm)　Mediterranean
This is the species from which the popular forms of garden and florists' hyacinths have been derived. These are obtainable in great variety, some treated by pre-cooling for early forcing. They are all intensely fragrant and all can be grown in bowls in bulb fibre indoors. The colour range includes white, yellow, pink, and crimson as well as various shades of blue and purple. Spring.

HYBRID

A hybrid is a cross between any two distinct plants, usually between species or forms of species. Sometimes two different genera produce a cross and the result is known as a bigeneric hybrid, e.g., × *Osmarea burkwoodii*, a bigeneric cross between *Osmanthus delavayii* and *Phillyrea decora*. Hybrids between species and genera are designated by a multiplication sign, ×.

HYDRANGEA

(Hydrangeaceae)
Hardy deciduous flowering shrubs, of which there are a large number of species, varieties, and cultivars, including climbing species. They all do particularly well in seaside districts.
Cultural requirements: Any ordinary garden soil in good heart with a situation in part shade for preference.
Propagation: From cuttings under glass in spring or in a cold frame in late summer. By suckers from plants in late autumn or spring.

H. macrophylla up to 6 ft or more (2 m)
Hortensia　　　　　　　　　　　Japan
This species includes the so-called florists' hydrangeas as well as the lovely lace-caps. They produce large heads of sterile florets, which as well as being highly decorative in the garden over a very long period, are superb for winter arrangements when dried.
　The blue forms will be pink or reddish-pink in alkaline soils. When grown in tubs or similar containers, they can be 'blued' by applications of alum, or one of the proprietary blueing compounds. It is impracticable to do this in the open ground, unless the soil is only mildly alkaline.

Hortensia cultivars

*'Altona', rose-pink with large florets;
'Ayesha', distinctive cultivar with pale pink flowers resembling those of a lilac;
'Europa', deep pink with large florets;
*'Général Vicomtesse de Vibraye', deep rose;
'Madame Emile Mouillière', one of the best whites;
*'Maréchal Foch', rose-pink, free flowering;
'Preziosa', a compact form with deep pink, smaller heads of bloom.

Lace-cap cultivars

'Bluewave', a central ring of blue fertile flowers, surrounded by a large ring of ray florets, varying in colour from pink to blue, according to soil;
'Lanarth White', a compact form with large flat heads of blue or pink flowers;
'Whitewave', the white counterpart of 'Bluewave' with flat heads of white sterile florets surrounding a central ring of blue fertile flowers.

All the above are in flower from summer into autumn.

H. paniculata 6 ft (2 m)   China and Japan
A shrub of medium size and compact habit, with large creamy-white heads of flowers that remain attractive over an exceptionally long period. 'Grandiflora' has much larger flowers than those of the type. Summer to autumn.

H. petiolaris up to 30 ft (9 m)   Japan and Korea
Another vigorous climbing species with flat heads of ivory-white flowers, profusely borne. The gold of the autumn foliage is very attractive. Midsummer.

H. quercifolia 6 ft (2 m)   S.E. U.S.A.
An attractive species with white flowers and oak-like leaves that colour magnificently in autumn. Slightly tender. Summer.

*Blue well when treated.

H. serrata 4 ft (1·2 m)   Japan and Korea
A compact species with flattened heads of blue or white fertile flowers surrounded by pink, white, or blue-tinted ray florets. There are two outstanding cultivars, 'Bluebird' with blue flowers (reddish-purple on alkaline soils) and 'Grayswood', with white ray florets that gradually turn crimson. Summer to autumn.

HYPERICUM
(Guttiferae) St John's Wort

Evergreen and deciduous shrubs and sub-shrubs, mainly hardy, but a few slightly tender. Flowers are chalice-like and bright golden-yellow.
Cultural requirements: Any ordinary garden soil, provided it is well-drained. Sunny or partly shaded situation.
Propagation: From seed or cuttings in cold frame. *H. calycinum* by division or suckers.

H. calycinum 1½ ft (45 cm)
Rose of Sharon   S.E. Europe
Evergreen suckering shrub with golden-yellow flowers. Excellent ground cover on hot dry banks and dry shady situations. Summer.

H. elatum 5 ft (1·5 m)   Garden origin
An erect growing species with small yellow flowers followed by scarlet, egg-shaped fruits. The plant in garden cultivation under this name is now known to be a hybrid, *H. × inodorum* 'Elstead'. Summer.

H. patulum 4 ft (1·2 m)   China and Japan
Semi-evergreen shrub with golden saucer-shaped flowers with striking central boss of stamens. 'Hidcote' is most outstanding form. Late summer.

H. × Rowallane 6 ft (2 m)   Garden origin
The finest of all the hypericums, semi-evergreen and slightly tender. The cup-shaped flowers, a deep buttercup-yellow, measure up to 3 in. (8 cm) across. Late summer.

IBERIS
(Cruciferae) Candytuft

Hardy annuals and perennials, the latter being useful rock garden plants. The perennial species are evergreen.
Cultural requirements: Annual and perennial kinds: Any ordinary garden soil and a sunny situation.

Propagation: Annual kinds: From seed sown outdoors in spring for summer flowering; in late summer for flowering early the following season.
   Perennials: From seed in a cold frame in spring; by cuttings of half-ripened shoots in a cold frame from late summer to autumn.

I. saxatilis 6 in. (15 cm)   S. Europe
Small evergreen sub-shrubs, useful in a sunny

Iberis (Candytuft)

This is the species from which most of the popular garden varieties and cultivars are derived.

Cultivars

'Ferox', hedgehog holly, with leaf surfaces as well as edges covered with prickles. Male;

'Golden King', broad leaves with yellow margin. Female;

'Golden Queen', similar to 'Golden King', but as inappropriately named, since it is male;

'J. C. van Tol', dark green polished leaves, practically spineless. Good berrying form. Female;

'Silver Queen', green leaves with a broad margin of silvery-white. Male.

IMPATIENS
(Balsaminaceae)

Greenhouse and hardy annuals and perennials. Many are equally effective as pot plants or for outdoor summer bedding.

Cultural requirements: Any ordinary garden soil and a sunny or shady situation.

Propagation: From seed under glass in heat in early spring.

I. balsamina 2½ ft (75 cm)
Balsam   India and China
Excellent as bedding or pot plants. The camellia-flowered double strains are particularly fine. Annual. Summer.

I. sultanii up to 1½ ft (45 cm)
Busy Lizzie   Zanzibar
The development of F_1 hybrid forms has greatly improved the flowering capacity and colour range of these useful greenhouse, room, or bedding plants. Among those worth growing are 'Elfin Mixed', 'Harlequin', and 'Baby Varieties' the last named a delightful dwarf strain, ideal for bedding or pot work. Half-hardy perennials. Summer.

INCARVILLEA
(Bignoniaceae) Chinese Trumpet Flower

Hardy herbaceous perennials with exotic looking trumpet flowers.

Cultural requirements: Rich, light, well-drained soil and a sunny sheltered situation.

Propagation: From seed under glass in moderate heat in spring; by division in autumn or spring.

I. delavayi 2 ft (60 cm)   China
Rose-pink trumpet flowers, three to six to a stem. Early summer.

I. grandiflora 1½ ft (45 cm)   China
Large rose-red trumpet flowers, suffused with orange at their throats. Summer.

INCENSE CEDAR – see *Libocedrus decurrens*

pocket on the rock garden. Small dark green linear foliage and white flowers. Late spring to midsummer.

I. sempervirens 1 ft (30 cm)
Perennial Candytuft   S. Europe
Dark evergreen foliage and clusters of pure white flowers. Early summer.

I. umbellata 1 ft (30 cm)   S. Europe
Useful hardy annuals, flowering quickly from seed. The flowers of the type are lilac-purple, but there are named strains with flowers in pink, carmine, lavender, and white. Summer.

ILEX
(Aquifoliaceae) Holly

Evergreen shrubs or small bushy trees of great beauty. Hollies are unisexual so that female kinds will have to be planted for berries, with male forms to pollinate them. Some hybrids and cultivars have leaves attractively variegated with gold or silver. Hollies make excellent hedging plants.

Cultural requirements: Any ordinary garden soil and a sunny or shady situation.

Propagation: From stratified seed planted in autumn; from cuttings of partly ripened wood under glass; by budding or grafting on to common holly for the variegated kinds.

I. aquifolium up to 30 ft (9 m)   Asia, N. Africa and Europe, including British Isles

INDIAN BEAN – see *Catalpa bignonioides*

INDIAN SHOT – see *Canna*

INDIARUBBER PLANT – see *Ficus*

INDIGOFERA
(Leguminosae)

Handsome slightly tender shrubs with pinnate foliage and clusters of pea flowers over a very long period.
Cultural requirements: Friable soil, rich in humus, and a sunny sheltered position, on a south or west wall for preference.
Propagation: From seed or cuttings under glass.

I. decora 1½ ft (45 cm)   China and Japan
A dwarf species, with pink flowers, excellent for the rock garden. There is also a white form, *alba*. Late summer.

I. gerardiana up to 4 ft (1·2 m)   Himalayas
Bright purple-rose flowers and elegant foliage. Summer to autumn.

I. potaninii 5 ft (1·5 m)   China
A shrub of medium size, with racemes of pink pea flowers. Summer to autumn.

INFLORESCENCE

The flowering part of a plant. An inflorescence can take a number of different forms according to the arrangement of the flowers on their stalks. For these see the following: corymb, cyme, panicle, raceme, spike, and umbel.

Ipomoea 'Heavenly Blue' (Morning Glory)

INSECTICIDES – see Pest Control

INULA
(Compositae)

Hardy perennials with daisy-like flowers, useful in herbaceous border.
Cultural requirements: Any ordinary garden soil rich in humus, and a sunny situation.
Propagation: From seed outdoors in spring; by division in spring or autumn.

I. ensifolia 1½ ft (45 cm)   S. Europe
A compact species with bright yellow daisy flowers. 'Golden Beauty' is a good named form. Summer.

I. hookeri 2 ft (60 cm)   Himalayas
Lemon-yellow rayed flowers, 3 in. (8 cm) across. Finely toothed downy foliage. Summer.

I. orientalis (syn. *I. glandulosa*)
2½ ft (75 cm)   Caucasus
Large golden-yellow daisy flowers with several rows of fringed ray florets. Summer.

IONOPSIDIUM
(Cruciferae)

Hardy annual, useful as an edging or carpeting plant and in the rock garden.
Cultural requirements: Any ordinary garden soil.
Propagation: From seed sown outdoors in spring, where plants are to grow.

I. acaule 3 in. (8 cm) Violet Cress   Portugal
Dwarf carpeting plant with lilac-blue flowers. Summer.

IPOMOEA
(Convolvulaceae)

Half-hardy annual climbers for the cold greenhouse or a sunny sheltered wall outdoors. Large trumpet flowers like those of an exotic convolvulus.
Cultural requirements: Light rich soil and a cool greenhouse or a sunny sheltered situation outdoors.
Propagation: From seed under glass in heat in early spring. Chipping the seed coat assists germination.

I. tricolor (syn. *I. rubro-coerulea*) up to 10 ft (3 m)
Morning Glory   Mexico
Enormous trumpet flowers, sky-blue with a yellow throat. The variety 'Heavenly Blue' has azure-blue flowers, shading to white at their centres. Summer.

There are also various perennial species suitable only for the heated greenhouse, including *I. batatus*, the sweet potato, whose tubers are edible.

Iris germanica 'Sunset'

IRIS
(Iridaceae)

Hardy bulbous-rooted and rhizomatous perennials. The genus is a large one with species suitable for a wide variety of garden purposes, including border, waterside, and rock garden.

The various types are divided up as follows, with numerous sub-divisions for exhibition and other purposes.

Bearded Irises

These include the popular 'Flag Iris', *I. germanica*; *I. pallida*, and the dwarf *I. pumila* and *I. variegata*, together with all their hybrids.

Beardless Irises

I. crocea, *I. chrysographes*, *I. cristata*, *I. sibirica*, and *I. unguicularis* are some of the better known species belonging to this section.

Cushion Irises

I. susiana, the 'Mourning Iris', is the best known species in this section.

Japanese Irises

These are the moisture-loving species that flourish at the edges of streams or garden pools. The two species in garden cultivation are *I. kaempferi* and *I. laevigata*.

Bulbous Irises

The main garden species of this section are *I. danfordiae*, *I. histrioides*, *I. tingitana*, *I. reticulata*, *I. xiphioides*, and *I. xiphium*.

Detailed descriptions of better known species and varieties.

Bearded and beardless kinds

I. chrysographes 2½ ft (75 cm)　　China
Large purplish-blue flowers springing from tufts of grassy foliage. 'Purple Wings' is an attractive form with violet-blue flowers. *I. chrysographes* likes moist soil conditions. Midsummer.

I. cristata 3 in. (8 cm)　　U.S.A.
A dainty dwarf that needs a moist sandy soil. The fringed flowers are blue, spotted with orange. Early summer.

I. crocea (syn. *I. aurea*) 4 ft (1·2 m)　　Kashmir
A strong grower and a moisture lover, with golden-yellow flowers. Midsummer.

I. foetidissima 2 ft (60 cm) Gladwin Iris　Britain
A native iris with flowers of a pale lilac-blue. The seedpods split open to reveal brilliant scarlet seeds in autumn. Moist soil and a shady situation. 'Lutea' has brownish-yellow flowers and orange-yellow seeds; 'Variegata' is a cultivar whose leaves are longitudinally striped with creamy-white. Midsummer.

I. germanica up to 4 ft (1·2 m) Flag Iris S. Europe
These should be planted in a sunny well-drained situation with the fleshy rhizomes only half-covered with soil. There are many different cultivars, changing all the time with many new introductions annually and reference should be made to current nursery catalogues. Early summer.

I. kaempferi 3 ft (1 m)　　Japan
This lovely Japanese species has large, orchid-like flowers, two or three to each stem. Colour varies from white, rosy-purple to deep purple. Can be grown as a bog plant. Good named cultivars include 'Attraction', purple and grey; 'Juno', rosy-purple; 'Purple Splendour', double; and 'Swan', double white. Summer.

I. laevigata 2 ft (60 cm)　　China
The flowers of this moisture-loving species can attain 5 in. (13 cm) across and are purple-blue or white in colour. It will grow at the edge of a pool and does not object to its roots being in standing water. Summer.

I. sibirica 3–4 ft (1–1·2 m)　　C. Europe
Forms dense clumps of narrow foliage and likes moist conditions although it will also thrive in the open border. There are various named forms, including 'Alba', white; 'Emperor', violet-blue; 'Mrs Rowe', pearl-grey; 'Perry's Blue', sky-blue; and 'Thelma Perry', china-blue.

I. unguicularis (syn. *I. stylosa*)
1 ft (30 cm)　　Mediterranean
Winter flowering species that does best in poor soil and a sunny situation. The flowers are lavender-blue and appear in batches over a long period. Winter.

Bulbous Irises

I. histrioides 6 in. (15 cm)　　Asia Minor
This delightful winter flowering species stands up to the severest weather to produce its blue flowers before the leaves in the depths of winter. Winter.

I. reticulata 6 in. (15 cm)　　Caucasus
This is similar in appearance to *I. histrioides* but taller and flowers somewhat later with short leaves. There are various named cultivars and hybrids between the two species of which the pale blue 'Cantab' is the best known. Spring.

I. xiphioides 2 ft (60 cm) English Iris　Pyrenees
This species, with its hybrids, are popular and easy to grow bulbous plants for an early summer display. They are obtainable in various shades of blue and purple, and there are also some good whites. Early summer.

I. xiphium 2 ft (60 cm) Spanish Iris　S. Europe
These flower a week or two earlier than the

Iris unguicularis (I. stylosa)
'Hermod'

English irises and, with their hybrids, have a wider colour range that includes some attractive browns and yellows. Early summer.

IRISH HEATH – see *Daboecia*

ITEA
(Iteaceae)

Evergreen and deciduous flowering shrubs of which one species of this small genus, *I. ilicifolia*, is most often seen in gardens.
Cultural requirements: Moist peaty soil and a sunny or partly shaded situation.
Propagation: From cuttings under glass in heat in late summer.

I. ilicifolia up to 15 ft (4·5 m)   W. China
Evergreen, slightly tender species that makes a good subject for a south or west wall. Holly-like foliage and pendent racemes of greenish-yellow flowers. Late summer.

IVY – see *Hedera*

IXIA
(Iridaceae)

Half-hardy corms with brilliantly coloured crocus-like flowers on dainty stems.
Cultural requirements: Light sandy soil, rich in humus. Ixias also make good pot plants for the cool greenhouse. Corms should be planted in late autumn or early winter, protecting those planted outdoors with a covering of ashes, compost, or bracken.
Propagation: By offsets.

I. campanulata 1 ft (30 cm)   S. Africa
Purple and crimson flowers, several to a stem. Summer.
I. maculata 1 ft (30 cm)   S. Africa
Orange-yellow flowers in gladiolus-like spikes; narrow grassy foliage. Spring.
I. viridiflora 1 ft (30 cm)   S. Africa
A species with green flowers, much in demand by flower arrangers. Spring.

Bulb specialists offer numerous cultivars in a wide range of colours, derived from the above mentioned species.

JACARANDA
(Bignoniaceae)

Flowering trees for the warm greenhouse with attractive fern-like foliage.
Cultural requirements: John Innes No. 2 or similar compost and a minimum winter temperature of 55 °F (12 °C). Plants in pots can stand outdoors in a sunny sheltered situation during summer.
Propagation: From seed under glass in late spring; by cuttings in late summer and autumn.

J. mimosaefolia up to 10 ft (3 m)   Brazil
Decorative greenhouse or house plants when young with delicate fern-like foliage. Established specimens bear attractive blue flowers. Trees in their native setting will reach a height of around 50 ft (15 m).

JACOBINIA
(Acanthaceae)

Flowering shrubs of exotic appearance, suitable for a warm greenhouse.
Cultural requirements: John Innes No. 2 or similar compost. Water freely in summer; sparingly at all other times. Minimum winter temperature 55 °F (12 °C).

Propagation: By cuttings of unripened shoots under glass in late spring.

J. carnea 3 ft (1 m)   Brazil
The plants bear cone-like clusters of pale rosy-pink flowers in great profusion. Late summer.
J. chrysostephana 3 ft (1 m)   Mexico
Winter flowering species with large clusters of orange-yellow flowers. Winter.

JACOB'S LADDER – see *Polemonium*

JAPANESE LAUREL – see *Aucuba japonica*

JAPANESE QUINCE – see *Chaenomeles*

JASMINE – see *Jasminum*

JASMINUM
(Oleaceae) Jasmine

Mainly climbing or trailing shrubs, hardy and tender.
Cultural requirements: Tender species: Well-drained pots or border in a greenhouse with winter temperatures not less than 45–50 °F (7–10 °C).

Hardy species: Any good garden soil and a sunny situation. *J. nudiflorum* can also be grown on a north wall.

Propagation: Tender species: By cuttings under glass in heat during summer.

Hardy kinds: By cuttings outdoors in a shady border in autumn or by layers.

J. nudiflorum up to 15 ft (4·5 m)
Winter Jasmine W. China
This popular winter flowering shrub is not a true climber but is normally grown as a wall shrub. It will thrive on any aspect. The bare bright green stems are thickly spangled with small yellow trumpet flowers throughout the winter months. Winter.

J. officinale up to 30 ft 9 m) N. India and China
Vigorous twining climber, good on a south or west wall or for scrambling through the branches of a tree. The small white flowers have an almost cloying fragrance. 'Grandiflorum' is a cultivar with larger flowers than the type and tinged with pink. 'Aureovariegatus' has leaves mottled with gold. Summer to early autumn.

J. polyanthum up to 25 ft (8 m) China
Vigorous twining species, too tender for outdoor planting except in mildest districts but an excellent plant for the cool greenhouse, provided growth is severely restricted by hard pruning. The white flowers, tinged with pink are intensely fragrant and are borne over a long period. Early to late spring.

JERUSALEM SAGE – see *Phlomis*

JEW'S MALLOW – see *Kerria japonica*

JUDAS TREE – see *Cercis siliquastrum*

JUNE BERRY – see *Amelanchier*

JUNIPER – see *Juniperus*

JUNIPERUS
(Cupressaceae) Juniper
An extensive genus of evergreen coniferous subjects, that includes many prostrate and creeping forms as well as medium-sized shrubs and tall trees.

Jacaranda

Jasminum nudiflorum 'Aureolus' (Winter Jasmine)

Cultural requirements: Any ordinary garden soil, including chalk. Sunny situation for preference.

Propagation: From seed in a cold frame in spring; from semi-hard stem cuttings with a heel in a cold frame in late summer.

J. communis (Various)   N. America, Asia, and Europe, including British Isles
A widely distributed and varied species, mostly of medium size. Many of the smaller forms make ideal plants for the rock or heath garden.

The following cultivars are all worth growing: 'Compressa', dwarf slim columnar form; 'Hibernica' (Irish juniper), dense growing, slender column up to 10 ft (3 m) in height; and 'Hornibrookii', dwarf creeping form, useful as ground cover.

J. horizontalis (Creeping)   N. America
Dwarf prostrate carpeting shrub, excellent as ground cover, with a spread of up to 10 ft (3 m) or more. Foliage is a striking glaucous-blue. Many named cultivars are known of which some of the best are 'Bar Harbour', grey-green; 'Glauca', steely-blue; 'Plumosa', feathery grey-green foliage, tinged with purple in winter; and 'Wiltonii' (syn. 'Blue Rug') whose name is sufficient description of its appearance and habit.

J. × *media* (*J. chinensis* × *J. sabina*)
up to 10 ft (3 m)   Hybrid of doubtful origin
This hybrid group contains some of the best and most useful of all the junipers, of small to medium size with ascending branches. 'Pfitzeriana' is the best known form. It makes an excellent lawn specimen with spreading branches of grey-green foliage. 'Pfitzeriana Aurea' has striking golden foliage.

J. sabina up to 10 ft (3 m)
Savin   S. and C. Europe
A species containing forms of widely varying character, mainly spreading or creeping in habit. *J. s. tamariscifolia* is the variety most commonly seen, a widely spreading conifer with feathery green foliage and a flattened top.

J. virginiana up to 40 ft (12 m)
Red Cedar   N. America
Medium to large conifers of conical appearance. The many fine cultivars include 'Grey Owl', with dainty sprays of grey foliage and 'Skyrocket', a pencil-slim column of blue-grey foliage.

KAFFIR LILY – see *Schizostylis coccinea*

KALANCHOË
(Crassulaceae)

Tender succulent plants with scented flowers, useful in the greenhouse or as room plants.
Cultural requirements: John Innes No. 2 or similar potting compost.
Propagation: from seed sown in sandy soil in spring or early summer. Winter temperature 45–50 °F (7–10 °C). From cuttings under glass in summer.

K. flammea, *K. blossfeldiana*, and *K. teretifolia* are three species suitable for the cool greenhouse. 'Brilliant Star', scarlet; 'Morning Sun', gold; and 'Tetra Vulcan', scarlet; are all good named kinds of hybrid origin.

KALE – see Kitchen Garden

KALMIA
(Ericaceae)

Evergreen ericaceous shrubs which are lime-haters and need similar soil conditions to rhododendrons.
Cultural requirements: Moist peaty soil and a sunny or partly shaded situation. Will not tolerate lime.
Propagation: From seed in a cold frame in spring; cuttings in summer; layers in autumn.

K. latifolia up to 10 ft (3 m) Eastern N. America
Similar in appearance to a rhododendron with large terminal clusters of pink lantern-like flowers set off perfectly by dark green foliage. 'Clementine Churchill' is a form with cerise flowers. Early summer.

KEEL
The lower petal of the flowers of legumes such as sweet peas, brooms, and lupins. So called from its resemblance to the keel of a boat.

KERRIA
(Rosaceae)

A genus of one species of useful deciduous flowering shrubs with a long and early flowering season.

Cultural requirements: Any good garden soil.

Propagation: By cuttings in a cold frame in summer; from layers in spring or from suckers.

K. japonica up to 10 ft (3 m)

Jew's Mallow   China and Japan

An excellent wall shrub for any aspect with golden-yellow flowers and apple-green stems which are decorative in winter. The showier double form 'Pleniflora' is the one most widely grown, but the type plant, with single buttercup flowers, has a charm of its own. Spring.

KITCHEN GARDEN

No matter how small it may be, a vegetable garden can be both a pleasurable and profitable experience for any gardener. This is particularly true in the present-day climate of constantly increasing food prices. In addition to saving money, those who grow their own have the enjoyment of eating flavour-fresh vegetables brought straight from garden to kitchen.

In the smaller gardens of today, the siting of a vegetable plot may present certain difficulties. If the plot is rectangular, it can be sited at the far end, screened by a hedge or a row of espalier or cordon apples or pears. Where the plot is wide enough, however, it is often better to site it to one side of the house, screening it with wattle hurdles or, more permanently, with a conifer hedge.

Where space is restricted it is better to concentrate on the more unusual and luxury vegetables, such as asparagus, seakale, calabrese, courgettes, sweet corn, and others that are either expensive or hard to come by in your neighbourhood shops. Space should always be found for a few short rows of lettuce and radishes and even those who do not enjoy the pleasures of a greenhouse can grow tomatoes outdoors against a sunny wall.

In the really tiny garden, crops such as globe artichokes and cardoons, which are decorative enough for the herbaceous border, can be grown. And there are few other climbing plants that give a more colourful and long lasting display of bloom than runner beans, especially if one of the varieties with pink or white flowers is grown.

Preparation of the site

Whether it consists of former pasture land, or whether it has already been in cultivation, the

Beetroots can be stored in a box of sand for winter eating, if the leaves and stalks are removed to about 1 in. (3 cm) above the root

Beetroot Crimson Globe

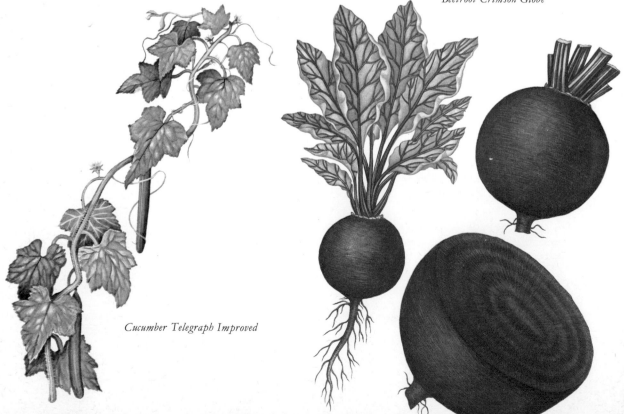

Cucumber Telegraph Improved

initial preparation of the site for vegetables is vital to success. Most vegetables thrive best in a deep well-dug soil, rich in humus and slightly on the alkaline side.

For an established plot, digging one spit deep will normally suffice but where a vegetable garden is being started from scratch, it will be better to practise double-digging or bastard trenching, if depth of soil allows.

Whenever possible, a spade should be used for this operation. It is only where the ground is too hard and stony that a fork should be used, although this latter tool is used to break up the lower spit of soil before the trenches are filled in. For heavy clay soils, a spade with a curved blade, known as a 'graft', can be useful. The soil does not stick to its blade as it does with a normal flat-bladed spade.

To dig one spit deep, the soil is taken from a strip, 1 ft (30 cm) wide, across the width of the plot and barrowed away to the opposite end. The soil from the next trench is then turned into the first, continuing in this manner until the other end of the plot is reached when the soil from the first strip will be used to fill the final trench.

Bastard trenching is a digging operation that ensures that the soil is well broken up to a depth of $1\frac{1}{2}$–2 ft (45–60 cm). A trench, 2 ft (60 cm) wide and one spit deep, is taken out and the soil is transferred to the opposite end of the plot as before. The bottom of the trench is then thoroughly broken up with a fork to the depth of another 1 ft (30 cm).

A second strip of a similar width is then marked out and the soil from this is transferred to the bottom of the first trench, taking care to remove any loose earth before breaking up the bottom of the trench with the fork. Once again the procedure continues until the back of the plot is reached and the last trench is filled in with soil from the first.

If the site is very wide, it may be more con-

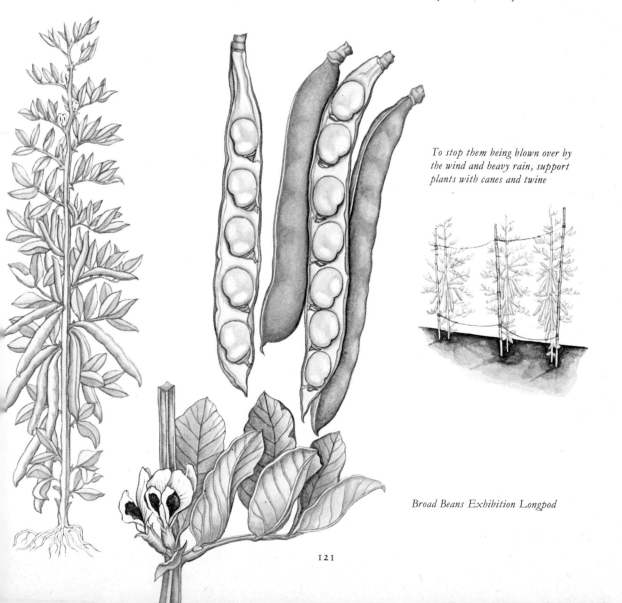

To stop them being blown over by the wind and heavy rain, support plants with canes and twine

Broad Beans Exhibition Longpod

Cabbage

venient to divide it in two lengthwise for digging, working up to one end and back again. If this method is adopted, the soil from the first trench will be dumped alongside it, at the point where digging will finish.

If manure or compost is being incorporated, it can be placed in the trenches as digging proceeds. Manure should always be in a well-rotted condition or it can cause damage to plant roots with which it comes into contact. Other fertilizers such as bonemeal, hoof and horn, or general fertilizers can be scattered on the surface and raked or lightly forked into the soil about a week before sowing or planting.

Where the site under cultivation is former pasture land, the turf should be skimmed off as each strip is being dug and placed, face down, in the bottom of the preceding trench. Alternatively, it can be stacked and composted.

Crop succession

Some vegetable crops take a good deal of nourishment out of the soil, others, such as peas and beans, leave a legacy in the form of nitrogen.

Growing the same crops in one position year after year encourages the spread of soil-borne diseases such as club root. For these reasons and to make the fullest use of available growing space, successional cropping should be practised.

To achieve this, the plot is normally divided up into three sections and succession is so planned that hardly any kind of crop occupies the same land at less than two-year intervals. Some crops need land that has been freshly manured, others respond better in soil that has first carried some other kind of crop.

Section 1: This is dug and manured ready for those crops that require rich soil.

Crops: Beans (Broad, French, and Runner), Peas, Onions, Lettuce, Leeks, Shallots, Spinach, and Celery.

Follow-ons: Carrots, Beetroots, and Turnips.

Section 2: This will be mainly reserved for root crops, including potatoes, which are worth growing where space permits. If this site has been previously manured, only light dressings of fertilizer will be needed.

Crops: Potatoes, Carrots, Beetroots, Parsnips, and Swedes.

Follow-ons: Onions, Spinach, Cabbages, Lettuces, and Spring Onions.

Section 3: This is used mainly for green crops, planted out in summer to provide winter and early spring greens. These will require a dressing of a general fertilizer, together with light applications of lime for the brassicas.

Crops: Cabbage, Brussels Sprouts, Kale, Cauliflowers, Broccoli, and Calabrese.

As these occupy the ground for the greater part of the year, there are no follow-on crops but part of this section could be devoted to a seed and nursery bed for raising brassica plants.

Individual crops

ASPARAGUS

Although asparagus is usually thought of as a luxury vegetable its cultivation is easy. A great deal depends on the proper initial preparation of the site since, once planted, asparagus must not be disturbed. It is a permanent crop that will pay handsome dividends over many years.

Asparagus likes a well-drained loamy soil best but will succeed in other types of soil (the possible exception being shallow chalk), provided that they are well-drained and rich in humus. If the soil is not normally sharply drained, deep digging is an essential part of the preliminary preparation, incorporating as much manure or compost as can be spared in the lower spit. Where there are doubts about drainage, asparagus should be grown in a bed raised 2 ft (60 cm) above the general level. A bed 4 ft (1·2 m) wide will accommodate two rows of plants $1\frac{1}{2}$ ft (45 cm) apart.

Plants can be raised from seed sown outdoors in spring. The resulting plants will provide a few spears for cutting in their third season but more rapid results are obtained by planting two- or three-year-old crowns. These will give small crops in their second season and a full yield the following year.

Cultivars

Connover's Colossal and Martha Washington.

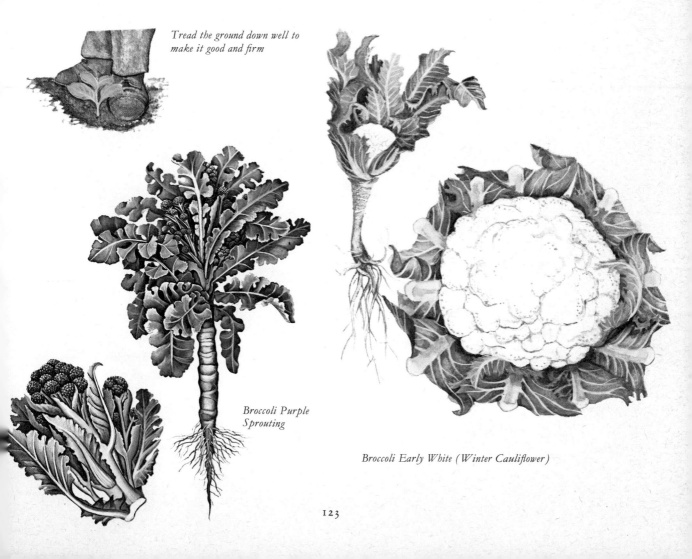

Tread the ground down well to make it good and firm

Broccoli Purple Sprouting

Broccoli Early White (Winter Cauliflower)

BEETROOT

Beetroot should be grown in ground previously manured for another crop. If necessary, a light dressing of a general fertilizer can be given a week or so before sowing. The seed is sown in drills (the round types) in late spring for early crops; maincrop sowings of long-rooted types are made from early to midsummer. A later sowing of the round type can be made a few weeks later to provide roots for pulling in midwinter.

The seedlings should be thinned to $4\frac{1}{2}$ in. (11 cm) when their first true leaves appear, continuing thinning until the plants are 9 in. (22 cm) apart. Distance between rows should be 1 ft (30 cm).

Early and late sowings should be pulled as required, maincrop sowings should be stored in boxes of moist sand or peat in a frost-proof shed or garage.

Cultivars

Round or Globe: Boltardy, Crimson Globe, and Little Ball.

Long varieties: Cheltenham Green Top, Long Red, and Housewives' Choice.

BROAD BEANS

For early crops sow in late autumn, choosing, if possible, a sheltered position. Maincrop sowings are made from late winter to early spring. Sow double rows, 9 in. (22 cm) apart, setting seed 3 in.

(8 cm) deep and 9 in. (22 cm) apart. Pinch out the tops of the plants when they are in full flower. This will produce better and earlier crops and minimize blackfly attacks.

Cultivars

Aquadulce, Giant Seville (for early sowings), Dreadnought, Rentpayer, Imperial Green Windsor. The Midget is a prolific dwarf sort, useful where space is restricted.

BROCCOLI
(Winter Cauliflower)

Broccoli need firm soil that has been only lightly forked over after removal of a previous crop. Before planting, a light dressing of a general fertilizer should be forked in.

Sow seed outdoors in late spring to produce plants that will go out, 2 ft (60 cm) apart with 3 ft (1 m) between the rows, around midsummer.

Cultivars

White: Matchless, Early March, and St George.

Sprouting: Calabrese, Early Purple Sprouting, and Early White Sprouting.

BRUSSELS SPROUTS

Brussels sprouts need firm ground and rich soil, with a light dressing of a general fertilizer forked in before planting. For early crops, seed can be sown under glass in late winter; main sowings are

Brussels Sprouts Perfection

Cabbage Greyhound

made outdoors in spring. Plant out in early summer 2–2½ ft (60–75 cm) apart with 3 ft (1 m) between the rows.

Cultivars

Rous Lench, Early Dwarf. Peer Gynt and Prince Askold are two newer F_1 hybrid varieties, both producing firm sprouts of medium size, excellent for the deep freeze.

CABBAGE AND KALE

For spring-sown cabbage to mature in summer and autumn, fork in a light dressing of well-rotted manure or compost. Autumn-sown cabbage, for use in spring, is planted on ground manured for a previous crop, without further digging.

Summer cabbage plants should go in 1 ft (30 cm) apart with 1½ ft (45 cm) between the rows; winter and spring varieties 2 ft (60 cm) with 2 ft (60 cm) between the rows.

Cultivars

Summer and Autumn: Early Ballhead, Greyhound, Velocity, and Winnigstadt.

Winter and Spring: Flower of Spring, Christmas Drumhead, January King, Savoy Cabbage, Best of All, and Ice Queen.

CARROTS

Carrots need deeply dug, well-drained soil that has been manured the previous season. Outdoor

Curly Kale Dwarf Green Curled

When the seedlings can be handled easily, thin them out leaving 18 in. (45 cm) between each

Carrot Early Nantes

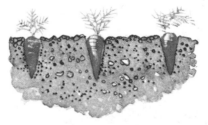

Thin to about 6 in. (15 cm) apart when the carrots are about 3 in. (8 cm) long

Cauliflower Early Snowball

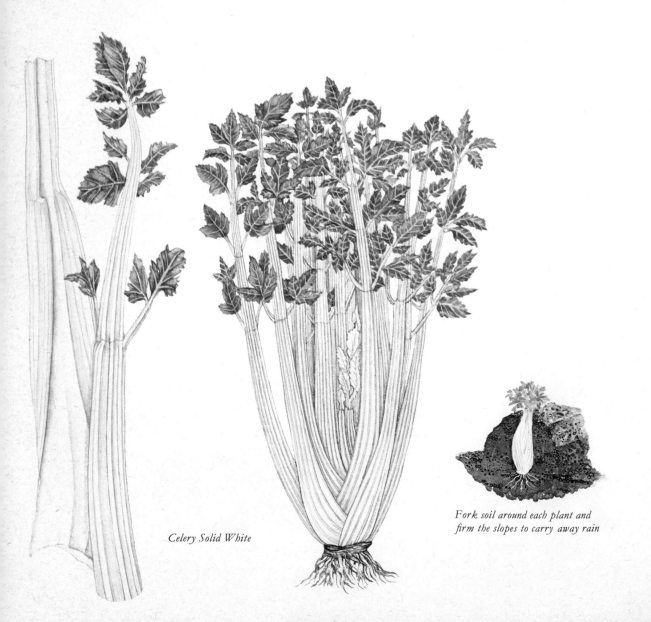

Celery Solid White

*Fork soil around each plant and
firm the slopes to carry away rain*

sowings can be made from early spring onwards; maincrop cultivars from spring to midsummer. Sow in drills 1 ft (30 cm) apart and thin as soon as the first pair of true leaves appears. Maincrop kinds should be lifted in autumn and stored in dry sand or earth in a shed or garage.

Cultivars

Intermediate, Autumn King, Scarlet Perfection, and St Valery.

CAULIFLOWER

Cauliflowers require deeply dug, well-manured and moist soil. Seed can be sown under glass in winter for early crops or outdoors from spring to early summer for maincrops. Plants should go in 2 ft (60 cm) apart, with the same distance between the rows.

Cultivars

All The Year Round, Early Snowball, Forerunner, South Pacific, and White Heart.

CELERY

Celery needs rich soil and plenty of moisture and is usually grown in shallow trenches. Seed should be sown in heat in late winter to produce plants ready to go out from early to midsummer. Celery plants must never lack for water. When they are about 1 ft (30 cm) in height they should be loosely tied with raffia and earthed up gradually as growth proceeds.

Cultivars

Prizetaker and Golden Self-blanching.

CRESS – see Kitchen Garden

CUCUMBER

Outdoor (ridge) cucumbers are the best type for the amateur gardener unless he has extensive greenhouse facilities. Seed is sown under glass in small pots. After hardening off, the plants should go out into rich soil, either on mounds or in well-prepared flat ground. For cultivation, see Marrows. Plants should be watered freely in dry weather. Gherkins, for pickling, can be grown in a similar manner.

Cultivars

Bedfordshire Prize Ridge, Burpee's Hybrid, Greenline. Prolific is good for gherkins.

KOHL RABI

This is one of the 'luxury' vegetables that are so well worth growing in the small garden. The swollen stems are eaten when they are about the size of a small turnip. They have a very delicate and distinctive flavour. Seed is sown outdoors in late spring, thinning the plants to 9 in. (22 cm).

Cultivars

Early Purple Vienna and Early White Vienna.

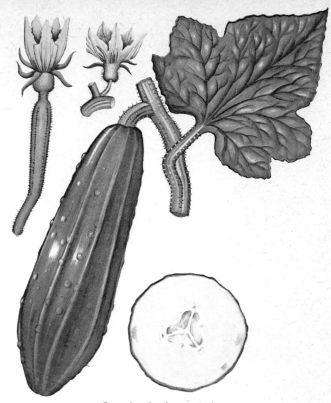

Cucumber Outdoor or Ridge

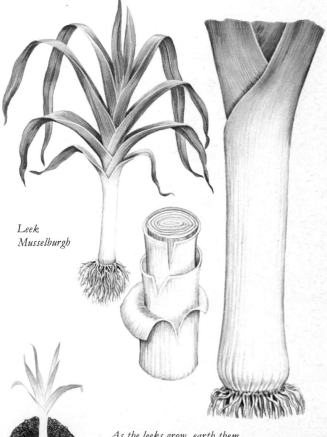

Leek Musselburgh

As the leeks grow, earth them each week to get the longest possible white stems

Lettuce Premier Great Lakes

*Cos Lettuce
Paris White*

*To get tight crisp hearts,
tie the leaves loosely
together when the lettuces
begin to make hearts*

LEEKS

Leeks are a valuable crop for bridging the hungry gap between winter and spring in the kitchen garden. Seed is sown outdoors during spring and the seedlings can either be thinned to 9 in. (22 cm) or planted out the same distance apart in holes made with a dibber. If leeks of exhibition quality are required, the holes can be filled with a mixture of sifted loam or with well-rotted compost.

Cultivars

Musselburgh, Marble Pillar, and Catalina.

LETTUCE

By a careful choice of cultivars and the help of cloches or cold frames, it is possible to have a succession of this valuable salad crop almost throughout the entire year. Outdoor sowings can begin in spring, on ground dug over and manured the previous autumn. Such sowings can be continued at fortnightly intervals until a week or two after midsummer. Subsequently, outdoor sowings can be made in late summer or early autumn of cultivars that will stand the winter to mature the following spring.

Sowings under glass

The first sowings under cloches or in a cold frame can be made in mid-autumn, the seedlings being thinned or transplanted 1 ft (30 cm) apart about six weeks later. Further sowings can be made in late winter to provide successive crops until the outdoor sowings start to mature.

Cultivars

Cabbage types: Minetto, Premier Great Lakes, Tom Thumb, Webb's Wonderful, Arctic King, May King, and Sea Queen.

Cos types: Lobjoit's Green, Winter Density, and Sugar Cos.

MARROWS AND COURGETTES

Vegetable marrows need a sunny situation and soil rich in humus. Plenty of well-rotted manure or compost should be dug in before planting. Marrows are traditionally grown on raised heaps of rotted turves or compost, but this method is not essential to success provided that the soil is in really good heart.

Seed is sown under glass in late spring, singly in small pots. The plants are hardened off to go out in early summer, when danger of frost is past. Outdoor sowings can also be made, where the plants are to grow, in early summer. Marrows should be cut when quite young, when their flavour and texture are at their best.

Bush cultivars

All Green, White Bush, and Zucchini F_1 Hybrid. (The last named is the best kind for producing

Marrow Green Bush

Marrow Courgette
F$_1$ Hybrid Zucchini

courgettes, which are cut when only 6 in. (15 cm) long.)

Trailing cultivars

Golden Delicious, Little Gem, and Long Green.

MUSHROOMS

Mushrooms can be cultivated successfully in any comparatively dry and well-ventilated building such as a greenhouse, shed, cellar or garage. An essential factor for success is the maintenance of an even temperature between 50° and 60 °F (10–15 °C). Darkness is not necessary, but they should not be grown in direct sunshine.

Mushrooms are normally cultivated in beds of compost made from straw, rotted down with stable manure. When the temperature of the compost heap has dropped to about 70 °F (21 °C), it can be made up into beds, 4 ft (1·2 m) wide and about 1 ft (30 cm) deep.

Proprietary preparations are obtainable for rotting down the straw without the use of stable manure. Mushroom spawn is inserted in the bed, about 3 in. (8 cm) below the surface. As soon as a greyish fluff and white threads (mycelium) appears on the surface, the beds should be cased, i.e. covered to a depth of 2 in. (5 cm) with a mixture of equal parts peat and sterilized soil.

Cropping can be expected 6–8 weeks later. The yield should continue for several months.

MUSTARD AND CRESS

Mustard and cress is a useful salad crop that is easily raised in boxes of sifted soil. Cress should be sown three days in advance of mustard, since the latter germinates more rapidly. The seed is sown thickly and pressed down on to the surface of the soil. It is then well watered and the boxes are covered with a sheet of glass or brown paper until germination takes place.

ONIONS

The site for onions should be dug over during winter, incorporating, in the process, liberal quantities of well-rotted manure or compost. Seed is sown in drills, 1 ft (30 cm) apart, in early spring.

Sowings can also be made under glass some weeks later to provide seedlings for planting out in mid-spring. Outdoor sowings can be made in late summer to stand the winter and produce crops the following year. Seedlings should be progressively thinned to 6 in. (15 cm).

Good crops of onions can also be raised from sets which are small bulblets specially prepared for planting in spring to produce early crops of onions and avoid the attack of onion fly.

Before onions are harvested, in late summer or early autumn, the top growth should be bent over to accelerate the ripening process. A week or two

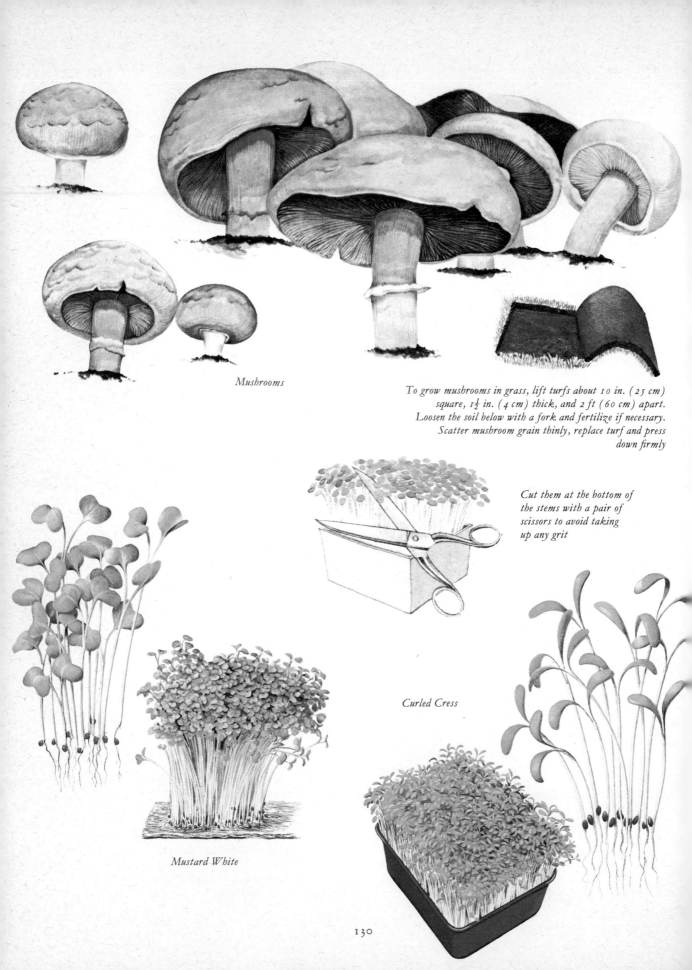

Mushrooms

To grow mushrooms in grass, lift turfs about 10 in. (25 cm) square, 1½ in. (4 cm) thick, and 2 ft (60 cm) apart. Loosen the soil below with a fork and fertilize if necessary. Scatter mushroom grain thinly, replace turf and press down firmly

Cut them at the bottom of the stems with a pair of scissors to avoid taking up any grit

Curled Cress

Mustard White

later, the bulbs can be lifted and stored in a well-ventilated shed or garage. Shallots are treated in a manner similar to onion sets.

Cultivars

Ailsa Craig, Autumn Queen, Bedfordshire Champion, Prizewinner, Yellow Globe. Spring onions: White Lisbon. Sets: All-Rounder.

PARSNIPS

Parsnips do best on ground that has been manured for a previous crop. Deep digging is essential for good results. Seed is sown in spring, in drills 15 in. (38 cm) apart and the seedlings are subsequently thinned to 6 in. (15 cm). Roots should be lifted for use as required.

Cultivars

Hollow Crown Improved and The Student.

PEAS

Peas should be grown on land that has been deeply dug and well-manured the previous autumn or winter. It is a crop that responds well to rich soil conditions. A light dressing of lime should be given a week or two before the seed is sown. Successive sowings can be made as required from early spring to midsummer. The seed should be sown in flat drills, 9–12 in. (22–30 cm) wide. Each drill will take three rows of seed spaced 2–3 in. (5–8 cm) apart in the rows. The plants should be supported with pea sticks or netting.

First Early cultivars

Feltham First, Kelvedon Wonder, Peter Pan, Progress No. 9, and Little Marvel.

Second Early cultivars

Early Onward, Kelvedon Monarch, and Kelvedon Spitfire.

Maincrop cultivars

Greensleeves and Onward.

POTATOES

Potatoes do best in soil that has been manured and dug over the previous autumn and given a dressing of a general fertilizer. They are also good for cleaning up new ground, although the crops will not necessarily be as heavy in these conditions.

Seed potatoes should be laid out in trays in a light, frost-proof place and allowed to sprout before planting. The sprouted tubers are planted in drills, 4–5 in. (10–13 cm) deep in rows 2 ft (60 cm) apart. Early cultivars should go in 1 ft (30 cm) apart in the rows, maincrop 15 in. (38 cm).

The plants should be earthed up as growth progresses. Around midsummer, maincrop potatoes should be sprayed with Bordeaux mix-

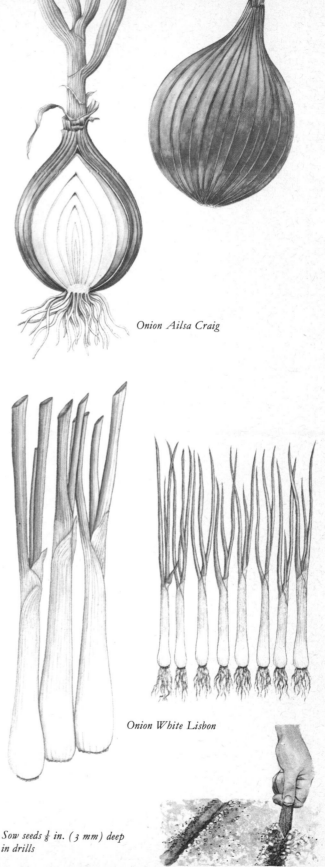

Onion Ailsa Craig

Onion White Lisbon

Sow seeds ⅛ in. (3 mm) deep in drills

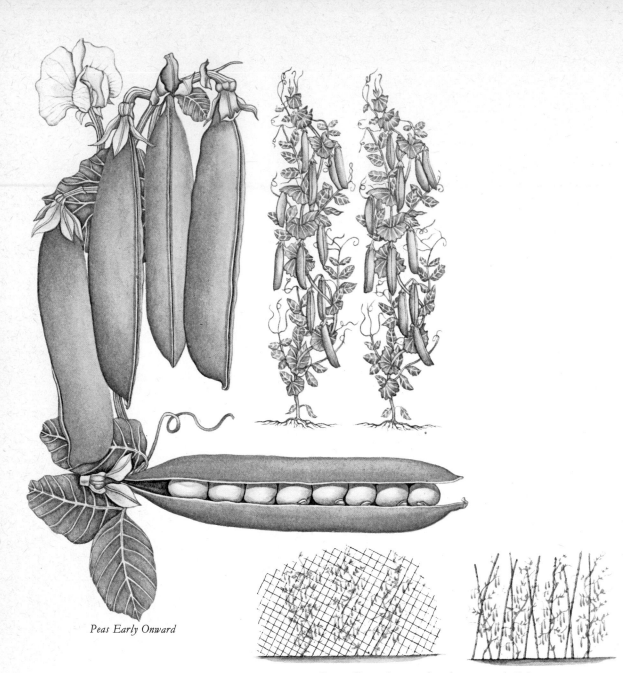

Peas Early Onward

Peas will grow better and produce more pods if they are supported by sticks, canes, or wire netting

ture or a liquid copper fungicide as a preventative against blight.

Early potatoes can be lifted as required. In autumn, maincrop cultivars should be lifted when the haulm has died down and stored in clamps out of doors or in sacks or boxes in a frost-proof shed or garage.

Cultivars

Early: Sharpes Express, Ulster Chieftain, and Arran Pilot.

Maincrop: Majestic, King Edward, and Golden Wonder.

RADISHES

Radishes can be grown in any well-cultivated soil out of doors or can be sown under glass for early crops from late winter to early spring. Successional outdoor sowings can be made from spring to early summer. In late summer, winter radishes can be sown to provide roots that can be lifted and stored or left in the ground for use as required. Seed should be sown thinly in drills 6 in. (15 cm) apart.

Forcing cultivars

Cherry Belle and Red Forcing.

Outdoor cultivars
French Breakfast and Sparkler.
Winter cultivars
China Rose, Mino, and Black Spanish.

RUNNER BEANS AND DWARF OR FRENCH BEANS

Both runner and dwarf beans need soil that has been deeply dug and has been given liberal quantities of well-rotted manure or compost.

Runner beans can be sown in boxes under glass in spring to provide plants for early cropping. Outdoor sowings are made in late spring or early summer. Seeds are sown 2–3 in. (5–8 cm) deep in double rows 1 ft (30 cm) apart. Sow seed 6 in. (15 cm) apart and thin to 1 ft (30 cm). The plants should be watered liberally during spells of dry weather and syringed overhead during the evening when they are in flower to encourage them to set pods.

Plants should be staked at an early stage, unless a dwarf kind, such as Hammond's 'Dwarf Scarlet', which needs no staking, is grown.

The cultivation for dwarf French beans is similar to the above, except that earlier crops can be obtained by growing them under cloches or in a cold greenhouse.

Cultivars

Runner beans: As Long As Your Arm, Cookham Dene, Scarlet Emperor, and Yardstick.

Dwarf French: Tendergreen, Masterpiece, and The Prince.

SHALLOTS

Shallots, which are treated in a similar way to onion sets, need the same kind of deeply dug and well-manured soil. The bulbs should be planted 6 in. (15 cm) apart in the rows, with only their tips showing above the soil surface. Choose a day in late winter when the soil is in good condition for planting.

When the leaves are starting to die down, the clusters of new bulbs are lifted and left for a few days on the surface of the soil to dry out. They are then tied in bundles and stored, in a similar manner to onions, in a dry and airy shed or garage.

SPINACH AND SPINACH BEET

Both these crops should be grown in ground that has been well-manured. Crops of spinach are used up as they mature, so that successional sowings should be made from spring to early summer in drills 1 ft (30 cm) apart, thinning the seedlings by stages to 6 in. (15 cm).

Spinach beet, also known as perpetual spinach, provides supplies of green leaves over a long

Parsnip Hollow Crown

Radish Scarlet Globe
Can be cut so they open out into
rosettes when put into iced water

*Dwarf French Bean
Tendergreen*

*Sew seeds in two parallel furrows 12 in. (30 cm) apart,
with sets of furrows 2 ft (60 cm) apart*

period from autumn to spring. The method of cultivation is the same as for spinach and leaves should be gathered regularly while they are young and tender. Seakale beet, or Swiss chard, is a very similar vegetable, except that the white fleshy midrib of the leaves can be cooked separately and served in a similar manner to asparagus or seakale.

Cultivars

Spinach: Longstanding Round (summer) and Longstanding Prickly (winter).

Spinach beet: Perpetual Spinach and Swiss Chard.

SWEET CORN

This is another of the 'luxury crops' and one that is becoming increasingly popular with gardeners since the introduction of new and earlier maturing cultivars. Early crops can be obtained from sowings in a warm greenhouse or heated frame in late spring to provide plants to go out, after hardening off, in early summer.

Outdoor sowings can be made in late spring or early summer, preferably under cloches.

Cultivars

Earliking, Kelvedon Glory, and North Star.

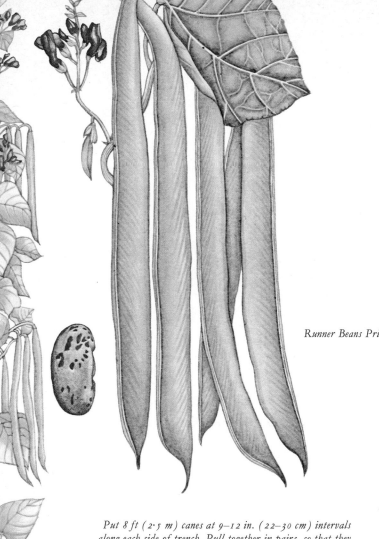

Runner Beans Prizewinner

*Put 8 ft (2·5 m) canes at 9–12 in. (22–30 cm) intervals
along each side of trench. Pull together in pairs, so that they
form a V 18 in. (45 cm) below the top, and rest another
cane along the top in the V. Put one seed 1 in. (3 cm) deep
at the base of each cane, and six or so at each end of the
row to replace any failures. Runner beans can also be
grown up tripods*

TOMATOES

This is one of the most valuable of kitchen garden crops and one, too, for which there should be space in even the smallest garden, even if no other vegetables are grown. Tomatoes can be grown in a heated or unheated greenhouse or against a sunny wall or fence outdoors.

Plants can be bought for any of these methods, but where heat and glass are available, it is more satisfying to raise one's own plants, since there will be a much wider choice of cultivars, many of better flavour and texture than those commonly offered by commercial growers.

Seeds to produce plants for growing on in a heated greenhouse should be sown in John Innes No. 1 or a similar seed compost in late winter, pricking the seedlings out into boxes and later transferring them to small pots. For unheated houses and for outdoor cultivation, sowings are made under glass about a month later.

The final spacing of the plants should be from 1½–2 ft (45–60 cm) and as soon as they start to set fruit, fortnightly applications of a proprietary fertilizer, specifically for tomatoes should be given. As a precaution against tomato blight, plants should be sprayed with a colloidal copper fungicide at midsummer, repeated a few weeks later. Any affected with mosaic or streak virus should be removed and burnt.

Cultivars

Greenhouse: Eurocross, Ailsa Craig, Alicante, Supersonic, and Golden Boy.

Outdoor: Sleaford Abundance and The Amateur.

TURNIPS

Early turnips can be grown on land manured the previous season, later kinds on ground cleared of an early crop such as peas or potatoes. Seed of early cultivars is sown in spring in drills 15 in. (38 cm) apart. Seedlings should be thinned to 6 in. (15 cm). For winter use, sow in late summer; for turnip tops sowings are made in early autumn. Garden swedes are treated in a similar manner to maincrop turnips.

Cultivars

Early White Milan, Golden Ball, Manchester Market, and Red Top Milan.

Swedes: Chignecto and Purple Top.

Leaf Beet Perpetual Spinach

Spinach Summer

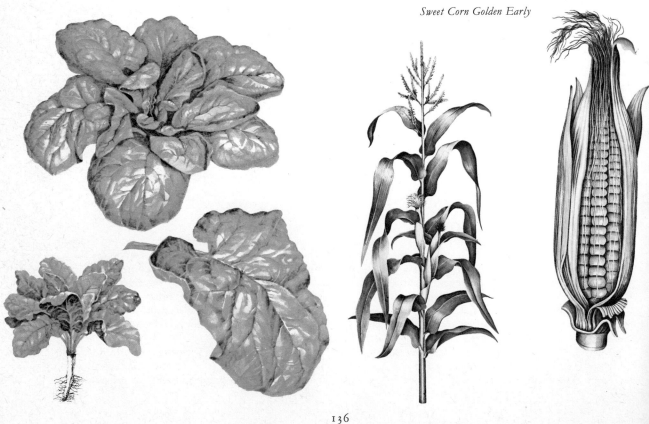

Sweet Corn Golden Early

Tomato Carters' Fruit

Turnip Golden Ball

To grow by ring culture, which gives a bigger and better crop: make a bed of fine gravel 1 ft (30 cm) deep. Stand bottomless rings 10 in. (25 cm) in diameter on it, 2 ft (60 cm) apart. Fill with potting compost, firmly place one plant in each and water it well in

Swede Prizewinner

Turnip Red Top Milan

KNAPWEED – see *Centaurea*

KNIPHOFIA

(Liliaceae) Red Hot Poker or Torch Lily
Hardy perennials of great value in the border.
Many are evergreen and all have handsome flower
spikes. Formerly found under generic name
Tritoma.
Cultural requirements: A rich loamy soil for
preference, but will thrive in heavy clay provided
it is well-drained. Plants should not be allowed to
dry out in summer.
Propagation: From seed in cold frame in spring;
division in spring or autumn.

K. caulescens 4 ft (1·2 m)   S. Africa
A handsome species with bold, yucca-like foliage
and reddish-salmon flowers. Midsummer.

K. galpinii 1½ ft (45 cm)   Transvaal
A slightly tender species with narrow, grass-like
leaves and orange-yellow flower spikes on slender
stems. Autumn.

K. uvaria 4 ft (1·2 m)   S. Africa
The best known species, and a parent of many
fine hybrid cultivars such as 'Bees Sunset', flame;
'Maid of Orleans', creamy-white; 'Royal
Standard', scarlet and gold; and 'Samuel's
Sensation', coral-red. Late summer to autumn.

KNOTWEED – see *Polygonum*

KOCHIA

(Chenopodiaceae) Summer Cypress
Half-hardy annuals forming a cylindrical conifer-
like bush of pale green foliage, that turns a
striking crimson in autumn.
Cultural requirements: Any ordinary garden
soil and a sunny situation.

Propagation: From seed, sown in gentle heat in
spring to provide plants for hardening off and
planting out in early summer.

K. trichophylla up to 3 ft (1 m)
Burning Bush   Europe and Asia
Neat oval bush of apple-green finely-cut foliage
turning a brilliant crimson and bronze in autumn.
Useful as focal plants in summer bedding schemes.

KOELREUTERIA

(Sapindaceae)
Attractive trees of slow growth and spreading
outline suitable for small to medium-sized gardens.
Cultural requirements: Any ordinary garden
soil and a sunny situation.
Propagation: By seeds in autumn or spring or
from layers in autumn.

K. paniculata up to 60 ft (18 m)   China
A broad-headed tree with handsome pinnate
foliage and yellow flowers followed by striking
bladder-like seedpods. Good autumn leaf colour.
Summer.

KOLKWITZIA

(Caprifoliaceae)
A genus of one deciduous hardy shrub of
moderate size with showy flowers like tiny
foxgloves.
Cultural requirements: Any good garden soil,
provided it is well-drained, and a sunny situation.
Propagation: From stem cuttings with a heel in
a cold frame in late summer or from seeds in
spring.

K. amabilis 5 ft (1·5 m)   China
A useful shrub for the border at midsummer.
Pale pink open-throated tubular flowers like
those of a weigela. 'Pink Cloud', with pink
flowers, is an attractive cultivar. Early summer.

LABURNUM

(Leguminosae)
Popular group of small deciduous flowering
trees, widely grown as garden specimens. The
leaves are trifoliate with pendent racemes of
yellow flowers.
Cultural requirements: Any ordinary garden
soil and a sunny situation.
Propagation: From seed outdoors in spring or

autumn; layers in autumn. The best cultivars are
budded or grafted on to seedling stocks of
common laburnum.

L. alpinum 20 ft (6 m)
Scotch Laburnum   C. and S. Europe
Small tree with compact head, trifoliate green
leaves and pendent clusters of yellow pea flowers.
Early summer.

Laburnum anagyroides

L. anagyroides (syn. *L. vulgare*) up to 30 ft (9 m)
Common Laburnum   C. and S. Europe
The well known summer flowering ornamental tree with masses of pendent yellow flowers and leaves of a dull green. It associates well with the pink and scarlet thorns which are in bloom during the same period. Early summer.

L. × *watereri* (*L. alpinum* × *L. anagyroides*)
up to 30 ft (9 m)   Garden origin
The finest result of this particular cross is 'Vossii', a free flowering laburnum, with golden racemes 1 ft (30 cm) or more in length. Early summer.

LACHENALIA
(Liliaceae) Cape Cowslip
Attractive free-flowering bulbous plants suitable for pot culture in the cool greenhouse.
Cultural requirements: John Innes No. 2 or similar potting compost. Water sparingly until growth gets well under way. Minimum winter temperature 45 °F (7 °C).

L. aloides 1 ft (30 cm)   S. Africa
Broad strap-shaped leaves, spotted with purple in some forms. Spikes of pendulous red and yellow tubular flowers. Spring.

L. orchioides 9 in. (22 cm)   S. Africa
Spikes of white or yellow tubular flowers, tinged with red or blue. Spring.

LACINIATE
A description of leaves cut into narrow sometimes pointed lobes. 'Laciniatum' is the botanical description, e.g., *Acer japonicum laciniatum*, a form of the Japanese maple with finely cut foliage.

LAD'S LOVE – see *Artemisia abrotanum*

LADY FERN – see *Athyrium filix-foemina*

LADY'S MANTLE – see *Alchemilla mollis*

LAGURUS
(Gramineae)
Hardy annual decorative grasses, good for drying for winter arrangements.
Cultural requirements: Any ordinary garden soil and a sunny open situation.
Propagation: From seed outdoors in spring where plants are to remain.

L. ovatus 1 ft (30 cm) Hare's Tail Grass
                        Europe, including British Isles
An ornamental grass with white fluffy inflorescences. Summer.

LAMBS' EARS – see *Stachys lanata*

LAMIUM
(Labiatae)
Hardy perennials, related to the wild deadnettles. They make good ground cover plants.
Cultural requirements: Any ordinary garden soil and a sunny or partly shaded situation.
Propagation: By root division in autumn or spring.

Lamiastrum galeobdolon 1 ft (30 cm) Yellow Archangel
The type plant is the wild yellow deadnettle with hooded flowers. The form commonly used as a vigorous cover plant is 'Variegatum' with leaves attractively variegated with silver. It is evergreen. Early summer.

L. maculatum 1 ft (30 cm)
Deep bottle-green wrinkled foliage with a central band of white. Pinkish-purple flower spikes. 'Roseum' has flowers of a bright rose-pink; 'Aureum', a much less vigorous cultivar, has striking golden foliage. Early summer.

LANCEOLATE
A term used to describe leaves that are lance-shaped; i.e., widening from the base before tapering to a pointed tip.

LANUGINOSE
Indicating plants with felted stems and/or foliage, woolly or cottony in texture.

LAPAGERIA
(Liliaceae)
Half-hardy greenhouse flowering climbers, suitable for a sheltered wall in milder districts.
Cultural requirements: For greenhouse cultivation, John Innes No. 2 or similar compost. Outdoors, a peaty soil, rich in humus.
Propagation: From seed under glass in heat in spring; by layers in spring or autumn.

L. rosea up to 15 ft (4·5 m)   Chile
An outstandingly beautiful flowering climber, with large waxy tubular flowers of a glowing rose-pink. Summer to autumn.

LARCH – see *Larix*

LARIX
(Pinaceae)
Hardy deciduous coniferous trees, largely grown for their timber.
Cultural requirements: Any well-drained soil. Larch will not thrive on heavy, damp, clay soils. They make attractive lawn specimens for the larger garden.
Propagation: From seed outdoors in spring.

L. decidua (syn. *L. europea*) up to 100 ft (30 m)
European Larch   Europe
Large trees with light green feathery foliage in spring. Semi-weeping in habit at maturity. One of our most important timber trees.

L. kaempferi (syn. *L. leptolepis*)
up to 100 ft (30 m) Japanese Larch   Japan
A vigorous tree, with narrow blue-green foliage and reddish twigs.

LARKSPUR – see *Delphinium*

LARVA

Caterpillar, grub, or maggot, many of which attack plants and are dealt with under Pest Control.

LATERAL

A term applied to the side or subsidiary shoots of branches of trees or shrubs – mainly used in connection with fruit.

LATHYRUS
(Leguminosae)

Hardy annual and perennial climbing plants. The former (sweet peas) are among the most popular garden plants for decoration, cutting, and exhibition and are also noteworthy for their delicate fragrance.

Cultural requirements: Deeply dug rich soil well supplied with rotted manure or compost, and a sunny situation. Support must be provided and liberal supplies of water in dry weather. Dead flowers should be promptly removed to prolong flowering season.

Propagation: Annual kinds from seed; perennials from seed or root division.

L. latifolius up to 10 ft (3 m)
Everlasting Pea   Europe
This perennial species has rose coloured or purple pea flowers, smaller than those of the annual kinds and scentless. 'Pink Beauty' and 'White Pearl' are two good forms whose names describe their colour. Summer to autumn.

L. odoratus up to 10 ft (3 m)
Sweet Pea   S. Europe
The number of cultivars of this popular garden plant are numerous and changing yearly. Consultation of seedsmen's catalogues will provide up-to-date information in this respect. In recent years, the introduction of low growing kinds, known variously as 'Jet Set' and 'Knee Hi' sweet peas, has reduced the labour of staking and tying since these new and shorter kinds need only the support of a few twiggy pea sticks and now have blooms of comparable size and quality to those of the taller kinds. Provided that faded

blooms are removed before they set seed, sweet peas will continue to bloom well into the autumn. Summer to mid-autumn.

LAUREL – see *Prunus laurocerasus* and *P. lusitanica*

LAURUS
(Lauraceae)

Evergreen shrubs or small trees of slightly tender constitution.

Cultural requirements: Any ordinary garden soil and a sheltered situation.

Propagation: From cuttings or layers in late summer.

L. nobilis 20 ft (6 m) Sweet Bay   Mediterranean
The sweet bay, with its aromatic foliage, widely used in cooking, makes an excellent tub plant that stands up well to clipping. In the milder and in coastal districts, it will make a handsome evergreen hedge.

LAVANDULA
(Labiatae)

Evergreen dwarf shrubs with sweetly aromatic flowers and foliage. Of great value for dwarf hedges and succeeding well in seaside districts.

Cultural requirements: Any ordinary light to medium soil and a well-drained, sunny, open situation. Prune in spring to counteract legginess, but do not cut back into old wood.

Lathyrus odoratus Giant Waved (Sweet Pea)

Lavatera trimestris 'Tanagra' (Summer Mallow)

Propagation: From cuttings in a cold frame or north border in early autumn.

L. spica (syn. *L. officinalis*) up to 3 ft (1 m)
Old English Lavender   Mediterranean
There are many clones and cultivars of this popular shrub including 'Alba', white; 'Loddon Pink', pale pink; and 'Rosea', lavender-pink. The type plant is tall and robust with flowers on long stems. For edging purposes dwarf forms such as 'Hidcote', with violet flowers or 'Munstead', lavender-blue, are more suitable. Summer.

LAVATERA
(Malvaceae)
Hardy shrubs, sub-shrubs and annuals with typical saucer-shaped mallow flowers.
Cultural requirements: Shrubby species: Light to medium rich soil and a warm sunny situation.
Annual species: As above.
Propagation: Shrubby species: From seed sown in gentle heat under glass in early spring or outdoors later.
Annual species: From seed outdoors in spring where plants are to grow, or in late summer for an early display the following season.

L. arborea up to 10 ft (3 m)
Tree Mallow   Europe, including British Isles
Sub-shrub, sometimes cultivated as a biennial, with pinkish-purple flowers, 3 in. (8 cm) across. Late summer to autumn.
L. trimestris up to 6 ft (2 m)   S. Europe
Tall growing hardy annual useful in the mixed border, with large rosy-pink flattened trumpet flowers. 'Loveliness' and 'Tanagra' are two outstanding forms. Late summer to autumn.

LAVENDER – see *Lavandula*

LAWNS
Nothing makes a greater contribution to the appearance of a garden than a green lawn, free of weeds and with a velvet sward that is springy to walk on. And the smaller the garden, the greater the need for perfection where a lawn is concerned.

Lawns in small gardens, however, get more than their share of wear and tear. But much can be done to make a tough resistant turf if the site is carefully prepared and the right seed is sown.

Early autumn is the best time for sowing grass seed, although a successful lawn can be made from a spring sowing if attention is paid to watering during dry spells when the young grasses are emerging. Unless the soil is heavy and waterlogged during winter, an indication that the site may need preliminary draining, it is not necessary to dig the site over to any great depth. Nine inches (22 cm) should be sufficient, unless the subsoil is heavy clay in which case the lower spit should be broken up with a fork as digging proceeds.

Light sandy soils will benefit from the addition of plenty of humus. Well-rotted garden compost or manure can be used, provided that they are free from dormant weed seeds.

All deep rooting perennial weeds such as docks, dandelions, and thistles should be removed as digging progresses. Others, such as nettles and couch grass, can be buried in the lower spit. They should not prove to be troublesome and any that do survive will be quickly destroyed by regular mowing.

The next thing is to make sure that the site is level. Unless it is, the grass may be skimmed off in places by the mower blades, leaving bare patches that are an open invitation to infestation by weeds and moss.

The surface should be raked and trodden several times until all hummocks and hollows have been levelled off. Where the prospective lawn is small, the eye should be a good enough guide for levelling. Larger expanses will require a set of levelling pegs, a length of board, and a spirit level.

The site should be given a week or two for the soil to settle. After a final raking, it should be ready for sowing or turfing. The cost of turfing is at least three to four times that of making a lawn from seed.

Turf is time-saving and trouble-free but seldom produces as fine a sward as is obtained from good quality grass seed. On the other hand, it will provide an established lawn in a matter of weeks instead of months.

Where seed is being used, a preliminary dressing of a good general fertilizer should be applied, at the rate of 2 oz. to the sq. yd about a week before sowing.

LAWSON'S CYPRESS
– see *Chamaecyparis lawsoniana*

LAYERING – see Propagation

LEAFMOULD
This is a good source of humus and can be obtained from leaves raked up in autumn and made into heaps and turned frequently to accelerate rotting-down. The heaps should be enclosed in wire netting to prevent the leaves from blowing away. Leafmould makes a good substitute for peat and partly rotted leaves can be dug into the soil or can be used as a mulch to suppress weeds and increase the humus content of the soil. Oak and beech leaves make the best leafmould.

LEATHERJACKETS – see Pest Control

LEEK – see Kitchen Garden

LEGUMINOUS
A term applied to plants which produce pods such as peas, beans, brooms, and laburnums.

LENTEN ROSE – see *Helleborus orientalis*

LEONTOPODIUM
(Compositae)
Hardy perennials with downy foliage and white flowers that make attractive plants for the rock garden.
Cultural requirements: Well-drained soil and a sunny situation in the rock garden. Also suitable for the alpine house.
Propagation: From seed in a cold frame in spring; by division in spring or autumn.

L. alpinum 6 in. (15 cm) Edelweiss   Alps
Small flower heads surrounded by silver-white downy bracts. Early summer.

L. sibiricum 6 in. (15 cm)   Siberia
A species with larger flowers than the former. Early summer.

LEOPARDSBANE – see *Doronicum*

LEPTOSIPHON
(Polemoniaceae)
Hardy annuals that make attractive edging plants, botanically known as *Gilia*.
Cultural requirements: Any ordinary garden soil and a sunny situation.
Propagation: From seed outdoors in spring where plants are to flower.

L. × hybridus 6 in. (15 cm)   Garden origin
This is the kind commonly offered by seedsmen. The colour range is wide and the star-like flowers are in shades that include cream, yellow, rose, orange, and red. 'Rainbow Mixture' and 'French Hybrids' are both good cultivars. Summer.

LEPTOSPERMUM
(Myrtaceae)
Slightly tender evergreen shrubs of Australasian origin.
Cultural requirements: Light well-drained neutral or acid soil and a protected sunny situation. Not hardy in colder districts.
Propagation: By cuttings under glass in autumn.

L. humifusum (syn. *L. prostratum*)   Tasmania
A low growing, mat-forming shrub with red stems and white flowers. Early summer.

L. scoparium up to 10 ft (3 m)
Manuka   New Zealand
Evergreen shrub of erect habit with small white flowers and myrtle-like leaves. There are several good cultivars, including 'Keatley', with larger pale pink flowers and 'Nicholsii', rosy-crimson. Early summer.

LETTUCE – see Kitchen Garden

LEUCOJUM
(Amaryllidaceae) Snowflake
Hardy bulbous plants with snowdrop-like flowers which, according to species, bloom in early or late spring or in autumn.
Cultural requirements: Any ordinary garden soil in good heart, and a sunny or shady situation. They are useful subjects for the wild or woodland garden and can be naturalized in grass.
Propagation: By offsets in summer.

L. aestivum 2 ft (60 cm) Summer Snowflake
          Europe, including British Isles
In spite of its popular name, the 'summer snowflake' flowers in spring, producing its white bell-like flowers on tall stems, several to each stem. Spring.

L. autumnale 6 in. (15 cm)
Autumn Snowflake   S.W. Europe
This species has smaller white flowers, tinged

with pink which appear before the leaves. The autumn snowflake prefers a warm sunny situation. Autumn.

L. vernum 8 in. (20 cm)
Spring Snowflake   Europe
The bell-like flowers of this species are most like those of the snowdrop. They are pure white, edged with green. Early spring.

LEWISIA
(Portulaceae)

Hardy perennial, rosette-forming plants, suitable for the rock garden or alpine house.
Cultural requirements: Light well-drained soil and a sunny situation in the rock garden.
Propagation: From seed under glass or by division, in spring.

L. brachycalyx 3 in. (8 cm)   W. U.S.A.
Fleshy leaf rosettes and large white flowers. Late spring.

L. cotyledon 9 in. (22 cm)   California
Evergreen fleshy rosettes in clusters with small heads of pale pink flowers.

L. tweedyi 3 in. (8 cm)   S.E. U.S.A.
Clumps of fleshy oval leaves surmounted by pale pink flowers up to 2½ in. (6 cm) across. Summer.

LEYCESTERIA
(Caprifoliaceae)

Hardy deciduous flowering shrubs that do particularly well in seaside districts.
Cultural requirements: Any ordinary garden soil and a sunny or partly shaded situation. Should be cut back hard in spring.
Propagation: From seed under glass in gentle heat in spring; by cuttings in a cold frame or by division in autumn.

L. formosa 6 ft (2 m)
Himalayan Honeysuckle   Himalayas
Stout stems bearing terminal clusters of white flowers with crimson-purple bracts 1½ in. (4 cm) long, followed by purple berries. Mid to late summer.

LIATRIS
(Compositae) Gay Feather

Decorative hardy perennials with grassy foliage useful in the border. The flower spikes have an unusual habit of opening from the tops downwards.
Cultural requirements: Preferably light, fairly poor soil and a situation in full sun.
Propagation: From seed outdoors in summer; by division in spring.

L. pycnostachya 4 ft (1·2 m)   N. America
Dense spikes of showy crimson-purple flowers. Summer.

L. spicata 3 ft (1 m)   N. America
Tall feathery spikes of rosy-mauve flowers. A useful border plant. Summer.

LIBOCEDRUS
(Pinaceae)

A small genus of evergreen conifers, not all of which are hardy enough for outdoor cultivation in colder districts.
Cultural requirements: Any well-drained soil and a sheltered situation for the more tender species.
Propagation: From seed under glass in autumn; by cuttings with a heel in late summer.

L. decurrens (syn. *Calocedrus decurrens*)
100 ft (30 m) Incense Cedar   W. America
This species is completely hardy and makes a densely clothed slender column of great architectural beauty, whether planted singly or in groups. Not suitable for smaller gardens.

LIGULARIA
(Compositae)

Handsome hardy perennials for waterside planting or moist situations, formerly included in genus *Senecio*.
Cultural requirements: Loamy soil and a moist partly shaded situation.
Propagation: From seed in summer; by division in spring or autumn.

L. dentata (syn. *L. clivorum*)
4 ft (1·2 m)   China and Japan
Magnificent plants with handsome heart-shaped leaves and large loose heads of orange daisy flowers. 'Desdemona' and 'Othello' have leaves suffused with purple; 'Gregynog Gold' has golden flowers with a bronze centre.

LIGUSTRUM
(Oleaceae) Privet

Evergreen or semi-evergreen shrubs widely used as hedging subjects.
Cultural requirements: Any ordinary garden soil and an open or shady situation.
Propagation: From cuttings under glass in summer, outdoors in autumn.

L. delavayanum (syn. *L. ionandrum*)
10 ft (3 m)   Yunnan
Evergreen shrub with small leaves and white flowers followed by black berries. Preferable to common privet for hedging in milder districts. Summer.

L. ovalifolium 10 ft (3 m)
Oval Leaved Privet   Japan
This species is the one most commonly used for garden hedging. It is evergreen in all but the coldest districts. It clips well to form a neat hedge

Lilium auratum

but, left unpruned, will exceed the height stated above. 'Aureum' is the attractive golden-leaved form.

L. vulgare 10 ft (3 m)
Common Privet   Europe, including British Isles
Semi-evergreen species, native to the hedgerows and woods of Britain. The white flowers are followed by clusters of shining black fruits in autumn.

LILAC – see *Syringa*

LILIUM
(Liliaceae)

An extensive family of hardy and half-hardy bulbous plants. The different species show wide variations in colour and form, from perfect trumpet flowers to others, like the turkscap lilies whose petals are recurved. Many have a rich fragrance.

Cultural requirements: Good drainage is of vital importance to all species and preferably a peaty soil rich in humus. Many are lime-haters, but the following can be successfully cultivated in mildly alkaline soils – *L. regale*, *L. candidum*, *L. martagon*, *L. henryi*, *L. chalcedonicum*, *L. croceum*, *L. testaceum*, and *L. umbellatum*. That most popular of lilies, *L. auratum*, is intolerant of lime, but any of the lime-haters can be successfully grown in tubs or pots containing a suitable lime-free compost.

Propagation: From seed sown as soon as it ripens or from offset bulblets or stem bulbils.

L. auratum 6 ft (2 m)
Golden-rayed Lily of Japan   Japan
One of the loveliest of lilies with large satin-white open trumpet flowers, rayed with crimson or gold, six or eight to a stem and intensely fragrant. Late summer.

L. candidum up to 5 ft (1·5 m)
Madonna Lily   E. Mediterranean
One of the loveliest and best known lilies cultivated as a garden plant since time immemorial. The flowers are white with conspicuous golden stamens. Unlike most other lilies, which require deep planting, *L. candidum* should be planted with the nose of the bulb just below soil level. It is very lime-tolerant. Summer.

L. hansonii up to 5 ft (1·5 m)   Korea
The golden-yellow, waxen-textured flowers of this species have attractively recurved petals. It prefers a partly shaded situation. Summer.

L. henryi up to 8 ft (2·5 m)   China
Turkscap-type flowers of bright orange, many to a stem. Vigorous grower. Late summer.

L. martagon 6 ft (2 m)
Turkscap Lily   Europe and N. Asia
Free flowering vigorous lily of easy cultivation often naturalizing itself if conditions are to its liking. Flowers vary in colour from pale purple to deep mahogany. Summer.

L. pardalinum 8 ft (2·5 m)
Leopard Lily   W. N. America
Turkscap flowers of crimson and orange, very easy to grow; likes moist soil conditions. Summer.

L. regale 5 ft (1·5 m) Regal Lily   China
One of the loveliest and most easily grown lilies. Flowers white, of a satiny texture, with yellow throat and maroon-tinged outside, up to eight on a stem. Will tolerate lime and is easy to raise from seed. Summer.

L. speciosum 5 ft (1·5 m)   China and Japan
A lovely lily, very similar in appearance to *L. auratum* and sharing its dislike of lime. White or pink flowers, spotted with crimson. Very free flowering. Late summer.

L. tigrinum 5 ft (1·5 m)
Tiger Lily   China and Japan
A showy orange turkscap lily; easy to grow, but susceptible to virus disease. Summer.

The above are the more popular and widely grown lily species, some of which have a number of forms or cultivars. There are also some superb hybrid strains, including 'Aurelian Hybrids', with widely flaring trumpet flowers in colours ranging from pale yellow through apricot to orange; 'Bellingham Hybrids', vigorous with brown and red turkscap flowers; and 'Parkmannii Hybrids', with fine strains such as 'Imperial Crimson', 'Pink Glory', and many others.

LILY – see *Lilium*

LILY-OF-THE-VALLEY
– see *Convallaria majalis*

LIME TREE – see *Tilia*

LIMNANTHES
(Limnanthaceae)

Dwarf hardy annuals useful as edging plants and in the rock garden.

Cultural requirements: Any ordinary garden soil and a sunny situation.

Propagation: From seed outdoors in spring, where plants are to flower, or in early autumn for an early display the following year.

L. douglasii 6 in. (15 cm)
Poached Egg Plant   California
The flowers get their popular name from their conspicuous yellow centres and white surrounds. If left undisturbed plants will seed themselves freely. Summer.

LIMONIUM
(Plumbaginaceae)

Hardy and half-hardy biennials and perennials, usually treated as half-hardy annuals. Formerly known as 'Statice'. The 'everlasting' flowers dry well.

Cultural requirements: Light sandy soil and a sunny situation.

Propagation: From seed sown under glass in gentle heat in spring.

L. bonduellii 1 ft (30 cm)   Algeria
Annual species with papery yellow flowers, useful in the border. Summer.

L. latifolium 3 ft (1 m)   Bulgaria
Large panicles of lavender-blue flowers that dry well. 'Grandiflorum' is an improvement on the type. Summer.

L. sinuatum 2 ft (60 cm)   Mediterranean
A perennial species treated as a half-hardy annual. In addition to the blue and cream forms there are several colourful strains that include pinks, yellows, and deeper blues. Late summer.

L. suworowii 1½ ft (45 cm)   Turkestan
Long spikes of lilac or pink flowers, of great value in flower arrangements. Summer.

Limonium Annual Mixed (Statice)

LINARIA
(Scrophulariaceae) Toadflax

Hardy annual and perennial plants, dwarf in character and useful in the rock garden and on walls and banks.

Cultural requirements: Any ordinary well-drained soil and a sunny situation.

Propagation: From seed, sown where plants are to flower.

L. maroccana up to 1 ft (30 cm)   Morocco
The type plant has purple flowers, marked with yellow, like those of a miniature snapdragon. There are a number of hybrids and more colourful strains, including 'Excelsior Hybrids' and 'Fairy Bouquet'. Summer.

L. purpurea 3 ft (1 m)   S. Europe
A perennial species that makes a good wall plant. The bluish-purple flowers are borne in long spikes. 'Canon J. Went' is a cultivar with attractive rose-pink flowers. Late summer to early autumn.

LING – see *Calluna vulgaris*

LINUM
(Linaceae) Flax

Hardy annuals and perennials with a variety of garden uses, including the rock garden.

Cultural requirements: Any ordinary garden soil and a sunny situation.

Linaria Fairy Bouquet

Propagation: Perennial species: From seed sown outdoors in spring or by division.

Annual species: From seed sown in spring where plants are to flower.

L. alpinum 6 in. (15 cm)   Europe
A dwarf perennial species with blue flowers, useful in the rock garden. Summer.

L. grandiflorum 2 ft (60 cm)
Scarlet Flax   Algeria
Easy to grow free flowering annuals. 'Rubrum' has flowers of a striking scarlet; and 'Album' has white flowers with crimson centres. Summer.

L. narbonense 2 ft (60 cm)   S. Europe
A perennial species with fine deep blue flowers. Early to late summer.

LIPPIA
(Verbenaceae)
Tender deciduous shrubs of which *L. citriodora* is the only species in common cultivation.
Cultural requirements: A warm south wall in milder districts or the protection of a cool greenhouse in less favoured areas.
Propagation: From cuttings under glass in heat in spring or summer.

L. citriodora (syn. *Aloysia citriodora*) up to
15 ft (4.5 m) Lemon-scented Verbena   Chile
Medium-sized shrub with aromatic lemon-scented foliage and small inconspicuous purple flowers. Late summer.

LIQUIDAMBAR
(Hamamelidaceae)
Hardy deciduous trees with maple-like foliage, noteworthy for their striking autumn colouring.
Cultural requirements: Deep, moist, loamy soil and a fairly sheltered situation.
Propagation: From seed outdoors in autumn or spring; by layering in spring.

L. styraciflua 100 ft (30 m)
Sweet Gum   E. U.S.A.
Large tree, ideal as a specimen on sheltered lawns in larger gardens where its handsome lobed leaves will provide a magnificent display of brilliant autumn colour.

LIRIODENDRON
(Magnoliaceae)
Flowering deciduous trees of great beauty and outstanding architectural form. Very fast growing and too large for the smaller garden.
Cultural requirements: Rich fertile soil and a fairly sheltered situation.
Propagation: From seed outdoors in autumn; by layers in spring.

L. tulipifera up to 100 ft (30 m)
Tulip Tree   N. America
A magnificent specimen tree, with curious leaves that have the appearance of having been cut off flat at their tips with scissors. The green and yellow tulip-like flowers are not borne until the tree is reaching maturity.

There are several named cultivars, including 'Aureomarginatum', leaves edged with yellow and 'Fastigiatum', of upright columnar habit. Summer.

LIRIOPE
(Liliaceae)
Hardy evergreen perennials with grass-like foliage.
Cultural requirements: Sandy well-drained soil and an open situation.
Propagation: By division in spring.

L. platyphylla (syn. *L. muscari*)
1½ ft (45 cm)   China
Evergreen grassy foliage in dense tufts and spikes of purple flowers, similar to those of a grape hyacinth. Autumn.

L. spicata (Prostrate)   China
A creeping species with pale lilac flowers. Autumn.

LITHOPS
(Aizoaceae) Living Stones
Evergreen greenhouse succulents whose popular name is derived from their resemblance to rounded stones or pebbles.
Cultural requirements: John Innes No. 2 or similar compost with the addition of crushed brick, mortar rubble or grit. The plants do best on a sunny greenhouse shelf or window-ledge indoors. Water should be withheld when plants are dormant. Minimum winter temperature 40 °F (4 °C).
Propagation: From seed under glass in heat, in spring or autumn.

L. lesliei 3 in. (8 cm)   S.W. Africa
Yellow daisy-like flowers. Autumn.

L. olivacea 3 in. (8 cm)   S.W. Africa
Olive-green 'stones' with yellow flowers. Autumn.

LITHOSPERMUM
(Boraginaceae) Gromwell
Dwarf prostrate flowering evergreen shrubs or sub-shrubs, some of which are on the tender side.
Cultural requirements: Sandy or light soil.
L. diffusum is a lime-hater.
Propagation: From seed in a cold frame in spring; by cuttings or layers in early autumn.

Lobelia String of Pearls Mixed

Propagation: Hardy perennials: From seed in a cold frame in autumn or in gentle heat in spring; by cuttings under glass or by division in spring.

Half-hardy kinds: From seed sown under glass in heat in early spring to provide plants to go out in early summer after hardening off.

L. cardinalis 3 ft (1 m)
Cardinal Flower   N. America
The type plant has green leaves and vivid scarlet flowers. The named cultivars are hybrids with *L. syphilitica* and *L. fulgens* as part of their parentage. They include 'Bees' Flame', brilliant scarlet; 'Purple Emperor', purple; 'Queen Victoria', scarlet, with beetroot-red foliage; and 'Russian Princess', salmon-pink. Summer.

L. erinus 6 in. (15 cm)   S. Africa
Half-hardy perennials, treated as half-hardy annuals, the popular blue lobelia is a favourite plant for summer bedding schemes, in which it is often associated with white alyssum. It is also useful in baskets and window-boxes. Seedsmen offer a host of named forms and strains including trailing varieties especially suited for baskets or window-boxes. 'Cambridge Blue' and the deeper violet-blue 'Mrs Clibran' are two of the most popular. 'Rosamond' has flowers of an unusual wine-red with a white eye. Summer.

L. diffusum 6 in. (15 cm)   S. Europe
Carpeting sub-shrubs that make good ground cover in rock garden; also excellent as wall plants. Gentian-blue tubular flowers are very striking. Good forms include 'Album', white; 'Grace Ward', larger blue flowers than the type; and 'Heavenly Blue', an apt description of its colour. Late spring to midsummer.

L. oleifolium 6 in. (15 cm)   Pyrenees
Grey silky foliage provides an attractive setting for sapphire-blue tubular flowers which are borne over a long period. A sheltered situation is advisable. Summer to early autumn.

L. rosmarinifolium 1 ft (30 cm)   Italy
A slightly tender species with narrow linear foliage and bright blue flowers. In colder districts the protection of a cold greenhouse is necessary. Winter to early spring.

LOBELIA
(Campanulaceae)
Hardy and half-hardy perennials used in bedding and in the border.
Cultural requirements: Hardy perennials: Any garden soil in good heart and an open sunny situation.

Half-hardy kinds: Usually treated as half-hardy annuals, otherwise requirements are similar.

Lobelia Pendula Sapphire

Lonicera periclymenum 'Belgica'

LOBSTER CLAW PLANT
– see *Clianthus puniceus*

LONDON PRIDE – see *Saxifraga × urbium*

LONICERA
(Caprifoliaceae)

An extensive genus of deciduous and evergreen shrubs, many of which are twining climbers. The shrubby species are mainly noteworthy for the dense small-leaved evergreen *L. nitida* which, together with its cultivars, makes a first class hedging plant.

Cultural requirements: Any garden soil in good heart and a cool, moist, root run. The climbing species do well on a north or north-west aspect.

Propagation: From cuttings in a shaded frame in summer, by layering in autumn. *L. nitida* will take from cuttings inserted almost anywhere and at any time.

L. caprifolium up to 20 ft (6 m)
        C. and S. Europe, and Asia Minor
Vigorous twiner, with fragrant creamy-white trumpet flowers. An old and popular species. Summer.

L. japonica up to 30 ft (9 m)   China and Japan
A vigorous twining honeysuckle with long white fragrant flowers. An ideal species for covering unsightly objects such as drainpipes. 'Aureo-reticulata' is a lovely form with vivid green leaves netted with gold. 'Halliana' is one of the most sweetly scented honeysuckles but the flowers are somewhat inconspicuous.

L. nitida 6 ft (2 m)   China
An excellent evergreen hedging shrub, almost equal to box provided it is clipped regularly to prevent legginess at the base. There are several named clones of distinctive appearance. 'Baggessen's Gold' has yellow leaves that turn to a medley of scarlet and gold in autumn and winter; 'Fertilis', which is stronger growing than the type, is the best form for hedging.

L. periclymenum up to 20 ft (6 m)
Woodbine   Europe, including British Isles
The common honeysuckle of our native hedgerows and woods of which cultivars with more striking colouring have been developed. 'Belgica', the 'Early Dutch' honeysuckle has reddish-purple, sweetly scented flowers. Those of 'Serotina' the 'Late Dutch' are very similar, but do not appear until some weeks later than those of the former kind. Early summer to autumn.

L. pileata 5 ft (1·5 m)   China
This is an attractive small semi-evergreen shrub with branches arranged in flat tiers and with clusters of violet berries in autumn.

L. tragophylla 30 ft (9 m)   China
A showy and vigorous climbing species that does best in a shady situation. The flowers are a bright yellow and very striking, borne in large clusters. Summer.

LOOSESTRIFE – see *Lysimachia* and *Lythrum*

LOVE-IN-A-MIST – see *Nigella*

LOVE-LIES-BLEEDING
– see *Amaranthus caudatus*

LUNARIA
(Cruciferae)

Hardy biennials and perennials whose seedpods are used for decorative purposes.

Cultural requirements: Any ordinary garden soil and a shady situation.

Propagation: From seed outdoors in spring.

L. annua (syn. *L. biennis*) 2 ft (60 cm)
Honesty   Europe
The purple flowers of this biennial species are followed by flattened disc-like seedpods which, when their covering is removed, are silvery-white inside and extremely decorative. There are also white and pale lilac forms. Early summer.

L. rediviva 2 ft (60 cm)   Europe
A perennial species with sweetly scented purple flowers and less showy narrower seedpods. Summer.

LUNGWORT – see *Pulmonaria*

LUPIN – see *Lupinus*

LUPINUS
(Leguminosae)

Hardy perennials and annuals of great decorative value in the borders in early summer.

Cultural requirements: Any ordinary garden soil in good heart and a sunny or lightly shaded situation.

Propagation: Annual species: From seed sown outdoors in spring where plants are to flower.

Perennial species: From seed outdoors in spring to provide flowering plants for following season; from cuttings under glass in early spring.

L. arboreus 6 ft (2 m) Tree Lupin   California
Shrubby species with fragrant yellow flower spikes. 'Golden Spire', deep yellow and 'Snow Queen', white, are both good named forms. Early to late summer.

L. hartwegii up to 3 ft (1 m)   Mexico
Annual species with spikes of blue flowers marked with white. There are several named forms and strains, including the attractive dwarf forms and strains, such as the dwarf 'Pixie Strain' with colours ranging from white through pink, blue, and lavender. Late summer.

L. polyphyllus up to 6 ft (2 m)   California
The perennial species from which the popular garden strains and named cultivars and hybrids

Lupinus

Lychnis Mixed (Campion or Viscaria)

have been developed. The Russell strains with chunky colourful flower spikes are the best known and there are also numerous named cultivars. Early to midsummer.

LUZULA
(Juncaceae) Wood Rush
Hardy perennials with grass-like leaves.
Cultural requirements: Any ordinary garden soil and a sunny or partly shaded situation.
Propagation: From seed outdoors in late spring; by division in autumn.

L. nivea 2 in. (5 cm)   Europe
An attractive species with creamy-white heads of bloom. Summer.

L. sylvatica 2½ ft (75 cm)   Europe
Dense clumps of rush-like foliage and clusters of brown flowers. A good ground cover plant. Summer.

LYCHNIS
(Caryophyllaceae) Campion
Hardy perennials that make attractive and useful border plants.
Cultural requirements: Any ordinary garden soil in good heart and a sunny open situation.
Propagation: From seed sown outdoors in late spring; by division in spring or autumn.

L. chalcedonica 3 ft (1 m) Maltese Cross   Russia
Fiery scarlet heads of flower on tall stems. There are also pink and white forms. Summer.

L. coronaria 2 ft (60 cm)
Rose Campion   S. Europe
Silver-grey felted leaves and stems and velvety-crimson flowers. There is also a white cultivar, 'Alba'. Summer.

L. flos-jovis 1 ft (30 cm) Flower of Love   Europe
A plant of semi-prostrate habit with hairy leaves and pink campion flowers. Summer.

L. viscaria (syn. *Viscaria vulgaris*)
1½ ft (45 cm)   Europe
Rose-red flowers on branching stems and grassy foliage. 'Albiflora' is an interesting white form and there is a good rose-red double, 'Splendens Plena'. Summer.

LYRE FLOWER – see *Dicentra spectabilis*

LYSICHITUM
(Araceae) Skunk Cabbage
Hardy perennials for the waterside or bog garden. The unpleasant odour of their flowers is the reason for their common name.
Cultural requirements: Moist boggy soil and a sunny or lightly shaded situation.
Propagation: From seed outdoors in moist soil when ripe or by division in early spring.

L. americanum 1½ ft (45 cm)   Western N. America
Huge paddle-shaped leaves up to 3 ft (1 m) long and large yellow arum-like spathes 1½ ft (45 cm) long. Spring.

L. camtschatcense 1½ ft (45 cm)   Japan
A smaller species with erect white spathes, 6 in. (15 cm) long and glaucous leaves appearing after the flowers. Spring.

LYSIMACHIA
(Primulaceae)
Hardy perennials of vigorous and fast-spreading habit.
Cultural requirements: Any garden soil provided it remains moist in summer. A position by the pool or waterside suits them well.
Propagation: From seed outdoors in late spring or by division in spring or autumn.

L. clethroides 3 ft (1 m)   China and Japan
Long curving spikes of white flowers and fine leaf colouring in autumn. Late summer.

L. ephemerum 3 ft (1 m)   S.W. Europe
Erect spikes of white, purple-tinged flowers, grey-green lanceolate foliage. Summer.

L. nummularia 2 in. (5 cm) Creeping Jenny
            N. Europe, including British Isles
Prostrate creeping plant of vigorous habit and

rapid spread with buttercup-yellow cup-shaped flowers. Good ground cover plant. Summer.

L. punctata 3 ft (1 m)
Yellow Loosestrife   Asia Minor
Favourite border plant, of rapid spread with yellow flowers in whorls on tall stems. Summer.

LYTHRUM
(Lythraceae) Purple Loosestrife
Hardy perennials that make attractive plants for the border or waterside planting.
Cultural requirements: Any ordinary soil and

a partly shaded situation. Moist soil conditions.
Propagation: By division in spring or autumn.

L. salicaria
3 ft (1 m)   Europe, including British Isles
Reddish-purple flower spikes on tall erect stems. Named cultivars include 'Brightness', rose-red and 'The Beacon', rosy-purple. Summer.

L. virgatum 2½ ft (75 cm)   Europe
A more compact species with dainty spikes of purple flowers. 'Dropmore Purple', rosy-purple and 'Rose Queen', bright rose-red, are both good cultivars. Summer.

MACLEAYA
(Papaveraceae) Plume Poppy
Hardy perennials of commanding stature for the back of the border. Formerly known as *Bocconia*.
Cultural requirements: Rich loamy soil and an open sunny situation.
Propagation: From root cuttings or by division in spring.

M. cordata up to 8 ft (2·5 m)   China and Japan
Deeply lobed foliage, glaucous on upper surface, silvery-white on reverse. Feathery white flowers, borne in loose panicles. Summer.

MADWORT – see *Alyssum*

MAGNOLIA
(Magnoliaceae)
Hardy deciduous and evergreen flowering trees and shrubs of great beauty and value in the garden. They make magnificent lawn specimens and are ideal for focal positions.
Cultural requirements: A rich, friable, loamy soil and a sunny sheltered situation. Magnolias will not thrive in light, dry, sandy soils or in wet, heavy clays.
Propagation: From seed in a cold frame in spring or autumn; by layering in summer or autumn.

M. denudata up to 30 ft (9 m) Yulan   China
Deciduous shrub or small tree of great beauty. The scented white cup-shaped blossoms measure 5 in. (13 cm) across. Mid-spring.

M. grandiflora up to 20 ft (6 m)   S. U.S.A.
The finest and best known evergreen species with handsome polished dark green leaves, rust-brown

on their reverse. The scented creamy-white flowers can measure up to 10 in. (25 cm) across. They do not flower until between ten and fifteen years old with the exception of 'Exmouth' and 'Goliath' which usually produce their blooms a few years earlier. In colder districts, *M. grandiflora* should be given the shelter of a south or west wall. Summer.

M. liliflora 10 ft (3 m)   China and Japan
Spreading shrub of medium size with creamy-white blossoms flushed with maroon outside. An excellent species for smaller gardens. 'Nigra' is a cultivar with flowers of a deeper purple. Late spring to early summer.

M. × *soulangeana* (*M. denudata* × *M. liliiflora*)
20 ft (6 m)   Garden origin
Beautiful and popular deciduous hybrid magnolias which flower when still quite young. The waxen-petalled flowers, like large tulips, are massed on the branches before the leaves appear. Will tolerate town and industrial conditions, but is averse to alkaline soils. There are several named cultivars in which the shape and colouring of the flowers vary from those of the type. Late spring.

M. stellata 10 ft (3 m) Star Magnolia   Japan
One of the loveliest of the deciduous magnolias compact enough for the smallest garden. The white flowers, star-shaped with overlapping strap-like petals, appear in advance of the leaves. 'Rosea' is a form whose flowers are flushed with pink. Early spring.

M. wilsonii 15 ft (4·5 m)   China
A lovely deciduous species of spreading habit with pendent white flowers and prominent crimson stamens. Early summer.

Magnolia × *soulangeana* 'Lennei'

MAHONIA
(Berberidaceae)

Valuable hardy evergreen shrubs, closely related to the barberries and formerly included in that genus. The foliage is pinnate with prickly holly-like compound leaves.

Cultural requirements: Any ordinary fertile garden soil and a sunny or shady situation.

Propagation: From seed under glass in summer; by suckers, layers, or cuttings.

M. aquifolium 3 ft (1 m)   N. America
One of the best of all shrubs for dense shade and an excellent ground cover plant under trees. Golden-yellow flower spikes are followed by purple berries which make a palatable preserve. Spring.

M. bealei 5 ft (1·5 m)   China
Often confused with *M. japonica*, but less striking, with shorter flower spikes. Late autumn.

M. japonica 5 ft (1·5 m)   China
One of the loveliest evergreen shrubs in cultivation with bold leathery dark green holly-like foliage and long racemes of butter-yellow, lily-of-the-valley scented flowers. It prefers a position in partial shade and makes a good tub plant. Early spring.

  'Charity', an elegant shrub with long pinnate leaves and bright yellow flowers, is a good hybrid cultivar, the other parent being *M. lomariifolia*.

M. lomariifolia 8 ft (2·5 m)   China
A handsome shrub, too tender for colder districts. The leaves are even more distinctive than those of the other species, being made up of fifteen or more leaflets. The flowers are deep yellow, borne on erect spikes. Winter.

MAIDENHAIR FERN – see *Adiantum*

MAIDENHAIR TREE – see *Ginkgo biloba*

MALCOLMIA
(Cruciferae)

Hardy annuals that make useful edging plants.

Cultural requirements: Any ordinary garden soil and a sunny situation.

Propagation: From seed outdoors in spring where plants are to flower.

M. maritima 6 in. (15 cm)
Virginian Stock   S. Europe
Colourful edging plants, seed of which is obtainable either in a mixture of colours which includes red, mauve, yellow, and white, or in separate colours. Summer.

MALE FERN – see *Dryopteris filix-mas*

MALLOW – see *Lavatera*, *Malope*, and *Malva*

MALOPE
(Malvaceae)

Hardy annuals, useful in the border and for cutting.

Cultural requirements: Any good garden soil and a sunny situation.

Propagation: From seed outdoors in spring where plants are to grow.

M. trifida 3 ft (1 m)   Mediterranean
Sturdy annuals with striking trumpet flowers of rosy-purple. There are also forms with white, rose, and crimson flowers. Summer.

MALUS
(Rosaceae)

Deciduous trees, formerly classified under *Pyrus* and including apples (see Fruit Garden). The flowering crabs are one of the glories of the garden in late spring, and are mainly of a size suitable for the smaller garden. Many are grown for the decorative value of their fruits in winter.

Cultural requirements: Any ordinary garden soil in good heart and a sunny open situation.

Propagation: Normally by grafting, but can also be raised from seed sown outdoors in March.

M. floribunda 20 ft (6 m) Japanese Crab   Japan
One of the loveliest of all flowering trees, *M. floribunda* makes an umbrella-shaped head with dense twiggy stems and branches that are smothered in white blossom, pink in bud. 'Atrosanguinea' is a form with deeper coloured flowers. Late spring.

M. × lemoinei 25 ft (8 m)   Garden origin
An outstandingly beautiful hybrid with coppery foliage and deep wine-red flowers.

Other first class members of the same group are 'Aldenhamensis', with bronzed foliage and purple flowers; 'Profusion', a splendid ornamental tree that flowers later than 'Lemoinei'; and 'Wisley Crab', a cultivar with wine-red flowers followed by large purple fruits. Late spring.

M. pumila
up to 30 ft (9 m) Europe, including British Isles
This is the wild crab-apple, sometimes known as *M. sylvestris*. Cultivars of this species provide the finest fruits for decorative effect and for crab-apple jelly. They include 'Golden Hornet', with striking yellow pear-shaped fruits. 'Montreal Beauty', with pink-tinged flowers and orange-scarlet fruits; and the popular 'John Downie', whose rosy-cheeked crab-apples are the best of all for preserves. Late spring.

M. × purpurea 30 ft (9 m)   Garden origin
A lovely hybrid with crimson flowers and purple-tinged foliage. Bushy-headed, with arching habit. Early spring.

There are also a number of excellent named hybrid cultivars including 'Almey', with red flowers and orange-red fruits; 'Dartmouth', a good variety for preserves; 'Eleyi', deep wine-purple foliage and flowers; 'Jay Darling', very showy with large wine-red flowers; and 'Simcoe', an introduction from Canada with coppery young foliage and purple-pink flowers.

MALVA
(Malvaceae) Mallow

Hardy perennials that make good plants for the middle of the border.

Cultural requirements: Any good garden soil and a sunny situation.

Propagation: From seed under glass in spring; by cuttings in a cold frame in late summer or division in spring.

M. alcea 3 ft (1 m)   Europe
Satiny rose-pink flowers and dainty foliage. 'Fastigiata', a slightly taller form, has flowers of a deeper colour. Midsummer to autumn.

MAMMILARIA
(Cactaceae) Nipple Cactus

Greenhouse succulents with cylindrical or globular stems covered with small spiny excrescences. The flowers are evanescent, lasting only a few hours.

Cultural requirements: John Innes No. 2 or similar compost with the addition of crushed

Malcolmia maritima (Virginian Stock)

brick, mortar rubble or grit. Water sparingly in summer and autumn, withholding water entirely in winter. Minimum winter temperature 50 °F (10 °C).

Propagation: From seed under glass in heat in spring; by cuttings or offsets.

M. compressa up to 8 in. (20 cm)   Mexico
Pinkish-purple flowers. Summer.

M. echinaria 6 in. (15 cm)   Mexico
Rose-pink flowers. Summer.

M. sempervivi 3 in. (8 cm)   Mexico
White flowers marked with red. Summer.

M. uncinata 4 in. (10 cm)   Mexico
Rounded pinkish-purple flowers. Summer.

MANURE – see Fertilizers

MAPLE – see *Acer*

MARANTA
(Marantaceae)

Evergreen perennials for the warm greenhouse, grown for their decorative foliage. They also make good house plants.

Cultural requirements: Rich well-drained compost and a moist shady situation. Minimum winter temperature 55 °F (12 °C).

Propagation: By division in spring.

M. arundinacea up to 4 ft (1·2 m)
Arrowroot   Tropical America
The form with variegated leaves is the best for greenhouse cultivation.

M. bicolor 1 ft (30 cm)   Brazil
Species with handsome olive-green foliage.

M. leuconeura 1 ft (30 cm)   Brazil
This, the most widely grown species, has pale green leaves with white and purple markings.

MARIGOLD – see *Calendula* and *Tagetes*

MARJORAM – see Herb Garden

MARSH MARIGOLD – see *Caltha palustris*

MATRICARIA
(Compositae) Feverfew

Hardy and half-hardy annuals and perennials with finely cut foliage and yellow flowers.

Cultural requirements: Any ordinary garden soil and an open sunny situation.

Propagation: Annual species: From seed under glass in spring.

    Perennial kinds: By cuttings or division in spring.

Matthiola bicornis (Night-scented Stock)

M. eximea (syn. *Chrysanthemum parthenium*)
1 ft (30 cm)   Europe
A short lived hardy perennial with deeply lobed foliage and masses of golden or white daisy flowers. The dwarf kinds make useful edging plants for summer bedding. 'Snow Ball' and 'Golden Ball' are recommended cultivars. Summer.

MATTEUCCIA
(Aspidiaceae)

Tall ferns with plumy foliage and an elegant outline.

Cultural requirements: Deep rich soil and a partly shaded moist situation.

Propagation: From ripe spores under glass; by division in spring.

M. struthiopteris up to 5 ft (1·5 m)
Ostrich Fern   Europe
A handsome fern with ostrich-plume-like foliage and an elegant vase-like shape. It makes a magnificent architectural plant for the wild or woodland garden or for the margins of a shady pool.

MATTHIOLA
(Cruciferae) Stock

Hardy and half-hardy annuals and biennials long popular in the garden for flowers and fragrance.
Cultural requirements: Rich deep soil with plenty of humus or well-rotted manure. Open sunny situation.
Propagation: Annual cultivars: Ten-week, bedding, and ordinary stocks; from seed under glass in spring to produce plants to go out in late spring. Sowings can also be made outdoors later, where plants are to flower.

Biennial stocks: Brompton and East Lothian stocks. Sow outdoors in summer to produce plants to flower the following spring.

M. bicornis 1 ft (30 cm)
Night-scented Stock   Greece
Old cottage favourite hardy annual with lilac flowers that distil their fullest fragrance on warm summer evenings. Sow seed outdoors in spring where plants are to flower. Summer.

M. incana up to 2 ft (60 cm)
Brompton Stock   S. Europe
Biennial species that is useful for early spring colour or as winter flowering greenhouse plants. The single and double flowers are very fragrant.

The popular summer bedding ten-week stock is a form of this species, grown as an annual. There are now various strains of seed from which 100% doubles are obtainable by retaining seed-lings with pale green leaves and removing those that are dark green.
Brompton stocks: Early to late spring.
Ten-week stocks: Summer.

MAY – see *Crataegus oxycantha*

MEADOW RUE – see *Thalictrum*

MECONOPSIS
(Papaveraceae)

Hardy perennials and biennials. Many of the first named are actually monocarpic, i.e. they form a rosette of leaves, flower when two to four years old and then die.
Cultural requirements: Moist rich soil and a partly shaded situation.
Propagation: From seed sown under glass when ripe or in early spring.

M. betonicifolia (syn. *M. baileyi*) up to 5 ft (1·5 m)
Himalayan Blue Poppy   Tibet
Sky-blue poppy flowers 2 in. (5 cm) in diameter with striking golden anthers. The leaves are hairy. Perennial. Early summer.

M. cambrica 1½ ft (45 cm)
Welsh Poppy   Europe, including British Isles
A charming little plant with yellow or pale orange-red flowers that will quickly naturalize itself if left undisturbed. The form 'Plena' has large semi-double flowers. Perennial. Early to midsummer.

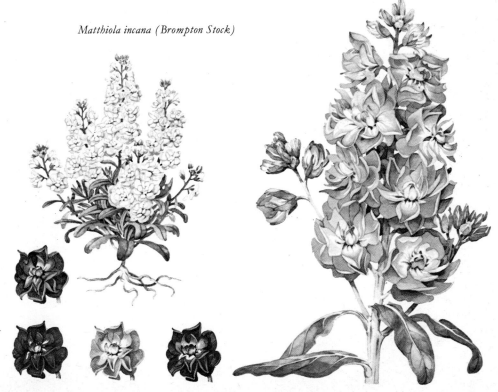

Matthiola incana (Brompton Stock)

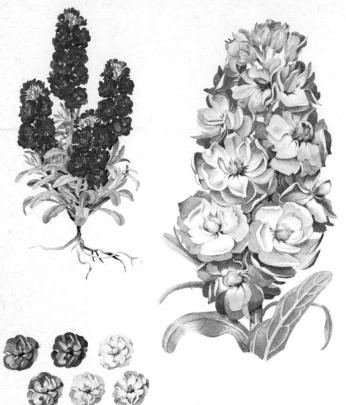

Matthiola (Ten-week Stock)

M. officinalis
3 ft (1 m)   Europe, including British Isles
Grown for its lemon-scented foliage that is used for flavouring and in pot-pourri, the yellow or white flowers are of secondary importance. Summer.

MENTHA
(Labiatae) – see also Herb Garden
Hardy perennials grown for their culinary uses and for their aromatic oils. The prostrate forms make useful plants for walls, paving, and the rock garden.
Cultural requirements: Moist soil and sunny or partly shaded situation.
Propagation: By division in autumn or spring.

M. × piperita 2 ft (60 cm)
Peppermint   Europe, including British Isles
Grown for its aromatic foliage. The flowers are purple. Late summer.

M. pulegium 6 in. (15 cm) Pennyroyal   W. Asia
An aromatic carpeting plant, useful on walls or in paving.

M. requienii 3 in. (8 cm)
Corsican Mint   Europe, including British Isles
An even more dwarf prostrate species than the above, *M. requienii* does not mind being walked on which makes it an ideal carpeting plant for growing in paving. The foliage is very aromatic.

M. rotundifolia 2 ft (60 cm)
Apple Mint   Europe, including British Isles
A taller mint with rounded hairy leaves, considered by many to be the best kind for mint sauce. The form 'Variegata' has foliage attractively variegated with creamy-white.

M. viridis (syn. *M. spicata*) 2 ft (60 cm)
Spearmint   Europe, including British Isles
The dark green pointed leaves of this species are widely used with new potatoes and peas. They also make a good mint sauce.

M. grandis 3 ft (1 m)   Tibet
Another Tibetan species similar to *M. betonicifolia*. The flowers are bluish-purple in bud, opening to deep blue; 'Branklyn' is a cultivar with gentian-blue flowers. Perennial. Early summer.

M. integrifolia 6 in. (15 cm)   Tibet
The rosettes of hairy leaves are golden and are averse to wet conditions in winter. The cup-shaped blooms are yellow. A monocarpic species. Summer.

M. regia 5 ft (1·5 m)   Nepal
Noteworthy for its attractive silver or gold winter rosettes. Bears yellow flowers on branching stems. Also monocarpic. Midsummer.

MELISSA
(Labiatae) Lemon Balm
Hardy perennial plants, often found in the herb garden but worthy of a place in the border by reason of their attractive lacy foliage.
Cultural requirements: Fairly light soil and a sunny open situation.
Propagation: From seed outdoors in spring; by division in spring or autumn.

MENTZELIA
(Loasaceae)
Hardy annuals with brilliant yellow flowers that make a magnificent display.
Cultural requirements: Any ordinary garden soil and a sunny situation.
Propagation: From seed outdoors in late spring.

M. lindleyi (syn. *Bartonia aurea*)
1 ft (30 cm)   California
Very conspicuous golden-yellow flowers with feathery stamens like those of the St John's Worts. Summer.

MERTENSIA
(Boraginaceae)

Hardy perennials, members of the borage family. Useful in the woodland garden.

Cultural requirements: Sandy peat or light rich loam and a partly shaded situation.

Propagation: From seed in a cold frame in autumn; by division in spring or autumn.

M. ciliata 2 ft (60 cm)   N. America
Glaucous foliage and blue campanulate flowers in clusters. Early summer.

M. virginica 1½ ft (45 cm)
Virginian Cowslip   U.S.A.
Blue-grey lanceolate leaves up to 6 in. (15 cm) long set off the drooping panicles of pale blue flowers to perfection. Early summer.

MESEMBRYANTHEMUM
(Aizoaceae)

Tender and half-hardy annuals that can be planted out in sunny borders in summer.

Cultural requirements: Sandy or medium soil and a sunny situation.

Propagation: From seed or from cuttings under glass in heat in spring.

M. criniflorum 3 in. (8 cm)
Livingstone Daisy   S. Africa
A colourful and vigorous half-hardy annual whose daisy flowers will brighten sunny banks or the rock garden over a very long period. A good seaside plant. Summer to autumn.

METASEQUOIA
(Taxodiaceae)

One of the two so-called fossil trees – *Ginkgo biloba* is the other – remains of which have been found in deposits from the carboniferous age. It is a monotypic genus and is deciduous, similar in appearance to the swamp cypress (*Taxodium distichum*).

Cultural requirements: Moist well-drained soil conditions.

Propagation: From seed outdoors in spring or early summer.

M. glyptostroboides up to 40 ft (12 m)   China
A vigorous deciduous conifer with linear feathery foliage that colours to an attractive cinnamon-brown in autumn.

MEXICAN ORANGE FLOWER
– see *Choisya ternata*

MICHAELMAS DAISY – see *Aster*

MIGNONETTE – see *Reseda odorata*

MILDEW – see Diseases

Mesembryanthemum criniflorum Mixed (Livingstone Daisy)

MILFOIL – see *Achillea*

MILLIPEDES – see Pest Control

MIMOSA
(Leguminosae)

Perennials for a warm greenhouse, best treated as half-hardy annuals. The popular spring flower mimosa is actually *Acacia dealbata* q.v.

Cultural requirements: John Innes No. 2 or similar potting compost. Water plants freely in summer, sparingly for rest of year.

Propagation: From seed under glass in heat in spring.

M. pudica 1½ ft (45 cm)   Brazil
Rose-pink flowers and feathery foliage that shrinks away when touched and is responsible for this plant's popular name 'Sensitive Plant'. Summer.

MIMULUS
(Scrophulariaceae) Monkey Flower

Hardy perennials, often treated as half-hardy annuals for use as summer bedding plants.

Cultural requirements: Any ordinary garden soil and a moist shady situation.

Propagation: From seed under glass in heat in early spring; by division in spring.

M. cardinalis 2 ft (60 cm)   N. America
Showy scarlet flowers freely borne over a long period. Summer.

M. guttatus 1½ ft (45 cm)   N. America
Bright yellow flowers spotted with purple. Spring to summer.

M. luteus 1½ ft (45 cm)   Chile
Bright yellow flowers and polished green foliage. An excellent waterside plant. Spring to summer.

MIND-YOUR-OWN-BUSINESS
– see *Helxine*

MINT – see *Mentha* and Herb Garden

MISCANTHUS
(Gramineae)
Tall clump-forming perennial grasses, useful as focal plants in the border.
Cultural requirements: Any ordinary garden soil and a sunny situation.
Propagation: By division of clumps in spring.

M. sacchariflorus up to 8 ft (2·5 m)   Japan
Elegant tall grass with narrow grey-green leaves. There is a slightly shorter variety, 'Aureus', with gold-striped leaves.

M. sinensis (syn. *Eulalia japonica*)
6 ft (2 m)   China and Japan
Dense erect clumps of tall stems bearing silver-green leaves with a central stripe of white. 'Variegatus' has a creamy-white stripe; 'Zebrinus' has leaves transversely banded with golden-yellow.

MOCK ORANGE – see *Philadelphus*

MOLUCELLA
(Labiatae)
Half-hardy annuals, with flowers that dry well.
Cultural requirements: Sandy or light soils and a sunny situation.
Propagation: From seed under glass in heat in spring or later outdoors where plants are to flower.

M. laevis 2 ft (60 cm) Bells of Ireland   Syria
The small white flowers, surrounded by shell-like green calyces, dry well for winter arrangements. Summer.

MONARDA
(Labiatae)
Hardy perennials with aromatic foliage.
Cultural requirements: Any ordinary garden soil and a sunny or partly shaded situation.

Propagation: From seed outdoors, by root division, in spring.

M. didyma 3 ft (1 m)
Bergamot or Bee Balm   N. America
Scarlet spidery flowers and coarse hairy foliage with a distinctive aroma when crushed. There are several good named cultivars, including 'Cambridge Scarlet', 'Croftway Pink', and 'Snow Maiden', whose names are all descriptive of their colour. Summer.

MONEYWORT – see *Lysimachia nummularia*

MONKEY FLOWER – see *Mimulus*

MONKEY PUZZLE – see *Araucaria*

MONKSHOOD – see *Aconitum*

MONOTYPIC
A group of plants that contains only one species.

MONSTERA
(Araceae)
Handsome climbing plants for the warm greenhouse that also make good house plants. The distinctive dark green glossy foliage, perforated when mature, with large irregularly shaped holes, is responsible for their popular name of 'Swiss Cheese Plant'.
Cultural requirements: John Innes No. 2 or similar compost. Minimum winter temperature 50 °F (10 °C).
Propagation: By stem cuttings under glass in heat.

M. deliciosa up to 10 ft (3 m) Tropical S. America
Large heart-shaped perforated leaves up to 2 ft (60 cm) or more in length. The yellowish-white flowering spathes are short lived and not particularly attractive. Early summer.

MONTBRETIA – see *Crocosmia* and *Tritonia*

MORINA
(Dipsaceae)
Hardy perennials whose tall flower spikes are attractive in the border and also dry well.
Cultural requirements: Light sandy soil and moist, partly shaded situation.
Propagation: From seed in a cold frame; by division in autumn.

M. longifolia 3 ft (1 m)   Himalayas
Large thistle-like leaves and erect spikes of white flowers that open to pink. The dried seedheads are very decorative. Summer.

MORNING GLORY – see *Ipomoea*

MORUS
(Moraceae) Mulberry

Attractive deciduous trees of medium size, grown as much for their decorative value as for their fruits. The leaves are used to feed silkworms. They make good lawn specimens.

Cultural requirements: Any ordinary garden soil, provided it is well drained and a sunny sheltered situation.

Propagation: From hardwood cuttings in a shady sheltered border outdoors or from layers, in autumn.

M. alba 40 ft (12 m)   China
Medium-sized tree with large heart-shaped leaves. The edible fruits are white changing to pink as they ripen.

M. nigra 30 ft (9 m) Black Mulberry   W. Asia
Long-lived trees of medium size, specimens reputed to be 300 or more years old still in existence in Britain. The blackish-crimson fruits are acid but palatable.

MOSS – see Lawns

MOSS ROSE – see *Rosa centifolia muscosa*

MOTHER OF THOUSANDS
– see House Plants

MOULD – see Diseases

MOUNTAIN ASH – see *Sorbus*

MOWERS – see Lawns

MUEHLENBECKIA
(Polygonaceae)

Slightly tender deciduous climbing or creeping plants of which *M. complexa* is the only species in common cultivation.

Cultural requirements: Any ordinary garden soil and a sunny sheltered situation.

Propagation: From cuttings in a cold frame in late summer; by seeds or division in spring.

M. complexa 15 ft (4·5 m)
Wire Vine   New Zealand
Twining plant with a tangle of fine stems that is equally useful on walls or scrambling over banks. The flowers are inconspicuous and are followed by small white fruits on female plants.

MULBERRY – see *Morus*

MULCHING

During the hot dry periods in summer, many garden plants appreciate regular mulching. This is one of the best ways of conserving soil moisture, but it is not its only virtue. Mulching can also be a great labour saver. Properly applied, mulches can cut down the summer chores of weeding and hoeing to a minimum. Later, the materials used will rot down and become assimilated in the soil, increasing its humus content and improving its texture.

To keep the soil in a moist condition and to prevent undue losses from evaporation, mulches should be applied as early on as possible in a dry spell. If dry weather persists, they should be renewed at intervals of about three weeks. In periods of severe drought, it may be necessary to water occasionally. When this is the case, the mulch should be drawn away from the base of the plants before water is applied.

There are many different materials suitable for use as a summer mulch. One of the finest of these is leafmould or partly rotted leaves. These have excellent moisture retaining properties and are almost completely free from the seeds of common garden weeds. They make an especially valuable mulch for lime-hating plants such as rhododendrons, azaleas, and heathers.

Bark fibre and shredded or moss peat are relatively inexpensive to buy in bulk, are clean to handle and completely sterile and weed-free. Grass mowings, too, make a good mulch, spread on the soil around plants to a depth of about 3 in. (8 cm). They should be turned occasionally in damp weather to prevent over-heating. Clippings from a lawn that has been treated with hormone weedkillers should not, however, be used for mulching for at least three weeks after application.

Garden compost, partly rotted down, makes one of the best mulches of all since it can be forked in in autumn to enrich and improve the texture of the soil. It may contain some weed seeds but these are easily removed by hand or hoe as soon as they germinate.

MULLEIN – see *Verbascum*

MUSA
(Musaceae)

Herbaceous perennials for hothouse cultivation. Included in the group are the banana and manilla hemp.

Cultural requirements: Rich well-drained potting compost containing well-rotted manure or compost. The plants are greedy feeders during their growing season. Minimum winter temperature 60 °F (15 °C).

Propagation: By suckers from base of plants.

M. Dwarf Cavendish up to 8 ft (2·5 m)
Canary Island Banana   Asia
Grown for its fruit. It needs a minimum temperature of 50–55 °F (10–12 °C) for successful

cultivation under glass. This is now known to be a dwarf form of *Musa acuminata*.

M. ensete up to 20 ft (6 m)   Abyssinia
This species, which is hardier than the rest, can be grown outdoors in tubs in a sheltered sunny situation during summer in favoured districts and transferred to a cool greenhouse for the rest of the year. It is grown for the decorative quality of its large polished leaves.

MUSCARI
(Liliaceae) Grape Hyacinth
Small bulbous plants, delightful in the garden from early to late spring and valuable in the rock garden.
Cultural requirements: Fairly rich soil and a sunny situation.
Propagation: From seed sown when ripe in a cold frame; by offsets.

M. botryoides 6 in. (15 cm)   Europe
Grape-like clusters of blue flowers. 'Heavenly Blue', with flowers of an intense sky-blue, is the best form. There is also a white cultivar, 'Album'. Spring.

M. comosum 8 in. (20 cm)   Europe
The flower spikes are feathery in the variety 'Monstrosum' (syn. 'Plumosum'). They make showy plants for the rock garden. Spring.

M. macrocarpum 10 in. (25 cm)   Mediterranean
A species with yellow scented flowers, twenty or more to a stem. Needs a warm sunny situation. Spring.

Myosotis Royal Blue (Forget-me-not)

M. tubergenianum 6 in. (15 cm)   Persia
Known as the 'Oxford and Cambridge' grape hyacinth from the appearance of its flowers of which the top halves are pale blue and the lower a deeper shade. Spring.

MUSHROOMS – see Kitchen Garden

MUSK – see *Mimulus*

MUSK ROSE – see *Rosa moschata*

MUSTARD – see Kitchen Garden

MYOSOTIS
(Boraginaceae) Forget-me-not
Hardy perennials, normally treated as hardy biennials and first rate for spring bedding in association with wallflowers, hyacinths, or tulips.
Cultural requirements: Moist soil and a partly shaded situation.
Propagation: From seed sown outdoors in spring or early summer.

M. alpestris up to 15 in. (38 cm)   Europe
The various selected forms of this species are those most commonly used for spring planting. They range in height from 6 in. (15 cm) – 'Ultramarine' and 'Blue Ball'; to 15 in. (38 cm) – 'Blue Bouquet'. 'Royal Blue' is a good early flowering variety of medium height; 'Rose Pink' is a compact form with attractive rose-pink flowers.

M. palustris up to 1 ft (30 cm)   Britain
This is a moisture loving species, ideal for pool or streamside planting. The flowers are sky blue and 'Grandiflora' is the best form. Early summer.

MYRTLE – see *Myrtus*

MYRTUS
(Myrtaceae)
Slightly tender evergreen shrubs, suitable only for mild districts or the shelter of a warm south wall in others.
Cultural requirements: Any ordinary well-drained soil and a sheltered sunny situation, or a south wall in colder districts.
Propagation: From cuttings under glass with bottom heat.

M. communis 12 ft (4 m)
Common Myrtle   W. Asia
Evergreen shrubs with aromatic foliage whose white flowers are followed by purplish-black fruits. There are several attractive cultivars – 'Flore Pleno', with double flowers; 'Microphylla', a more miniature form; and 'Variegata', with creamy-white variegation. Late summer.

NANDINA
(Berberidaceae)

A genus of one species of evergreen shrub resembling bamboos in appearance.

Cultural requirements: Any well-drained soil and a sunny sheltered situation.

Propagation: From cuttings under glass with bottom heat in late summer.

N. domestica 8 ft (2·5 m)

Sacred Bamboo   China and Japan

Medium-sized shrubs with handsome compound foliage and white flowers. Summer.

NARCISSUS
(Amaryllidaceae)

This extensive group of hardy spring flowering bulbs includes daffodils, jonquils, and various other species and hybrids. As far as the gardener is concerned the terms daffodil and narcissus are often interchangeable although the former is correctly applied only to those with trumpet flowers.

The kinds most widely grown are the large flowered hybrids. These are divided into sections for exhibition purposes. The divisions (which are again sub-divided according to colour and form) are as follows: Trumpet, Large-cupped, Small-cupped, Double, Triandrus and hybrids, Cyclamineus and hybrids, Jonquils, Tazetta, Poeticus, and Miscellaneous.

The lists that follow contain a representative selection of those kinds currently available in commerce. It is a list that is constantly changing as new kinds are introduced, but many included here have proved their worth over many years.

1. Trumpet
(*a*) Yellow trumpet and perianth: Arctic Gold, Golden Harvest, Hunter's Moon, King Alfred, Rembrandt, and Spanish Gold.
(*b*) Bi-coloured trumpets: Foresight, Norway, Queen of Bi-colours, and Trousseau.
(*c*) White trumpets: Beersheba, Cantatrice, Glacier, and Mount Hood.

2. Large-cupped
(*a*) Yellow perianth, coloured corona: Carlton, Fortune, Vulcan, and Yellow Sun.
(*b*) White perianth, coloured corona: Duke of Windsor, Flower Record, Semper Avanti, and Tudor Minstrel.

(*c*) White perianth and corona: Castella, Ice Follies, and Snowshill.

3. Small-cupped narcissi
(*a*) Perianth and corona coloured: Chungking and Doubtful.
(*b*) Perianth white, corona coloured: La Riante, Merlin, and Rockall.
(*c*) Perianth and corona white: Engadine and Verona.

4. Double narcissi
Acropolis, Anne Frank, Candida, Irene Copeland, and Texas.

5. Cyclamineus hybrids
Charity May, Dove Wings, February Gold, and Peeping Tom.

6. Triandrus hybrids
Dawn, April Tears, Silver Chimes, and Thalia.

7. Jonquils and hybrids
Baby Moon, Nirvana, Sugarbush, and Suzy.

8. Poetaz
Bridal Crown, Cheerfulness, and Geranium.

9. Poeticus
Actaea, Old Pheasant's Eye, and Queen of Narcissi.

Cultural requirements: Outdoors: Any ordinary garden soil. Bulbs should be planted from late summer to late autumn, 5 in. (13 cm) deep in heavy soils, 6 in. (15 cm) deep in light soils. Bulbs naturalized in grass should be planted in holes 3 in. (8 cm) deep, replacing the turf after planting. The grass should not be cut until the leaves of the bulbs have practically died off.

Pots and bowls: Bulbs in pots can go into good garden soil. The pots should be plunged under 6 in. (15 cm) of soil or ashes for about twelve weeks before bringing them into a cool greenhouse, cold frame, or unheated room where they should remain until the flowers start to show colour.

Bulbs can also be grown in fibre. This should be kept moist and never be allowed to dry out. The bowls should be treated similarly to pots, as described above.

Propagation: Bulbs will normally need lifting and division every third season. Offset bulbs should flower in the first or second season after planting.

NASTURTIUM – see *Tropaeolum*

Nemesia Rainbow Mixed

NAVELWORT – see *Omphalodes*

NEMESIA
(Scrophulariaceae)
Half-hardy annuals, useful and colourful summer bedding plants.
Cultural requirements: Any ordinary garden soil and a sunny well-drained situation.
Propagation: From seed under glass in gentle heat in spring for planting out in early summer.

N. strumosa up to 1 ft (30 cm) S. Africa
This species has given rise to many colourful cultivars, including 'Blue Gem', lavender-blue; 'Fire King', crimson-scarlet; 'Carnival', a semi-dwarf strain with a wide colour range; and 'Triumph', a mixture with larger flowers in a range of striking colours. Summer.

NEMOPHILA
(Hydrophyllaceae)
Hardy annuals, popular as an edging plant for summer bedding.
Cultural requirements: Any ordinary garden soil, moist conditions, and a sunny situation.
Propagation: From seed sown outdoors in spring where plants are to flower or in late summer to provide an early display the following season.

N. menziesii (syn. *N. insignis*) 6 in. (15 cm)
Baby Blue Eyes California
Sometimes known as the Californian bluebell,

this attractive and easy to grow hardy annual has light blue and white flowers. There is also a white form, 'Alba'. Summer.

NEPETA
(Labiatae) Catmint
Hardy perennials with small serrated silver-grey foliage and lavender-blue flower spikes. They make excellent edging plants in the herbaceous border.
Cultural requirements: Any ordinary garden soil and a sunny, well-drained situation.
Propagation: From seed sown in spring where plants are to grow; by division in early spring.

N. × faassenii 1 ft (30 cm) Garden origin
Although commonly referred to as *N. mussinii*, the catmint most commonly seen in gardens is in fact a hybrid form. It is an attractive plant with silver-grey soft foliage and pale mauve flowers that remain decorative over a long period. Early to late summer.

NERINE
(Amaryllidaceae)
Half-hardy bulbous plants, some species of which can be grown outdoors in milder districts. The flowers make a valuable contribution to the garden in autumn.
Cultural requirements: Light, rich, sandy soil and a sunny sheltered situation at the foot of a south or west wall. Plants will benefit from a

summer mulch of peat, well-rotted compost or leafmould. Nerines dislike disturbance.
Propagation: By offsets.

N. bowdenii 2 ft (60 cm)   S. Africa
This is the only species hardy enough to be grown outdoors in safety. The flowers, which are borne in large umbels, vary in colour from deep pink almost to white. 'Fenwick's Variety' has larger flowers than those of the type. Early autumn.

NERIUM
(Apocynaceae) Oleander

Evergreen shrubs for the cool house, usually grown in pots or tubs.
Cultural requirements: John Innes No. 2 or similar potting compost. Plants should be pruned hard back in winter to induce bushiness and increase flowering potential.
Propagation: By cuttings under glass in heat in spring or summer.

N. oleander up to 10 ft (3 m)
Oleander or Rose Bay   China and Japan
The flowers of the type are usually single, white or pink in colour and exceptionally beautiful. There are also various cultivars with double flowers and a wide colour range that includes cream, yellow, pink, red, and purple. Summer to autumn.

NEW ZEALAND FLAX
– see *Phormium tenax*

NICANDRA
(Solanaceae) Shoo Fly Plant

Hardy annuals reputed to act as fly repellents indoors. Also known as 'Apple of Peru'.
Cultural requirements: Any ordinary garden soil and a sunny situation.
Propagation: From seed outdoors in spring.

N. physaloides 3 ft (1 m)   Peru
The bell-shaped flowers are pale lavender-blue and are followed by small apple-like fruits. Summer.

NICOTIANA
(Solanaceae)

Half-hardy annuals, of which the species *N. tabacum* is the tobacco of commerce. There are also numerous attractive garden forms many of which are noteworthy for their distinctive and delightful fragrance, particularly at night.
Cultural requirements: Rich moist soil and a sunny situation.
Propagation: From seed under glass in heat in spring.

Nemophila menziesii (Baby Blue Eyes)

Nicotiana Sensation Hybrids

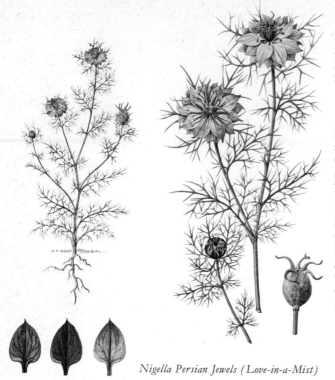

Nigella Persian Jewels (Love-in-a-Mist)

N. alata (syn. *N. affinis*) up to 2½ ft (75 cm)
Sweet Tobacco   Brazil
Free-flowering plants with long white tubular flowers, exceptionally fragrant from dusk to dawn. Named forms include 'Lime Green', with greenish-yellow flowers; 'Dwarf White Bedder', a compact cultivar with white flowers that stay open during the day; and 'Sensation Mixed', a fine strain with colours that include mauve, pink, crimson, yellow, and white. Summer to mid-autumn.

N. sylvestris 3 ft (1 m)   Argentine
Handsome plants with pale green leaves and tall stems, bearing clusters of white tubular flowers. They make good border plants. Summer.

NIEREMBERGIA
(Solanaceae)
Half-hardy and hardy perennials of prostrate or bushy habit. They are useful as pot plants or for summer bedding outdoors.
Cultural requirements: Well-drained rich soil; John Innes No. 2 compost for pot culture.
Propagation: From seed under glass in heat in spring. For outdoor culture, treat as half-hardy annuals.

N. caerulea (syn. *N. hippomanica*)
6 in. (15 cm)   Argentine
Lavender-blue flowers and narrow leaves. 'Purple Robe' is a good form, with yellow-centred purple flowers. Summer.

N. rivularis (syn. *N. repens*) 2 in. (5 cm)   Chile
A prostrate species, good for planting in crevices in paving or in the rock garden. The cup-shaped flowers are white. Summer.

NIGELLA
(Ranunculaceae) Love-in-a-Mist
Hardy annuals with feathery foliage and flowers surrounded by a green ruff.
Cultural requirements: Any ordinary garden soil and an open sunny situation.
Propagation: From seed outdoors in spring.

N. damascena 1½ ft (45 cm)   S. Europe
Sometimes also known as 'Devil-in-a-Bush' from the curious seedheads that follow the flowers. Both flowers and seedheads make decorative cutting material. Good named forms include 'Miss Jekyll', sky-blue; 'Persian Rose', pink; and 'Persian Jewels', a colourful mixed strain. Summer.

NIGHT-SCENTED STOCK
– see *Matthiola bicornis*

NOMOCHARIS
(Liliaceae)
Hardy bulbous plants, close relations of the lilies and fritillarias, they bear flowers resembling exotic orchids.
Cultural requirements: Moist peaty soil in good heart but not freshly manured. Sunny or partly shaded situation.
Propagation: From seed under glass in late winter.

N. mairei 4 ft (1·2 m)   W. China and Tibet
Pendulous white open trumpets with spotted and fringed petals. Summer.

N. pardanthina 3 ft (1 m)   W. China
Pendulous pink flowers deeper in colour and spotted at their centres, up to 4 in. (10 cm) across. Summer.

N. saluenensis 3 ft (1 m)   W. China
Pale pink cup-shaped flowers held erect with up to six flowers to each stem. Summer.

NOTHOFAGUS
(Fagaceae) Southern Beech
Hardy or slightly tender evergreen and deciduous trees or large shrubs, suitable only for milder districts.
Cultural requirements: Moist lime-free soil and a sheltered situation.
Propagation: By layers in spring.

N. antarctica 30 ft (9 m) Antarctic Beech   Chile
A fast growing deciduous tree with rounded heart-shaped leaves that colour attractively in autumn.

N. obliqua 50 ft (15 m)   Chile
Fast growing deciduous tree with handsome foliage.

N. procera 50 ft (15 m)   Chile
Another fast growing species, with deeply veined leaves that colour well in autumn.

NOTOCACTUS
(Cactaceae)

Greenhouse succulents forming spiny hummocks, with yellow flowers. They need a well-drained compost with plenty of grit or coarse sand. Water moderately in summer and autumn, withhold water in winter.

Propagation: From seed under glass in heat in spring; by cuttings or offshoots.

N. mammulosus 6 in. (15 cm)   S. America
Round ribbed spiny cushions with yellow flowers. Summer.

NYMPHAEA
(Nymphaceae) Water Lily

Greenhouse and hardy aquatic perennials, more commonly seen outdoors in pools or water gardens.

Cultural requirements: Water-lilies are placed in small wicker baskets or plastic containers filled with a suitable soil and are lowered into the water until they touch the bottom. Choice should be made of species or cultivars suitable for the depth and area of water available.

Propagation: By division in spring.

Hardy species

N. alba Common Water-Lily
    Europe, including British Isles
This native species has white flowers. There is also a variety with pink flowers, *N. a. rosea*. Summer.

N. × laydekeri   Garden origin
Hybrid water-lilies, compact enough for tub culture and also good for shallow pools. There are various good named cultivars, including 'Lilacea', with sweetly scented deep rose flowers; 'Fulgens', brilliant crimson; and 'Purpurata', wine-red. Summer.

N. odorata   N. America
The type plant of this species has white flowers. There are also several good named cultivars, including 'Alba', a scented white form ideal for small pools; 'Minor', which is even more compact; 'Eugène de Land', a pink water-lily with golden stamens; and 'Sulphurea', soft sulphur-yellow. Summer.

N. pygmaea (syn. *N. tetragona*)
The smallest water-lily with white flowers and miniature leaves. It will thrive in tubs, bowls, or very shallow pools. 'Helvola' is its yellow counterpart. Midsummer.

In addition to the above, there are many beautiful hybrids of which the following form a representative selection: 'Escarboucle', wine-red; 'Fire Crest', pink; 'James Brydon', carmine; and 'Sunrise', golden-yellow.

NYSSA
(Nyssaceae)

Hardy deciduous trees noteworthy for the beauty of their scarlet autumn leaf colour. Good for waterside planting.

Cultural requirements: Moist lime-free soil.

Propagation: By layers in autumn.

N. sylvatica 50 ft (15 m) Tupelo   N. America
Slow growing tree of medium-size and pyramidal habit. The dark green glossy foliage assumes a colourful medley of scarlet and orange tints in autumn.

OAK – see *Quercus*

OBEDIENT PLANT – see *Physostegia*

ODONTOGLOSSUM
(Orchidaceae)

A large genus of orchids. It contains many species and there are also numerous colourful hybrids.

Cultural requirements: Many odontoglossums will thrive in a cool greenhouse, with minimum night temperatures of 45–50 °F (7–10 °C). Potting compost, osmunda fibre, sphagnum moss, leafmould, and sand.

Propagation: By division.

O. bictoniense 3 ft (1 m)   Guatemala
Sprays of yellowish-green flowers with white or pale pink lips. Autumn.

O. cariniferum 4 ft (1·2 m)   Panama
Greenish-red flowers on tall stems, each bearing four to five blooms. Spring.

O. crispum 2 ft (60 cm)   Colombia
White or rose-tinted flowers with ruffled petals and toothed edges, blotched with brown. Any season.

O. grande 4 ft (1·2 m) Tiger Orchid   Guatemala
Large flowers, four to seven to a spray, with petals and sepals banded with yellow and brown. Late autumn.

O. pulchellum 1½ ft (45 cm)   Guatemala
Small white waxen-textured flowers, six or seven to a spray with a scent of lilies-of-the-valley. Spring.

OENOTHERA
(Onagraceae) Evening Primrose
Hardy biennials and perennials, many of which, in spite of their popular name, flower during the day.
Cultural requirements: Light to medium soil and a sunny situation.
Propagation: From seed under glass in spring or outdoors in early summer; perennial species also by root division in spring.

O. biennis 4 ft (1·2 m)   N. America
This biennial species has naturalized itself in Britain. The yellow, scented flowers open at dusk. Mid to late summer.

O. fruticosa 2 ft (60 cm)   N. America
Perennial species with deep yellow flowers up to 2 in. (5 cm) in diameter, opening in the evening. Summer.

O. missouriensis (syn. *O. macrocarpa*)
9 in. (22 cm)   N. America
Trailing perennial species with carpets of leafy stems spangled with large yellow flowers. Summer.

O. tetragona (syn. *O. youngii*)
2 ft (60 cm)   N. America
Perennial species with shining glaucous foliage and a succession of lemon-yellow flowers. There are several named forms of which 'Fireworks', with yellow flowers, is the best. Summer.

OLD MAN – see *Artemisia abrotanum*

OLEARIA
(Compositae) Daisy Bush
A race of hardy and partly tender evergreen shrubs from Australia and New Zealand. The majority are grey leaved and do particularly well in seaside districts.
Cultural requirements: Any ordinary garden soil, provided it is well-drained, and a sunny situation. The tender kinds should have the protection of a south wall. They cannot be grown in colder districts.
Propagation: From hardwood cuttings in summer; layers in autumn or spring.

O. haastii 6 ft (2 m)   New Zealand
This is the hardiest species which will stand up to seaside gales. The oval leaves are grey and leathery and massed with daisy-like flowers in summer. Summer.

O. macrodonta 15 ft (4·5 m)
New Zealand Holly   New Zealand
Partly tender species with handsome holly-like leaves, silvered on their undersides and panicles of fragrant white and yellow daisy flowers. An ideal seaside shrub. 'Major' has larger leaves and flowers than the type. Midsummer.

O. mollis 3 ft (1 m)   New Zealand
Compact shrubs of rounded habit with oval, serrated grey foliage. The large heads of bloom appear early. A first rate foliage plant. Early summer.

OMPHALODES
(Boraginaceae)
Hardy annuals and perennials of creeping habit that make useful subjects for the rock garden.
Cultural requirements: Any ordinary garden soil in good heart and a partly shaded situation.
Propagation: From seed sown outdoors in spring; perennial species by division in spring.

O. cappadocica 9 in. (22 cm)   S. Europe
Creeping plants with rich blue flowers in forget-me-not-like sprays. Early summer.

O. linifolia 6 in (15 cm)
Venus's Navelwort   S. Europe
Hardy annual with white flowers that makes a good edging plant. Midsummer.

O. luciliae 6 in. (15 cm)
Rock Forget-me-not   Asia Minor
Another useful creeping perennial for the rock garden, with blue-grey foliage and sprays of china-blue flowers. Summer.

O. verna 6 in. (15 cm)
Creeping Forget-me-not   Europe
A creeping perennial with forget-me-not flowers of a striking blue. Late spring to early summer.

ONION – see *Allium* and Kitchen Garden

ONOPORDON
(Compositae)
Hardy perennial and biennial thistle-like plants of impressive appearance; striking plants for the back of the border.
Cultural requirements: Any ordinary well-drained soil in good heart and a sunny situation.
Propagation: From seed outdoors in spring. The plants are transferred to their flowering position in autumn.

O. acanthium 8 ft (2·5 m)
Scotch Thistle   Europe, including British Isles

Handsome plants for the larger border or as specimens for focal planting. The prickly leaves and stems are silvered with fine hairs and the large thistle heads are purple. Summer.

O. arabicum 8 ft (2·5 m)   S. Europe
Biennial species, similar in habit and appearance to the above. Summer.

ONOSMA
(Boraginaceae)
Small bushy or semi-prostrate hardy perennials, useful in the rock garden.
Cultural requirements: Well-drained gritty soil and a sunny situation in the rock garden.
Propagation: From seed under glass in a cool greenhouse or frame in spring; by cuttings under glass in summer.

O. albo-roseum 6 in. (15 cm)   Asia Minor
An attractive plant with hairy leaves and dainty clusters of white flowers that turn pink as they mature. Summer.

O. tauricum 9 in. (22 cm) Golden Drop   Europe
A taller variety with sprays of pendent yellow flowers. Early summer.

OPUNTIA
(Cactaceae) Prickly Pear
Greenhouse and hardy succulent plants with flattened oval or pear-shaped spiny stems known as pads.
Cultural requirements: Hardy species: Well-drained sandy soil and a sunny situation in the rock garden.

Greenhouse species: Potting compost John Innes No. 2 with the addition of crushed brick, mortar rubble, or grit. Water sparingly in summer and early autumn, withhold water in winter. Minimum winter temperature 40 °F (4 °C).
Propagation: From seed under glass in heat in spring; by cuttings.

Hardy species
O. englemannii 6 in. (15 cm)   U.S.A.
Yellow flowers. Early summer.

O. vulgaris 1 ft (30 cm) Barbary Fig   U.S.A.
Yellow flowers. Summer.

Greenhouse species
O. ficus-indica
up to 15 ft (4·5 m)   Tropical America
Yellow flowers. Early summer.

O. phaeacantha up to 5 ft (1·5 m)   S. U.S.A.
Flattened oval stems with sharp spines. The flowers are yellow but this species seldom flowers in greenhouse cultivation. Summer.

ORANGE BALL TREE – see *Buddleia globosa*

ORIGANUM
(Labiatae) Marjoram
Perennial herbs with aromatic foliage. Used for culinary purposes.
Cultural requirements: Light sandy soil and a sunny situation.
Propagation: From seed sown outdoors in early summer; by division of roots in spring.

O. hybridum 1 ft (30 cm)   Garden origin
Rosy-purple flowers and aromatic grey foliage. Summer.

O. vulgare 1 ft (30 cm)
                Europe, including British Isles
Purple flower clusters and dark green aromatic leaves. There is an attractive golden cultivar 'Aureum' that makes a useful edging plant. Summer.

ORNITHOGALUM
(Liliaceae)
Hardy and tender bulbous plants.
Cultural requirements: Tender species: John Innes No. 2 or similar potting compost; sunny position in greenhouse.

Outdoor species: Light soil in good heart and a sunny situation. Plant bulbs late summer to autumn.
Propagation: From offsets in autumn and winter.

O. arabicum 2 ft (60 cm)   S. Europe
White scented flowers marked at their throats with black. Can be grown outdoors in a sheltered situation in mild districts. Summer.

O. thyrsoides 1½ ft (45 cm)
Chincherinchee   S. Africa
Popular South African florists' flower that can be grown outdoors for summer flowering. The flowers are white with yellow stamens and last for an exceptionally long time when cut. Summer.

O. umbellatum 6 in. (15 cm) Star of Bethlehem
                Europe, including British Isles
Fragrant white star-like flowers on short stems. A useful plant for the rock garden. Early summer.

OSMANTHUS
(Oleaceae)
Evergreen shrubs with small white flowers, deliciously fragrant in many species.
Cultural requirements: Light to medium loam and a sunny situation. In colder districts, they appreciate the protection of a south or west wall.
Propagation: From seed in a cold frame in spring; by cuttings of partly ripened shoots in a cold frame in summer.

O. delavayi (syn. *Siphonosmanthus delavayi*)
8 ft (2·5 m)   China
An evergreen shrub with polished dark green

foliage and a bushy habit. The jasmine-like flowers are very sweetly scented. Spring.

O. heterophyllus (syn. *O. ilicifolium*)
10 ft (3 m)   Japan
Slow growing evergreen shrub with holly-like foliage. The small white flowers are fragrant and there are numerous named forms, including 'Gulf Tide', white and 'Variegatus', with leaves edged with creamy-white. Autumn.

× *Osmarea burkwoodii* is a bigeneric hybrid between *Osmanthus delavayi* and *Phillyrea decora*. It has the best qualities of both its parents, including polished dark green foliage and very fragrant white flowers. Early spring.

OSMUNDA
(Osmundaceae)
Tall and stately ferns, of which the royal fern, *O. regalis*, is the one most commonly found in cultivation.
Cultural requirements: Rich peaty soil and a moist situation in shade or partial shade. An excellent plant for the waterside.
Propagation: From spores in a cool greenhouse; by offsets in late spring.

O. regalis 6 ft (2 m) Royal Fern
   Africa, U.S.A., Europe, including British Isles
The royal fern is now a protected wild plant in Britain. It likes boggy conditions and its enormous leaves are very striking, their beauty enhanced by the rust-coloured fertile fronds.

OSTRICH FERN – see *Matteuccia struthiopteris*

OSTROWSKIA
(Campanulaceae)
Hardy perennials of campanula-like habit and appearance.
Cultural requirements: Rich sandy loam and a sunny sheltered situation.

Propagation: From seed outdoors in spring for plants to flower the following season.

O. magnifica 4 ft (1·2 m)   C. Asia
Tall spikes of pale blue campanula-like flowers, up to 6 in. (15 cm) across. Early summer.

OVATE
A term used to describe leaves that are egg-shaped, i.e., broadest at the middle.

OXALIS
(Oxalidaceae) Wood Sorrel
Hardy annuals and perennials of prostrate habit useful as edging or in the rock garden.
Cultural requirements: Light sandy soil and a sunny situation.
Propagation: From seed under glass in gentle heat in spring; by division or offsets in spring.

O. adenophylla 4 in. (10 cm)   Chile
Grey-green clover-like foliage and lilac-pink funnel-shaped flowers. Early summer.

O. inops 3 in. (8 cm)   S. Africa
A delightful rock perennial of even more compact growth than the above. The pink flowers, yellow at their throats, are set off perfectly by the dainty trifoliate leaves. Late spring to early summer.

OXYDENDRUM
(Ericaceae)
Monotypic genus which makes a small tree or large shrub.
Cultural requirements: Any good garden soil, provided it is lime-free.
Propagation: From seed in spring in a cold house or frame.

O. arboreum 20 ft (6 m) Sorrel Tree   U.S.A.
White flowers in pendulous terminal clusters and lanceolate foliage that colours magnificently in autumn. Summer.

PACHYSANDRA
(Buxaceae)
Hardy evergreen dwarf shrubs or sub-shrubs of creeping habit.
Cultural requirements: Sandy loam or peat and a shady situation.
Propagation: From cuttings or division.

P. terminalis 1 ft (30 cm) Japanese Spurge Japan
Dwarf evergreen shrub with inconspicuous white flowers that makes excellent ground cover for moist shady positions under trees and shrubs. The form 'Variegata', with silver-variegated foliage, is less rampant than the type. Early spring.

Paeonia 'Beersheba'

PAEONIA
(Paeoniaceae) Peony

Hardy perennial and shrubby plants of great decorative value in the border and thriving equally well in sun or part shade.

Cultural requirements: A deep soil enriched with well-rotted farmyard manure or compost. As little disturbance as possible after planting. Plant with dormant buds not more than 2 in. (5 cm) below the soil surface.

Propagation: Herbaceous kinds: From seed sown in a cold frame in autumn; by division; tree peonies from seed, by grafting or layers.

P. delavayi 5 ft (1·5 m) W. China
Shrubby species with deep crimson flowers and impressive golden anthers, followed by decorative seedheads with black fruits. Early summer.

P. lactiflora (syn. *P. albiflora*)
up to 2½ ft (75 cm) Siberia
It is from this species, with white fragrant flowers, that the lovely cultivars and hybrids, sometimes known as Chinese peonies, have been raised. They are hardy perennials and a representative selection is as follows:

Doubles: 'Albert Crousse', shell-pink; 'Duchesse de Nemours', white; 'Festiva Maxima', pure white marked with red; 'Kelway's Glorious', glowing white; 'Kelway's Supreme', blush-pink, turning to white; and 'Marie Crousse', salmon-pink.

Singles: 'Beersheba', rose-pink; 'Kelway's Gorgeous', salmon-rose; 'Queen Elizabeth', flesh-pink; and 'The Bride', pure white.

Imperial Peonies: 'Bowl of Beauty', pale pink and cream; 'Gleam of Light', carmine-pink; 'Kelway's Majestic', cherry-rose; and 'King George VI', bright rose.

Early to midsummer (according to cultivar).

P. × lemoinei up to 6 ft (2 m)
(*P. lutea × P. suffruticosa*) Garden origin
This splendid cross has produced plants with huge yellow flowers as well as others with striking combinations of colour. Among these are 'Alice Harding', canary-yellow, double; 'Chromatella', double sulphur-yellow; 'L'Esperance', single yellow, blotched with carmine; and 'Souvenir de Maxime Cornu', a vivid golden-yellow double whose petals are edged with carmine. Early summer.

P. lutea up to 6 ft (2 m) Yunnan
Finely cut foliage and large yellow flowers with golden stamens like those of a large kingcup. The variety *Ludlowii* is an improvement on the type with larger and more distinctive flowers.

P. mlokosewitschii 2 ft (60 cm) Caucasus
This herbaceous species is one of the loveliest, bearing cup-shaped flowers of citron-yellow, set off to perfection by glaucous foliage. Late spring.

P. officinalis 2 ft (60 cm) S. Europe
This is the old-fashioned peony of the cottagers' garden. It flowers a few weeks before most of the *lactiflora* cultivars and hybrids and there are white, rose-pink, and crimson forms, all with fully double blooms. Late spring.

P. suffruticosa up to 8 ft (2·5 m) Moutan China
One of the loveliest of all flowering shrubs and an absolute 'must' for those on alkaline soils and unable to grow azaleas. The moutans do equally well in sun or part shade but should be protected from early morning sun after night frosts in spring to prevent damage to the opening buds.

The type plant has enormous white or blush-pink flowers, with a central blotch of maroon surrounding the conspicuous golden stamens. There are also a number of superb named cultivars, including 'Duchess of Kent', bright rose; 'King George V', scarlet flecked white; 'Lord Selborne', salmon-pink; and 'Taiyo', brilliant red. Late spring to early summer.

PAMPAS GRASS – see *Cortaderia*

PANICLE
A raceme (q.v.) with branching stems bearing flowers (e.g., *Gypsophila paniculata*).

PANSY – see *Viola tricolor*

Papaver nudicaule (Iceland Poppy)

PAPAVER
(Papaveraceae) Poppy

Hardy annuals and perennials, easy to grow and extremely popular.

Cultural requirements: Any good garden soil and a sunny situation.

Propagation: Annual species: From seed sown outdoors in spring where plants are to grow.

Perennial species: From seed outdoors or by division in spring; from root cuttings in winter.

P. alpinum 1 ft (30 cm) Alpine Poppy   Europe
Delightful rock perennial that is like a miniature Iceland poppy; long flowering in shades of yellow, orange, and pink as well as white. Summer.

'Lord Lambourne', orange-scarlet; 'Mrs Perry', salmon-pink, blotched at centre with black; 'Perry's White', white with dark blotches; and 'Salmon Glow', a salmon-pink double. Early summer.

P. rhoeas 1½ ft (45 cm)
Corn Poppy   Europe, including British Isles
The scarlet corn poppy is a parent of the lovely Shirley poppies with their extensive colour range that includes many bi-colours. Midsummer to autumn.

P. somniferum 3 ft (1 m)
Opium Poppy   Europe and Asia
The lovely peony-flowered poppies, with their long lasting double flowers were derived from

Papaver orientale

P. nudicaule 2 ft (60 cm) Iceland Poppy   Arctic
Colourful biennial poppies that can be flowered as annuals if early sowings are made under glass. The brilliant colour range includes pink, salmon, apricot, yellow, orange, and scarlet as well as some interesting bi-colours. 'Sunbeam Art Shades' and 'Champagne Bubbles' are two outstanding cultivars, the latter F_1 hybrids. Early to late summer.

P. orientale 3 ft (1 m) Oriental Poppy Asia Minor
Showy perennials with enormous satin-petalled flowers in a variety of brilliant shades, which, in the type, are orange-scarlet. Various named cultivars include 'King George', brilliant scarlet;

this species, better known perhaps, for its more sinister associations with drug traffic. Once again the range of colour in the cultivars is superb and brilliant. *P. somniferum* is a hardy annual. Summer.

PAPHIOPEDILUM
(Orchidaceae)

Terrestrial or epiphytic orchids. Numerous species and hybrids are grouped under this heading. They are sometimes incorrectly referred to as cyprepediums, the generic name of the hardy North American slipper orchids.

Cultural requirements: Many kinds will thrive in a comparatively cool temperature, with a minimum of 55–60 °F (12–15 °C). For the more

tender tropical species and their hybrids, a minimum temperature of 65 °F (18 °C) is necessary.
Propagation: By division when the plants have made four to six growths.

There are very many different species and hybrids with mainly evergreen foliage and the characteristic lady's slipper-type of flower. Specialist catalogues should be consulted for the kinds currently in commerce.

PARROT'S BILL – see *Clianthus puniceus*

PARROTIA
(Hamamelidaceae)
A hardy deciduous tree renowned for its brilliant autumn leaf colour.
Cultural requirements: Any good garden soil and an open situation. Makes a good lawn specimen.
Propagation: By layering in autumn or spring.

P. persica up to 30 ft (9 m)　　　　Persia
Large shrub or small tree with an attractive spreading habit. The flowers are of crimson stamens only. Leaves colour magnificently in autumn to orange-red and scarlet.

PARSLEY – see Herb Garden

PARSNIP – see Kitchen Garden

PARTHENOCISSUS – see *Vitis*

PASQUE FLOWER – see *Pulsatilla vulgaris*

PASSIFLORA
(Passifloraceae) Passion Flower
Self-clinging climbers, most of which are too tender for outdoor planting. Others however, and these are some of the loveliest, will succeed outdoors on a sheltered south or west wall in any but the coldest districts. The structure of the flowers is curious, with a tubular calyx, five sepals and five petals surrounding a ring of thread-like filaments. All these parts of the flower have been assigned a religious significance linked to the crucifixion of Christ.
Cultural requirements: Any ordinary garden soil rich in humus and a sheltered position on a south or west wall. The greenhouse species need a winter temperature of not less than 50 °F (10 °C).
Propagation: From seed under glass in heat in spring; outdoor species by cuttings in a cold frame in summer or from layers.

P. caerulea Blue Passion Flower　　　S. Brazil
A vigorous evergreen climber for milder districts, forming a dense curtain of leaves and stems when grown on a south or west wall. The flowers are greenish-white in colour with a curious central corona of bluish-purple. In hot summers these are sometimes followed by pale orange ovoid fruits. Summer to autumn.

P. edulis Granadilla　　　　S. America
A tender greenhouse climber with flowers similar to those of *P. caerulea* but not as large. The yellowish-purple fruits that follow are edible. In tropical climates it is grown for its passion fruit. Summer.

PASSION FLOWER – see *Passiflora*

PATHS
One of the most important jobs to be tackled in a new garden is the provision of suitable paths. Paths are for walking on. This may seem obvious although in some gardens they are made so narrow that even one person can scarcely use them in comfort.

Paths in regular use should be sufficiently wide for two people to walk abreast. This means a width of at least 4 ft (1·2 m). They should also lead from one garden feature to another, preferably by the shortest possible route. In larger gardens, a certain amount of latitude is permissible but in the smaller plot, paths should, wherever practicable, take the shortest distance between two points.

Any path that is likely to get a good deal of use and certainly those along which mowers or wheelbarrows are going to be pushed, needs a solid foundation, if only to ensure adequate drainage. On the surface of a badly constructed path on heavy soils, water will collect after heavy rain. With sticky clay soils, it may be necessary to lay land drains underneath the path to dispose of surplus water.

Normally, however, a 6 in. (15 cm) layer of rubble, covered with 1–2 in. (2–5 cm) of clinker, will be sufficient to provide adequate drainage. Gardeners today enjoy a wide choice of surfacing materials for paths. These include gravel, bricks, paving slabs of natural or artificial stone, cobbles, pebbles, and crazy paving. Attractive surfaces can also be made from a combination of such materials – for example, bricks alternating with paving, flagstones in square or rectangular patterns, or large seaside pebbles set in concrete.

In the vegetable garden one of the best and cheapest surfacing materials for the paths is ashes. A cinder path is always clean to walk on, discourages slugs and snails and is easy to maintain. All that is needed to keep it tidy and weed-free is a hoeing and raking over once a month during the summer.

Nearer to the house, surfacing materials should

Plants to grow on walls and between paving stones:
(top, l. to r.) Erinus alpinus, Dianthus deltoides, Alyssum
montanum; (bottom, l. to r.) Thymus serpyllum, Saxifrage,
Sedum Mixed, Sempervivum

be chosen with greater care. They should not only be suitable to their surroundings but also in harmony with the materials of which the building is constructed. Bricks or random paving are a perfect complement to the rustic charm of a country cottage; Victorian-style houses look more at home with gravel. Contemporary homes, on the other hand blend well with pre-cast concrete paving slabs. These are easy to lay and comparatively inexpensive.

They can either be laid 'dry' or in a setting of 3–6 in. (8–15 cm) of concrete. To lay paving 'dry', the site for the path will first have to be dug out to a depth of 4–6 in. (10–15 cm). The bottom of this excavation is then filled with clinker, hardcore, or rubble rammed or rolled down firmly. This is covered with a layer of sand, in which the paving slabs are bedded.

They must be perfectly level after laying; the slightest irregularity can cause them to rock or even crack. This type of path is ideal where there will not be a great deal of wear and tear. For paths in harder and more constant use, the slabs or other materials should be laid in concrete.

The concrete should be levelled with the edge of a board and tamped down lightly. This will leave a layer of almost pure liquid cement on the surface. The paving material is lightly bedded into this while it is wet, checking for levels as the work proceeds.

Concrete itself, properly laid, can make serviceable and good looking paths. Thin battens can be inserted at intervals as dividers and removed when the concrete is partly set or the surface can be deeply scored with a trowel to simulate rectangular or random paving.

PEA – see Kitchen Garden

PEA, Everlasting – see *Lathyrus latifolius*

PEA, Sweet – see *Lathyrus odoratus*

PEACH – see *Prunus persica* and Fruit Garden

PEAR – see Fruit Garden

PEARL BUSH – see *Exochorda*

PEAT – see Fertilizers

PELARGONIUM
(Geraniaceae)

An extensive group of greenhouse and hardy evergreen perennials. It includes the popular zonal pelargoniums often incorrectly called geraniums as well as many fancy greenhouse species and decorative ivy-leaved kinds together with others with aromatic foliage.

Cultural requirements: Zonal pelargoniums: Any good garden soil and sunny open beds or borders. Zonal pelargoniums of all kinds make bedding plants *par excellence*.

Greenhouse species (show, fancy, and regal pelargoniums): John Innes No. 2 or similar potting compost and a winter temperature of not less than 40 °F (4 °C).

Propagation: From cuttings in late summer in a cold frame or greenhouse. Zonal pelargoniums can also be raised from seed sown in heat under glass in spring.

All the bedding and greenhouse kinds of pelargoniums are hybrids of a number of different species and various named cultivars are offered by specialist growers whose catalogues should be consulted for up-to-date information.

Popular named forms: Zonal pelargoniums: 'Gustav Emich', vivid red; 'King of Denmark', rose-pink, semi-double; 'Muriel Parsons', bright pink; 'Paul Crampel', scarlet; and 'Xenia Field', white, with a scarlet eye. 'Mrs Henry Cox' and 'The Czar' are grown for their strikingly marked foliage.

Regal pelargoniums: 'Aztec', white marked with crimson; 'Braque', shrimp-pink; 'Grand Slam', reddish-crimson; and 'Renoir', orange-pink.

PELLETED SEED

The pelleting of seed is a comparatively new process which is fast growing in popularity with the amateur gardener. Pelleting is a technique by which a coating is applied to small seeds to increase their size considerably, thus making them much easier to handle and to sow. By planting at suitable distances in the rows or seed boxes the need for thinning and transplanting is practically done away with so that the seedlings develop better and more quickly without any check to growth.

There are, however, certain procedures which must be followed for success with pelleted seed. Firstly, the soil in which the seed is sown must be moist and friable in order that the coating can dissolve quickly. Secondly, the top inch of soil must *never* be allowed to dry out during the germination period.

Among the seeds – and their numbers increase yearly – that are now available in pelleted form are alyssum, ageratum, asters, candytuft, cornflower, godetia, stocks, sweet williams, and wallflowers. Vegetables obtainable in this form are carrots, parsnips, leeks, tomatoes, lettuces, and onions, among others.

PELTIPHYLLUM
(Saxifragaceae)

Hardy perennials that make useful plants for pool or waterside planting and other moist situations.

Cultural requirements: Moist, fertile soil and a sunny or partly shaded situation.

Propagation: From seed outdoors in late spring or by division in spring.

P. peltatum 3 ft (1 m) Umbrella Plant California
Sometimes known as *Saxifraga peltata*, this moisture loving perennial has large clusters of white or pale pink flowers which appear before the handsome rounded leaves unfurl. It is a vigorous plant of invasive habit. Spring.

PENNISETUM
(Gramineae)

Hardy perennial grasses that cut and dry well for winter arrangements.

Cultural requirements: Light, sandy, well-drained loam and a sunny situation.

Propagation: From seed outdoors or by division in spring.

P. alopecuroides 4 ft (1·2 m) China
Decorative perennial grass with narrow bright green leaves and feathery purplish flower heads. Late summer.

P. villosum 2 ft (60 cm) Abyssinia
Slightly tender perennial species that needs a sheltered situation. The leaves are narrow and arching and the purplish feathery plumes of blossom are very striking. Summer.

PENSTEMON
(Scrophulariaceae)

Hardy and half-hardy perennials of great value as border and bedding plants. There are also dwarf species suitable for the rock garden. The flowers are tubular and profusely borne.

Cultural requirements: Ordinary soil, preferably rich in humus, and a sunny well-drained situation.

Propagation: From seed under glass in gentle heat in early spring; by division in spring; by cuttings in a cold frame in late summer.

P. barbatus (syn. *Chelone barbata*) 3 ft (1 m)
Turtle Head Mexico
Coral-red tubular flowers and narrow, lanceolate foliage. Summer.

P. hartwegii 1½ ft (45 cm) Mexico
Deep red tubular flowers and narrow leaves. Summer.

P. heterophyllus 1 ft (30 cm) California
A species with flowers of a brilliant azure-blue. 'Blue Gem' is a good named form. Summer.

P. newberryi 9 in. (22 cm) N.W. America
A good species for the rock garden, forming dense mats of foliage and bearing a profusion of scarlet flowers. Midsummer.

P. scouleri 1 ft (30 cm)   N.W. America
Another species of prostrate habit, useful in the rock garden. The long tubular flowers are lilac-purple. Early summer.

All the above mentioned species are hardy.

PEONY – see *Paeonia*

PEPEROMIA
(Piperaceae)

Tender perennials for the heated greenhouse which are also popular as house plants. They are grown for their decorative foliage.
Cultural requirements: John Innes No. 2 or similar potting compost and a shady position in the greenhouse or on a window-ledge. Winter temperature of not less than 50 °F (10 °C).
Propagation: From cuttings under glass in heat in spring.

P. argyreia 6 in. (15 cm)   Brazil
Large oval leaves banded with green and white. Susceptible to cold draughts.

P. hederaefolia 6 in. (15 cm)   S. America
Deeply veined heart-shaped foliage and long whitish flower spikes. Suitable as a house plant.

P. obtusifolia 9 in. (22 cm)
Oval leaves, dark green and margined with red. The form 'Variegata', whose leaves are edged with cream, makes a striking house plant.

PERENNIAL

Any plant whose life span is more than two years. Generally used of herbaceous perennials although the term also includes shrubs and trees.

PERIWINKLE – see *Vinca*

PERNETTYA
(Ericaceae)

Hardy evergreen shrubs needing a lime-free soil. Densely clothed with prickly foliage and with small white bell-shaped flowers followed by striking berries. They associate well with heathers. Some forms are unisexual, others are self-fertile.
Cultural requirements: Moist, peaty, acid soil, and a sunny or partly shaded situation.
Propagation: From seed outdoors in peaty soil in autumn; by layers in spring.

P. mucronata up to 3 ft (1 m)   Chile
The most widely planted species and one of the showiest of dwarf evergreens. The masses of white flowers are followed by a profusion of marble-sized berries, ranging in colour from white to deep purple. Group planting ensures a good crop of these. The following cultivars are more striking than the type: 'Alba', white berries tinged with pink; 'Bell's Seedling', an hermaphro-

dite form with large red berries; 'Davis's Hybrids', a good strain with large berries in a variety of colours; 'Lilacina', reddish-lilac berries; and 'Pink Pearl', lilac-pink.

PEROVSKIA
(Labiatae)

Grey-leaved aromatic sub-shrubs, useful for their late flowering character.
Cultural requirements: Any ordinary garden soil, provided it is well-drained, and a sunny situation.
Propagation: From cuttings in a frame in summer.

P. atriplicifolia up to 5 ft (1·5 m)
Russian Sage   Afghanistan
A delightful grey-leaved shrub with tall spikes of lavender-blue flowers. 'Blue Spire' has even larger spikes of flower than the type. Late summer to autumn.

PERUVIAN LILY – see *Alstroemeria*

PEST CONTROL

Plant pests and diseases probably account for more gardening disappointments than bad weather, poor soil, and indifferent cultivation put together.

The control of pests requires year-long vigilance. Methods of dealing with the main offenders are described in the alphabetical list that follows:

Aphids

These come in assorted colours – green, black, blue, pink, and brown. Those which cause most trouble to gardeners are the greenflies and black-flies. The former attack roses and many other garden plants; blackfly plays havoc among the broad beans, runner beans, and asters.

These sap-sucking insects not only weaken the plants but are also responsible for introducing virus diseases into the systems of the plants on which they feed.
Treatment: Spraying with malathion or fentro (the latter a liquid replacement for DDT), liquid derris, or a systemic insecticide. Dust with nicotine, gamma-BHC, or malathion.

Caterpillars

Fruit trees can be badly affected by the caterpillars of the winter moth, which feed on the young leaves and shoots in spring. Other caterpillars affect rose bushes, bush fruits, trees, shrubs, and flowering plants.
Treatment: For winter moth, spray with fentro or thiol, for others, fentro, derris, or a systemic insecticide. Dust with derris or Sevin.

The female of the winter moth lays its eggs in the bark of fruit trees during winter. Grease-banding will trap it on its way to this operation.

Earwigs

This pest is one of the banes of the dahlia grower's existence, but control is a simple matter.
Treatment: Spray the plants and surrounding soil with Lindex or dust with gamma-BHC or Sevin.

Flea Beetles

This pest attacks the emerging seedlings of turnips, brassicas, and wallflowers. Tiny shot-holes in the first leaves indicate its presence. Attacks can prove fatal and, in any case, cause a severe check to growth.
Treatment: Dust with Sevin, gamma-BHC, or derris as soon as the seedlings appear above ground; repeat twice at five-day intervals.

Leaf Miners

These are larvae that tunnel under the surface of the leaves. Their attacks are mainly confined to chrysanthemums. Severe attacks can seriously weaken the constitution of the plants and result in poor quality blooms.
Treatment: Spray with Lindex or malathion. Mild attacks can be checked by locating the larva (at the end of its trail) and squashing it between thumb and forefinger.

Leatherjackets

These are the grey, rubbery-looking larvae of the cranefly. They feed on the roots of many flowers and vegetables and can be especially damaging to newly sown lawns.
Treatment: Fumigation of the soil with napthalene flakes or, in the case of lawns, applications of Sevin dust in summer, bulked with four times its weight in sand or sifted soil.

Millipedes

These must not be confused with centipedes, which are quick moving and brown and beneficial in the garden. Millipedes are dark grey or blackish and curl up when disturbed. They feed on roots, bulbs, and tubers and are found in large numbers in newly cultivated pasture land.
Treatment: The napthalene treatment as for leatherjackets or Sevin dust, worked into the top 4 in. (10 cm) of soil before planting.

Raspberry Beetle

This beetle is the cause of maggoty fruits in raspberries. Its larvae hatch from eggs laid in the flowers during early summer. They later eat their way into the fruits.
Treatment: Spray or dust with derris just before and after flowering.

Red Spider

This is not a true spider but a sap-sucking mite that attacks the leaves of plants outdoors and under glass. It can be particularly troublesome in the greenhouse and is encouraged by a dry atmosphere.
Treatment: Outdoors: DNC winter wash at bud-break stage, systemic insecticides during spring and summer.
   Under glass: Azobenzene aerosol or systemic insecticide spray.

Slugs and Snails

The former remedy of Meta fuel, mixed with bran or tea-leaves, has been largely superseded by various proprietary brands of slug bait, usually in pellet form. These will prevent the ravages of slugs and snails, if scattered among plants and crops that are susceptible and renewed at regular intervals.

Wireworms

These yellow, thread-like grubs are the larvae of the click beetle. Like leatherjackets and millipedes, they are found in large numbers in newly turned pasture. They feed on the roots of plants and can play havoc with vegetable seedlings.
Treatment: Pieces of carrot or potato, impaled on pointed sticks and buried just below the soil surface can be used to trap this somewhat elusive pest. Fumigation of the soil with napthalene is also useful.

PETASITES
(Compositae)

Rapid spreading invasive carpeting plants whose flowers appear in winter.
Cultural requirements: Any ordinary garden soil and a shady situation.

P. fragrans 6 in. (15 cm)
Winter Heliotrope   Mediterranean
The pale lilac, heliotrope-scented flowers of this practically evergreen hardy perennial appear in winter before the new leaves. The latter are rounded and slightly toothed. An excellent ground cover plant for the wild or woodland garden but too invasive for other parts. Winter.

PETIOLE

The stalk of a leaf.

PETUNIA
(Solanaceae)

Half-hardy perennials, normally treated as half-hardy annuals and invaluable as summer bedding plants. The garden forms in general cultivation are hybrids and are obtainable in singles, doubles, dwarfs, and an exceptionally wide range of

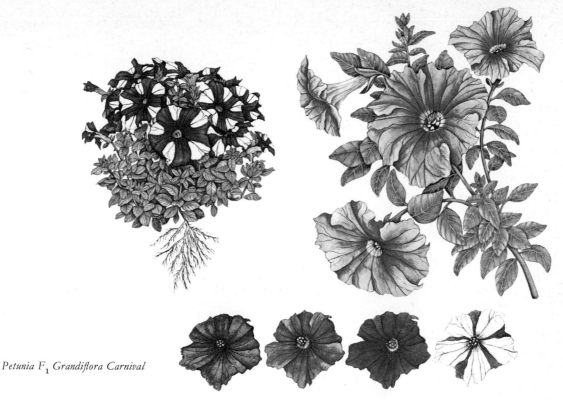

Petunia F₁ Grandiflora Carnival

colours. The double kinds, many of which have attractively fringed petals, are particularly suitable for pot, tub, and window-box culture.

Cultural requirements: Any ordinary garden soil rich in humus and a sunny open situation.

Propagation: From seed sown in gentle heat under glass in spring to produce plants to go out when danger of frost is past.

P. × hybrida up to $1\frac{1}{2}$ ft (45 cm)

Garden forms that are hybrids between *P. axillaris*, *P. integrifolia*, and *P. violacea*, all of which are Argentine species. There are many fine named cultivars and current seedsmen's catalogues should be consulted for these. These include such outstanding F₁ hybrids as 'Brass Band', primrose-yellow; 'Pink Bountiful', salmon-pink; and 'Star-fire', scarlet and white; together with small flowered doubles like 'Cherry Tart' and strains of large flowered hybrids such as 'Colour Parade'.

PHACELIA
(Hydrophyllaceae)

Hardy annuals of great beauty with blue or white flowers.

Cultural requirements: Any ordinary garden soil rich in humus and a sunny or partly shaded situation.

Propagation: From seed sown outdoors in spring where plants are to grow.

Phacelia campanularia

Philadelphus coronarius

P. campanularia 1 ft (30 cm)   S. California
An attractive dwarf annual for edging or the rock garden. The bell-shaped flowers are an intense gentian-blue. 'Blue Bonnet' is an outstandingly good cultivar, slightly taller than the type. Summer.

P. tanacetifolia 2 ft (60 cm)
Wild Heliotrope   California
Clusters of small pale blue or lilac flowers, good for bees. Summer.

PHALARIS
(Gramineae)
Hardy annual and perennial ornamental grasses.
Cultural requirements: Any ordinary garden soil, a sunny situation for the annual species; the perennial kind will thrive in sun or part shade.
Propagation: From seed sown outdoors in spring. Perennial species can also be increased by division of plants in autumn or spring.

P. arundinacea
4 ft (1·2 m)   Temperate N. Hemisphere
A tall and vigorous perennial grass with purplish spikes and narrow green leaves. The form most commonly seen in gardens is 'Picta' (syn. 'Variegata') whose leaves are longitudinally striped with white. This grass is variously known as 'Gardener's Garters' and 'Ribbon Grass'.

P. canariensis 1½ ft (45 cm)
Canary Grass   S. Europe
A decorative annual grass with graceful plumy flowers.

PHILADELPHUS
(Philadelphaceae)
Hardy deciduous shrubs with white flowers intensely fragrant in many species. Often incorrectly called syringa.
Cultural requirements: Any ordinary garden soil. Philadelphus succeed even on poor chalk soils and in a sunny or partly shaded situation.
Propagation: From softwood cuttings in a cold frame in late summer; from hardwood cuttings outdoors in late autumn and from rooted suckers.

P. coronarius up to 15 ft (4·5 m)   S. Europe
The original species and the one most commonly seen in gardens. A shrub of rather coarse habit, vigorous, with creamy-white richly fragrant blossoms. Summer.

P. × lemoinei up to 8 ft (2·5 m)   Garden origin
The original cross between *P. coronarius* and *P. microphyllus* from which M. Lemoine of Nancy raised so many fine cultivars at the turn of the present century. Among these, 'Avalanche', 'Coupe d'Argent', and 'Manteau d'Hermine' are still widely grown. Summer.

P. × virginalis up to 10 ft (3 m)   Garden origin
Another group of hybrids which includes such lovely cultivars as 'Enchantment', 'Glacier', and 'Snowflake'. Summer.

PHILLYREA
(Oleaceae)
Handsome hardy evergreen shrubs, related to the osmanthus.
Cultural requirements: Any ordinary garden soil and a sunny or partly shaded situation. They make good seaside subjects.
Propagation. From cuttings of ripened wood in a cold frame in autumn.

P. decora 10 ft (3 m)   W. Asia
Broadly spreading evergreen shrub with glossy leathery leaves and small but very fragrant white flowers. Early summer.

PHILODENDRON
(Araceae)
Climbing perennials for the warm greenhouse, grown for the decorative qualities of their leaves. They make excellent house plants.
Cultural requirements: John Innes No. 2 or similar compost. Water freely at all times. Minimum winter temperature 45 °F (7 °C).

P. andreanum (Climber)   Colombia
Heart-shaped leaves, up to 6 in. (15 cm) long at the juvenile stage increasing to 3 ft (1 m) on mature plants. The leaves are dark green and gold on their upper surfaces, purplish-pink on reverse.

P. hastatum 8 ft (2·5 m)   Brazil
A slow growing species with dark green spear-shaped leaves.

P. laciniatum (Climber)   Brazil
Rampant climber, needing plenty of space. Deeply lobed leaves.

P. scandens (Climber)   W. Indies
The most widely grown species and popular as a house plant. It is vigorous and will climb to 10 ft (3 m) or more.

PHLOMIS
(Labiatae)
Hardy perennials and evergreen sub-shrubs, most of which have grey woolly leaves.
Cultural requirements: Well-drained light soil and a sunny situation.
Propagation: From seed under glass in early spring; herbaceous species by division in spring or autumn; shrubby kinds from cuttings in late summer.

P. fruticosa 4 ft (1·2 m)
Jerusalem Sage   Mediterranean
Evergreen shrub with yellow deadnettle flowers. Midsummer.

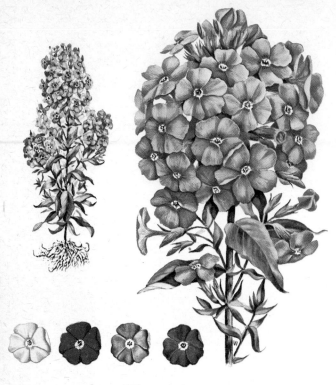

Phlox paniculata

P. viscosa 4 ft (1·2 m)   Syria
A perennial species very similar in habit and
appearance to the above. Tall spikes of yellow
flowers, in whorls, rise from a basal rosette of
large grey-green leaves. Midsummer.

PHLOX
(Polemoniaceae)
Hardy perennials and half-hardy annuals, invaluable in summer beds and borders.
Cultural requirements: Generally speaking,
phlox thrive in any fertile soil except stiff heavy
clay.
Propagation: Annual kinds from seed under
glass in gentle heat in spring or outdoors later;
perennial species from stem cuttings in late
summer or early autumn or by division in spring
or autumn. Root cuttings of *P. paniculata* can be
taken in spring as a precaution against eelworm,
to which this species is susceptible.

P. amoena 6 in. (15 cm)   N. America
An attractive rock phlox, smothered in reddish-
purple or white flowers, 1 in. (3 cm) in diameter
over a long period. Hardy perennial. Early
summer.

P. divaricata 1 ft (30 cm)   Eastern N. America
Somewhat similar in character to *P. amoena*, but
with masses of lavender-blue flowers. Hardy
perennial. Early summer.

P. douglasii 6 in. (15 cm)   Western N. America
A good carpeting hardy perennial for the rock
garden or for dry walls. There are a number of
good named forms, including 'Beauty of Rosen-
dorf', deep pink; 'Boothman's Variety', mauve;
'May Snow', pure white; and 'Rose Queen',
silvery-pink.

P. drummondii up to 1 ft (30 cm)   Texas
This delightful half-hardy annual species makes
an excellent summer bedding plant. There are
some colourful mixtures, including 'Dwarf
Beauty', with large flowers in a wide colour
range, whose size makes it useful for edging;
'Globe Mixed', another good edger of compact
habit; and 'Carnival', a taller strain with large
flowers in shades of pink, rose, salmon, scarlet,
and violet. Summer.

P. paniculata (syn. *P. decussata*)
up to 4 ft (1·2 m)   U.S.A.
Most of the perennial border phloxes are cultivars
or hybrids of this species. They all have a long
flowering season, flowers with an unusual tangy
fragrance and will succeed in partial shade. Good
named forms include 'Brigadier', orange-red;
'Eva Foerster', salmon-pink with white eye; 'Mia
Ruys', a dwarf white; 'Otley Purple', violet;
'Rosa Spier', soft pink with crimson eye; and
'Starfire', brilliant carmine-red. Summer to early
autumn.

P. subulata 4 in. (10 cm)   N. America
A rock garden species forming mossy mats of
foliage that are completely covered with bloom
in early summer. Good named forms include
'Betty', salmon-pink; 'Sensation', deep pink; and
'Temiscaming', reddish-purple. Early summer.

PHORMIUM
(Liliaceae)
Evergreen plants from New Zealand with hand-
some broadsword leaves and magnificent spikes
of bronzy-red flowers up to 10 ft (3 m) in height.
Cultural requirements: Any fertile garden soil.
Does well in exposed maritime districts and hardy
in any but the coldest districts.
Propagation: From seed in a cold greenhouse or
frame or by division in spring.

P. colensoi 3 ft (1 m)   New Zealand
The smaller of the two phormium species; the
leaves are narrower and more lax and the flowers
yellowish in colour. Summer.

P. tenax (syn. *P. cookianum*) up to 10 ft (3 m)
New Zealand Flax   New Zealand
Handsome evergreen of great architectural value,
either in the border, or as a specimen. The leaves
are glaucous and sword-like. In addition to the
type, there are the following cultivars: 'Purpureum', with bronzy-purple leaves; 'Variega-

tum', leaves edged with creamy-white; and 'Veitchii', whose foliage is striped with creamy-yellow. The flowers of all these are bronzy-red on spikes up to 15 ft (4·5 m) tall. Summer.

PHYGELIUS
(Scrophulariaceae)
Slightly tender South African sub-shrubs with penstemon like flowers. Grown against a south or west wall, they may reach 8 ft (2·5 m) but in the open border seldom exceed half that height.
Cultural requirements: Light well-drained soil rich in humus and a sunny situation.
Propagation: From seed in a cold frame or by division in spring.

P. capensis up to 6 ft (2 m)   S. Africa
Small semi-evergreen sub-shrub with yellow-throated scarlet tubular flowers in upright spikes. 'Coccineus', with crimson-scarlet flowers, is a good form. Late summer to autumn.

PHYLLITIS
(Aspleniaceae)
Hardy evergreen ferns with leathery strap-like foliage.
Cultural requirements: Any kind of soil and a moist shady situation.
Propagation: From spores under glass in heat; by division in spring.

P. scolopendrium (syn. *Scolopendrium vulgare*) 1½ ft (45 cm) Hart's Tongue Fern
                Europe, including British Isles
Handsome native ferns with long, narrow, glossy green leaves. 'Undulatum', with fronds with waved edges, is an especially good form.

PHYLLODOCE
(Ericaceae)
Dwarf ericaceous shrubs that associate well with heathers.
Cultural requirements: Peaty, lime-free soil and a cool moist root run.
Propagation: From seed or by cuttings in summer; by layers in autumn.

P. aleutica 6 in. (15 cm)   Aleutians and Japan
Dwarf mat-forming shrub with urn-shaped greenish-yellow flowers. Early summer.
P. breweri 1 ft (30 cm)   California
Large terminal clusters of rosy-purple flowers. Summer.
P. empetriformis 9 in. (22 cm)   W. U.S.A.
Clusters of reddish-purple campanulate flowers and tufted leaves. Late spring.
P. nipponica 8 in. (20 cm)   Japan
A delightful rock garden plant for acid peaty soils. Attractive clusters of white or pink-tinged flowers freely borne. Early summer.

PHYLLOSTACHYS
(Gramineae)
One of the three main groups of bamboos and less invasive than most. Partly tender and suitable only for milder areas.
Cultural requirements: Light rich soil and a moist sheltered situation.
Propagation: By division in late spring or early summer.

P. aurea 15 ft (4·5 m)   Japan
A species with bright green canes that mature to yellow; green leaves.
P. flexuosa 8 ft (2·5 m)   China
Dark green leaves and slender bright green canes darkening as they mature. The young shoots are edible.
P. nigra up to 14 ft (4·2 m)   China and Japan
A bamboo of elegant arching habit with green canes turning to dark brown and finally to black. There are several named cultivars – 'Boryana', with masses of arching leafy stems and edible young shoots; 'Henonis', with bright green canes maturing to brownish-yellow, also edible; and 'Punctata', whose green canes are mottled with black.

PHYSALIS
(Solanaceae) Chinese Lantern Plant
and Cape Gooseberry
Hardy perennials, the fruits of which are edible, but better known for their decorative qualities.
Cultural requirements: Any garden soil, preferably rich in humus, and a sunny situation.
Propagation: From seed sown outdoors in spring; by root division in spring.

P. franchettii
up to 2 ft (60 cm)   S.E. Europe and Asia
A vigorous and invasive plant whose orange-red fruits in their scarlet lantern-like calyces are highly decorative in winter arrangements.

PHYSOSTEGIA
(Labiatae)
Hardy perennials with creeping rootstocks. Useful in the border or as waterside plants.
Cultural requirements: Any light friable soil and a partly shaded moist situation.
Propagation: From seed outdoors in spring; by division in spring or autumn; from root cuttings in late winter.

P. virginiana up to 3 ft (1 m)
Obedient Plant   N. America
Deeply toothed leaves and spikes of rosy-lilac tubular flowers. The plant gets its popular name from the fact that each floret appears as if on a kind of ball-and-socket joint and will stay put when moved. Summer to early autumn.

PHYTOLACCA
(Phytolaccaceae) Pokeberry
Hardy perennials whose flowers are followed by blackish-purple berries and whose leaves provide a colourful autumn display.
Cultural requirements: Any good garden soil and a sunny or partly shaded situation. Good plants for the wild or woodland garden.
Propagation: From seed outdoors or by division, in spring or autumn.

P. americana 6 ft (2 m) N. America
Tall white flower spikes succeeded by glossy black berries. These are poisonous as also are the roots. Summer.

P. clavigera 6 ft (2 m) China
This species differs from the former in having reddish-purple stems and pink flowers. Its tall columns of jet-black berries are very striking. Summer.

PICEA
(Pinaceae) Spruce
Hardy evergreen conifers with short needle-like foliage arranged spirally on the stems. A very large genus that includes the Christmas trees and kinds that are grown for timber.
Cultural requirements: Most types of soil with the exception of shallow chalk or very dry ones.
Propagation: From seed sown in a cold frame in early spring or outdoors later. Special forms by grafting.

P. abies (syn. *P. excelsa*) up to 120 ft (36 m)
Norway Spruce N. and C. Europe
Large trees of broadly pyramidal habit with drooping branches. Popularly known as Christmas trees. There are many forms, differing in appearance and habit, including some lovely dwarfs suitable for the rock or heather garden. Two of the most attractive of the latter are 'Nidiformis', growing only about 3 ft (1 m) tall and with a curious nest-like depression at its centre and 'Pygmaea', 2½ ft (75 cm), a dense pygmy spruce with dark green needles and a broadly conical shape.

P. breweriana 100 ft (30 m) N.W. California
Considered by many to be the loveliest of all conifers although slow to reach its fully decorative maturity. The main branches have slender pendent branchlets clothed with green needles like the fringe on a Spanish shawl.

P. omorika up to 100 ft (30 m)
Serbian Spruce C. Europe
Slender conifer of spire-like character, well clad with needles to ground level.

P. pungens 50 ft (15 m) Blue Spruce Colorado
Slow growing conifer with stiff prickly needles, grey-green or glaucous. The blue-leaved forms

'Glauca' and 'Kosteriana' are outstandingly beautiful and make fine lawn specimens.
P. sitchensis 60 ft (18 m) Western N. America
Fast growing conical tree grown for its timber and widely used in afforestation. The foliage is bluish-green.

PIERIS
(Ericaceae)
Lime-hating evergreen shrubs with clusters of pitcher-shaped, lily-of-the-valley-type flowers. Some species are noteworthy for the brilliant colouring of their young foliage.
Cultural requirements: Lime-free loamy soil rich in humus and a sheltered partly shaded situation.
Propagation: From seed in a cold frame late autumn or early spring; by layers in autumn.

P. formosa 8 ft (2·5 m) E. Himalayas
Handsome evergreen shrub with finely toothed dark green foliage and creamy-white urn-shaped flowers in drooping clusters. Young foliage is copper tinged. In the variety *forrestii*, these young growths are a striking scarlet, and are especially brilliant in the form known as 'Wakehurst', whose vivid young foliage makes a colourful foil for the white flowers. Spring.
P. japonica 15 ft (4·5 m) Japan
This species is hardier than *P. formosa*, with slightly larger flowers, borne in great profusion. 'Variegata' is a dwarf, slow growing form whose leaves are variegated with white. Spring.
P. taiwanensis 10 ft (3 m) Formosa
Medium-sized shrub, similar to the former species but with larger leaves and flowers. The young leaves are bronzy-red. Mid-spring.

PIGSQUEAK – see *Bergenia*

PILEA
(Urticaceae)
Perennials for the warm greenhouse that also make good house plants. They are grown for the decorative qualities of their leaves.
Cultural requirements: John Innes No. 2 or similar compost. Water freely in summer, sparingly for the rest of year. Minimum temperature 55 °F (12 °C).
Propagation: By cuttings in a propagating case in spring; by division in late winter.

P. cadierei up to 9 in. (22 cm) Aluminium Plant
The oval dark green leaves are strikingly veined with silver.
P. microphylla (syn. *P. muscosa*) 1 ft (30 cm)
Artillery Plant Tropical America
A small plant with finely divided leaves. It

derives its popular name from the fact that the flowers, if sprinkled with water, produce small explosions due to the discharge of pollen. Summer.

PINCUSHION FLOWER – see *Scabiosa*

PINE – see *Pinus*

PINK – see *Dianthus*

PINNATE

A term used to describe compound leaves in which the leaflets are arranged on either side of a central stalk.

PINUS

(Pinaceae) Pine

Evergreen coniferous trees important for their timber and in the garden. Certain species, such as the Scots pine, *P. sylvestris* and *P. nigra* are useful in shelter belts.

Cultural requirements: Well-drained soil and a sunny situation.

Propagation: From seed in a cold greenhouse or frame in spring or outdoors in late spring. Special kinds are grafted.

P. nigra up to 150 ft (45 m)
Austrian Pine   Europe
A widely planted species, often used for windbreaks and fairly tolerant of chalky soils. 'Hornibrookiana' is an attractive, very slow growing dwarf form.

P. radiata (syn. *P. insignis*)
100 ft (30 m)   California
Fast growing tree, used for screening, especially in seaside districts. Branches are horizontal with bright green needles.

P. sylvestris 100 ft (30 m)
Scots Pine   Europe, including British Isles
A handsome tree, native to Britain with a straight reddish-brown trunk and a crown of horizontal branches. The leaves are grey-green. There are a number of good garden forms, including some interesting dwarfs. The Scots pine makes an excellent windbreak that is resistant to salt spray.

P. wallichiana (syn. *P. excelsa*) up to 100 ft (30 m)
Bhutan Pine   Himalayas
A large tree with a broad head and horizontal lower branches that makes a distinctive specimen tree where sufficient space is available. The long grey-green needles are particularly decorative.

PISTIL

The female part of a flower consisting of style, stigma, and ovary.

PITTOSPORUM

(Pittosporaceae)

Tender evergreen shrubs suitable for outdoor cultivation in milder districts. Grown primarily for their decorative foliage.

Cultural requirements: Any well-drained garden soil. In colder districts the protection of a south or west wall will be needed.

Propagation: From cuttings under glass with bottom heat in summer.

P. crassifolium 20 ft (6 m)   New Zealand
One of the hardier species of pittosporum. The leaves are leathery and grey-brown on their reverse. It makes an attractive hedging plant for milder areas. Flowers are deep purple. Spring.

P. tenuifolium 20 ft (6 m)   New Zealand
The hardiest species, upright in habit with pale green fluted foliage. The latter is widely used for decorative purposes. The flowers are brownish-purple and there are several attractive cultivars, some with white or cream-variegated leaves. Spring.

PLANE TREE – see *Platanus*

PLANTAIN LILY – see *Hosta*

PLATANUS

(Platanaceae)

Large trees with maple-like foliage that stand up magnificently to town conditions. Their bark is shed in winter. Extensively used for city planting, but too large for the average-sized garden.

Cultural requirements: Any kind of soil with the exception of shallow chalky kinds.

Propagation: From seed outdoors in autumn; by cuttings in late autumn.

P. × hispanica (syn. *P. × acerifolia*)
up to 100 ft (30 m)
London Plane   Origin unknown
This tree, popular for street and park planting, is a hybrid of *P. orientalis* and *P. occidentalis*.

PLATYCODON

(Campanulaceae) Chinese Bellflower
or Balloon Flower

Hardy perennials, related to the campanulas and useful plants for the front of the border or the rock garden.

Cultural requirements: Well-drained soil and a sunny situation.

Propagation: From seed outdoors in spring or by division.

P. grandiflorum up to 1 ft (30 cm) China and Japan
When in bud, the flowers resemble small balloons. They open cup-shaped and are borne several to a stem. 'Albus' is a tall form with almost white

flowers; 'Apoyama', with violet-blue flowers and *mariesii*, blue, are more compact kinds, suitable for the rock garden. Late summer to early autumn.

PLEIONE
(Orchidaceae) Indian Crocus
Dwarf orchids, with flowers on short stems that often open before the leaves appear.
Cultural requirements: Potting compost of peat, chopped sphagnum moss, and coarse sand, with plenty of broken crocks for drainage. The plants need plenty of water when growth is at its peak but should be watered sparingly when growth slows down and not at all when growth is dormant. They are hardy in a cold greenhouse and can be grown outdoors in milder districts, given winter protection.
Propagation: By division after the plants have finished flowering.

P. formosana 4 in. (10 cm)   Formosa
Pale rosy-crimson flowers with a fringed cream lip. There are several good cultivars, including 'Alba', white with a yellow lip and 'Pricei' ('Oriental Splendour'), purple-red. Spring.

PLUMBAGO
(Plumbaginaceae)
Evergreen shrubs for the warm greenhouse.
Cultural requirements: John Innes No. 2 or a similar compost. The plants need a shady situation and should be cut back hard after flowering. Water freely in summer, sparingly for rest of year. Minimum temperature 45 °F (7 °C).

P. capensis up to 15 ft (4·5 m)
Cape Leadwort   S. Africa
A greenhouse wall shrub with sky-blue flowers. There is also a white form, 'Alba'. Summer and autumn.

PLUME POPPY – see *Macleaya cordata*

PLUMS – see Fruit Garden

POACHED EGG PLANT
– see *Limnanthes douglasii*

POINSETTIA – see *Euphorbia pulcherrima*

POLEMONIUM
(Polemoniaceae)
Hardy perennials, useful in the border and rock garden, mainly with blue flowers.
Cultural requirements: Any ordinary garden soil and a sunny open situation.
Propagation: From seed outdoors in spring or by division in spring or autumn.

P. caeruleum 2 ft (60 cm)
Jacob's Ladder   Europe, including British Isles
An attractive perennial with decorative foliage and blue flowers. Early summer.

P. foliosissimum 2½ ft (75 cm)   U.S.A.
Blue campanulate flowers in clusters against a background of dense foliage. Long flowering period. Late spring to early autumn.

POLYANTHUS – see *Primula × media*

POLYGONATUM
(Liliaceae) Solomon's Seal
Cultural requirements: Any ordinary soil in good heart and a shady situation.
Propagation: By division in spring or autumn.

P. × hybridum (*P. multiflorum × P. odoratum*), the commonest garden 'Solomon's Seal', often grown as *P. multiflorum*. It is a more vigorous plant than its first parent. Early summer.

P. multiflorum 3 ft (1 m)
Solomon's Seal   Europe, including British Isles
Elegant plants for shady borders or for the wild or woodland garden. Small white pendent flowers on arching stems.

POLYGONUM
(Polygonaceae)
The knotweeds are a large family of hardy plants, that includes annuals, perennials, and climbers.
Cultural requirements: Any ordinary garden soil and a sunny situation.
Propagation: Annual kinds from seed outdoors in spring; perennial species from seed or by division; shrubby species from stem cuttings in a frame in late summer.

P. affine 1 ft (30 cm)   Himalayas
Attractive mat-forming plant for moist soils. Rose-pink flowers in spikes and foliage that colours to coppery-bronze in autumn. 'Darjeeling Red' is a form with crimson flowers; 'Donald Lowndes' is more compact, with more prominent spikes of rose-coloured flowers which persist and deepen in colour as they mature. Summer to autumn.

P. amplexicaule 3 ft (1 m)   Himalayas
A taller species, useful in the border, with bright crimson poker-like spikes of bloom on slender erect stems. There are several good cultivars, including 'Album', white, tinged pink; and 'Firetail', crimson-scarlet. Late summer to early autumn.

P. baldschuanicum Russian Vine   S.E. Russia
Sometimes known also as the 'Mile-a-Minute' vine, this vigorous climber is ideal for covering unsightly sheds, dead trees and other similar

objects. The pinkish-white flowers are borne profusely in feathery panicles, over a long period. Summer to autumn.

P. bistorta 2 ft (60 cm) Bistort   Europe
Erect spikes of soft pink flowers. 'Superbum' is taller, with flowers of a paler pink. Summer.

P. campanulatum 3 ft (1 m)   Himalayas
Pale pink flowers in loose pendent panicles. A good plant for the wild or woodland garden. Midsummer to autumn.

P. cuspidatum (syn. *Reynoutria japonica*)
up to 8 ft (2·5 m) Japanese Knotgrass   Japan
A handsome but extremely rampant and invasive species, difficult to eradicate once established. Suitable only for the wild or woodland garden. The white plumes of blossom are attractive as also are the crimson hollow stems. Late summer.

P. orientale up to 6 ft (2 m)   Tropical Asia
A lovely annual species with clusters of drooping pink flowers. Summer.

P. vaccinifolium 6 in. (15 cm)   Himalayas
A shrubby, mat-forming species that likes a well-drained but moist situation and that makes a good rock garden plant. The rose-pink heather-like flowers are borne on wiry stems.

POLYPODIUM
(Polypodiaceae)
Hardy ferns.
Cultural requirements: Humus-rich soil and a shady situation.
Propagation: From spores under glass; or, more usually, by division in spring.

P. vulgare 1 ft (30 cm)   Britain
The common polypody is an evergreen fern, found on walls and banks throughout the British Isles, particularly where the soil is on the chalky side. 'Pulcherrimum' is a form whose fronds are more deeply waved than those of the type.

POMEGRANATE – see *Punica granatum*

PONTEDERIA
(Pontederiaceae) Pickerel Weed
Hardy aquatic plants with arrow-head leaves and spikes of blue or white flowers.
Cultural requirements: Plant in rich bottom soil in about 6 in. (15 cm) of water.
Propagation: By division in spring.

P. cordata 2 ft (60 cm)   N. America
This species has blue, white, and green flowers. The variety *angustifolia* has bright blue flowers. Summer.

POOLS – see Water Gardens

POPLAR – see *Populus*

POPPY – see *Meconopsis* and *Papaver*

POPULUS
(Salicaceae)
Hardy deciduous trees, many of which are of exceptionally rapid growth. Suitable as screens but not in the vicinity of buildings as their roots can cause serious damage to foundations. Many species have attractive catkins and fragrant foliage.
Cultural requirements: Any type of soil except dry chalky ones which most species dislike. They like moist conditions.
Propagation: By cuttings, layers, or suckers in autumn.

P. alba up to 90 ft (27 m) White Poplar
        W. Asia, and Europe, including British Isles
Also known as 'Abele', a large tree with leaves that are felted with white on their undersides.

P. balsamifera up to 100 ft (30 m)
Balsam Poplar   N. America
A large tree of erect habit, whose young leaves distil a pleasing aromatic fragrance in their neighbourhood. This aroma is common to several other poplars, including *P. candicans*, the 'Balm of Gilead'.

P. nigra up to 100 ft (30 m)
Black Poplar   Europe and W. Asia
Large trees, heavily branched with diamond-shaped leaves and red catkins. *P. n.* 'Italica' (syn. 'Pyramidalis'), is the well known slender and columnar Lombardy poplar.

P. tremula 50 ft (15 m) Aspen
A tree of medium size with leaves on slender flattened stalks that cause them to be almost perpetually in motion. Good yellow autumn colour.

PORTUGAL LAUREL – see *Prunus lusitanica*

PORTULACA
(Portulaceae)
Delightful half-hardy annuals with fleshy leaves and colourful single or double flowers in shades of scarlet, pink, purple, and yellow as well as white.
Cultural requirements: Any good garden soil, well-drained, and a sunny situation.
Propagation: From seed in gentle heat under glass in spring or outdoors later where plants are to flower.

P. grandiflora 6 in. (15 cm)   Brazil
Richly coloured blooms in great profusion make this an excellent plant for the rock garden in summer, or for edging. The double forms are especially attractive. 'Sunglo', an F$_1$ hybrid strain, has double flowers, 2½ in. (6·5 cm) across, in a blend of brilliant shades. Summer to mid-autumn.

POTATOES – see Kitchen Garden

POTENTILLA
(Rosaceae) Cinquefoil
Hardy perennials and shrubby plants with strawberry-like foliage and flowers.
Cultural requirements: Herbaceous and shrubby kinds: Ordinary fertile soil and a sunny situation.
Propagation: Herbaceous kinds: From seed outdoors in late spring; by division in autumn.

Shrubby species: From seed outdoors in spring; by cuttings in a cold frame in late summer or autumn.

P. atrosanguinea 1½ ft (45 cm)　　　　Himalayas
Dark crimson flowers on branching stems and strawberry-like foliage. 'Etna' and 'Gibson's Scarlet' are both improvements on the type. Hardy perennial. Summer.

P. fruticosa
up to 4 ft (1·2 m) Europe, Asia, and N. America
The shrubby cinquefoils are noteworthy for their exceptionally long flowering season, being seldom without bloom from late spring to autumn.

Their restricted size makes them ideal shrubs for the smaller garden and they associate well with hardy perennials. There are numerous named forms of which 'Farrer's White'; 'Katherine Dykes', primrose-yellow; 'Sunset', deep orange; 'Tangerine', coppery-orange; and 'Vilmoriniana', creamy flowers and an erect habit, are all worthy of note. Late spring to autumn.

POTTING
An important operation in the development of young plants, either from seed or from cuttings. The first pots, often known as thumb pots, should not exceed 3 in. (8 cm) in diameter at the top. As plants develop and the pots fill with roots, they are potted-on into larger sizes, 5 in. (13 cm), 7 in. (17 cm), and in special cases up to 9 or 10 in. (22–25 cm). Care should be taken to move plants on to a larger size before the roots become pot-

Seedlings pricked out 2 in. (5 cm) apart into boxes of potting compost for growing on.

bound. The correct stage for this operation is normally when roots begin to appear at the drainage holes.

PRICKING OUT
Another gardening operation that consists of transferring overcrowded seedling plants to fresh boxes or from a seed bed to a properly spaced row outdoors.

PRIMROSE – see *Primula vulgaris*

PRIMULA
(Primulaceae)
An extensive genus of perennials of great value for spring bedding in the rock garden and by the waterside. The tender kinds make superb pot plants for the cool greenhouse.
Cultural requirements: Greenhouse species: John Innes No. 2 or similar potting compost and a shaded well-ventilated cold frame in summer, a temperature of 50–55 °F (10–12 °C) in the greenhouse in winter.

Hardy species: A soil rich in humus and abundant supplies of moisture. Most kinds, including primroses and polyanthus, like a partly shaded situation.
Propagation: Greenhouse species: From seed under glass in a temperature of 50–55 °F (10–12 °C); *P. sinensis* and *P. obconica* in spring, *P. malacoides* at midsummer.

Hardy species: From seed under glass in gentle heat in early spring or in a cold frame later. Germination tends to be erratic unless seed is sown as soon as ripe.

P. auricula 9 in. (22 cm) Auricula
Rock garden or border plants with fleshy leaves, covered, in many kinds, with a white or yellowish waxy farina. Good named forms include 'Blairside Yellow', dwarf yellow; 'Celtic King', yellow with white eye; 'Dusty Miller', yellow, leaves with a dense white farina; 'Mrs J. H. Wilson', lilac-mauve with yellow eye; and 'Queen Alexandra', pale yellow and cream. Spring.

P. beesiana 2 ft (60 cm)　　　　W. China
Candelabra type primulas with lilac-purple flowers

Re-pot plants as roots begin to appear at the drainage holes

Primula obconica Giant Flowered Mixed

in erect whorled spikes. Moist soil and partial shade. Good for waterside planting. Early summer.

P. bulleyana 2 ft (60 cm)   Yunnan
Another attractive candelabra species with striking apricot-orange flowers. Moist soil and partial shade. Summer.

P. denticulata 1 ft (30 cm)
Drumstick Primula   Himalayas
Popular early flowering hardy perennial with large spherical drumstick heads of lilac flowers. 'Alba' is an interesting white form; 'Prichard's Ruby', a rich ruby-red. Sun or partial shade. Early spring.

P. florindae 3 ft (1 m)
Himalayan Cowslip   S.E. Tibet
A magnificent and stately hardy primula, with heads of pendent scented sulphur-yellow flowers. Very moist, even boggy soil and sun or partial shade. Summer.

P. japonica 1½ ft (45 cm)   Japan
Easy to grow moisture loving hardy primula, suitable for sun or partial shade. The reddish-purple flowers are borne in whorls on erect stems. Late spring to early summer.

P. malacoides 1 ft (30 cm) Fairy Primula   China
A greenhouse perennial of delicate beauty with dainty flower clusters, lavender in the type but now obtainable in pink, purple, carmine, and white, and in various attractive cultivars. 'Perfection' produces robust plants with candelabra-like stems and large flowers in blush-pink, rose, cerise, crimson, lavender, and mauve. Winter temperature 45–55 °F (7–12 °C). Make good house plants. Winter and spring.

P. × media (*P. veris* × *P. vulgaris*)
up to 1 ft (30 cm) Polyanthus   Garden origin
Among the most colourful of spring bedding plants, polyanthus, particularly the giant-flowered kinds, also make excellent greenhouse pot plants that can be taken indoors when in flower.

There are many fine cultivars in single or mixed colours, including 'Pacific Super Giants', 'Pacific Hybrids', 'Pacific Giants Blue Shades', and 'Giant Yellow'. Outdoors, a cool, moist, shady border suits them best. Spring.

P. obconica 1 ft (30 cm)   China
Another greenhouse species with larger flower trusses produced over an exceptionally long period. They also make first class house plants. Obtainable in a wide colour range that includes white, light and dark blue, pink, salmon, and crimson. 'Apple Blossom', salmon-pink; 'Goliath', cerise-red with individual flowers 2½ in. (6·5 cm) across; and 'True Blue', lavender-blue, are all outstanding named forms. Spring.

Primula × media (Polyanthus)

P. pulverulenta 3 ft (1 m)　　　　　　W. China
An attractive moisture loving candelabra-type hardy species with deep claret-red flowers on tall mealy stems. They will quickly naturalize themselves, given conditions to their liking. 'Bartley Strain' has flowers of a soft pink. Summer.

P. rosea 6 in. (15 cm)　　　　　　Himalayas
Delightful little perennials for a damp position at the margins of a stream or pool. The flowers are a bright rose-pink with a yellow eye and are borne in clusters on short stems. Spring.

P. vulgaris 4 in. (10 cm) Primrose　　British Isles
The simple yellow primrose of our hedgerows and streamsides has undergone some striking changes in the hands of the plant breeders and many hybrid strains are now obtainable with colours ranging from white through shades of yellow, pink, cerise, crimson, and scarlet to deep blue and violet. Some of these make excellent pot plants for the greenhouse or indoors, especially 'Mother's Day', a strain with extra large flowers up to 2 in. (5 cm) across. Spring.

PRIVET – see *Ligustrum* and Hedges

PROPAGATION

Among the various ways of propagating plant material, the best known and most commonly practised is from seed. Annuals, biennials, perennials, shrubs, and trees can all be reproduced by this means, but it is less commonly used for the two last named groups than for the rest. In any case, not all plants will breed true from seed so that other means have to be used to produce plants that are exact replicas of their originals.

Stocks of herbaceous perennials are, in most instances, easily increased by division or, in some cases, of which phlox and oriental poppies are examples, by root cuttings. Trees and shrubs are normally increased by stem cuttings, layers, or offshoots.

These are all economical methods by which the amateur gardener can increase his stocks of plants. Many shrubs root easily from cuttings even without the help of special equipment such as a heated propagating frame.

The advantage of heat and glass, however, is that stocks can be more easily increased from softwood cuttings. These consist of lengths of stem, 2–3 in. (5–8 cm) long, taken from young shoots of the current year's growth. They should be cut off cleanly with a sharp knife or secateurs, just below a leaf joint. Before inserting them into the rooting medium, the lower pairs of leaves should be removed.

They are then firmly inserted and kept covered with a sheet of glass or polythene until roots begin to form. This process usually takes from three weeks to a month. The use of a rooting compound, in which the base of the cuttings are dipped, will increase the chances of successful rooting.

Various kinds of rooting media can be used, including pure sand, peat, vermiculite, and proprietary formulae. A good home-made compound consists of one part sterilized loam, two parts peat, and three parts sharp sand. For plants that like lime, such as viburnums, ¾ oz. (21 g) of ground chalk or limestone can be added to each barrow-load of material.

If the cuttings are in a frame, it should be kept closed until roots have formed, except for a short period daily to dry out condensation which can cause damping-off. Where only a few cuttings are being taken, the easiest procedure is to insert them round the edges of a 4, 5 or 6 in. (10–15 cm) pot and then enclose the pot in a polythene bag.

When rooting has taken place, the cuttings should be hardened off before transferring them to 3 in. (8 cm) pots. After the transfer, the pots should be shaded until the young roots recover from the shock of transplantation.

The best time for taking softwood cuttings is around midsummer. An easier method for the novice is by means of semi-ripe or hardwood cuttings. The former can be taken in late summer, those from fully ripened wood are best taken in autumn. Many popular shrubs, such as deutzias, buddleias, spiraeas, and viburnums root readily from semi-ripe cuttings.

These strike well in a cold frame where they can be left *in situ* to overwinter. They should be ready for planting out the following spring.

The easiest method of all is by hardwood cuttings, although the scope is restricted to a narrower choice of shrubs. The chances of success are increased if such cuttings are taken with a 'heel'. This is a portion of the older wood, usually roughly elliptical, that comes away when the side shoot is pulled off its parent stem. It should be trimmed with a sharp knife or razor blade before the cutting is inserted.

Hardwood cuttings should be shortened to between 6 and 12 in. (15–30 cm). Any unripe wood at their tips should be removed. They will then be ready for inserting in V-shaped trenches, with ½ in. (1 cm) of sharp sand trickled into the bottom.

After they go in, 1–2 in. (2·5–5 cm) apart, the cuttings should be well firmed to ensure that there are no air pockets below soil level that might inhibit root formation. A position at the foot of a north facing wall is best. This will lessen the risk of damage due to a rapid thaw after severe frost. Alternatively, they can go into a shady north facing border.

Among the shrubs that strike easily from hardwood cuttings are clerodendrum, deutzias, summer and winter jasmines, laurels, privet, mock orange, flowering currant, roses, rosemary, willows, skimmias, snowberry, lilacs, and viburnums.

PRUNING

Before we go into action with the secateurs, it is as well to know the reasons for carrying out the important operation of pruning.

In the first place, we prune to induce more vigorous growth, to increase the production of flowers and, in the case of fruit trees and bushes, to concentrate their energies on the production of bigger and better fruit. Also, with established subjects, we prune to keep the plants shapely, to remove dead and diseased wood and to get rid of unwanted shoots and branches.

A pair of sharp secateurs is an essential tool for this operation. There are various kinds obtainable, most of them equally effective but none of which will give the essential clean cut if their blades are blunt. A pruning saw can also be useful for dealing with stouter branches.

Many shrubs such as camellias, magnolias, and rhododendrons will seldom, if ever, need pruning but the more vigorous deciduous shrubs and climbers will benefit from regular annual attention. As a rule-of-thumb guide to pruning, those that flower on the previous year's growths are cut back as soon as the flowers have faded; those that bloom on the current season's growth are cut back in early spring or late winter.

Certain shrubs such as lavender, heathers, and brooms will not tolerate drastic pruning. The procedure with these is to prune regularly but lightly, always avoiding cutting back into old wood.

The pruning of roses is a thorny subject in more senses than one. Opinions are divided as to the best time for this operation and many gardeners recommend early spring as the ideal time for the job. In actual fact, however, newly planted roses can be pruned at any time from the beginning of winter up to the end, provided that growth is dormant. This can be an advantage where large numbers of roses are grown. It spreads the operation over several months and allows full advantage to be taken of spells of fine weather.

The objects of pruning are threefold. Roses, although we sometimes tend to overlook the fact, are shrubs. Left to their own devices, they will produce a tangle of shoots, bearing flowers of only average size and quality.

We prune in the first place, therefore, to produce fewer but finer blooms. This aim is achieved by concentrating the upward flow of sap in spring into a smaller number of dormant 'eyes' or buds, thus allowing each of the resulting shoots to develop without competition and overcrowding.

Also where roses, as they so often are, are being used for bedding, pruning will ensure that the plants attain approximate uniformity of height, although, where several different cultivars are being grown, there are still bound to be considerable variations.

The best pruning tool for the amateur is a pair of good quality secateurs. These, if kept in good condition and sensibly used, will make clean cuts without snags or torn stems. Where older and stouter growths have to be dealt with, a small pruning saw can be an advantage.

Many expert rose growers prefer to use a pruning knife, but practice is necessary before this can be used effectively. With only a few exceptions, newly planted roses need cutting back hard in their first season. The easiest way is to carry out this initial pruning before the bushes go in, cutting out all weak and twiggy growths and shortening the stronger stems to about 6 in. (15 cm) in the case of hybrid teas and 8–9 in. (20–22 cm) for floribundas.

On light sandy soils, however, which are often

lacking in humus, it is better merely to tip the shoots of new plants lightly and to encourage growth during their first season by generous mulching with peat, leafmould, well-rotted garden compost or manure.

The other exceptions are newly planted climbing forms of bush roses. These are obtained as mutants or sports from hybrid teas and floribundas, which, in isolated cases, develop a climbing habit. Too severe pruning of these in their first season can cause them to revert to bush form.

Among the roses needing this kind of treatment are the climbing versions of 'Ena Harkness', 'Shot Silk', 'Spek's Yellow', and other popular kinds like that loveliest and most fragrant of pale pink roses, 'Lady Sylvia'. The majority of these climbing sports are much less vigorous than climbers proper and they seldom exceed 10–12 ft (3–4 m) in height.

The pruning procedure after rose bushes have completed their first season's growth is quite different. In order to obtain blooms of exhibition size and quality, drastic pruning, allied to an intensive feeding programme, will be necessary. For ordinary garden and cutting purposes, however, more moderate procedures can be practised.

The former method consists of cutting back all the stems to within 4–5 in. (10–13 cm) of soil level. Moderate pruning entails cutting back hard all inward growing and crossing stems and shortening all other main and lateral growths by half.

The position of the pruning cut is of vital importance. It should be made just above an outward pointing bud at an angle of approximately 45 degrees, but not close enough to cause damage to the dormant bud.

Established floribundas require a different pruning technique from hybrid teas. Annual pruning should consist of cutting back lightly any main shoots that have appeared from the base during the season. At the same time, older and weaker shoots are pruned back to one or two buds.

PRUNUS
(Rosaceae)
Ornamental deciduous and evergreen shrubs and trees grown primarily for the beauty of their blossom in spring and early summer. The genus includes the lovely Japanese cherries, the flowering almonds and peaches, and the bird cherries and cherry laurel.

Cultural requirements: For culture of peaches and nectarines, see Fruit Garden. Ornamental species, in the main, will thrive in any ordinary garden soil but prefer those in which lime is present. They also like a sunny, well-drained situation.

Propagation: Mainly by budding, except where species or raising new cultivars are the objectives, when new kinds are grown from seed.

P. × amygdalo-persica (*P. dulcis* × *P. persica*)
20 ft (6 m)   Garden origin
This hybrid between the peach and almond is normally represented by the cultivar 'Pollardii', a beautiful small tree which is an improvement on the almond, having larger flowers of a more intense pink. Early spring.

P. avium 50 ft (15 m) Gean and Mazzard
Europe, including British Isles, and W. Asia
One of the loveliest of our native trees, the wild cherry has masses of white cup-shaped flowers in nodding clusters, appearing as the leaves unfurl. 'Plena' is a double form that makes an attractive garden specimen. Spring.

P. cerasifera up to 20 ft (6 m) Myrobalan or Cherry Plum   Caucasus and W. Asia
Small trees with white, wide open blooms, followed on mature trees by rounded cherry-like fruits which are edible but not of particularly interesting flavour. Makes a useful hedging plant. 'Atropurpurea' is a form with coppery-purple foliage. It is better known as 'Pissardii'. Early spring.

P. conradinae up to 30 ft (9 m)   China
Early flowering cherry species that makes a good specimen tree for the small garden. The flowers are pink in bud, opening to white. 'Semiplena' is a good semi-double form. Late winter.

P. dulcis (syn. *P. amygdalus*) up to 30 ft (9 m)
Common Almond   S. Europe and N. Africa
The popular flowering almond is one of the first trees to bloom in spring. The single flowers are pink and there is also a showier double form, 'Roseoplena'. Early spring.

P. incisa 15 ft (4.5 m) Fuji Cherry   Japan
A small spreading tree that flowers early. The small flowers are white, tinged with pink in bud and the toothed foliage colours attractively in autumn. 'Moerheimii' is a cultivar of weeping habit. Early spring.

P. laurocerasus up to 20 ft (6 m)
Common Laurel   E. Europe and Asia Minor
Vigorous evergreen shrubs with dark leathery polished foliage, useful as screens or as hedges in larger gardens. The creamy-white flowers are small and almond-scented and are followed by red cherry-like fruits that later turn black. There are various cultivars, including 'Angustifolia', with narrower leaves than the type; 'Otto Luyken', a compact form of upright habit; 'Rotundifolia', the best hedging laurel; and 'Variegata', an

interesting form with leaves splashed with creamy-white. Early summer.

P. lusitanica up to 20 ft (6 m) Spain and Portugal
Evergreen tree or large shrub, a useful alternative to *P. laurocerasus* on shallow chalky soils. Attractive dark green foliage and spikes of scented white flowers. Midsummer.

P. padus up to 50 ft (15 m) Bird Cherry
Europe, including British Isles, and N. Asia
A valuable tree for the wild or woodland garden with clusters of white scented flowers appearing soon after leaves unfurl. There are several cultivars, including 'Watereri', that are an improvement on the type. Spring.

P. persica up to 30 ft (9 m) China
The garden forms of peach are small trees or large shrubs producing pale pink blossom on the bare branches early in the year. There are many named cultivars including 'Alba' and 'Alboplena', with single and double white flowers respectively and 'Klara Meyer', the most popular form, with double peach-pink blossom.

P. sargentii (syn. *P. serrulata sachalensis*)
up to 20 ft (6 m) Japan
This is one of the loveliest of the Japanese cherries, round-headed and massed with single pink blossom. The foliage opens coppery-bronze, turning green as it matures and changing again to brilliant hues of scarlet and orange in autumn. Early spring.

P. serrulata up to 30 ft (9 m) Origin unknown
This small spreading tree with a flattened head and white double flowers, is the parent of many of the so-called Japanese cherries most of which are hybrids of this species and of *P. speciosa*. Among the many lovely named cultivars, the following are outstanding:

'Amanogawa' (syn. *P. serrulata erecta*), a fastigiate form that makes a slender column, massed with vanilla-scented double pale pink flowers;

'Fugenzo', a tree of compact habit, flat-topped with large double rose-pink flowers in pendent clusters;

'Hisakura', a small tree with single deep pink flowers;

'Hokusai', widely spreading habit, its branches massed with semi-double pink flowers. The young foliage is coppery-bronze;

'Kanzan', the most popular of all the Japanese cherries, popular for street planting. Upright ascending branches and double flowers of a rather coarse pink. Often confused with 'Hisakura';

'Kiku-shidare Sakura', a lovely weeping cherry with pendent branches to ground level, wreathed in masses of double pink blossom;

'Pink Perfection', raised in Britain and a form of

great beauty with pink flowers in long clusters;

'Shimidsu Sakara' (syn. *P. serrulata longipes*), a lovely cherry with a wide spreading umbrella-shaped head and double white flowers with fringed petals, pale pink in bud;

'Ukon', an unusual cultivar with yellowish-green flowers seen to best advantage against a background of dark conifers.

The flowering period of the above mentioned cultivars varies between early to late spring.

P. subhirtella up to 30 ft (9 m) Japan
A species containing trees of small to medium size and forms of varying habit and flowering periods. 'Autumnalis' is a cultivar with semi-double white flowers that appear in succession throughout the winter during mild spells. 'Autumnalis Rosea' has flowers of a pale pink. There are also several attractive weeping forms, including 'Pendula' and 'Pendula Rosea'. These are of very modest proportions and flower in early spring. Winter or early spring.

P. triloba 12 ft (4 m) Garden origin
A delightful deciduous flowering shrub seen at its best on a wall. The double form, 'Multiplex', is most commonly seen. It has erect stems thickly clustered with small pink rosette flowers. Early spring.

PSEUDOTSUGA
(Pinaceae) Douglas Fir
Small genus of evergreen conifers of which the most important is *P. menziesii* (syn. *P. taxifolia*). They are stately trees of broadly pyramidal habit and are valuable as timber trees.
Cultural requirements: Any moist well-drained soil with the exception of chalk.
Propagation: From seed in a cold frame or outdoors in spring.

P. taxifolia (syn. *P. douglasii*) 200 ft (60 m)
Douglas Fir Western N. America
Although the type plant is too large for gardens of small to average size, there are cultivars of sufficiently modest dimensions for the smallest plot. 'Fletcheri' is a slow growing cultivar with blue-green foliage not exceeding 6 ft (2 m) in height. 'Holmstrup' and 'Nana' are similarly of dwarf character with deep green and glaucous-blue foliage respectively. 'Brevifolia' and 'Densa' are two other miniature slow growing bush forms that look well in the rock or heather garden.

PTERIS
(Pteridaceae)
Tender ferns suitable for outdoor culture in milder districts but best in a cool greenhouse or as room plants.
Cultural requirements: Indoors: Compost of

Prunus subhirtella autumnalis 'All Winter'

equal parts fibrous loam, leafmould, peat and sand, and a shady part of the greenhouse, conservatory, or a shady cool window-sill.

Outdoors: Any ordinary soil, preferably rich in humus, and a shady situation.

Propagation: From spores or by division.

P. cretica 1 ft (30 cm)   Tropics and sub-tropics
Pale green leathery fronds; there are also crested and silver-variegated kinds.

P. serrulata (syn. *P. multifida*) 1½ ft (45 cm)
Ribbon Fern   China and Japan
This fern with its varieties makes an excellent pot plant for indoors, or the cool greenhouse. The narrow, ribbon-like fronds have attractively fluted edges.

PULMONARIA
(Boraginaceae) Lungwort
Hardy perennials useful in the border for their early flowering character.

Cultural requirements: Any ordinary moist garden soil and a sunny or partly shaded situation.

Propagation: From seed outdoors in spring; by division in spring or autumn.

P. angustifolia 9 in. (22 cm)   Europe
Spikes of gentian-blue flowers rising from rosettes of dull green foliage. A rapid spreader that makes a good ground cover plant. Early to late spring.

P. rubra 9 in. (22 cm)   Transylvania
A species with flowers of a bright terracotta. Spring.

P. saccharata up to 1 ft (30 cm)
Bethlehem Sage   Europe
The foliage is bright green, marbled with white. The flowers are blue, changing to pink as they open. Cottagers knew them as 'Soldiers-and-Sailors'. 'Mrs Moon' and 'Pink Dawn', with pink flowers, are both improvements on the type. Spring.

PULSATILLA
(Ranunculaceae) Pasque Flower
Hardy perennials formerly classified under 'Anemone'. Useful spring flowering border or rock garden subjects.

Cultural requirements: Well-drained soil and a sunny situation.

Propagation: From seed in a cold frame when ripe in spring; by careful root division in spring or autumn.

P. vernalis 4 in. (10 cm)   European Alps
Blue-tinged white flowers covered with a silky down. A choice plant for the rock garden. Spring.

P. vulgaris
9 in. (22 cm)   Europe, including British Isles
A delightful native plant, with nodding bell-shaped lavender flowers, covered with silky hairs and followed by decorative seedheads. 'Alba' is an attractive white form. Spring.

PUNICA
(Punicaceae)
Shrubs or small trees on the tender side. Normally grown on a warm sheltered wall in all but the most favoured districts of Britain.

Cultural requirements: Well-drained soil and a really sheltered sunny situation.

Propagation: From seed under glass in gentle heat in spring; by cuttings in summer.

P. granatum up to 15 ft (4·5 m)
Pomegranate   Mediterranean and Middle East
Deciduous shrubs with slightly spiny stems. Funnel-shaped orange-scarlet fleshy flowers, seldom followed by fruit in Britain. There are several good cultivars, including 'Albo-pleno', with double ivory-white flowers; 'Flore Pleno', with double orange-red flowers; and 'Nana', an attractive dwarf form not exceeding 2 ft (60 cm) in height. Summer.

PUSCHKINIA
(Liliaceae)
Pretty small hardy bulbous plants, with bluebell-like flowers.

Cultural requirements: Light sandy soil and a sunny situation.

Propagation: From seed in a cold frame in summer; by offsets in autumn.

P. scilloides 4 in. (10 cm)
Striped Squill   Asia Minor
Spikes of very pale blue flowers, striped with a deeper blue at the centres of the petals. 'Alba' is an attractive white form. They make good rock garden plants. Spring.

PYRACANTHA
(Rosaceae) Firethorn
Hardy evergreen flowering and berrying shrubs useful as specimens, for hedging or as wall subjects.

Cultural requirements: Any ordinary well-drained soil and a sunny or partly shaded situation. Will flower and fruit on north or east walls, and can be hard pruned into shape.

Propagation: From seed in a cool greenhouse or frame in spring; by cuttings in a frame or shady border in late summer.

P. atalantioides (syn. *P. gibbsii*)
up to 20 ft (6 m)   China
Large glossy leaves and a profusion of orange-scarlet berries. Very vigorous. 'Aurea' (syn. 'Flava') is a cultivar with striking yellow fruits. Early summer.

P. coccinea
up to 15 ft (4·5 m)   S. Europe and Asia Minor
White flowers followed by coral-red berries, set off to perfection by the dark green glossy foliage. 'Lalandei', the most widely grown of all the firethorns, is more vigorous than the type. Early summer.

P. rogersiana 15 ft (4·5 m)   S.W. China
Creamy-white flowers and large crops of reddish-orange berries. Smaller glossy leaves. 'Flava' has yellow fruits. Early summer.

PYRETHRUM – see *Chrysanthemum coccineum*

PYRUS
(Rosaceae)

The ornamental pears are trees of small to medium size with grey-green foliage in many species.

Pyrus communis is the ordinary fruiting pear (see Fruit Garden). With the exception of the willow-leaved pear, *P. salicifolia*, the ornamental kinds are not widely grown.
Cultural requirements: Any type of garden soil. The ornamental pears are tolerant of both drought and moisture and succeed well in cold districts and industrial areas.
Propagation: By grafting or layering.

P. salicifolia 30 ft (9 m)
Willow-leaved Pear   Caucasus
A species with narrow, willow-like leaves, silvery when young but turning a duller grey as they mature. Creamy-white flowers in spring followed by small inedible yellow fruits. An excellent lawn specimen or focal plant.

'Pendula' is a form of weeping habit.

QUERCUS
(Fagaceae) Oak

Hardy deciduous and evergreen trees and occasionally, shrubs, forming a large and widely distributed genus, mostly large for the garden of small to medium size.
Cultural requirements: Deep rich soil, but will not succeed on shallow chalky ones.
Propagation: From seed (Acorns) stratified in winter and sown outdoors in spring.

Q. cerris 120 ft (36 m)
Turkey Oak   Europe, and Asia Minor
One of the finest of the deciduous oaks with deeply lobed handsome foliage up to 5 in. (13 cm) long. 'Laciniata' has much more finely cut foliage than the type.

Q. coccinea 50 ft (15 m) Scarlet Oak   E. U.S.A.
Bold deeply lobed leaves that turn a fiery scarlet in autumn. One of the finest trees for autumn colour where space is available.

Q. ilex 60 ft (18 m) Holm Oak   S.W. Europe
Large evergreen trees, among the finest in garden cultivation. Makes an excellent screen in seaside areas and is equally useful as an elegant lawn specimen. Dark glossy green leaves, grey on reverse and tolerant of all soil conditions. Stands up well to clipping.

Q. robur 100 ft (30 m) Common Oak
Europe, including British Isles, and Asia Minor
The oak most commonly native to Britain. A stately and long lived tree whose leaves have shallow lobes.

There are many named cultivars, including weeping, columnar, and variegated kinds, 'Pendula', 'Fastigiata', and 'Variegata' respectively.

QUICKTHORN – see *Crataegus*

QUINCE – see *Chaenomeles*

RACEME
A type of inflorescence in which there is a main stem bearing flowers on non-branching stalks.

RADISH – see Kitchen Garden

RAMONDA
(Gesneriaceae)
Hardy alpine perennials suitable for the shady crevices of the rock garden.
Cultural requirements: Well-drained gritty soil, rich in humus, and a northerly or partly shaded vertical crevice.
Propagation: From seed in a cool greenhouse or frame in spring; by division of plants or from leaf cuttings.

R. myconi (syn. *R. pyrenaica*)
6 in. (15 cm)   Pyrenees
Pale mauve flowers with overlapping petals rising from a basal rosette of flat leaves. Summer.

RANUNCULUS
(Ranunculaceae)
A varied genus of which the common buttercup, *R. acris*, is a member. There is a double form of this in garden cultivation. The genus includes hardy border and alpine perennials, tuberous-rooted and aquatic plants.
Cultural requirements: Any ordinary garden soil rich in humus.
Propagation: From seed in a cool greenhouse or cold frame in autumn; herbaceous kinds by division in spring or autumn.

R. amplexicaulis 1 ft (30 cm)   Pyrenees
Dainty white flowers with golden-yellow centres. A useful plant for the sunny slopes of a rock garden. Late spring to early summer.
R. asiaticus up to 1 ft (30 cm)
Turban Ranunculus   S. Europe
Tuberous species with strains in a wide range of colours. Popular florists' flowers, long-lasting when cut. Tubers, which have claw-like ends should be planted, claws downwards, in a sunny sheltered situation. They can also be grown in a cool greenhouse for earlier flowers. Late spring to early summer.

RAOULIA
(Compositae)
Carpeting perennials of Australasian origin useful in the rock garden or alpine house.
Cultural requirements: Well-drained sandy soil and a sunny situation in the rock garden.
Propagation: From seed or by division, in spring.

R. australis ½ in. (1 cm)   New Zealand
Small silvery rosettes of leaves forming mats, topped by clusters of tiny white flowers. Spring.
R. glabra ½ in. (1 cm)   New Zealand
Close carpet of green leaves spangled with yellow flowers. Spring.

RASPBERRIES – see Fruit Garden

REBUTIA
(Cactaceae)
Low growing spherical cacti with small spines and red, yellow, or purple flowers.
Cultural requirements: John Innes No. 2 or similar potting compost with the addition of crushed brick, mortar rubble, or grit. Water sparingly in summer, withhold water in winter.
Propagation: From seed under glass.

R. minuscula up to 3 in. (8 cm)   Argentine
Globular spiny cushions with red trumpet-shaped flowers that appear from the base of the plants. Summer.
R. xanthocarpa up to 6 in. (15 cm)   Bolivia
Similar to the above mentioned species but with orange-red flowers. Summer.

RED CURRANTS – see Fruit Garden

RED HOT POKER – see *Kniphofia*

RED SPIDER – see Pest Control

REDWOOD – see *Sequoia*

REED MACE – see *Typha latifolia*

RESEDA
(Resedaceae) Mignonette
Hardy annuals with scented flowers.

Reseda (Mignonette)

Cultural requirements: Any ordinary garden soil.
Propagation: From seed sown outdoors in spring where plants are to flower.

R. *odorata*
up to 2 ft (60 cm)   N. Africa and Egypt
Cottage garden favourite with spikes of reddish flowers that are very fragrant. Summer.

RHEUM
(Polygonaceae)
Hardy perennials that make handsome foliage plants. The culinary rhubarb is a member of this genus.
Cultural requirements: Any ordinary garden soil rich in humus and a sunny situation.
Propagation: From seed outdoors in spring; by division in winter.

R. *palmatum* 6 ft (2 m)
Sorrel Rhubarb   N.E. Asia
Huge rounded lobed leaves and imposing spikes of deep red flowers. It makes a good plant for the waterside. R. *p. tanguticum* is a variety with larger leaves. Midsummer.

RHIPSALIDOPSIS
(Cactaceae)
Fairly small flat-stemmed succulents with pink flowers.
Cultural requirements: Richer compost than for most cacti which must be well-drained. Water throughout the whole of the year. Minimum temperature 50 °F (10 °C).
Propagation: By cuttings in summer.

R. *rosea* 9 in. (22 cm) Easter Cactus   Brazil
Rosy-pink flowers on flat spineless stems. Spring.

RHIZOME
Underground stems, bearing roots as well as leaves as in the bearded irises.

RHODODENDRON
(Ericaceae)
This genus, which now includes the azaleas, provides some of our finest garden shrubs. There is only one stipulation, namely that the soil in which they are grown must be completely lime-free. In addition to the evergreen rhododendrons and azaleas, there are deciduous kinds of the latter, many of whose leaves colour magnificently in autumn. The more tender azaleas make superb pot plants for indoors and the cool greenhouse.

There are numerous rhododendron species, but it is the hardy hybrids, with their extensive colour range and forms that are most widely grown. The more dwarf and compact kinds are useful in the rock garden and many kinds make first rate tub plants. This is an excellent way for the gardener on alkaline soils to enjoy their beauty.

R. *ponticum*, the common purple rhododendron, has naturalized itself in Britain and makes an ideal subject for screens and hedges.
Cultural requirements: Moist well-drained soil, rich in humus and free from lime. Most rhododendrons thrive in a partly shaded situation but many kinds of hardy hybrids are quite happy in full sun. Rhododendrons are surface rooting so that it is better to apply an annual mulch of peat, partly rotted leaves or bracken than to disturb the roots by forking over the soil in their vicinity. Plants will benefit by the removal of spent flower heads before they set seed.

They are extremely tolerant of town conditions and industrial pollution and therefore make excellent planting material for town gardens.

Hardy Hybrid Rhododendrons
The named forms of these colourful hybrids run into hundreds. A very restricted representative selection would include such popular kinds as

Rhododendron Langworth

'Betty Wormald', rose-pink; 'Britannia', crimson-scarlet; 'Cynthia', rosy-crimson; 'Goldsworth Yellow', primrose-yellow; 'Loderi', white to cream or pale pink; 'Mother of Pearl', blush-pink, fading to white; 'Mrs Furnival', pale rose-pink; and 'Pink Pearl', pale pink, probably the most widely planted of all rhododendrons.

More compact kinds are represented by the following, among countless others: 'Bluebird', violet-blue; 'Blue Tit', lavender-blue; 'Carmen', dark crimson; 'Elizabeth', dark red; 'Humming Bird', carmine; and 'Praecox', rosy-purple and one of the earliest to come into flower.

Deciduous Hybrid Azaleas

These are represented by the 'Ghent', 'Knaphill', and 'Exbury' hybrids, all of which flower in late spring or early summer. The first group have richly scented flowers. The foliage of many colours brilliantly in autumn.

There are also many named cultivars in each of the above mentioned groups including 'Harvest Moon', yellow; 'Klondyke', orange-gold; 'Strawberry Ice', flesh-pink; and 'Superbum', pink and apricot.

Evergreen Hybrid Azaleas

This group, too, includes an exceptionally large number of named cultivars of which the Kurume azaleas are the most widely planted. Popular kinds include 'Hatsugiri', crimson-purple; 'Hinodegiri', crimson; 'Hinomayo', pink; 'Kirin', deep rose; 'Palestrina', white tinged with pale green; and 'Vuyk's Scarlet', bright red.

RHOICISSUS
(Vitidaceae)

Greenhouse climbing perennials that are also popular as house plants since they stand up well to indoor conditions.

Cultural requirements: John Innes No. 2 or similar potting compost. Water freely in spring and summer, sparingly at other times. Minimum temperature 45 °F (7 °C).

Propagation: From partly ripened shoots in summer.

R. rhomboidea   Natal
Trifoliate dark green leaves and a dense habit of growth. Pinching out the growing points of young shoots will induce a more bushy habit. This plant rarely flowers in cultivation.

RHUBARB – see *Rheum*

RHUS
(Anacardiaceae) Sumach

Hardy deciduous flowering shrubs and trees grown primarily for their handsome pinnate foliage which colours brilliantly in autumn. Several species, formerly included in this genus, have now been transferred to *Cotinus* q.v.

Cultural requirements: Any ordinary garden soil and a sunny situation.

Propagation: From cuttings, suckers, or layers in autumn.

R. typhina up to 25 ft (8 m)
Stag's Horn Sumach   E. U.S.A.
Small tree or large shrub grown for the decorative quality of its large pinnate leaves, up to 2 ft (60 cm) long and divided into many smaller leaflets. The foliage colours to a brilliant scarlet and yellow in autumn and the crimson fruits, in conical panicles, found only on female plants, are very striking. Mid-spring.

It is worth noting that poison ivy, *Rhus toxicodendron*, is a member of this genus and that other species can cause skin irritations in those allergic to them.

RIBBON GRASS – see *Phalaris arundinacea*

RIBES
(Saxifragaceae)

Hardy deciduous shrubs that include gooseberries and black, red, and white currants whose culture is dealt with in the Fruit Garden section. There are also several ornamental kinds of great value in the garden in early spring.

Cultural requirements: Any ordinary garden soil and a sunny situation. Cut back flowering shoots when blooms have faded.

Propagation: By cuttings of ripened wood outdoors in autumn.

R. sanguineum 8 ft (2·5 m)
Flowering Currant   Western N. America
Medium-sized shrub whose flowers and leaves have a pungent black currant aroma. The flowers are a deep rose-pink borne in drooping clusters and are followed by small black fruits of no decorative value. The best known named cultivars are 'Atrorubens', deep crimson; 'King Edward VII', crimson; and 'Pulborough Scarlet', deep red. Spring.

R. speciosum 8 ft (2·5 m)
Fuchsia-flowered Gooseberry   California
An attractive shrub, that makes a good wall specimen, with small reddish-crimson fuchsia-like flowers, hanging in rows under the branches like those of a gooseberry. Hardy, but needs a warm sheltered situation to flower freely. Spring.

RICINUS
(Euphorbiaceae)

Half-hardy annuals grown for their handsome

palmate foliage. They also make good greenhouse pot plants.

Cultural requirements: Any garden soil rich in humus and a sunny situation.

Propagation: From seed under glass in heat in early spring to produce plants to go outdoors, after hardening off, in early summer.

R. communis 4 ft (1·2 m)
Castor Oil Plant   Tropical Africa
Handsome foliage plants with large maple-like leaves that vary in colour from green to coppery-bronze or purple. Widely used as accent plants in summer bedding schemes. There are several named cultivars including 'Gibsonii', with red-flushed leaves and stems and 'Zanzibarensis', with bright green leaves.

ROBINIA
(Leguminosae)

Hardy deciduous trees and large shrubs with attractive pinnate leaves and clusters of pea flowers.

Cultural requirements: Any ordinary garden soil and a sunny well-drained situation. The wood of robinia is brittle and exposed, windy positions should be avoided.

Propagation: From seed outdoors in late autumn; from rooted suckers in autumn. Choice cultivars by grafting.

R. hispida 8 ft (2·5 m) Rose Acacia   S. U.S.A.
Shrub or small tree with pinnate foliage up to 10 in. (25 cm) long and with racemes of pink pea flowers. Early summer.

R. pseudoacacia 40 ft (12 m)
False Acacia   N. America
Deciduous trees with spiny branches and pendent racemes of fragrant white flowers. There are several named cultivars of which the following are worthy of note: 'Aurea', golden-yellow leaves turning green later; 'Frisia', much smaller than the type with permanently golden leaves; and 'Inermis', small with a compact rounded head. Early summer.

ROCHEA
(Crassulaceae)

Greenhouse succulents, closely allied to the crassulas. They also make good house plants.

Cultural requirements: John Innes No. 2 compost with the addition of crushed brick or extra sand. Water very sparingly in winter. Minimum temperature 45 °F (7 °C).

Propagation: From seed under glass in heat in spring; by cuttings under glass in summer.

R. coccinea 1 ft (30 cm)   S. Africa
Grey-green fleshy leaves and scarlet flowers. Summer.

R. jasminea 9 in. (22 cm)   S. Africa
White flowers. Spring.

ROCK CRESS – see *Aubrieta*

ROCK GARDENS

Rock gardens can bring rich rewards but they are the kind of garden feature that needs constant attention where maintenance is concerned. In the average sized garden, however, there is no need, or, in fact, opportunity, to work on the grand scale. A too ambitious project tends, in any case, to throw the entire garden design out of balance.

In many cases, it should be possible to take advantage of the natural contours of the land. But if the garden is flat, it will be necessary to excavate and throw up mounds to give the necessary Alpine effect.

Where space permits, a small pool will enhance the attraction of a rock garden. The soil taken from the hole will also be useful for providing different levels. In any event, careful preliminary preparation of the site is important. The whole should be dug over, one spit deep. As far as possible, the fertile topsoil should be kept apart from any sub-soil that is excavated. The former can then go back to where it will do most good, on the surface.

All perennial weeds should be removed as digging proceeds, especially such persistent subjects as docks, thistles, creeping buttercup, ground elder, horsetail, and bindweed. As far as the choice of stone for the rocks is concerned, natural stones such as York, Westmorland, or Purbeck provide the most pleasing and authentic appearance. Choice, however, may have to be dictated by the kinds available locally as transport can add considerably to the cost.

Slabs of broken concrete can also be used to quite good effect. It does not, of course, have the same appearance as natural stone, but its artificial look is quickly camouflaged by trailing and creeping plants.

A good rule, when siting the rocks, is to think of icebergs. Only the tips of the stones should be showing in the iceberg ratio of one-eighth above to seven-eighths below. This may seem to be a wicked waste of stone, but rocks must be buried really deeply if an almond-cake effect is to be avoided.

Each stone should slope downwards and backwards into the soil. This will help to channel rain to the roots of the plants. Where natural stone is being used, the strata markings should all run in the same direction – normally horizontally.

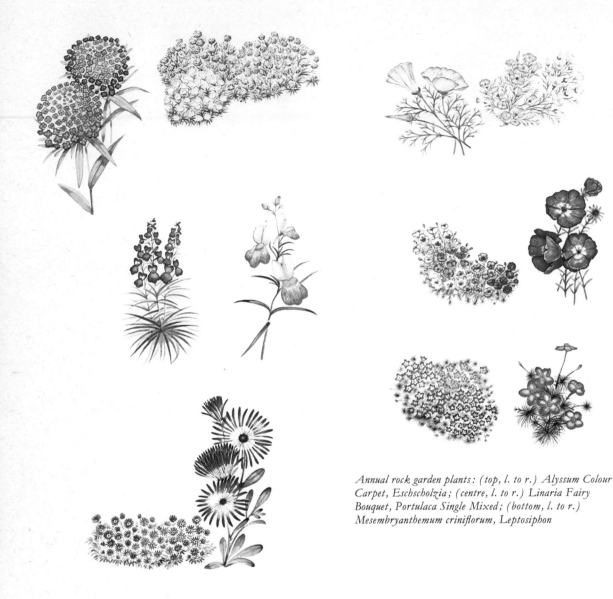

Annual rock garden plants: (top, l. to r.) Alyssum Colour Carpet, Eschscholzia; (centre, l. to r.) Linaria Fairy Bouquet, Portulaca Single Mixed; (bottom, l. to r.) Mesembryanthemum criniflorum, Leptosiphon

Once the construction is complete, planting can begin after the soil has had a few weeks to settle. Although most rock plants – except the tender and temperamental kinds – can go in from autumn to early spring, those with grey or felted foliage are best left until spring, especially if the soil is on the heavy side. If doubts exist about the drainage of the site, small pebbles or granite chippings can be used to improve the texture and porosity of the soil. This is particularly important in the case of alpines whose natural habitat is on the screes.

Among those with a liking for such conditions are *Leontopodium*, better known as edelweiss, the national flower of Switzerland, many of the saxifrages and various kinds of rock pinks. Spreaders and creepers should be planted so that they can overspill the sides of the rocks. Aubrieta, rock phloxes, and the prostrate forms of thyme are all good for this purpose.

A good basic planting for the newcomer to rock gardening would be three plants each of

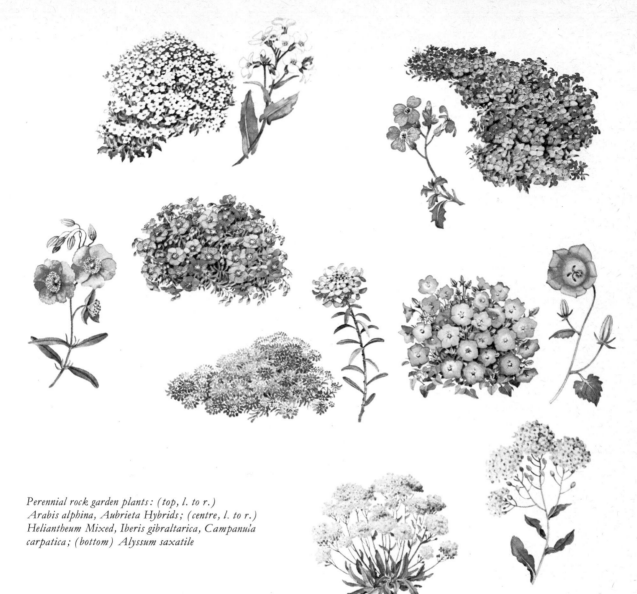

Perennial rock garden plants: (top, l. to r.)
Arabis alphina, Aubrieta Hybrids; (centre, l. to r.)
Heliantheum Mixed, Iberis gibraltarica, Campanula
carpatica; (bottom) Alyssum saxatile

aubrieta, the yellow *Alyssum saxatile* and the white perennial candytuft, *Iberis sempervirens.* All of these can be relied on for a first rate display of bloom each spring.

In late spring and early summer the display in the rock garden reaches its zenith. Rock phloxes will spread their colourful carpets of blossom and this, too, is the season of the many lovely species and cultivars of saxifrage, with their wide variety of flowers, form, and foliage.

A rock garden need not be without interest as summer progresses. Dwarf campanulas will take over where other plants leave off, with miniature geraniums and the sun roses in their extensive range of glowing colours.

For more continuing interest, there are many forms of dwarf conifer ideally suitable for planting in the rock garden. These are mentioned in the appropriate sections.

As the rock gardener grows in experience, so will his desire to grow some of the lovelier but more temperamental alpine plants.

ROCK ROSE – see *Helianthemum*

ROCKET – see *Hesperis*

RODGERSIA
(Saxifragaceae)

Hardy perennials with handsome palmate leaves and feathery inflorescences.

Cultural requirements: Moist peaty soils and a sheltered sunny or shady situation.

Propagation: By division in spring.

R. aesculifolia 4 ft (1·2 m)   China
Bronzy leaves like those of a horse chestnut and long white flower clusters. Summer.

R. pinnata 4 ft (1·2 m)   China
Clear pink flowers in many branched panicles and handsome bronze-tinged leaves. Summer.

R. podophylla 4 ft (1·2 m)   Japan
Cream flowers in large spreading clusters and striking lobed palmate foliage. Summer.

ROMNEYA
(Papaveraceae) Tree Poppy

Slightly tender shrubby perennials with handsome deeply cut leaves and large poppy-like flowers with a prominent boss of golden stamens.

Cultural requirements: Light soil rich in humus and a sunny sheltered situation. Romneyas resent disturbance.

Propagation: From root cuttings or suckers under glass in winter.

R. coulteri 4 ft (1·2 m)   California
Deeply divided glaucous foliage and white satin-textured flowers with striking golden stamens. Midsummer to autumn.

R. trichocalyx 4 ft (1·2 m)   California
Similar to former species but with more erect stems and bristly flower buds. Summer.

ROSA
(Rosaceae)

The roses are, without doubt, the most popular of all garden plants, thriving, as they do, in such a wide variety of soils, situations, and climatic conditions.

Although the emphasis is on the hybrid teas and floribundas, with their magnificent shapely flowers in an extensive range of colours, the old rose species and shrub roses still retain the affection of many gardeners for their unsophisticated beauty and their ease of cultivation. Climbing species and hybrids too are invaluable for covering walls or for decorative effect on pillars and pergolas, while the more vigorous kinds can be allowed to scramble through the branches of trees in a combination that enhances the beauty of both host plant and guest.

Cultural requirements: The optimum soil conditions are a deep fertile soil, enriched with well-rotted manure or compost. Roses, however, will give good results in a variety of soils provided that attention is paid to manuring, mulching, and feeding. A sunny open situation suits them best although some, like the climbing rose 'Mermaid', will flower and flourish even on a north wall.

Propagation: New cultivars are obtained from seed, sown in a cold frame in spring or outdoors later. Cultivars are budded on to stocks of R. rugosa, R. canina, and others, but many can also be raised from cuttings outdoors in a shady border in autumn. This is an economical way for the amateur to increase his favourites.

Pruning: Hybrid teas, floribundas, climbers, and ramblers are normally cut back hard each winter in accordance with the habits and requirements of each type. Rose species and the old-fashioned roses are treated in a similar manner to flowering shrubs; with them, pruning will be directed at maintaining a shapely bush and the removal of dead or diseased wood and any shoots that are overcrowding the plants.

Rose species and hybrids: These are so numerous that only a representative selection of the best garden kinds can be given. This applies also to the old and new shrub roses, and to the hybrid teas and floribundas.

R. banksiae up to 25 ft (8 m)
Banksian Rose   China
A vigorous semi-evergreen climber which needs a warm sunny wall to succeed. The slender stems are thornless and the foliage practically evergreen. The small rosette-like flowers, white in the type plant, are delicately scented. 'Lutea' is a form with double yellow flowers.

R. bracteata   China
This species is noteworthy mainly as a parent of the superb climber 'Mermaid', with evergreen foliage and sulphur-yellow single flowers, mentioned above.

R. centifolia 6 ft (2 m)   Caucasus
One of the oldest roses known in cultivation noteworthy for its delicious fragrance and multi-petalled pink flowers. There are many forms of the old cabbage rose and it has also played a part in the development of many hybrids.

R. chinensis 4 ft (1·2 m) China Rose   China
A 'perpetual flowering' species that most of the present-day hybrids can claim as an ancestor. The flowers are crimson or pink, followed by scarlet heps. They are very sweetly scented.

R. damascena 4 ft (1·2 m)
Damask Rose   Origin uncertain
An intensely fragrant semi-double rose, varying in colour from white to red whose petals are used

Rosa 'Super Star'

in the manufacture of Attar of Roses and other perfume essences. R. *d.* 'Versicolor', with pink and white flowers, is the York and Lancaster rose.

R. *filipes*   W. China
A vigorous rambling rose that will climb to the tops of tall trees. The white flowers, borne profusely in clusters, are sweetly scented. 'Kiftsgate' is an exceptionally vigorous form whose flower clusters consist of 100 or more flowers. These are followed by red fruits.

R. *gallica* 4 ft (1·2 m)   C. and S. Europe
This is another rose that has played a major role in the development of the present-day garden roses. The flowers are red, followed by rounded, sealing wax red heps. R. *g.* 'Versicolor', better known as 'Rosa Mundi', is an attractive form with semi-double blooms attractively striped with red and white.

R. *moschata* 12 ft (4 m)
Musk Rose   Origin uncertain
This is a vigorous rose whose creamy-white flowers have a strong musky fragrance. It flowers on into the autumn.

R. *moyesii* 10 ft (3 m)   W. China
A rose of erect habit with elegant arching stems and velvety crimson flowers followed by decorative flagon-shaped heps. 'Geranium' is an interesting form with flowers of a striking geranium-red.

R. *pimpinellifolia* (syn. R. *spinosissima*) 3 ft (1 m)
Burnet Rose   Europe and N. Asia
A small shrub, native to parts of Britain with small single yellow flowers appearing in late spring or early summer.

R. *rubiginosa* (syn. R. *eglanteria*) 9 ft (2·7 m)
Sweet Briar   Europe
Vigorous rose with aromatic foliage and sweetly scented pink flowers. The parent of many hybrids including the Penzance briars which make such excellent hedging plants.

R. *rubrifolia* 6 ft (2 m)   C. and S. Europe
This rose species is grown for the decorative effect of its brilliant coppery-purple foliage. The small pink flowers are comparatively insignificant and are followed by small red heps.

R. *rugosa* 6 ft (2 m)
Ramanas Rose   China and Japan
Perpetual flowering shrub rose with rough foliage and sweetly scented crimson-purple flowers followed by conspicuous scarlet heps. Among the delightful cultivars are such well known ones as 'Blanc Double de Coubert', with semi-double paper-white blooms; 'Frau Dagmar Haastrup', rose-pink; and 'Roserie de l'Hay', crimson-purple with creamy stamens.

R. *wichuraiana* 12 ft (4 m)   Japan
A trailing semi-evergreen species and the parent of the 'Wichuraiana Hybrids', which include such

well known ramblers as 'Albéric Barbier', 'Albertine', and 'Dorothy Perkins'.

Newer Shrub Roses

Chinatown 6 ft (2 m)
A perpetual flowering deep yellow rose, tinged with coppery-pink in bud.

Constance Spry 6 ft (2 m)
A shrub rose of loose and arching habit with large rose-pink blooms in the old cabbage-rose tradition.

Fritz Nobis up to 5 ft (1·5 m)
A fine modern shrub rose with salmon-pink flowers up to 4 in (10 cm) across.

Frühlingsgold 8 ft (2·5 m)
Free-flowering and vigorous hybrid with semi-double or single creamy-yellow flowers massing the arching stems in late spring and early summer.

Nevada 8 ft (2·5 m)
A rose reputedly of R. *moyesii* parentage, with an arching vigorous habit of growth. Perpetual flowering with creamy-white single flowers lavishly borne.

Penelope 6 ft (2 m)
Hybrid musk rose, delicately scented of 'Ophelia' parentage. The semi-double flowers are a rich creamy-pink with golden stamens.

Hybrid Teas and Floribundas

Any list of the above mentioned roses is bound to be only of limited value since new introductions in large numbers supersede the older ones annually. Those that follow are roses that have stood the test of time and show signs of becoming what is known in the world of pop music as standards.

Hybrid Teas for General Garden Purposes

*'Blue Moon', lilac-silver;
*'Ena Harkness', crimson-scarlet;
*'Fragrant Cloud', geranium-red – exceptionally fragrant;
'Gail Borden', rose-pink, shaded yellow on reverse;
*'Josephine Bruce', crimson-scarlet, velvety texture;
'King's Ransom', yellow;
*'Lady Seton', deep rose-pink;
'Mischief', salmon-pink;
'Pascali', white;
'Peace', pale yellow, tinged pink;
'Perfecta', cream, shaded rosy-red;
'Piccadilly', scarlet, shaded yellow on reverse;
*'Prima Ballerina', deep pink;
'Rose Gaujard', white, flushed carmine;
*'Silver Lining', pale rose-pink, silvered on reverse;

*Very Fragrant

Rosa 'Mermaid'

*'Super Star', salmon-orange flowers;
*'Sutter's Gold', orange, shaded red on reverse;
'Tzigane', orange-red, creamy-yellow on reverse;
*'Wendy Cussons', cerise, flushed with scarlet.
*Very Fragrant

Floribundas

'Allgold', golden-yellow;
'Chanelle', cream, suffused peach;
*'Dearest', salmon-pink;
'Dorothy Wheatcroft', bright red;
*'Elizabeth of Glamis', pale salmon-pink;
'Evelyn Fison', red;
'Frensham', deep crimson-scarlet;
'Iceberg', pure white;
'Lilli Marlene', scarlet;
'Masquerade', yellow, pink, and red;
'Paddy McGredy', carmine, paler on reverse;
'Paprika', lacquer red;
'Pink Parfait', pink, suffused yellow;
'Queen Elizabeth', clear pink;
'Sea Pearl', pale orange and pink, yellow reverse;
'Violet Carson', pink, silver reverse.

Climbing Roses (Repeat flowering)

*'Danse du Feu', orange-scarlet;
*'Maigold', bronzy-yellow;
'Mermaid', creamy-yellow;
*'New Dawn', pale pink;
'Pink Perpetué', clear pink, deeper on reverse;
*'Zephyrine Drouhin', bright pink.

There are also various climbing sports of hybrid tea and floribunda roses.

Rambler Roses (Summer flowering only)

*'Albéric Barbier', creamy-white;
*'Albertine', salmon-pink, shaded copper;
'American Pillar', rose-pink with white eye;
'Chaplin's Pink', bright pink;
'Dorothy Perkins', rose-pink;
'Emily Gray', pale golden-yellow;
'Excelsa', rosy-crimson;
'Paul's Scarlet', bright crimson-scarlet.
*Fragrant

ROSE – see Rosa

ROSE ACACIA – see Robinia hispida

ROSE OF SHARON – see Hypericum calycinum

ROSE MALLOW – see Lavatera

ROSEMARY
– see Rosmarinus and Herb Garden

ROSMARINUS
(Labiatae) Rosemary
Hardy evergreen shrubs, decorative in the garden and of great value as culinary herbs.

Cultural requirements: Any well-drained garden soil and a sunny situation.
Propagation: By cuttings of partly ripened wood in summer.

R. *officinalis* up to 6 ft (2 m)
Common Rosemary   S. Europe and Asia Minor
Dense shrubs with rich green linear foliage, silvered on the reverse. The leaves are aromatic and a traditional ingredient of a *bouquet garni*. Lavender-blue flowers are borne in the leaf axils. Among the many good forms are 'Albus', with white flowers; 'Fastigiatus', of erect habit and also known as 'Miss Jessup's Variety'; and 'Tuscan Blue', with flowers of a deeper blue than those of the type. Early summer.

ROWAN – see Sorbus aucuparia

ROYAL FERN – see Osmunda regalis

RUBUS
(Rubaceae) Bramble
Hardy deciduous flowering shrubs and perennials. The genus includes raspberries, for which see Fruit Garden.
Cultural requirements: Any good garden soil and a sunny or partly shaded situation.
Propagation: Shrubby species by layering; herbaceous kinds by division in spring.

R. *biflorus* up to 10 ft (3 m)   Himalayas
Grown for the beauty of its stems in winter, which have the appearance of being whitewashed, thanks to the white waxy bloom with which they are covered. The small white flowers are followed by edible yellow fruits. Early summer.

R. *cockburnianus* (syn. R. *giraldianus*)
up to 10 ft (3 m)   China
Another white-stemmed species with inconspicuous rosy-purple flowers, followed by black fruits with a waxy patina. Early summer.

R. *deliciosus* up to 10 ft (3 m)   Rocky Mountains
An attractive shrub with thornless stems and large white flowers like those of a dog rose. Early summer.

R. *tricolor* (Prostrate)   China
An evergreen creeping species with long trailing bristly stems and dark green foliage, silvered on reverse. Makes a good ground cover plant especially for shady situations when established. The white flowers are followed by red edible fruits.

R. Tridel (R. *deliciosus* × R. *trilobus*)
10 ft (3 m)   Garden origin
Vigorous shrub with thornless stems bearing large white flowers with a prominent cluster of golden stamens. Early summer.

RUDBECKIA
(Compositae) Cone Flower
Hardy annuals and perennials whose daisy-like flowers have raised centres in contrasting colours.
Cultural requirements: Any ordinary garden soil, preferably moist and not too light.
Propagation: Annual and biennial kinds: From seed sown under glass in spring or outdoors later.
  Perennial species: From seed outdoors in spring or by division.

R. fulgida deamii (syn. *R. deamii*)
3 ft (1 m)   S.E. U.S.A.
Deep yellow daisy flowers with a dark centre. Similar to *R. speciosa* but with a more erect habit of growth. Summer to early autumn.

R. hirta 2½ ft (75 cm)
Black-eyed Susan   N. America
A biennial species normally treated as an annual. Flowers are golden-yellow with a very dark brown centre. Tetraploid forms have given rise to the so-called 'Gloriosa Daisies' which are easy to grow and flower from seed in a single season and which have magnificent double or semi-double flowers up to 7 in. (17 cm) across, in a wide range of colours.

R. purpurea – see *Echinacea purpurea*

R. sullivantii 2½ ft (75 cm)   N. America
Large yellow daisy flowers with a black centre. 'Goldsturm' has larger flowers, is more vigorous, and an improvement on the type. Summer to autumn.

RUE – see *Ruta graveolens*

RUSCUS
(Liliaceae)
Evergreen sub-shrubs whose small oval, spine-tipped leaves are actually flattened stems known as cladodes. They have the virtue of thriving in dry dense shade, where few other plants will flourish.
Cultural requirements: Any type of soil and a sunny or shaded situation.
Propagation: From suckers or by division in spring.

R. aculeatus 3 ft (1 m) Butcher's Broom   Britain
This sub-shrub, native to Britain, has spiny tipped cladodes and gets its popular name for reputedly being used to scour down butchers' chopping blocks – a kind of living Brillo pad. If plants of both sexes are grown, the small greenish flowers will be followed by bright red berries on the female kinds.

RUSSIAN SAGE – see *Perovskia atriplicifolia*

RUTA
(Rutaceae)
Aromatic shrubs with attractive ferny foliage.
Cultural requirements: Any ordinary garden soil and a sunny situation.
Propagation: From seed outdoors in late spring; by cuttings in a cold frame in late summer.

R. graveolens 3 ft (1 m)   S. Europe
Small evergreen shrub with finely cut blue-grey leaves and clusters of yellow flowers. 'Jackmans' Blue' is an outstanding form with glaucous foliage; 'Variegata' has leaves variegated with creamy-white. Summer.

SAGE – see *Salvia officinalis* and Herb Garden

ST DABEOC'S HEATH
– see *Daboecia cantabrica*

ST JOHN'S WORT – see *Hypericum*

SAINTPAULIA
(Gesneriaceae) African Violet
Warm greenhouse perennials that are popular as house plants. The leaves are rounded and slightly felted; flowers are borne in clusters.
Cultural requirements: John Innes No. 2 or similar compost and warm, shaded, moist conditions. Minimum temperature 60 °F (15 °C).
Propagation: From seed or by leaf cuttings.

S. ionantha 4 in. (10 cm)   E. Africa
Greenhouse or house pot plants with single or double violet, white or pink flowers in clusters. Sudden changes of temperature should be avoided indoors. Summer to autumn.

SALIX
(Salicaceae) Willow and Sallow
A large and varied group of hardy deciduous trees and shrubs, that include prostrate kinds suitable

Salvia splendens 'Blaze of Fire'

for the rock garden as well as large trees. The weeping forms are especially beautiful.
Cultural requirements: Any ordinary loamy soil; light sandy soils do not suit them, but they like moist conditions and most of the larger kinds make ideal subjects for waterside planting.
Propagation: From cuttings in damp soil in autumn and winter.

S. alba 60 ft (18 m)   N. Asia, N. Africa, and White Willow   Europe, including British Isles
A large tree of pyramidal habit and with slightly pendent branches. Narrow silvery foliage and attractive catkins in spring. Vigorous and fast growing. 'Chermesina' is a striking form with brilliant orange-scarlet branches. 'Vitellina' is equally eye-catching in winter with bright yellow stems.

S. babylonica 50 ft (15 m) Weeping Willow China
An interesting tree of weeping habit with narrow green leaves, glaucous blue on reverse and brown stems. The catkins appear with the leaves in spring.

S. caprea 20 ft (6 m) Goat Willow and Sallow
      W. Asia and Europe, including British Isles
The popular sallow, native to Britain, whose catkins are gathered as Palm or Pussy Willow in spring. The male catkins are yellow, those of the female trees are silvery.

S. × chrysocoma (syn. *S. alba tristis*) 50 ft (15 m) Weeping Willow
      Europe, including British Isles, N. Asia
One of the loveliest of weeping trees, particularly beautiful in winter, when the yellow stems are at their most attractive and in spring when the young golden foliage first starts to unfurl. Not suitable for small gardens.

S. daphnoides 40 ft (12 m)
Violet Willow   N. Europe and C. Asia
Vigorous tree of medium size with purple-violet shoots and decorative catkins on bare stems.

S. matsudana 40 ft (12 m)
Pekin Willow   N. China and Korea
Medium-sized tree of pyramidal habit that thrives in drier soil conditions. 'Tortuosa' is an interesting form whose stems and branches are twisted and contorted into a corkscrew appearance.

S. repens up to 3 ft (1 m) Creeping Willow
      N. Asia and Europe, including British Isles
A prostrate creeping shrub with narrow leaves, silvered on the reverse. Catkins are profusely borne.

SALLOW – see *Salix caprea*

SALPIGLOSSIS
(Solanaceae)
Half-hardy annuals that are excellent for summer bedding and also make good pot plants.
Cultural requirements: Any good garden soil and a sunny situation sheltered from winds.
Propagation: From seed sown in gentle heat under glass in spring or outdoors later where plants are to flower.

S. sinuata 2 ft (60 cm)   Chile
Beautiful funnel-shaped flowers in a colour range that includes gold, scarlet, rose, crimson, mahogany, blue, and purple. The petals are attractively veined and the new F_1 hybrid strains are a great improvement on the type. Summer.

SALVIA
(Labiatae)
A wide and varied genus of shrubs, sub-shrubs, hardy and half-hardy annuals and perennials.
Cultural requirements: Any ordinary fertile garden soil and a sunny situation.
Propagation: *S. splendens* the scarlet bedding salvia and *S. patens*, its blue counterpart, are both half-hardy perennials that can be treated as half-hardy annuals to flower in the same season. Seed is sown in heat under glass to produce plants to go outdoors in summer. Sage (*S. officinalis*) and other shrubby species from seed or cuttings; hardy herbaceous kinds by division in spring.

S. azurea 4 ft (1·2 m)
A useful late flowering sub-shrub with bright blue flower spikes. Late summer to autumn.

S. haematodes 3 ft (1 m)   Greece
A summer flowering perennial with violet-blue flowers in long spikes. Often treated as a biennial on account of its short lived character. Summer.

S. horminum 1½ ft (45 cm) Clary   S. Europe
Hardy annuals whose beauty lies in their long lasting, brightly coloured bracts. There are many good strains including 'Colour Blend', a mixture of white, pink, blue, and violet, 'Blue Bird', with deep violet-blue bracts; and 'Pink Cloud', bright pink. Summer.

S. officinalis up to 3 ft (1 m)
Common Sage   S. Europe
In addition to the ordinary form with greyish corrugated leaves used as a culinary herb, there are several more decorative forms suitable for the border or rock garden. These include 'Alba', with white flowers; 'Icterina', with green and gold variegated leaves; 'Purpurascens', with purple leaves and stems; and 'Tricolor', with grey-green foliage splashed with creamy-white and purple.

S. patens up to 2½ ft (75 cm)   Mexico
This half-hardy perennial species has flowers of a pure gentian-blue and is one of the loveliest of blue-flowered plants. The tuberous roots can be overwintered in a similar manner to those of dahlias. Summer.

S. splendens up to 1 ft (30 cm)   Brazil
Brilliant half-hardy perennials, normally treated as half-hardy annuals and among the most popular of summer bedding plants, both for their brilliant colour and their exceptionally long flowering period. Among the many named forms 'Blaze of Fire', 'Tetra Scarlet', and 'Tom Thumb', the last named a dwarf cultivar, are all outstanding. 'Royal Purple' is a newer introduction with spikes of rich deep purple. Summer to autumn.

S. × superba (syn. *S. virgata nemorosa*)
3 ft (1 m)   Garden origin
Bold spikes of purple flowers that remain attractive even after they have faded. A first rate border perennial. Summer.

S. uliginosa 5 ft (1·5 m)   Brazil
A fine late flowering perennial for the back of the border, producing spikes of azure-blue flowers on tall stems. Late summer to autumn.

SAMBUCUS
(Caprifoliaceae) Elder
Hardy deciduous shrubs or small trees. There are a number of garden forms more attractive than the common elder, *S. nigra*.

Cultural requirements: Any ordinary garden soil and a sunny or partly shaded situation.
Propagation: From hardwood cuttings of ripened shoots in autumn.

S. nigra up to 20 ft (6 m)
Common Elder Europe, N. Africa, and W. Asia
The common elder is native to Britain and is widely found in woods and hedgerows. The flat heads of creamy-white flowers have a vanilla-like scent and are followed by large clusters of black berries. 'Aurea' is an attractive cultivar with bright golden-yellow foliage; 'Laciniata' has finely divided lacy leaves. Summer.

S. racemosa 12 ft (4 m)
Red-Berried Elder   Europe and W. Asia
Terminal panicles of creamy-white flowers, followed by bright red fruits. 'Plumosa Aurea', with deeply cut golden foliage, is a superb form. Spring.

SANSEVERIA
(Liliaceae)
Evergreen clump forming or creeping perennials for the warm greenhouse, grown for their striking foliage. They are popular house plants.
Cultural requirements: John Innes No. 2 or similar potting compost. Water freely in summer, very sparingly at other times. Minimum temperature 50 °F (10 °C) but will stand lower temperatures if kept dry in winter.

S. grandis up to 3 ft (1 m)   Tropical Africa
Handsome dark green leaves, up to 3 ft (1 m) in length. This species needs higher temperatures than the others and is not, therefore, suitable as a room plant.

S. thyrsiflora 1½ ft (45 cm)   S. Africa
The leaves of this species are banded with pale green.

S. trifasciata 2 ft (60 cm)
Mother-in-Law's Tongue   Tropical Africa
The tall and narrow pointed leaves are banded with dark and light green. 'Laurentii' is a good form, with golden marginal variegation.

SANTOLINA
(Compositae) Cotton Lavender
Compact evergreen sub-shrubs with aromatic foliage.
Cultural requirements: Light sandy soil and a sunny open situation.
Propagation: By cuttings in spring or autumn.

S. chamaecyparissus (syn. *S. incana*)
2 ft (60 cm)   Mediterranean
Dwarf shrubs with silver-felted deeply cut foliage and buttonheads of golden-yellow flowers. 'Corsica' (syn. 'Nana') is dwarfer than the type. Summer.

S. neapolitana 2 ft (60 cm) · Italy
A sub-shrub similar to the former species but with a looser, more plumy habit. Lemon-yellow flowers. Summer.

SANVITALIA
(Compositae)
Hardy annuals of creeping habit that make good carpeting or edging plants.
Cultural requirements: Any ordinary garden soil and a sunny situation.
Propagation: From seed under glass in spring or outdoors later where the plants are to flower.

S. procumbens 6 in. (15 cm) Mexico
Carpeting plants whose small yellow daisy flowers have a central cone of black. There is also a double form, 'Flore Pleno'.

SAPONARIA
(Caryophyllaceae) Soapwort
Hardy annuals and perennials, many of which make useful plants for the rock garden.
Cultural requirements: Any ordinary garden soil and a sunny situation for the rock garden species. *S. officinalis* does equally well in sun or partial shade.
Propagation: Annual species: From seed outdoors in spring or in late summer for early flowering the following year.
Perennial species: From seed under glass in gentle heat in spring or outdoors later; by division in autumn and winter.

S. caespitosa 3 in. (8 cm) Pyrenees
Dwarf green hummocks spangled with large pink flowers. A useful rock garden perennial. Early summer.

S. ocymoides 6 in. (15 cm)
Rock Soapwort Europe
Spreading mats of foliage with masses of bright pink or purplish-pink flowers. 'Rubra Compacta' is the best form. Perennial. Summer.

S. officinalis 3 ft (1 m)
Bouncing Bet Europe, including British Isles
Hardy perennials with pink or white flowers. The double forms, 'Alba Plena' and 'Rosea-plena', are showy but invasive plants. Late summer.

SAXIFRAGA
(Saxifragaceae) Saxifrage
An extensive group of plants, extremely useful in the rock garden. There are many species and hybrids which can usefully be divided into four separate groups.
Cultural requirements: Well-drained soil and a sunny situation for most kinds.
Propagation: From seed, division, or from cuttings in late summer.

Silver or Encrusted Saxifrages
These have silvery-white rosettes and flowers in small clusters.
S. aizoon (syn. *S. paniculata*)
up to 9 in. (22 cm) Europe
The flowers of the type are white; 'Lutea' has pale yellow flowers; *rosea*, pink; and *minor* is an even dwarfer form with white flowers. Spring to early summer.

The section contains some magnificent hybrids such as 'Dr Ramsey', 'Southside Seedling', and 'Tumbling Waters'.

Kabschia or Cushion Saxifrages
The kabschias form very compact mounds of silvered foliage and flower from late winter to spring. They need well-drained gritty soil and make excellent subjects for the alpine house.
S. ferdinandi-coburgii 3 in. (8 cm) Bulgaria
Bright yellow flowers rising from silver rosettes of foliage. Late winter to spring.
S. × jenkinsae up to 3 in. (8 cm) Garden origin
An attractive hybrid with silvery rosettes and pale pink flowers. Best grown in the alpine house.
'Riverslea' is another distinctive hybrid with purplish-pink flowers, up to 3 in. (8 cm) in height. Spring.

Engleria or Bell Saxifrages
These also have silvery basal rosettes of leaves with short-stemmed flower clusters.
S. grisebachii 6 in. (15 cm) Greece
White-encrusted silver rosettes and small pink flowers. It makes a good plant for the alpine house but can also be grown in the rock garden in the scree or in clefts. *S. g.* 'Wisley', with crimson flowers, is the best form. Spring.

Mossy Saxifrages
These make large mats of evergreen foliage, massed with bloom over a long period in colours ranging from white through shades of pink to deep crimson. *S. moschata* is the parent of many garden hybrids, including 'Stormont', pink; 'Pixie', deep red; and 'Peter Pan', deep pink. Spring.

S. peltata – see *Peltiphyllum peltatum*

× urbium (syn. *S. umbrosa*) up to 1 ft (30 cm)
London Pride Europe, including British Isles
Feathery sprays of pale pink flowers rising from rosettes of dark green leathery leaves. Not a choice plant, but good as ground cover in shady situations. Early summer.

SCABIOSA
(Dipsaceae) Pincushion Flower
Hardy annuals and perennials, with long-stemmed flowers that cut well.

Scabiosa

Schizanthus (Butterfly Flower)

Cultural requirements: Any ordinary garden soil in good heart, but they do best in alkaline soils and like a sunny situation.

Propagation: Annual species: From seed in gentle heat under glass in spring or outdoors later.

Perennial species: By division in spring.

S. atropurpurea 3 ft (1 m)　　　　S. Europe
This annual species has cushion-shaped flowers of purple, blue, crimson, pink, and white. Seedsmen offer strains with varying heights and colour range, including 'Blue Moon', lavender-blue; 'Coral Moon', salmon-pink; and 'Giant Hybrids', with double flowers larger than those of the type. Summer.

S. caucasica 2 ft (60 cm)　　　　Caucasus
The well known perennial scabious with large flat heads of lavender-blue flowers. The best named forms are 'Clive Greaves', mauve; 'Miss Willmott', pure white; and 'Loddon Anna', pale blue. Summer to autumn.

SCABIOUS – see *Scabiosa*

SCARBOROUGH LILY – see *Vallota*

SCHIZANTHUS
(Solanaceae) Butterfly Flower
Greenhouse annuals that make superb pot plants with brightly coloured flowers borne in great profusion. In milder districts can be used for summer bedding.

Cultural requirements: John Innes No. 2 or similar potting compost and winter temperatures not lower than 45 °F (7 °C).

Propagation: From seed sown in early spring for flowers in summer and autumn or in late summer for spring flowering.

Most of the kinds in general cultivation are hybrids or strains of *S. hybridus pinnatus* (syn. *grandiflorus*) such as 'Butterfly', with large orchid-like flowers in a wide range of colours; 'Hit Parade', a compact dwarf strain; and 'Pansy-flowered', with large rounded flowers. Spring and summer.

SCHIZOSTYLIS
(Iridaceae) Kaffir Lily
A monotypic genus with gladiolus-like flowers, valuable as a late autumn and early winter flowering subject.

Cultural requirements: Moist rich soil and a sunny situation. Crowns should be protected in severe winter weather by a covering of ashes or bracken.

Propagation: By division of rhizomes in spring.

S. coccinea up to 3 ft (1 m)　　　　S. Africa
Scarlet, crimson, or pink flowers, many to each stem. Good named forms include 'Mrs Hegarty', rose-pink and 'Viscountess Byng', pale pink. Autumn to early winter.

Schlumbergera × *buckleyi (Zygocactus truncatus)*

SCHLUMBERGERA
(Cactaceae)
Greenhouse succulents, with branched and flattened spineless stems. Also known as the 'Easter Cactus', a name it shares with *Rhipsalidopsis rosea*.
Cultural requirements: Slightly richer soil than usual for cacti. Water freely in summer, sparingly for the rest of the year. Minimum temperature 45 °F (7 °C).
Propagation: By cuttings in sandy soil in spring.

S. gaertneri 9 in. (22 cm)   Brazil
The flowers are bright red. It is now known as *Rhipsalidopsis gaertneri*. Early summer.

SCILLA
(Liliaceae) Squill
Hardy bulbous plants that include in their ranks the native bluebell, *S. non-scripta*. The dwarf species make excellent early flowering plants for the rock garden.
Cultural requirements: Light soil rich in humus and a sunny situation.
Propagation: From seed in a cold frame or outdoors in autumn; by offsets.

S. bifolia 6 in. (15 cm)   Europe
Royal-blue stellate flowers very early in the year, narrow strap-shaped leaves. Early spring.

S. hispanica (syn. *S. campanulata*,
Endymion hispanicus) 1 ft (30 cm)   Europe
A taller species with blue, white, pink, or lavender flowers. Spring.

S. non-scripta (syn. *S. nutans*, *Endymion non-scriptus*) 1 ft (30 cm)
Bluebell   Europe, including British Isles
The English bluebell now has several good garden forms, with larger flower spikes than the type. There are white- and pink-flowered kinds. Spring.

S. sibirica 8 in. (20 cm)   Asia Minor
A delightful dwarf early flowering bulb, valuable for the intense gentian-blue of its nodding flowers in late winter. 'Atrocaerulea' (syn. 'Spring Beauty') is an outstanding vigorous form. Late winter.

S. tubergeniana 6 in. (15 cm)   Persia
This species has very pale blue flowers with a darker blue streak down the centre of their petals. It will naturalize freely, given conditions to its liking. Early spring.

SCIRPUS
(Cyperaceae)
Hardy perennial bog or waterside plants.
Cultural requirements: Any ordinary garden soil and a waterside situation in marshy conditions.
Propagation: By division in spring or autumn.

S. cernuus 1 ft (30 cm) Club Rush
Although this species is hardy, it is normally grown as a greenhouse pot plant. It has attractive drooping stems.

S. tabernaemontani up to 5 ft (1·5 m)   Europe
A handsome rush with reddish inflorescences and glaucous leaves. The variety 'Zebrinus', the zebra rush, is very decorative with leaves banded with cream and green.

SCOLOPENDRIUM – see *Phyllitis*

SCOTCH THISTLE – see *Onopordon*

SEA BUCKTHORN
– see *Hippophae rhamnoides*

SEA HOLLY – see *Eryngium*

SEA LAVENDER – see *Limonium latifolium*

SEA PINK – see *Armeria maritima*

SEDUM
(Crassulaceae)
Hardy evergreen succulent plants – annual, biennial, and perennial.
Cultural requirements: Any ordinary well-drained garden soil and a sunny border or rock garden. The dwarf kinds make good wall plants.
Propagation: From seed outdoors in spring; by division in autumn.

S. acre 3 in. (8 cm)
Stonecrop   Europe, including British Isles
This perennial species forms spreading mats of succulent foliage with masses of yellow star flowers. Too invasive for the rock garden, but excellent in dry walls and paving. Summer.

S. caeruleum 3 in. (8 cm)   Mediterranean
Annual species with pale blue star flowers having a white eye.

S. maximum 1½ ft (45 cm) Ice Plant   Europe
A perennial species with flattish greenish-white flower heads. 'Atropurpureum', with deep reddish-purple leaves and stems and pink flowers, is the best garden form. Late summer.

S. spathulifolium 4 in. (10 cm)   N. America
A dwarf perennial for the rock garden or dry wall whose leaves are dusted with a white farina. The flowers are yellow and there is a variety, 'Purpureum', with broad purple leaves. Early summer.

S. spectabile 1½ ft (45 cm)   Japan
Popular perennials with fleshy succulent glaucous foliage, valuable for late colour in the border. The flat heads of mauve flowers attract butterflies. 'Brilliant' is a fine form with larger flower heads. 'Autumn Joy' has salmon-rose flowers, and the

hybrid 'Ruby Glow', growing only 1 ft (30 cm) tall, has flowers of a deep ruby-red. Late summer to autumn.

SEED SOWING – see Propagation

SEMPERVIVUM
(Crassulaceae) Houseleek

The houseleeks are a varied group of fleshy-leaved plants that make ideal subjects for the rock garden or for dry walls. The flower spikes rise from densely packed basal rosettes of leaves.

Cultural requirements: Light sandy soil and an open sunny situation.

Propagation: From seed under glass in gentle heat in spring; by offsets in summer or by leaf cuttings, left to dry out for a short period and then inserted in John Innes No. 2 or a similar compost.

S. arachnoideum 3 in. (8 cm)
Cobweb Houseleek S. Europe
Small rosettes with rose-red flowers. The rosettes give the impression of being cobweb covered. Summer

S. tectorum 6 in. (15 cm)
Common Houseleek Europe and Asia
The species sometimes seen growing on the roofs of cottages and farm buildings, with pinkish-purple flowers. *Calcareum* has glaucous leaves, tipped with purple. Summer.

SENECIO
(Compositae)

Hardy annuals, evergreen perennials, and shrubs.

Cultural requirements: Any ordinary garden soil in good heart and a sunny situation. Although not completely hardy, the shrubby species make excellent plants for maritime districts and stand up well to wind.

Propagation: Annual species: From seed outdoors where plants are to grow.

Shrubby species: From semi-hard stem cuttings in a cold frame in late summer.

S. elegans (syn. *Jacobaea elegans*)
1½ ft (45 cm) S. Africa
Hardy annual species with single and double flowers in a colour range that includes mauve, purple, crimson, rose, and white. Good for cutting. Summer.

S. greyi 5 ft (1·5 m) New Zealand
Evergreen shrub with felted silver-grey foliage and yellow daisy flowers in terminal clusters. Summer.

S. laxifolius 5 ft (1·5 m) New Zealand
Similar to above species but with more rounded leaves and slightly more tender. Summer.

S. maritima (syn. *Senecio cineraria*)
1½ ft (45 cm) Mediterranean
A half-hardy evergreen sub-shrub with silver-frosted foliage that is useful for summer bedding. It is normally treated as a half-hardy annual but survives mild winters outside. 'Candicans' and 'Dwarf Silver' are both good forms; 'White Diamond' has intensely white-felted leaves.

SEPAL
A segment of the calyx of a flower. Normally green, but sometimes coloured.

SEQUOIA
(Taxodiaceae)
A genus containing one species of large evergreen conifers.

Cultural requirements: Deep rich soil and a sunny situation.

Propagation: From seed in a cold frame in spring.

S. sempervirens
up to 350 ft (115 m or more) N. California
A majestic tree with reddish-brown spongy bark and yew-like linear foliage rarely exceeding 150 ft (45 m) in Britain. 'Adpressa', a dwarf form with cream-coloured tips to the young shoots. It often reverts to type. 'Prostrata', another unusual dwarf kind with wide spreading branches.

SEQUOIADENDRON
(Taxodiaceae)
A genus containing one species, formerly included with *sequoia*.

Cultural requirements: As for sequoia.

Propagation: From seed or cuttings.

S. giganteum up to 300 ft (100 m)
Wellingtonia California
Another magnificent conifer, not as tall as the sequoia, but greater in girth. It rarely exceeds 100 ft (30 m) in Britain.

SERRATED
With a saw-like edge as applied to the margins of leaves.

SESSILE
A term applied to flowers and leaves without stalks.

SETACEOUS
Covered in bristles like the stems of raspberries and some brambles.

SHADBUSH – see *Amelanchier canadensis*

SHALLOTS – see Kitchen Garden

Sinningia speciosa Invincible Mixed (Gloxinia)

SHASTA DAISY
– see *Chrysanthemum maximum*

SHIELD FERN – see *Dryopteris filix-mas*

SHOO FLY PLANT
– see *Nicandra physaloides*

SHRIMP PLANT – see *Beloperone guttata*

SIBERIAN WALLFLOWER
– see *Cheiranthus allionii*

SIDALCEA
(Malvaceae)

Hardy perennials with mallow-like flowers, useful for their long flowering period and first rate border plants.

Cultural requirements: Any ordinary garden soil and a sunny open situation.

Propagation: From seed outdoors in spring; division in spring or autumn.

S. malvaeflora 3 ft (1 m)   California
A perennial with tall spikes of lilac-pink flowers. The best garden forms are hybrids of this species and the white-flowered *S. candida* and include named forms such as 'Croftway Red', reddish-pink; 'Brilliant', crimson; 'Rev. Page Roberts', shell-pink; and 'William Smith', salmon-red. Summer to early autumn.

SILENE
(Caryophyllaceae)

Hardy annuals, biennials, and perennials many of which make good rock garden plants.

Cultural requirements: Any ordinary well-drained garden soil and a sunny situation.

Propagation: Annual and biennial species: From seed outdoors in spring where plants are to flower or later to flower following season.

Perennial species: From seed in a cold frame in spring; by division in spring.

S. acaulis 2 in. (5 cm) Moss Campion   Alps
Cushion-forming rock perennial with stemless pink campion flowers. Early summer

S. alpestris 6 in. (15 cm)   Alps
An attractive perennial with pure white frilled flowers and tufted narrow leaves. Mid to late summer.

S. armeria 1½ ft (45 cm)   S. Europe
Annual species with pink flowers. Summer.

S. maritima 6 in. (15 cm)   Europe
An attractive trailing rock perennial with glaucous leaves and masses of pink campion flowers. Early summer.

S. schafta 4 in. (10 cm)   Caucasus
Mat-forming rock perennial with masses of rosy-red flowers. Autumn.

SINNINGIA
(Gesneriaceae)

Tuberous-rooted deciduous plants for the warm greenhouse. Best known species is *S. speciosa* (syn.

SISYRINCHIUM

Gloxinia speciosa), parent of the many lovely strains of gloxinia in garden commerce.
Cultural requirements: John Innes No. 2 or similar potting compost and a greenhouse temperature of not less than 50 °F (10 °C).
Propagation: From seed in heat under glass in spring; from stem or leaf cuttings under glass in heat.

S. speciosa up to 1 ft (30 cm) Gloxinia Brazil
Exotic greenhouse pot plants with large trumpet flowers of a velvety texture in striking colours that include white, blue, rose, crimson, and red shades. Unsurpassed as summer flowering greenhouse or house plants. Late summer to autumn.

SISYRINCHIUM
(Iridaceae)
Evergreen hardy perennials, bearing tufts of sword-like or grassy foliage. The dwarf varieties make delightful alpine plants.
Cultural requirements: Any garden soil in good heart and a sunny situation.
Propagation: From seed or by offsets in spring.

S. angustifolium 1 ft (30 cm)
Blue-Eyed Grass N. America
Pale violet flower spikes arising from grass-like tufts of foliage. Summer.

S. striatum 2 ft (60 cm) Argentine
A vigorous and popular perennial with a long flowering season. The erect stems carry close-packed spikes of purple-veined yellow flowers above sword-like fans of foliage. Summer.

SKIMMIA
(Rutaceae)
Hardy evergreen shrubs with fragrant inconspicuous flowers followed by striking scarlet berries. The male and female flowers are borne on separate plants in most species so that forms of both sexes will need to be planted to enjoy the beauty of the berries.
Cultural requirements: Any ordinary soil in moist condition and a sunny or partly shaded situation. Excellent plants for maritime districts and exposed positions.
Propagation: From seed in a cold frame in spring; by cuttings under glass in spring or summer and by layers in autumn.

S. japonica 4 ft (1·2 m) Japan
A small shrub suitable for any garden with elliptical leathery leaves and terminal clusters of small creamy-white flowers of penetrating fragrance. The last-named are followed by scarlet berries on the female plants, lasting right through the winter.
There are several interesting named forms, including 'Foremanii', with extra-vivid red fruits;

'Nymans', very free-fruiting with larger berries than the type; and 'Rubella', a male form whose distinctive reddish buds open into white sweetly scented blossom.

SKUNK CABBAGE – see *Lysichitum*

SLUGS – see Pest Control

SMOKE BUSH – see *Cotinus coggygria*

SNOW-IN-SUMMER
– see *Cerastium tomentosum*

SNOWBERRY – see *Symphoricarpos*

SNOWDROP – see *Galanthus*

SNOWDROP TREE – see *Halesia*

SNOWY MESPILUS – see *Amelanchier*

SOIL
To grow plants successfully, a knowledge of soil type and condition is of great help to the gardener. Most garden soils fall into one of five categories – clay, loam, sand, peat, and chalk.
Clay soils are made up of superfine particles that stick together like glue, especially when wet. Air cannot readily circulate between these particles and since oxygen is essential to healthy root action, many plants are unable to thrive in these conditions.
When clay soils get wet, the particles bind together into a sticky unworkable mass. They are also colder than other soil types and dry out more slowly in spring. On the credit side, they have the power to retain the essentials for plant growth better and are usually, basically, more fertile.
The addition of lime helps to break up the particles and the texture can be improved even more by the incorporation of liberal quantities of rotted straw, farmyard manure, compost, peat, or leafmould. There are also proprietary soil conditioners that fulfil a similar function if they are raked into the surface but the cost of these makes them only a practicable proposition for restricted areas.
Early autumn and late spring are the best times for cultivating heavy clay soils. In autumn, it helps to throw up the soil in ridges. This makes it easier for wind and frost to break down the lumps. Once dug and raked down, the surface of clay soils should be walked on as little as possible.
Loam soils vary a great deal in consistency. The best for gardeners is medium loam; this will contain between 50% and 60% clay. All loams will benefit from applications of animal manure or

other humus-rich materials, especially sandy loams, since humus will improve their capacity for holding moisture. The addition of humus also causes the finer particles to bind together into a coarser granular texture. Where animal manure or compost is not easily obtainable, leafmould, peat, or spent hops all make good substitutes.

Those who garden on chalk are restricted to growing plants that are lime-tolerant. It is a waste of time and effort to attempt to grow calcifuges – the technical term applied to lime-hating plants – such as azaleas and rhododendrons, although, on a restricted scale, the effect of such soils can be counteracted by applications of sequestrene iron.

Fortunately, however, for those on alkaline soils, there are countless lovely and attractive subjects that will grow well even in soils over-lying pure chalk, particularly if the chalk is broken up and plenty of humus is added.

Although sandy soils are a joy to work at all times, even after heavy downpours, their moisture retaining properties are unsatisfactory and plants tend to suffer badly during prolonged dry spells. Any kind of fertilizer, organic or inorganic, is rapidly leached out by rain. The secret of success with this type of soil is to dig in as much organic matter as possible to help to retain moisture and plant nutrients. In addition to the usual materials, mulching with peat, leafmould or lawn mowings and green manuring in late summer will all help.

Peaty soils are normally acid soils and although this condition can be corrected by the addition of lime, it would be unwise to take such action until the possibilities of growing the many lovely lime-hating plants has been fully explored. These include azaleas, rhododendrons, heathers, camellias, and magnolias. As well as these, vigorous shrubs such as buddleias, forsythias, philadelphus, and flowering currants will also flourish in acid peaty soils, together with most herbaceous perennials and annuals. Most vegetables, particularly members of the cabbage family, will need a dressing of lime to grow well.

SOLANUM
(Solanaceae)

An extensive group that includes culinary plants such as the potato, *S. tuberosum* and the aubergine, *S. melongena*. The climbing species are those most commonly grown for decorative purposes, to-gether with the winter cherry, a berry-bearing greenhouse shrub that makes a good house plant for winter decoration.

Cultural requirements: Climbing species: If grown in greenhouse borders, a soil rich in humus; in pots, John Innes No. 2 or similar compost. In milder districts, the climbing species, *S. crispum* and *S. jasminoides* can be grown out-doors with the protection of a south or west wall.

Berrying species: John Innes No. 2 or similar compost, minimum temperature 55 °F (12 °C).

Propagation: Fruiting species: From seed under glass in heat in early spring.

Climbing species: By cuttings under glass in late summer.

S. capsicastrum 1½ ft (45 cm)

Winter Cherry   Brazil

Dwarf bushes with white flowers, followed by rounded scarlet berries.

S. crispum up to 20 ft (6 m)

Climbing Potato   Chile

Climbing species with purple flowers like those of a potato with a yellow stamen 'beak'. They are followed by small yellowish fruits. 'Glasnevin' is the best form, with a longer flowering season than that of the type. Early summer to autumn.

S. jasminoides up to 20 ft (6 m)   Brazil

Slightly more tender than the former species. It must have the protection of a south wall out of doors. The flowers are slaty-blue and there is also a white form, 'Album'. Summer.

SOLIDAGO
(Compositae) Golden Rod

Popular hardy perennials, useful in the border in late summer.

Cultural requirements: Any ordinary garden soil and a sunny or shady situation.

Propagation: From seed outdoors in spring; by root division in spring or autumn.

S. virgaurea

3 ft (1 m)   Europe, including British Isles

The common golden rod, an invasive and com-paratively uninteresting plant, has been super-seded by numerous clones and cultivars that are a great improvement on the type. These include 'Golden Gate', bright yellow; 'Goldenmosa', golden-yellow mimosa-like flowers, both around 3 ft (1 m) in height; a taller form, 'Ballardii', with branching heads of golden flowers that is ideal for the back of the border, and several more compact kinds such as 'Brachystachys', 'Golden Thumb', and 'Laurin'. Late summer to autumn.

SOLOMON'S SEAL
– see *Polygonatum multiflorum*

SOPHORA
(Leguminosae)

Deciduous and evergreen trees and shrubs with attractive pinnate foliage and pea flowers.

Cultural requirements: A well-drained loamy soil and a sunny sheltered situation. *S. tetraptera* succeeds well on a south or west wall.

Propagation: From seed in a cold frame in spring; from stem cuttings in a frame in late summer or by layering in autumn.

S. japonica 50 ft (15 m)
Japanese Pagoda Tree   China
Medium- to large-sized hardy tree with handsome pinnate leaves up to 1 ft (30 cm) long. The creamy-white pea flowers do not appear until the trees reach maturity. Late summer to autumn.

S. tetraptera 25 ft (8 m) Kowhai   New Zealand
Large shrub or small tree requiring wall protection in Britain except in milder areas. Deep yellow tubular pea flowers in clusters and fern-like pinnate foliage. Early summer.

SORBARIA
(Rosaceae)

Hardy deciduous shrubs, formerly included in genus *spiraea* and with the typical plumy blossom of the latter.
Cultural requirements: Any ordinary garden soil and a sunny situation. Prune back hard each spring.
Propagation: From seed outdoors in spring; by cuttings of ripened wood or suckers.

S. aitchisonii up to 10 ft (3 m)   Afghanistan
A handsome shrub of medium size with pinnate toothed foliage and large conical feathery flower spikes of creamy-white. Summer.

S. arborea up to 18 ft (5 m)   China
A taller and more vigorous species of similar appearance with leaves composed of numerous toothed leaflets and long panicles of creamy-white blossom. Summer.

SORBUS
(Rosaceae)

A very large genus containing numerous deciduous shrubs and trees of exceptional value in the garden. Many are grown for their ornamental foliage as well as for their colourful autumn berries. They include the whitebeams as well as the rowans or mountain ashes.
Cultural requirements: Any ordinary well-drained garden soil including chalk, and a sunny situation.
Propagation: From stratified seed and by layers. Special kinds are grafted.

S. aria up to 50 ft (15 m)
Whitebeam   Europe, including British Isles
Deciduous trees of medium height with compact rounded heads and distinctive ovate foliage, silver-grey when young and felted with white on its underside. The clusters of creamy-white flowers are followed by scarlet autumn fruits. 'Decaisnea' is an outstanding form with larger leaves and berries.

S. aucuparia up to 50 ft (15 m) Rowan or Mountain Ash   Europe, including British Isles
Popular trees, native to Britain with attractive pinnate foliage, creamy-white scented flowers in clusters and handsome berries in early autumn, which are unfortunately an early target for birds. The fruit makes an edible, if somewhat astringent preserve. There are numerous named forms, including 'Edulis', with larger and more palatable fruits; 'Pendula', a weeping form; and 'Xanthocarpa' a variety with yellow fruits. Summer.

S. discolor (syn. *S.* 'Embley') 30 ft (9 m)   China
Small to medium-sized tree of erect habit, particularly noteworthy for the brilliant autumn colouring of its leaves and its striking orange-scarlet berries.

S. Joseph Rock 30 ft (9 m)
                    Origin uncertain (probably China)
An excellent small tree which colours brilliantly in autumn, its orange and scarlet leaf colouring providing a perfect setting for the pale yellow fruits which unlike the red kinds, appear to offer less attraction to birds.

S. sargentiana 30 ft (9 m)   China
This makes a magnificent specimen tree with reddish-brown sticky buds like those of a horse chestnut, followed by extra large pinnate leaves up to a foot in length, that colour to a vivid crimson-scarlet in autumn. The small scarlet fruits are produced in large rounded clusters.

SOUTHERNWOOD – see *Artemisia abrotanum*

SPADIX

A spike with both male and female flowers in the centre of a spathe as in arum lilies.

SPARAXIS
(Iridaceae)

South African half-hardy bulbous plants of dwarf stature well suited for a sheltered pocket on the rock garden, or against a warm wall.
Cultural requirements: Rich sandy soil and a sunny sheltered border. Should be covered with bracken or litter in the winter.
Propagation: From offsets.

S. grandiflora up to 2 ft (60 cm)   S. Africa
The flowers of the type are violet-purple but nurserymen offer strains in a wide variety of colours including some interesting tri-colours. Spring.

SPARTIUM
(Leguminosae)

A genus of one species allied to the brooms *cytisus* and *genista*.
Cultural requirements: Any well-drained garden soil, but succeeds in dry sandy soils and

revels in an open sunny situation. Prune lightly in spring, taking care not to cut back into old wood.
Propagation: From seed outdoors in spring or autumn, transferring seedlings to pots until they are ready for planting out.

S. junceum up to 10 ft (3 m)
Spanish Broom   S. Europe
Rush-like bright green stems closely packed with scaly leaves, golden-yellow fragrant pea flowers. An exceptionally useful late flowering shrub. Late summer to autumn

SPATHE
A leaf-like bract, often coloured, enclosing the spadix (q.v.). Example: Arum Lily.

SPECIES
Section of plants subsidiary to a genus, e.g. *Rosa* (genus) *canina* (species).

SPEEDWELL – see *Veronica*

SPIDER FLOWER – see *Cleome*

SPIDERWORT – see *Tradescantia*

SPINACH – see Kitchen Garden

SPINDLE TREE – see *Euonymus europaeus*

SPIRAEA
(Rosaceae)
Hardy flowering shrubs of great value in the garden at different seasons.
Cultural requirements: Any ordinary well-drained garden soil in good heart and a sunny open situation. Those flowering on current season's wood should be cut back hard in spring (*S. japonica*, *S.* × *bumalda*). Those flowering early on previous season's wood should be pruned hard after flowers have faded (*S.* × *arguta*, *S. thunbergii*). *S.* × *vanhouttei*, which flowers later, should be lightly pruned during winter.
Propagation: By cuttings in a cold frame in summer; by offshoots in autumn.

S. × *arguta* (*S. multiflora* × *S. thunbergii*)
6 ft (2 m) Bridal Wreath   Garden origin
Elegant hybrid shrub of medium size with graceful arching habit. The pure white flowers mass the branches in late spring. Late spring to early summer.

S. × *bumalda* (*S. albiflora* × *S. japonica*)
1½ ft (45 cm)   Garden origin
Moderately dwarf shrub with toothed foliage and flat heads of carmine-pink flowers. 'Anthony Waterer', with deep crimson flowers, is the form

most commonly seen. It blooms over a long period. Summer.

S. japonica 5 ft (1·5 m)   China and Japan
The most popular species with flattened heads of rosy-red flowers. Good named forms include 'Alpina', a dwarf spiraea only about 1½ ft (45 cm) in height, with masses of rose-pink flowers. Mid to late summer.

S. thunbergii 5 ft (1·5 m)   China
Medium-sized compact shrub whose slender branches are massed with pure white flowers in early spring. Dense and twiggy with wiry stems. Early spring.

SPIT
Term used in digging to indicate a spade's depth.

SPLEENWORT – see *Asplenium*

SPREKELIA
(Amaryllidaceae) Jacobean Lily
Greenhouse bulbous plants with exotic scarlet flowers.
Cultural requirements: John Innes No. 2 or similar compost and a winter temperature of not less than 45 °F (7 °C). In mild districts it can be planted out in summer in a warm sunny situation.
Propagation: From seed in heat under glass in early spring; by offsets.

S. formosissima 2 ft (60 cm)   Mexico
Deep scarlet flowers up to 5 in. (12 cm) across, on 1 ft (30 cm) stems.

SPRING SNOWFLAKE – see *Leucojum vernum*

SPRUCE – see *Picea*

SPUR
Short gnarled twigs on fruit trees usually bearing clusters of fruit buds; the curved tubular portion of flowers such as aquilegias and nasturtiums.

SPURGE – see *Euphorbia*

STACHYS
(Labiatae)
Hardy perennials, some of which make useful plants for the border or rock garden. One species, *S. tuberifera*, the Chinese artichoke, is a vegetable.
Cultural requirements: Any ordinary garden soil and a sunny situation.
Propagation: By division in spring or autumn.

S. corsica 1 in. (3 cm)   Corsica
Carpeting plant for the rock garden, spangled with pale pink flowers. Summer.
S. lanata 1½ ft (45 cm) Lamb's Ears   Caucasus
Low growing clumps of silver-felted flannel-

textured leaves from which arise spikes of rather uninteresting purplish-pink flowers. A good ground cover plant, the best form of which is the non-flowering 'Silver Carpet'. Summer.

S. macrantha (syn. *Betonica grandiflora*)
1½ ft (45 cm) Betony   Europe and Asia Minor
The oval leaves of this species are hairy and wrinkled. The purple-violet flowers are borne in whorls on erect stems. 'Rosea' is an attractive pink form. Late spring to early summer.

STACHYURUS
(Strachyuraceae)

A small group of attractive late winter flowering deciduous shrubs.
Cultural requirements: Any ordinary garden soil in good heart and a sunny or partly shaded sheltered situation.
Propagation: By cuttings under glass with bottom heat in summer.

S. chinensis up to 12 ft (4 m)   China
The primary attraction of this shrub is its drooping racemes of yellow flowers that fringe the bare branches in winter. Late winter or early spring.

S. praecox up to 10 ft (3 m)   Japan
Similar in habit and appearance to the above but with larger leaves and shorter flower clusters. Late winter or early spring.

STAMEN

The male organ of a flower, made up of the pollen-bearing anther lobes and supporting stalk or filament.

STANDARD

The upper petal of a pea-type flower.
   A term used to describe trees or bushes on a tall unbranched stem.

STAR OF BETHLEHEM
– see *Ornithogalum umbellatum*

STAR OF THE VELDT – see *Dimorphotheca*

STATICE – see *Limonium*

STELLATE

Star-shaped, as applied to flowers, e.g., *Magnolia stellata*.

STEPHANOTIS
(Asclepidiaceae)

Evergreen climbing shrubs for the warm greenhouse, noteworthy for the rich and exotic fragrance of their flowers.
Cultural requirements: John Innes No. 2 or similar compost, enriched with well-rotted

manure. Water freely in summer and autumn, sparingly for the rest of year.
Propagation: By cuttings in a propagating case in spring or summer.

S. floribunda 10 ft (3 m)
Madagascar Jasmine   Madagascar
Vigorous climber with leathery oval leaves and very fragrant white waxen-textured flowers in clusters. Spring and summer.

STERNBERGIA
(Amaryllidaceae)

Hardy bulbous plants that produce their leaves after the flowers in autumn.
Cultural requirements: A good garden soil and a sunny situation.
Propagation: By offsets in late autumn.

S. lutea 9 in. (22 cm)   Asia Minor
Deep yellow flowers, like those of a crocus, followed by narrow, rush-like foliage. Autumn.

STEWARTIA
(Theaceae)

Attractive deciduous hardy ornamental shrubs and trees, closely related to the camellias and, like them, needing lime-free soil and a partly shaded situation. They make good plants for the woodland garden.
Propagation: By cuttings outdoors in a shady border in autumn or by layers.

S. koreana 20 ft (6 m)   Korea
A small tree with white flowers the foliage of which colours well in autumn. Late summer.

S. malacodendron up to 20 ft (6 m)   S.E. U.S.A.
A large shrub with oval leaves and white flowers with purple stamens. Late summer.

S. pseudocamellia 20 ft (6 m)   Japan
A small tree with interesting flaking bark and white flowers. The leaves colour well in autumn. Summer.

S. sinensis up to 30 ft (9 m)   China
A large shrub or small tree with decorative bark and fragrant cup-shaped white flowers. Summer.

STIPA
(Gramineae) Feather Grass

Hardy perennial flowering grasses that dry well for winter arrangements.
Cultural requirements: Any ordinary garden soil and a sunny situation.
Propagation: From seed outdoors; by division in spring.

S. gigantea 3 ft (1 m)   Europe
Feathery gold-tinged inflorescences on tall stems, rising from dense clumps of foliage. Summer.

Streptocarpus Choice Hybrids

S. pennata 2 ft (60 cm)   Europe
Dense panicles of feathery bloom and dense tufts
of grassy foliage. Summer.

STOCK – see *Matthiola*

STOCKS FOR FRUIT TREES
– see Fruit Garden

STOKESIA
(Compositae) Stokes' Aster
Attractive hardy perennials with large cornflower-
like blooms.
Cultural requirements: Any ordinary garden
soil and a sunny well-drained situation.
Propagation: By root division in spring.

S. laevis (syn. *S. cyanea*) 1 ft (30 cm)   N. America
An attractive plant for the edge of the border
with large lavender-blue flowers. There are also
pink and white forms. Late summer.

STOLON
Underground stems which produce roots and
subsequently new plants.

STOMATA
Pores on the surface of leaves through which the
plants 'breathe' and transpire water vapour.

STONECROP – see *Sedum*

STRANVAESIA
(Rosaceae)
Hardy evergreen trees and shrubs, with interesting foliage, white flowers, and decorative fruits.
Cultural requirements: Any ordinary garden
soil, provided it is well-drained. Good for town
planting and industrial areas.
Propagation: By cuttings of partly ripened
shoots under glass in late summer.

S. davidiana up to 30 ft (9 m)   China
Vigorous shrub or small tree with leathery, dark
green leaves and white flowers followed by
clusters of red fruits which the birds ignore.
There is also a semi-prostrate form, 'Prostrata',
as well as one with bright yellow fruits, 'Fructu-
luteo'. Midsummer.

STRATIFICATION
A process for hastening the germination of hard-
coated seeds in which they are placed between
layers of moist peat or sand and subjected to
chilling either outdoors or in a refrigerator.

STRAWBERRY – see Fruit Garden

STRAWBERRY TREE – see *Arbutus*

STRELITZIA
(Musaceae)

Exotic evergreen perennials for a warm greenhouse.

Cultural requirements: John Innes No. 2 or similar compost and a sunny situation in the greenhouse. Winter temperature of not less than 55 °F (12 °C).

Propagation: From seed sown in heat under glass in spring; by division or offsets in spring.

S. reginae 4 ft (1·2 m)
Bird of Paradise Flower   S. Africa
Long-stemmed crested flowers of blue and orange-yellow that look like the head of an exotic tropical bird. There is a variety 'Citrina', with purer yellow and blue flowers. Spring.

STREPTOCARPUS
(Gesneriaceae) Cape Primrose

Greenhouse perennials of great beauty of which the hybrid kinds make decorative pot plants for the warm greenhouse.

Cultural requirements: John Innes No. 2 or similar compost and a position near the glass.

Propagation: From seed in heat under glass in early spring.

S. hybridus 1 ft (30 cm)
The hybrids of *S. rexii* and *S. dunnii* are the ones most widely grown and seedsmen offer strains in a wide range of colours. They are usually treated as annuals to flower in the summer after they are sown. 'Prize Strain' has large trumpet flowers in white, lavender, deep blue, rose, and red. Summer.

STRIPED SQUILL – see *Puschkinia scilloides*

STYLE

The stalk uniting stigma to ovary in the pistil of a flower.

STYRAX
(Styracaceae)

Hardy deciduous flowering shrubs with pendent snowdrop-like flowers.

Cultural requirements: Moist lime-free soil and a sunny or partly shaded situation.

Propagation: From seed under glass in spring; by cuttings of partly ripened wood in summer or by layers in autumn.

S. japonica up to 25 ft (8 m)   Japan
A large shrub or small tree of outstanding beauty. Ovate leaves and white bell-shaped flowers hang from the underside of the branches. Midsummer.

SUCKER

Shoots or stems that spring from the base of plants or directly from the roots as in raspberries and grafted roses.

SUMACH – see *Rhus*

SUMMER CYPRESS – see *Kochia trichophylla*

SUMMER HYACINTH
– see *Galtonia candicans*

SUMMER SNOWFLAKE
– see *Leucojum aestivum*

SUN ROSE – see *Helianthemum*

SUNFLOWER – see *Helianthus*

SWAMP CYPRESS – see *Taxodium distichum*

SWAN RIVER DAISY
– see *Brachycome iberidifolia*

SWEDE – see Kitchen Garden

SWEET BAY – see *Laurus nobilis*

SWEET GUM – see *Liquidambar styraciflua*

SWEET PEA – see *Lathyrus odoratus*

SWEET SULTAN – see *Centaurea moschata*

SWEET TOBACCO – see *Nicotiana affinis*

SWEET WILLIAM – see *Dianthus barbatus*

SWEET WIVELSFIELD – see *Dianthus*

SYCAMORE – see *Acer pseudoplatanus*

SYMPHORICARPOS
(Caprifoliaceae)

Deciduous shrubs grown primarily for the beauty of their winter fruits. Most species will do well in dense shade even under the drip from trees.

Cultural requirements: Any type of garden soil and a sunny or shady situation.

Propagation: From cuttings of ripened wood outdoors in autumn and winter; by suckers.

S. albus up to 10 ft (3 m) Snowberry N. America
A dense suckering shrub with inconspicuous pinkish flowers, much loved by bees, that are followed by glistening white berries that persist through the winter. The variety *laevigatus* has larger berries than the type. There are also several striking hybrids, including 'Magic Berry', with

rose-pink fruits; 'Mother of Pearl', white berries flushed pink; and 'White Hedger', a good hedging shrub with smaller white berries in large clusters.

SYMPHYTUM
(Boraginaceae) Comfrey

Hardy perennials useful for damp shady borders or for waterside planting in wild or semi-wild conditions.

Cultural requirements: Any ordinary soil, provided it is moist, and a sunny or shady situation.

Propagation: By division in spring.

S. grandiflorum 8 in. (20 cm)   Caucasus
An attractive plant of creeping habit with pale yellow drooping flowers, tipped with red in bud and borne in clusters. Spring to early summer.

S. × uplandicum (*S. asperum × S. officinale*)
3 ft (1 m)   Garden origin
A handsome plant for the wild or water garden. Sometimes listed as *S. × peregrinum*. It is similar in appearance to the common comfrey (*S. officinale*), but growing taller. The drooping pink flowers turn to blue or bluish-purple as they open. Summer.

SYRINGA
(Oleaceae)

Although often mistakenly applied to the phila-delphus, or mock oranges, *Syringa* is, in fact, the correct generic name for lilacs. They are a group of hardy, showy, deciduous flowering shrubs.

Cultural requirements: Any ordinary garden soil in good heart. Lilacs need annual dressings of compost or well-rotted manure to flower prolifically.

Propagation: By layers in spring or autumn; by cuttings of partly ripened wood under glass in late summer.

S. vulgaris up to 20 ft (6 m) Lilac   E. Europe
This makes a large shrub or small tree of vigorous and rapid growth with panicles of intensely fragrant bloom. The garden forms most common-ly seen are cultivars of this species many of which were introduced by the Lemoines of Nancy at the turn of the present century.

Good named kinds include the following:

Singles

'Ambassadeur', lilac with a white eye;
'Maréchal Foch', carmine-rose;
'Maud Notcutt', pure white, extra large panicles;
'Souvenir de Louis Spath', wine-red.

Doubles

'Belle de Nancy', purplish-red, opening to lilac-pink;
'Charles Joly', dark purple-red;
'Katherine Havemeyer', one of the best doubles with lavender-purple flower trusses turning to paler lavender-pink as they mature;
'Madame Abel Chatenay', broad panicles of creamy-white bloom;
'Madame Antoine Buchner', rosy-lilac flowers in loose clusters;
'Madame Lemoine', one of the best of the white doubles.

Early summer

In addition to these there are some useful late flowering hybrids, raised by Miss Isabella Preston and known as 'Canadian Hybrids' (*S. × prestoniae*). These are vigorous and very hardy with large panicles of bloom on the current year's growth. Most of these are reddish-purple or lilac-pink. Early summer.

TAGETES
(Compositae) Marigold

Half-hardy annuals that are popular as summer bedding plants. The group includes the French and African marigolds as well as many new and striking F_1 hybrid strains.

Cultural requirements: Any good garden soil rich in humus and a sunny situation.

Propagation: From seed under glass in spring or outdoors later where plants are to flower.

T. erecta up to 3 ft (1 m)
African Marigold   Mexico
The flowers of the species are single and yellow or orange in colour but there are also many fine double cultivars both tall and dwarf in stature. Of the latter, 'First Lady', with large double primrose-yellow blooms, 3½ in. (9 cm) across; 'Gay Ladies', a blend of similar kinds in orange and yellow; and 'Gold Galore', a striking form with shapely double flowers 4 in. (10 cm) or more

Tagetes Golden Gem

in diameter are all outstanding. Taller kinds are well represented by 'Doubloon', primrose-yellow; 'Sovereign', golden-yellow; and 'Double Eagle', bright orange.

All the above are F$_1$ hybrid cultivars, specially bred for uniformly vigorous growth and size of flowers. Summer to autumn.

T. patula up to 1 ft (30 cm)
French Marigold   Mexico
The French marigolds too, have undergone extensive development in the past decade and the older small flowered orange, red, and brown kinds are fast being replaced with the spectacular F$_1$ hybrids between the French and African species. Among the newer kinds are 'Orange Nugget' and 'Gold Nugget', whose petals are attractively ruffled; 'Seven Star Gold' and 'Seven Star Red', with double flowers up to 3$\frac{1}{2}$ in. (9 cm) across; and 'Showboat', with large yellow carnation-like flowers. Summer to autumn.

T. tenuifolia (syn. *T. signata*)
6 in. (15 cm)   Mexico
A dwarf species with feathery foliage and small yellow or orange flowers, widely used as an edging plant in summer bedding schemes. 'Carina', tangerine; 'Lemon Gem', bright yellow; and 'Paprika', mahogany-red and gold are all good named kinds. Summer to autumn.

TAMARISK – see *Tamarix*

TAMARIX
(Tamaricaceae)
Hardy evergreen and deciduous flowering shrubs, highly wind resistant and ideal for maritime districts.
Cultural requirements: Any ordinary garden soils with the exception of shallow chalky ones.
Propagation: By cuttings out of doors in autumn.

T. pentandra up to 15 ft (4·5 m)   W. and C. Asia
A shrub or small tree with arching branches bearing plumy branchlets composed of tiny pointed scale leaves. The flowers are pink, in short spikes. A good late flowering subject especially suitable for seaside areas. 'Rubra' is a form with darker flowers. Late summer.

T. tetrandra up to 15 ft (4·5 m)   S.E. Europe
Similar in many ways to the above-mentioned species, but the pink flowers appear earlier in the year. Early summer.

TAXODIUM
(Taxodiaceae)
Deciduous large conifers with fern-like foliage that can be grown in waterlogged soils and are thus ideal for lakeside planting.
Cultural requirements: A moist rich soil – not

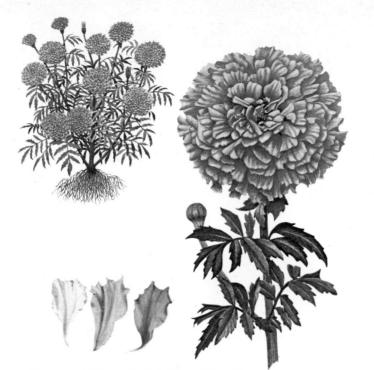

Pluck off any faded heads to help produce flowers for as long as possible

Tagetes erecta 'Crackerjack' (African Marigold)

chalk – or a situation at the margins of large pools, lakes, or rivers.

Propagation: From seed in a cold frame in spring; by cuttings of ripened wood in a shaded frame in autumn and by layering in spring.

T. distichum up to 100 ft (30 cm)
Swamp Cypress   S. U.S.A. (Florida)
A large tree with reddish-brown peeling bark and pale green spring foliage, turning rusty-red in autumn. When grown by the waterside, the swamp cypress produces knobbly knee-like protuberances from its roots.

TAXUS
(Taxodiaceae) Yew

The yews are a small genus of evergreen conifers that bear fleshy scarlet fruits instead of the more usual cones. The fruits each contain a single seed which is poisonous.

Cultural requirements: Any type of soil or situation, including dry soils and dense shade.

Propagation: From seed outdoors in spring; by cuttings in a cold frame in autumn; by grafting on to common yew for special kinds.

T. baccata up to 60 ft (18 m)
Europe, including British Isles, and N. Asia
One of Britain's three native conifers; very slow growing and living to a great age. Unsurpassed

as a hedging plant or for topiary work. There are various forms, including 'Fastigiata', the Irish yew, which makes a broad-based columnar tree of great architectural beauty; 'Standishii', a dwarf golden yew of columnar habit; and 'Variegata', a form whose ascending branches are clothed with silver-margined foliage.

TECOMA – see *Campsis*

TEUCRIUM
(Labiatae)

Hardy perennials and slightly tender small shrubs.

Cultural requirements: Any well-drained garden soil and a sunny open situation.

Propagation: Shrubby species: By cuttings in a frame in late summer; perennial kinds by division.

T. fruticans 6 ft (2 m)
Shrubby Germander   S. Europe
Small evergreen shrub with silvered stems and leaves. The blue flowers appear over a very long period. Early to late summer.

T. polium 4 in. (10 cm)   S. Europe
Grey-leaved tufted sub-shrub with yellow or purple flowers. Summer.

T. pyrenaicum 4 in. (10 cm)   S. Europe
Pale green hairy foliage and mauve and white hooded flowers. Summer.

Tagetes patula 'Naughty Marietta' (French Marigold)

THALICTRUM
(Ranunculaceae) Meadow Rue

Hardy perennials that make good border plants. The leaves are finely divided, like those of a maidenhair fern.

Cultural requirements: Any ordinary garden soil in good heart.

Propagation: By division in spring.

T. aquilegifolium up to 5 ft (1·5 m)   Europe
A tall growing species with pale lilac flowers in loose clusters. 'Purple Cloud' is a more compact form with rosy-purple flowers and there is also a white variety, 'Album'. Summer.

T. dipterocarpum up to 5 ft (1·5 m)   W. China
Tall and stately plants for the back of the border with finely cut ferny foliage and tall spikes of lavender flowers. 'Hewitt's Double' is a good cultivar, and the white 'Album' is also attractive. Late summer.

T. glaucum up to 6 ft (2 m)   S. Europe
This species has distinctive blue-grey foliage and loose clusters of yellow flowers. Summer.

T. minus (syn. *T. adiantifolium*)
3 ft (1 m)   Europe, including British Isles
A popular border plant, with maidenhair-like foliage and bronzy flowers. It can, however, be invasive. Early summer.

THORN – see *Crataegus*

THRIFT – see *Armeria*

THUJA
(Pinaceae)

Hardy evergreen conifers with aromatic scaly foliage and mainly of pyramidal habit. The dwarf forms make attractive specimen plants for the rock or heath garden.

Cultural requirements: Any ordinary garden soil, provided it is well-drained, and an open situation.

Propagation: From seed under glass in gentle heat in spring; by cuttings in a cold frame in late summer.

T. occidentalis up to 50 ft (15 m)   N.E. America
The American arborvitae is a handsome conifer of medium size that is sometimes used for hedging. It is a tree of broadly columnar habit and the species includes many garden forms and cultivars. There are kinds of upright habit such as 'Fastigiata' and 'Buchananii', dwarfs like 'Compacta' and 'Pygmaea' as well as the widely grown 'Rheingold', a semi-dwarf type with rich brownish-gold foliage that makes it an excellent plant for the rock or heather garden.

T. orientalis up to 40 ft (12 m)   China
A species of more modest dimensions which also contains forms of widely varying character. The type plant is columnar in habit when young, broadening out as it comes to maturity.

T. plicata (syn. *T. lobbii*)
100 ft (30 m)   Western N. America
The western red cedar is a vigorous, fast growing

conifer with mahogany-red bark and a horizontal branch structure. This is a conifer that has been widely used for hedging until recently, since when it has been largely superseded by the faster growing *Cupressocyparis* × *leylandii*.

'Zebrina', whose foliage is striped with creamy-yellow, is one of the most striking cultivars.

THUJOPSIS
(Cupressaceae)

A single species of conifers, closely related to *Thuja*.

Cultural requirements: Any ordinary soil, including chalk, provided that it is well-drained.

Propagation: From seed under glass in gentle heat in spring; by cuttings in a cold frame in late summer.

T. dolabrata up to 50 ft (15 m)　　　　Japan
This conifer, with dark green scaly foliage in flattened sprays, makes a good lawn specimen. 'Nana', a compact spreading variety, is an interesting dwarf.

THUNBERGIA
(Acanthaceae)

Tender perennials that are usually treated as annuals. Suitable for the warm greenhouse or for a sunny sheltered wall.

Cultural requirements: John Innes No. 2 or similar compost.

Propagation: From seed under glass in heat in early spring.

T. alata up to 6 ft (2 m)
Black-eyed Susan　　　　　　　　S. Africa
An attractive twining plant that is also useful in hanging baskets or window-boxes. The flowers are white, cream, or orange, with black centres. Summer.

T. gibsonii 10 ft (3 m)　　　　E. and S. Africa
Twining plants, similar to the former species but with orange, waxen-textured flowers. Summer.

THYME – see *Thymus* and Herb Garden

THYMUS
(Labiatae)

Hardy evergreen shrubs and sub-shrubs with aromatic foliage, some of which have culinary uses as herbs.

Cultural requirements: Any ordinary well-drained garden soil and a sunny situation.

Propagation: From seed outdoors in spring; by division in spring or by cuttings in summer.

T. × *citriodorus* 1 ft (30 cm)
Lemon Thyme　　　　　　　Garden origin
Lemon-scented foliage and small green leaves. Summer.

T. herba-barona 3 in. (8 cm)　　　　Corsica
A dwarf form with purple flowers and leaves with the aroma of carraway seed. Summer.

Tagetes patula 'Petite Mixed'
(French Marigold)

T. serpyllum 1 in. (3 cm)
Wild Thyme   Europe, including British Isles
Dwarf creeping plants with small leaves, useful in the rock garden or for crevices in walls or paving. The flowers of the type, which smother the plants in blossom throughout summer, are rosy-purple. Other forms include 'Alba', white; 'Coccineus', deep crimson; 'Pink Chintz', pink; and 'Lanuginosus', an interesting form with grey woolly leaves and pink flowers. Summer.

T. vulgaris 9 in. (22 cm)   S. Europe
This species is widely used as a culinary herb. In addition to the type with purple flowers, there are forms such as 'Aureus', with bright yellow foliage and 'Silver Queen', whose leaves are variegated with white. Summer.

TIARELLA
(Saxifragaceae) Foam Flower
Hardy perennials of creeping habit that make good ground cover plants for a shady or partly shaded situation.
Cultural requirements: Any ordinary garden soil and a shady situation.
Propagation: From seed or by division in spring.

T. cordifolia 9 in. (22 cm)   Eastern N. America
A creeping plant, invaluable as ground cover in shade, smothered in feathery white bottle brush flowers in early summer. The foliage turns bronze in autumn. Early summer.

T. wherryi 9 in. (22 cm)   Eastern N. America
This species has feathery spikes of creamy-white flowers and bronzed rounded leaves that turn red in autumn. Late spring to summer.

TIBOUCHINA
(Melastomataceae)
Evergreen flowering shrubs for the warm greenhouse that can also be grown outdoors in very favoured districts.
Cultural requirements: John Innes No. 2 or similar compost. Water freely in summer, more sparingly for rest of year. Minimum temperature 50 °F (10 °C).
Propagation: By cuttings under glass in heat.

T. semidecandra (syn. *Lasiandra macrantha*)
up to 10 ft (3 m)   Brazil
Striking greenhouse shrubs with purple satiny flowers, 4 in. (10 cm) across, over an exceptionally long period. Early autumn to winter.

TIGRIDIA
(Iridaceae) Tiger Flower
Half-hardy bulbs with colourful flowers that are borne in succession several to a stem. Individual blooms last only one day.

Cultural requirements: Rich well-drained soil and a sunny situation at the foot of a south wall.
     Greenhouse culture: John Innes No. 2 or similar potting compost.
     Bulbs should be stored in a frost-free shed or garage after the foliage has died down.
Propagation: By offsets.

T. pavonia 1½ ft (45 cm)   Mexico
Brilliant hued butterfly-like flowers up to 6 in. (15 cm) in diameter. Leaves like those of a gladiolus. Summer.

TILIA
(Tiliaceae) Lime and Linden Tree
Hardy long lived deciduous trees, mostly too large for the average sized garden but sometimes restricted to pleached form as a boundary or dividing hedge.
Cultural requirements: Any ordinary garden soil and a sunny open situation.
Propagation: From seed in a cold frame in spring; by layers in autumn.

T. × euchlora 60 ft (18 m)
An attractive hybrid with dark green lustrous foliage and small creamy-yellow scented flowers. It is semi-weeping in habit. Summer.

T. petiolaris 90 ft (27 m) Weeping Silver Lime
An elegant large weeping tree of uncertain origin with dark green leaves, silvery-white on their reverse. The flowers are richly fragrant. Summer.

T. platyphyllos 100 ft (30 m)
Broad-leaved Lime   C. and S. Europe
This makes a fine specimen tree for parks or large gardens. It has a large rounded head. 'Rubra', the red-twigged lime, has young stems of a bright crimson-red that are decorative throughout the winter. It is of fairly erect habit and widely used for street planting.

TILTH
A term used to describe the condition of the soil surface when it has a fine granular structure and is in a suitable condition for seed sowing. The surface of heavy soils is best broken down by exposure to frost and wind in winter. It can then be raked down to a tilth fine enough for the above mentioned operations. There are also certain proprietary products that are useful for producing a good tilth over a restricted area. Dressings of lime, too, will help to break down the lumps in heavy clay soils.

TOAD FLAX – see *Linaria*

TOBACCO PLANT – see *Nicotiana*

TOMATO – see Kitchen Garden

Tropaeolum canariense (Canary Creeper)

TOMENTOSE

A term describing the leaves and stems of plants which are woolly or cottony in texture, e.g., *Cerastium tomentosum*.

TORENIA
(Scrophulariaceae)

Annuals for the cool greenhouse, with musk-like flowers.

Cultural requirements: John Innes No. 2 or similar compost. The plants are suitable for pots or hanging baskets.

Propagation: From seed under glass in heat in spring.

T. fournieri 1 ft (30 cm)   Indo-China
Pale blue snapdragon flowers, marked with yellow at their base. 'Grandiflora', with larger flowers, is an improvement on the type.

TRACHELOSPERMUM
(Apocynaceae)

Rather tender self-clinging evergreen twining shrubs with jasmine-like flowers.

Cultural requirements: A well-drained loamy soil, rich in humus, and a sheltered south or west wall. Given these conditions, trachelospermums will thrive outdoors in any but the coldest districts.

Propagation: By cuttings of partly ripened wood under glass in summer.

T. jasminoides 10 ft (3 m) Chinese Jasmine China
A lovely climber with creamy-white, richly scented jasmine-like flowers. 'Variegatum' is an attractive cultivar with creamy-white variegated foliage. Late summer.

TRACHYMENE – see *Didiscus*

TRADESCANTIA
(Commelinaceae) Spiderwort

Hardy and greenhouse perennials, the latter grown primarily for their foliage and making easy but attractive house plants.

Cultural requirements: Greenhouse species: John Innes No. 2 or similar potting compost and a minimum winter temperature of 55 °F (12 °C).

Hardy kinds: Any ordinary garden soil and a sunny or partly shaded situation.

T. × andersoniana (syn. *T. virginiana*)
2 ft (60 cm)   N. America
Hardy perennials with violet-blue, three-petalled

flowers borne in the centre of bold grassy foliage and valuable for their exceptionally long flowering season. There are several cultivars with more prominent flowers than those of the type, including 'Alba', white; 'Flore Pleno', semi-double mauve; 'Iris Prichard', lilac, shaded pink; 'J. C. Weguelin', pale blue; and 'Purple Dome', deep violet-purple. Summer to autumn.

T. blossfeldiana 1 ft (30 cm)
A more erect species with olive-green, hairy leaves, deep reddish-purple beneath. Terminal heads of small pink flowers appear at intervals during the year.

T. fluminensis 6 in. (15 cm)
Wandering Jew   S. America
Popular house plant, used also in hanging baskets in greenhouse or conservatory. The ovate leaves are striped with green and cream.

TREE HOLLYHOCK – see *Hibiscus syriacus*

TREE OF HEAVEN
– see *Ailanthus altissima*

TREE PEONY – see *Paeonia suffruticosa*

TREE POPPY – see *Romneya*

TRICUSPIDARIA – see *Crinodendron*

TRIFOLIATE

Having leaves composed of three separate leaflets to a stem, e.g., clover, trefoil, and laburnum.

TRILLIUM
(Liliaceae) Wood Lily
Tuberous-rooted perennials with trifoliate leaves and three-petalled flowers.
Cultural requirements: Moist soil rich in humus and a shady situation.
Propagation: From seed in a cold frame when ripe; by division of tubers in autumn.

T. grandiflorum 1 ft (30 cm)
Wake Robin   N. America
Large white, three-petalled flowers 3–4 in. (8–10 cm) across. The bold leaves make an attractive setting for the flowers. Late spring.

T. undulatum 1 ft (30 cm)
Painted Wood Lily   N. America
In this species, the petals are red at their base. The coppery-brown foliage makes an attractive foil for the flowers. Early summer.

TRITONIA
(Iridaceae)
Hardy and half-hardy corms, formerly known as *montbretia*. The common orange-flowered montbretia is *Crocosmia × crocosmiiflora* q.v.
Cultural requirements: Light well-drained soil and a sunny situation.
Propagation: By offsets.

T. crocata 2 ft (60 cm)   S. Africa
Spikes of bright orange flowers. Summer.
T. flavida 2 ft (60 cm)   S. Africa
Yellow flower spikes. Summer.

Tropaeolum majus 'Gleam Hybrids'
(Nasturtium)

T. rosea 3 ft (1 m)   S. Africa
The flowers of this species are red, marked with
yellow at the base of the petals. Summer.

TROLLIUS
(Ranunculaceae) Globe Flower
Hardy perennials with single or double large
buttercup-like flowers, useful on account of their
early flowering habit.
Cultural requirements: Moist soil and a partly
shaded or sunny situation.
Propagation: From seed in a shady bed outdoors
or by division in spring or autumn.

T. europaeus
2 ft (60 cm)   Europe, including British Isles
Pale yellow globular flowers on 2 ft (60 cm) stems.
There are a number of hybrid forms which are
more striking in appearance than the type. They
include 'Golden Queen', bright orange; 'Gold-
quelle', with buttercup-yellow flowers; and
'Orange Princess', with large orange-yellow
spheres. Early summer.

TROPAEOLUM
(Tropaeoleaceae)
An extensive group of hardy and slightly tender
annuals and perennials that includes the popular
nasturtium, *T. majus*, and the almost hardy canary
creeper, *T. canariensis*.
Cultural requirements: Nasturtiums: Any
ordinary garden soil and a sunny situation.

Canary creeper: Treat as a half-hardy annual,
giving it the protection of a wall or fence. It will
thrive in sun or partial shade.

Propagation: Nasturtiums: From seed outdoors
in spring where plants are to grow.

Canary creeper: From seed under glass in heat
in spring to produce plants to go out when
danger of frost is past, or sown *in situ*.

T. canariense up to 10 ft (3 m)   Peru
Pale green deeply lobed leaves and attractively
fringed yellow flowers.

T. majus varying heights up to 10 ft (3 m)
Nasturtium   Peru
Easy to grow annuals that succeed in almost any
soil conditions. The semi-double bush cultivars
are the most widely grown although the climbing
types are useful for covering banks, tree stumps,
etc. Popular among the bush varieties are the
'Gleam' hybrids, with sweetly scented flowers.
There are also some good dwarf kinds (*T. nanum*),
such as 'Tom Thumb' and 'Cherry Rose'. Summer.

T. speciosum up to 10 ft (3 m)
Chilean Flame Flower   Chile
A fast growing but slender climber best grown
through an evergreen shrub. The neat rounded
leaves are composed of several small leaflets.
Bright scarlet flowers appear near the stem tips
and are composed of stalked, rounded, and
waved petals. Summer to autumn.

TRUMPET VINE – see *Campsis*

TSUGA
(Pinaceae) Hemlock
Large evergreen coniferous trees of elegant habit,
pyramidal in shape with semi-weeping branches.

Tropaeolum majus Giant Climbing Mixed
(Nasturtium)

The foliage is rather like that of the yews.
Cultural requirements: Deep rich soil and an open situation.
Propagation: From seed outdoors in spring; by cuttings in a cold frame in autumn.

T. canadensis 90 ft (27 m)
Canadian Hemlock   Eastern N. America
Broadly spreading trees that fork low down. Tolerant of alkaline soil conditions and a valuable specimen conifer for large gardens.

T. heterophylla up to 200 ft (60 m)
Western Hemlock   Western N. America
An important timber tree that is now being widely planted for afforestation purposes. It also makes an attractive lawn specimen, conical in habit and fast growing.

TUBER

A fleshy underground stem with buds known as 'eyes', e.g., potato, or swollen roots which may or may not bear a few eyes at the top, e.g., dahlia.

TULIP – see *Tulipa*

TULIPA
(Liliaceae)

An extensive genus of popular spring flowering bulbous plants with kinds ranging in height from the early spring flowering species, less than 6 in. (15 cm) tall, to the stately early summer flowering hybrids at 2½ ft (75 cm). There are about 100 different species, of which some of the most popular, together with the hybrid cultivars, are dealt with below.
Cultural requirements: Any good garden soil rich in humus and a sunny open situation. Tulips can be naturalized in grass but do not respond as well as daffodils or crocuses to these conditions. Bulbs can be cultivated in pots or bowls, using John Innes No. 2 or a similar compost for the former purpose, bulb fibre for the latter. For cultural procedure, see Hyacinths.
Propagation: From seed in a cold frame in early spring; by offsets in late autumn.

T. clusiana 1 ft (30 cm)
Lady Tulip   Afghanistan and Persia
A graceful early-flowering species with narrow, grass-like leaves and white flowers vertically striped with crimson. Early spring.

T. fosteriana 2 ft (60 cm)   Turkestan
A species with very large scarlet blooms yellow at the base and up to 10 in. (25 cm) in diameter when fully open. There are several attractive named hybrids, including 'Golden Eagle', yellow and red; 'Mme Lefeber' (syn. 'Red Emperor'), vivid

scarlet; 'Purissima', white; and 'Tender Beauty', white and rosy-red. Spring.

T. greigii 2 ft (60 cm)   Turkestan
Large scarlet flowers with black or yellow base to petals. A distinctive feature and one passed on to many of its hybrids, is the vertical stripes of chocolate-brown on the leaves. Good named hybrids include 'Ali Baba', grey-green striped foliage and vermilion flowers; 'Red Riding Hood', scarlet; 'Segwun', salmon-pink and cream; and 'Trinket', lemon-yellow and red. Spring.

T. kaufmanniana 6 in. (15 cm)
Waterlily Tulip   C. Asia
These are among the earliest of the tulips to come into flower, the type plants having conical blooms of ivory and crimson, with a deep gold centre to the flowers when they open. There are various attractive hybrids such as 'Alfred Cortot', brilliant red with a black centre; 'Fritz Kreisler', coral-pink, ivory, and red; 'Stresa', scarlet, crimson, and gold; and 'The First', carmine, ivory, and gold. Early spring.

T. tarda (syn. *T. dasystemon*)
3–4 in. (8–10 cm)   Turkestan
A delightful dwarf species, suitable for the rock garden where it will naturalize itself if conditions are to its liking. The flowers are creamy-white, marked with bright yellow at the base of the petals. Early spring.

The hybrid tulips, of which there are numerous sorts, flowering from early spring to early summer, according to type, are too numerous to mention here individually. Reference to current bulb catalogues will give details of the cultivars at present in commerce.

TULIP TREE – see *Liriodendron tulipifera*

TUPELO – see *Nyssa sylvatica*

TYPHA
(Typhaceae) Cat Tail or Reed Mace

Hardy aquatic perennials, often incorrectly referred to as bulrushes.
Cultural requirements: Marshy ground, up to 6 in. (15 cm) deep in water. A situation in the shallows of ponds or rivers suits them well.
Propagation: By division in spring.

T. latifolia
8 ft (2·5 m)   Europe, including British Isles
This species has long reddish-brown velvety spikes that can be cut for winter arrangements. Summer.

T. minima 1½ ft (45 cm)   E. Europe
A dwarf species with smaller and neat oval brown spikes which cut equally well for similar purposes. Summer.

ULEX
(Leguminosae) Furze or Gorse
Hardy evergreen shrubs with very spiny foliage, flowering over many months and flourishing in the poorest soils.
Cultural requirements: Poor acid soil and a dry, hot, sunny situation.
Propagation: From seed outdoors in spring. The double form does not set seed and is increased by cuttings in a cold frame in late summer. Seedlings or cuttings should be pot-grown.

U. europaeus up to 6 ft (2 m)
        W. Europe, including British Isles
A dense spiny evergreen shrub with yellow pea flowers at almost all times of the year with the display reaching its peak in late spring and early summer. The more compact double form, 'Plenus', is particularly striking. Late spring to early summer.

U. gallii 2 ft (60 cm) Hedgehog Gorse
        W. Europe, including British Isles
This forms a dense spiny cushion spangled with yellow pea flowers in late summer. Late summer.

ULMUS
(Ulmaceae) Elm
Hardy deciduous trees with inconspicuous reddish flowers borne before the leaves appear. They are followed by green winged fruits. Although there are numerous species, those most commonly seen are the English, Dutch, and Wych elm. In recent years, the first named of these has fallen victim to the Dutch elm disease, a fungus disease spread by wood beetles. This has killed off practically all elms in some districts of Britain and is still spreading at the time of writing.
Cultural requirements: Fairly rich soil in good heart and a sunny situation.
Propagation: From seed outdoors in spring; by suckers or layers in autumn.

U. carpinifolia 90 ft (27 m)
      Europe, including British Isles, and N. Africa
A large and graceful tree, roughly pyramidal in habit with small glossy leaves. The hybrid *U.×sarniensis*, the so-called 'Jersey Elm', is conical in shape and has small leaves that colour to a vivid yellow in autumn and is being used as a

replacement planting for the disease-prone English elm. There is also a cultivar, 'Variegata', with leaves mottled with white.

U. glabra 100 ft (30 m) Wych Elm
        Europe, including British Isles, and Asia
A large tree, native to Britain, which is seen at its best in the weeping forms 'Camperdownii' or 'Pendula'. The leaves are large and rough and the greenish disc-like fruits are attractive in spring. The wych elms are among the finest deciduous trees for exposed situations in maritime areas.

U. procera up to 150 ft (45 m) English Elm
        W. Europe, including British Isles
Large and stately trees which, apart from the present difficulties with Dutch elm disease are among the finest deciduous trees for landscape effect. The toothed leaves turn a deep yellow before they fall. 'Argentovariegata' has leaves mottled with silver; 'Louis van Houtte' is a cultivar with golden-yellow foliage.

UMBEL
A type of inflorescence, normally flat-topped, in which all the flowers spring from the same point, e.g., polyanthus.

UMBRELLA PLANT
– see *Peltiphyllum peltatum*

URSINIA
(Compositae)
A genus of South African daisy-flowered half-hardy annuals.
Cultural requirements: Any ordinary garden soil and a sunny sheltered situation.
Propagation: From seed under glass in early spring or outdoors later where plants are to flower.

U. anethoides 1 ft (30 cm)   S. Africa
Vivid orange daisy-like flowers with a zone of chestnut-red at their centres. There are hybrid cultivars such as 'Sunshine Blend' with a wider colour range, including some self-colours. Summer.

U. pulchra (syn. *U. versicolor*)
9 in. (22 cm)   S. Africa
Orange daisy flowers with a darker centre. 'Golden Bedder', light orange with a darker orange centre, is a good form. Summer.

VACCINIUM
(Ericaceae)

Evergreen and deciduous ericaceous shrubs that include the bilberries, blueberries, and whortleberries. They are noteworthy for the colouring of their foliage in autumn.

Cultural requirements: Moist, peaty, lime-free soils and a shady or partly shaded situation.

Propagation: From seed in gentle heat under glass in spring; by cuttings, layers, or division.

V. arctostaphylos 9 ft (2·7 m)   Caucasus
Deciduous species with white waxy-textured lily-of-the-valley flowers followed by black berries. The leaves colour well in autumn. Summer.

V. corymbosum 6 ft (2 m)
Swamp Blueberry   N. America
A deciduous shrub of medium size with bright green leaves turning scarlet in autumn. The urn-shaped flowers are tinged with pink and are followed by large blue-black edible berries. Early summer.

V. myrtillus 1½ ft (45 cm)
Bilberry   Europe, including British Isles
The bilberry or whortleberry is native to Britain's heath and moorlands with bright green stems and small oval leaves. The blue-black berries that follow the small globular pink flowers are edible. A good ground cover plant for shade. Spring.

V. nummularia 1½ ft (45 cm)   Himalayas
Dwarf evergreen shrub with hairy stems and glossy green foliage. The flowers are pink and are borne in clusters, followed by edible black berries. A good foliage plant but rather tender for colder districts. Spring.

V. vitis-idaea 6 in. (15 cm)
Cowberry   N. America, Asia, and Europe
Prostrate evergreen shrub that makes good ground cover for shady places. Small box-like leaves; pink-tinged white flowers followed by red berries. Summer.

VALERIANA
(Valerianaceae)

Hardy herbaceous perennials, closely related to *Kentranthus*.

Cultural requirements: Any ordinary garden soil and a sunny situation.

Propagation: From seed outdoors in spring; by division in autumn.

V. phu 2 ft (60 cm) Cretan Spikenard   Caucasus
Useful border plants with white flowers. The golden-leaved form, 'Aurea', is particularly attractive in spring. Late summer.

V. saxatile 4 in. (10 cm)   Europe
Dwarf perennials with pale pink flowers, useful in the rock garden. Summer.

VALLOTA
(Amaryllidaceae) Scarborough Lily

Greenhouse bulbous plants that also make decorative house plants.

Cultural requirements: John Innes No. 2 or similar compost and a sunny situation. Minimum winter temperature 40 °F (4 °C).

Propagation: By offsets.

V. speciosa up to 3 ft (1 m)   S. Africa
Brilliant scarlet trumpet flowers, three or more to a 2 ft (60 cm) stem. Strap-shaped leaves. Autumn.

VARIETY

A distinct and usually true-breeding variant or form occurring naturally in a species.

VEGETABLES – see Kitchen Garden

VENIDIO-ARCTOTIS
(Compositae)

Bigeneric hybrids that are a cross between *Venidium* and *Arctotis*. They are tender perennials with showy and daisy-like flowers. Until recently, resulting crosses were sterile but strains have now been raised that will set viable seed. Colours include pink, orange, copper, and crimson. Summer.

VENIDIUM
(Compositae)

Half-hardy annuals and perennials. The latter are normally treated as half-hardy annuals.

Cultural requirements: Any ordinary garden soil and a sunny situation.

Propagation: From seed under glass in gentle heat in spring.

V. fastuosum 3 ft (1 m)
Monarch of the Veldt   S. Africa
Brilliant orange daisy flowers marked with jet

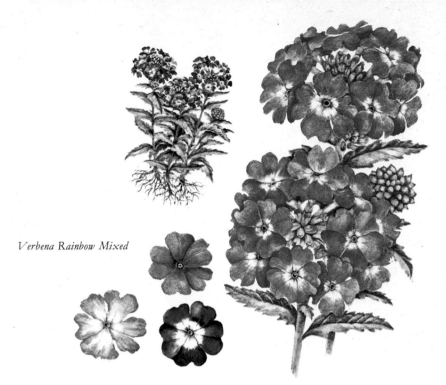

Verbena Rainbow Mixed

black at their centres and 4 in. (10 cm) or more across. Summer.

VERATRUM
(Liliaceae) False Hellebore
Hardy perennials with handsome foliage that make attractive plants for the wild garden.
Cultural requirements: Medium to heavy moist soil and a partly shaded situation.
Propagation: From seed under glass in early spring; by division in spring or autumn.

V. nigrum 4 ft (1·2 m)   Europe
Large and handsome dark green ribbed leaves and long pyramidal panicles of deep purple flowers. Summer.

V. viride 4 ft (1·2 m)   N. America
A species with large plantain-like leaves and clusters of greenish flowers. Summer.

VERBASCUM
(Scrophulariaceae) Mullein
Hardy biennials and perennials with tall spikes of bloom rising from a basal cluster of foliage. Some kinds seed themselves freely.
Cultural requirements: Any ordinary garden soil and a sunny situation.
Propagation: From seed outdoors in spring. Perennial species can also be increased by division or root cuttings.

V. bombyciferum (syn. *V. broussa*)
6 ft (2 m)   Europe
The leaves of this biennial species are thickly felted with white and the tall flower spikes are bright yellow. 'Arctic Summer' is an attractive form with flowers of a paler yellow. Early summer.

V. chaixii 3 ft (1 m)   S.W. Europe
A hairy-leaved short-lived perennial species with large branching spikes of yellow flowers. Summer.

V. dumulosum up to 1 ft (30 cm)   Asia Minor
Dwarf shrubby species with bright yellow flowers on short spikes. The flowers have a reddish eye. The plants need winter protection in wet cold areas and make excellent subjects for the alpine house. Summer.

In addition to the foregoing there are a number of hybrids of *V. phoeniceum* of great value in the herbaceous border. These include 'Cotswold Queen', apricot; 'Gainsborough', canary-yellow; and 'Pink Domino', rose-pink. Summer.

VERBENA
(Verbenaceae)
Half-hardy perennials, formerly popular as greenhouse pot plants but now widely grown as summer bedding plants with a long flowering season.
Cultural requirements: Any good garden soil and a sunny situation.

Propagation: The bedding hybrids are treated in a similar way to half-hardy annuals. Seed is sown in heat in early spring to produce plants to go out in early summer.

V. bonariensis 1½ ft (45 cm)   S. America
Attractive border plants with spikes of purple flowers that cut well. Summer to autumn.

V. peruviana 4 in. (10 cm)   S. America
A tender perennial that needs a sunny sheltered situation and overwintering in a warm greenhouse in colder districts. It is a prostrate species and the scarlet flowers are very striking.

V. rigida (syn. *V. venosa*) 1½ ft (45 cm) Argentine
A first rate bedding perennial with fleshy roots that, in colder districts, can be lifted and stored like those of dahlias. The showy violet-purple flowers are profusely borne over a very long period. Summer to autumn.

There are also many attractive hybrid cultivars, ideal for summer bedding. These include 'Amethyst', violet-blue; 'Delight', coral-pink; 'Firelight', scarlet; 'Sparkle', scarlet with a white eye; and 'Rainbow Mixture', with as wide a colour range as its name implies.

VERONICA
(Scrophulariaceae) Speedwell
Hardy perennials of great value in the border. The shrubby species are now classified as Hebe, q.v.
Cultural requirements: Any ordinary garden soil in good heart and a sunny situation.
Propagation: From seed outdoors in spring; by division in spring or autumn.

V. exaltata 5 ft (1·5 m)   Origin uncertain
Lavender-mauve flowers on tall erect stems. Narrow, toothed leaves. Late summer.

V. gentianoides 2 ft (60 cm)   Caucasus
Pale blue flowers in narrow spikes and glossy green basal foliage. Early summer.

V. prostrata (syn. *V. tenerium* and *V. rupestris*)
up to 8 in. (20 cm)   Europe and W. Asia
A lovely veronica for rock gardens, dry walls, or paving. The creeping mats of small leaves are massed with spikes of bright blue flowers. There are several good named cultivars, including 'Mrs Holt', with pink flowers; 'Shirley Blue', deep blue; and 'Trehane', an interesting form with pale blue flowers and golden foliage. Mid to late summer.

V. spicata up to 2 ft (60 cm)
     Europe, including British Isles
Dense spikes of pale blue flowers and narrow, toothed leaves. Named forms include 'Crater Lake Blue', ultramarine and 'Pavane', deep pink with grey foliage. Summer.

'Wendy' (2 ft – 60 cm) is an attractive hybrid with silver-grey foliage and slender erect spikes of blue flowers in late summer.

VIBURNUM
(Caprifoliaceae)
The viburnums are one of the most valuable groups of shrubs for garden decoration. The genus includes both evergreen and deciduous species and hybrids flowering at many different seasons. Several have attractive fruits.
Cultural requirements: Any kind of soil and for most, a sunny situation although some species are tolerant of partial shade.
Propagation: From cuttings of partly ripened wood under glass in late summer; by layers in autumn.

V. betulifolium 15 ft (4·5 m)   China
Large deciduous shrubs with clusters of creamy-white flowers followed by outsize bunches of scarlet translucent berries.

V. bitchiuense 8 ft (2·5 m)   Japan
A shrub of medium size, similar to *V. carlesii* but of looser and more open habit. Dark green foliage and clusters of fragrant pink flowers. Deciduous. Midsummer.

V. × *bodnantense* (*V. fragans* × *V. grandiflorum*)
8 ft (2·5 m)   Garden origin
Winter flowering deciduous species with clusters of white tubular flowers, pink tinged in bud and very fragrant. 'Dawn' is the best form. Winter to early spring.

V. × *burkwoodii* (*V. carlesii* × *V. utile*)
8 ft (2·5 m)   Garden origin
Evergreen or semi-evergreen shrub with dark lustrous foliage, felted with grey on reverse. The white richly scented flowers, pink in bud, are produced in large clusters. Spring.

V. carlcephalum (*V. carlesii* × *V. macrocephalum*)
8 ft (2·5 m)   Garden origin
Another splendid *carlesii* hybrid with larger heads of scented bloom and a vigorous habit of growth. Deciduous. Spring.

V. carlesii up to 6 ft (2 m)   Korea
A widely grown spring flowering shrub with attractive foliage and spherical clusters of pink-budded white flowers with a delicious clove fragrance. 'Aurora' and 'Diana' are selected forms of even greater beauty. Spring.

V. davidii up to 5 ft (1·5 m)   China
Compact evergreen species grown primarily for the beauty of its dark green glossy foliage, deeply etched with darker veins. If several specimens are planted, the small white flowers will be followed by turquoise-blue berries.

Viburnum tinus (Laurustinus)

Viola Choice Mixed

V. fragrans (syn. *V. farreri*)
up to 10 ft (3 m)   China
Slow growing deciduous species, and one of the most popular winter flowering shrubs. The clusters of white flowers, pink in bud, open in mild spells throughout the winter and are freely produced. Their fragrance is intense and will scent the air for a considerable distance around the plants on mild days in winter. Winter to early spring.

V. × *juddii* (*V. bitchiuense* × *V. carlesii*)
6 ft (2 m)   Garden origin
A medium-sized hybrid that is an improvement on both its parents. It is more vigorous and bushy than *V. carlesii*, with 3 in. (8 cm) clusters of white scented flowers, tinged with pink at the bud stage. Semi-evergreen. Spring.

V. lantana up to 15 ft (4.5 m)
Wayfaring Tree   Europe, including British Isles
Large deciduous shrub or small tree native to Britain and growing widely on chalky downlands. The creamy-white flower clusters are followed by crimson fruits which turn to black as they mature. The leaves often colour to a vinous purple in autumn. Early summer.

V. opulus sterilis up to 15 ft (4.5 m)
Guelder Rose   Europe, Asia, and N. Africa
A vigorous moisture loving deciduous shrub with lobed maple-like leaves that colour well in autumn. The flat-topped flower clusters are white and are followed by translucent red fruits. The best known form is the 'Snowball Bush', sterile, with globular flower heads, greenish-white in bud and opening to pure white. As its name implies, it bears no fruits. Midsummer.

V. plicatum 10 ft (3 m)
Japanese Snowball   China and Japan
This deciduous species has rounded heads of sterile florets produced along the branches. The botanical variety *tomentosum* is of great architectural value by reason of the layered structure of its branches. The double rows of creamy-white lace-cap flower clusters decorate the branches in the manner of a stylized Japanese painting. Fruits are red, turning to black. 'Lanarth' and 'Mariesii' are both excellent cultivars. Early summer.

V. rhytidophyllum 8 ft (2.5 m)
A vigorous evergreen shrub with large matt sage-green foliage deeply etched with darker veins. If more than one specimen is planted the loose

clusters of creamy-white flowers will be followed by oval red fruits that turn to black. Early summer.

V. tinus 10 ft (3 m) Laurustinus Mediterranean
One of the most popular evergreen shrubs. The flattened heads of bloom start to colour in autumn and reach their peak in late winter and early spring. It is a first rate hedging shrub that is tolerant of shade. 'Eve Price' and 'St Ewe' are cultivars superior to the type. Late winter to spring.

VINCA
(Apocynaceae) Periwinkle

The periwinkles are evergreen trailing shrubs that are widely used as ground cover plants.

Cultural requirements: Any ordinary garden soil and a sunny or shaded situation.

Propagation: By division or from rooted runners in spring.

V. difformis 1 ft (30 cm) S.W. Europe
Slightly tender species, with pale blue trumpet flowers and oval evergreen leaves. Useful for its winter flowers. Late autumn and winter.

V. major up to 2 ft (60 cm)
Europe, including British Isles
Very vigorous species with arching and trailing stems that root as they run. The oval leaves are dark green and glossy and the bright blue funnel-shaped flowers are borne in the leaf axils over a long period.

'Variegata' is a striking form, with leaves mottled with creamy-white. Spring to late summer.

V. minor
6 in. (15 cm) Europe, including British Isles
More prostrate and mat-forming than *V. major* but equally good as ground cover. The leaves of this species are smaller and narrower and the blue flowers on a correspondingly reduced scale. Among the named forms are a sky-blue double, 'Azurea Flore Pleno'; 'Gertrude Jekyll', a good white; 'Multiplex', plum-purple; and 'Variegata', with blue flowers and creamy-white variegated foliage. Spring to summer.

VINES – See *Vitis*

VIOLA
(Violaceae)

Hardy perennials that include pansies, violas or tufted pansies, and violets.

Cultural requirements: Any good garden soil rich in humus. Violets are grown in a shady border during summer and transplanted into sunny cold frames in September for winter flowers.

Propagation: From seed in a greenhouse or cold frame; by basal cuttings in a cold frame in late summer; by division in autumn.

V. cornuta 4 in. (10 cm) Horned Violet Pyrenees
Useful rock garden species with large violet flowers up to 1½ in. (4 cm) across. There are several attractive named forms, including 'Alba', white; 'Ardross Gem', blue and gold; and 'Northfield Gem', violet-purple. Late spring to summer.

V. gracilis 4 in. (10 cm) Asia Minor
This species forms large spreading clumps with masses of yellow-centred purple flowers over a very long period. 'Major' has larger flowers than the type. Summer.

V. odorata 4 in. (10 cm)
Sweet Violet Europe, including British Isles
The sweet violet is native to Britain's woods and hedgerows and is the parent of the larger flowered florists' hybrids including 'Violette de Parme' ('Parma Violet') and 'Princess of Wales'. Winter and spring.

V. tricolor 6 in. (15 cm)
Pansy Europe, including British Isles
Hardy perennials normally treated as biennials. The colour range is very wide and the flowers are large and velvety. There are many fine named cultivars, including the newer F_1 hybrids, 'Roggli Giants' and 'Engelmann's Giant', 'Westland Giant', and 'Swiss Giant'. Seed is also obtainable of self-colours. Late spring to summer.

V. × williamsii 4 in. (10 cm)
Violetta Garden origin
Hybrids of *V. cornuta* that make attractive small plants, massed with bloom over a long season.

Viola tricolor (Pansy)

There are several good named forms, including 'Buttercup', yellow; 'Lady Sackville', violet-purple; and 'Lorna', lavender-purple.

VIOLET – see *Viola odorata*

VIOLET CRESS – see *Ionopsidium acaule*

VIPER'S BUGLOSS – see *Echium*

VIRGINIAN COWSLIP – see *Mertensia*

VIRGINIAN STOCK – see *Malcolmia*

VIRUS DISEASES – see Diseases of Plants

VISCARIA – see *Lychnis*

VITIS
(Vitaceae) Vine

Climbing shrubs, some of which are grown for their grapes, others for their decorative value as climbers. A number of plants formerly under this heading are now classified as *Ampelopsis* but are included here for convenience.

Cultural requirements: Ornamental kinds: Any ordinary garden soil in good heart, enriched with well-rotted manure or compost and a sunny south or west wall.

Fruiting varieties under glass: A well-drained greenhouse border, enriched with bonemeal and well-rotted manure or compost. Good ventilation is essential.

Propagation: By cuttings in a cold frame or shady border in autumn.

V. brevipedunculata
(*Ampelopsis brevipedunculata*)   Asia
A vigorous climber with three-lobed heart-shaped leaves and small blue fruits in autumn.

'Tricolor' is an attractive form whose leaves are marbled with pink and white.

V. coignetiae Giant Vine   Japan
A magnificent climber with leaves measuring as much as 1 ft (30 cm) across and colouring brilliantly in autumn. The fruits are black, with a purple bloom.

V. henryana (*Parthenocissus henryana*)   China
An attractive, self-clinging climber less rampant than the virginian creepers and with three- to five-lobed leaves of green or bronze, veined with white and colouring magnificently in autumn.

V. inconstans
(*Parthenocissus tricuspidata*)   China and Japan
A vigorous self-clinging creeper often mistakenly referred to as virginian creeper and known in the U.S.A. as 'Boston Ivy'. It is one of the fastest climbers for covering house walls and like most other vines, colours magnificently in autumn. In the selected form 'Veitchii' (syn. *Ampelopsis tricuspidata* 'Veitchii'), the young leaves are tinged with purple.

V. quinquefolia
(*Parthenocissus quinquefolia*)   E. U.S.A.
This is the true virginian creeper. It is self-clinging and the five-lobed leaves, of a dull sage-green, colour brilliantly to orange and scarlet in autumn.

V. vinifera Grape   Asia Minor
This is the fruiting grape of which, however, several kinds are now grown primarily for their value as decorative wall climbers.

These include 'Incana', the 'Dusty Miller' grape, whose grey-green leaves are covered in a white farina; 'Brandt', a good outdoor fruiting vine with purple-black grapes and leaves that turn purple in autumn; and the 'Teinturier Grape', *V. vinifera* 'Purpurea', with deep red foliage turning a dark purple in autumn.

WALLFLOWER – see *Cheiranthus cheiri*

WAND FLOWER – see *Dierama pulcherrimum*

WATER GARDENS
Water is a great asset to any garden. Garden pools attract birds and give a refreshing sense of coolness on sweltering summer days. At one time, their construction entailed really hard work.

Nowadays, thanks to a wide choice of prefabricated plastic and fibreglass models, the 'instant' pool has become a practical proposition for anyone capable of digging a hole.

With such prefabricated pools, all that is required is a hole that conforms as closely as possible to the size and shape of the container. The latter is dropped in and there is a ready-made water feature.

This, of course, is over-simplifying the operation. The container will still have to be firmly bedded down into position, filled with water and stocked with suitable plants and livestock.

Fibreglass pools are normally guaranteed for ten years against damage by frost or ice. They are pre-moulded to provide varying water levels, to allow for the planting of bog and moisture loving plants in the shallower areas around their edges. The deeper water at the centre will accommodate water-lilies and other bottom-rooting aquatic plants.

Larger pools can be constructed from reinforced PVC sheeting or from the stronger and longer lasting plastic sheeting specially manufactured for the purpose. The latter material is guaranteed for ten years but with reasonable care and regular maintenance it should last much longer.

Installation is a simple matter. The lining material will take the shape of the hole and is held in position by the weight of the water. A flap, 2 ft (60 cm) wide, should be left all round at surface level so that the sheeting can be anchored with paving slabs or bricks.

To calculate the amount of lining material needed, twice the depth is added to the overall length to arrive at the length and the same with the breadth to calculate the required width. It is not necessary to make any allowance for the overlap since the elasticity of the material will take care of this.

The hole for the pool site is excavated to a depth of between 1½ ft (45 cm) and 2 ft (60 cm). The sides of this hole should slope gently outwards with a shallow shelf, about 4 in. (10 cm) deep at the edges. This will permit the cultivation of marginal and bog plants. When digging is completed, stones and any other material that might pierce the sheeting must be removed.

The surface of the excavated area is then covered with a thin layer of sand to provide a reasonably flat surface for the liner to rest on. The liner is then placed over the hole, stretched fairly taut and held temporarily in position with heavy stones or bricks.

The pool can then be filled with water. The weight of the water will stretch the plastic and mould it to the contours of the hole. All that remains to be done is to trim off any surplus sheeting at the edges and cover with the bricks or paving slabs.

If more elaborate water features are required the attraction of the pools described can be enhanced by fountains and cascades operated by a submersible electric pump.

There will, of course, be the problem of disposing of the spoil from the excavation. This can be used for levelling up any low-lying areas in the garden or failing this, can be used to create a rock garden, either at the poolside or in some other part of the garden.

Stocking the Pool

Once the construction work is finished, the pool will need stocking with plants and fish. Since pure water is essential to both, the first thing necessary is to provide it with plants that oxygenate the water and keep it clean and sweet for plant and fish life. As well as the floating and submerged oxygenators, there are three other types of water plant – moisture lovers for the damp margins, bog plants for the swamp areas, and aquatics for the deeper water.

Water-lilies should be chosen with the area of the pool in mind. The larger species and cultivars soon cover broad expanses of water and are suitable only for lakes or large ponds, but there are a number of dwarf kinds, some of which will thrive even in a tub of water. These are ideal for the small garden pool.

Other types of water plants are dealt with in the appropriate sections of the text.

WATER HAWTHORN
– see *Aponogeton distachyus*

WATER LILY – see *Nymphaea*

WAX PLANT – see *Hoya carnosa*

WAYFARING TREE – see *Viburnum lantana*

WEED CONTROL

In spite of the great strides made in the development of modern weedkillers, there are still some garden conditions in which their use is impracticable without danger to growing plants. Examples of these are in the rock garden and in summer bedding schemes.

The only effective way of keeping such areas of the garden weed-free is by a combination of chemical control, hoeing, and hand-weeding. For the rock garden, the short-handled onion hoe is an ideal tool for the job. Where larger areas are involved there is a wide choice of hoes, including many newer designs that break away completely from the traditional Dutch push hoe and the swan-necked draw type.

Whatever kind of hoe is used, the object of the exercise should be to slice off the weeds just below the surface of the soil. The best time for carrying out hoeing operations is during spells of dry weather, when the soil surface is crumbly and the weeds have less chance of survival.

Modern weedkillers act in a variety of ways; it is essential, therefore, to choose the kind most suited to the job in hand. Some will make a clean sweep of both weeds and garden plants, others are more selective and will kill off certain types of plant without harming others.

Some, too, have long-term effects and will continue to be deadly to plant life for many months. Ground that has been treated with these will need to lie fallow for six months or more, until the toxic properties of the weedkiller have been dissipated. This is where the newer kinds based on the chemical paraquat, are so useful. This enters plants through their leaves and stems but is rendered inactive as soon as it comes into contact with the soil. This is an ideal way of dealing with weeds in rose beds and under shrubs and fruit trees and bushes.

Sodium chlorate is one of the oldest and best known of the persistent weedkillers. It is the perfect answer to weeds on paths, drives, and paving and can be applied either dry or in solution at the rate of 2–4 oz. to a gallon (12–25 g per litre) of water.

It can, however, be dangerous to use. If applied too generously, rain can wash it into neighbouring beds and borders in which case it can get rid of more than weeds.

Science has provided us with an imposing range of chemicals for use in the war against lawn weeds. Selective weedkillers are marketed under a number of different brand names but most are based on three chemicals, fortified with mecoprop to take care of the more highly resistant clover.

These are obtainable in liquid or powder form. The latter are easier to apply and are often suplied mixed with a lawn fertilizer that stimulates the growth of the grass and ensures that it fills in bare patches more quickly where weeds have died.

Wind drift is one of the biggest hazards where these chemicals are being used. With the liquid kinds, it is best to use a watering-can equipped with what is known as a dribble bar. This produces sizeable droplets that are not easily dispersed by wind on to neighbouring beds and borders.

Distribution of powdered lawn weedkillers is best carried out by means of a wheeled or hand spreader. Great care, too, should be taken to make sure that any containers used for weedkillers are thoroughly washed out after use.

This applies particularly to the persistent weedkillers of which a very weak solution can cause serious damage especially to plants that are unduly sensitive.

WEIGELA
(Caprifoliaceae)
Hardy deciduous flowering shrubs, formerly included under the generic name *Diervilla*.

Cultural requirements: Any ordinary garden soil rich in humus and a sunny or partly shaded situation.
Propagation: By softwood cuttings under glass in spring; by cuttings of ripened wood in a shady border in autumn.

W. florida 8 ft (2·5 m) China and Japan
This species, together with various cultivars and hybrids, is the one most commonly seen in our gardens. The type plant has rose-pink funnel-shaped flowers and there is a delightful form, 'Variegata', grown for its foliage, having leaves edged with creamy-white and strawberry-pink flowers.

Among the best known cultivars and hybrids are 'Abel Carrière', rose-carmine; 'Eva Rathke', crimson-red; 'Mont Blanc', white; and 'Newport Red', a lighter red than 'Eva Rathke'. Early to midsummer.

WILLOW – see *Salix*

WINTER ACONITE – see *Eranthis*

WINTER BARK – see *Drimys winteri*

WINTER CHERRY
– see *Solanum capsicastrum*

WINTER HELIOTROPE
– see *Petasites fragrans*

WINTERSWEET – see *Chimonanthus praecox*

WIRE NETTING BUSH
– see *Corokia cotoneaster*

WIREWORMS – see Pest Control

WISTERIA
(Leguminosae)
Hardy deciduous climbing flowering shrubs that cling by twining stems and are spectacularly beautiful when in flower. They have pinnate foliage and long racemes of scented pea flowers.
Cultural requirements: Any garden soil in good heart and rich in humus. A position in full sun is essential and they make ideal plants for a south or west wall, for sunny pergolas, or for scrambling through the branches of old trees.
Propagation: From seeds in spring or layers in spring or summer.

W. floribunda up to 20 ft (6 m) Japan
The finely divided pinnate foliage of this species consists of up to ten leaflets. The violet-blue flower spikes which are borne lavishly, measure

up to 1 ft (30 cm) in length. The form 'Macro-botrys' is even more striking with lilac tassel-like flowers as much as 3 ft (1 m) in length. Other attractive cultivars include 'Alba', white; 'Rosea', pale rose-pink; and 'Violacea Plena', a double form with violet-blue flowers. Early summer.

W. sinensis up to 50 ft (15 m)　　　　China
This is the most popular and widely grown species with spicily fragrant mauve tassels up to 1 ft (30 cm) long that first appear before the leaves unfurl. 'Alba', white; 'Black Dragon', deep purple; and 'Plena', double lilac are interesting variations on the type. Early summer.

WITCH HAZEL – see *Hamamelis mollis*

WOOD OLIVE – see *Elaeagnus*

WOOD RUSH – see *Luzula*

WOOD SORREL – see *Oxalis*

WOODBINE – see *Lonicera*

WOODRUFF – see *Asperula*

WORMWOOD – see *Artemisia abrotanum*

XERANTHEMUM
(Compositae)
Hardy annuals with single and double 'ever-lasting' flowers, useful in winter arrangements.
Cultural requirements: Any ordinary garden soil and a sunny open situation.

Propagation: From seed outdoors in spring where plants are to flower.

X. annuum 2 ft (60 cm)　　　　S. Europe
Single and double purple flowers that should be picked and dried as soon as they are fully open. 'Amethyst' is a good double form. Summer.

YARROW – see *Achillea*

YEW – see *Taxus*

YUCCA
(Liliaceae)
Hardy and tender evergreen shrubs with rosettes of broadsword leaves and magnificent flower spikes of exotic appearance.
Cultural requirements: Hardy species: Ordinary, well-drained soil and a sunny situation.
Propagation: By offsets or root cuttings in spring.

Y. filamentosa up to 6 ft (2 m)　　S.E. U.S.A.
Clumps of spreading sword-like foliage of bluish-green edged with white, thread-like filaments. The creamy-white bell flowers are borne in handsome erect spikes, up to 6 ft (2 m) in height. Late summer.

Y. flaccida up to 4 ft (1·2 m)　　S.E. U.S.A.
Similar to the above species, but slightly hardier. 'Ivory', with green-tinged creamy-white flowers, is the best form. Late summer.

Y. gloriosa up to 8 ft (2·5 m)
Adam's Needle　　　　　　　S.E. U.S.A.
A handsome species whose leaf clusters are borne on stout erect trunks. The leaves are broad, stiff, and spine-tipped and the creamy-white flowers are borne in 6 ft (2 m) spikes. Late summer to autumn.

Y. recurvifolia 6 ft (2 m)　　　　S.E. U.S.A.
This is one of the hardiest species, with leaves up to 3 ft (1 m) long curving downwards at their tips. Mature plants develop stout, trunk-like stems. The creamy-white flowers are borne in close-packed panicles, up to 3 ft (1 m) in height. Late summer.

ZANTEDESCHIA
(Araceae) Arum Lily

Rhizomatous perennials for the cool greenhouse, hardy outdoors in favoured districts.

Cultural requirements: Under glass: John Innes No. 2 or similar compost.

Outdoors: Rich moist soil and, for preference, a waterside situation.

Propagation: From seed under glass in heat in spring; by division or from offsets.

Z. aethiopica (syn. *Richardia africana*)
3 ft (1 m)   S. Africa
The well known arum or calla lily, with large white spathes and a central yellow spadix has wide religious associations. 'Crowborough' is a form that is hardier and that needs less moisture than the type. Spring.

ZAUSCHNERIA
(Onagraceae)

Half-hardy perennials or sub-shrubs of spreading habit.

Cultural requirements: Well-drained soil and a sunny situation. Cuttings should be over-wintered in a greenhouse or frame to replace losses in hard winters.

Propagation: From seed under glass in spring to provide plants to go outdoors later; by cuttings in a shady border in early autumn.

Z. californica 9 in. (22 cm)
Californian Fuchsia   California
Dense clumps of grey foliage with scarlet tubular flowers, useful in the rock garden. Late summer.

Z. cana 2 ft (60 cm)   California
This differs from the former species in having

Zinnia Mammoth Mixed

narrow leaves. The flowers are similar. Late summer.

ZEBRINA
(Commelinaceae) Wandering Jew

Evergreen trailing plants for the warm greenhouse that also make good house plants. They are closely allied to the tradescantias.

Cultural requirements: John Innes No. 2 or similar compost. Water freely in summer and autumn, more sparingly for rest of year. Minimum temperature 40 °F (4 °C).

Propagation: From tip cuttings of young stems at any time.

Z. pendula (syn. *Tradescantia zebrina*)
Wandering Jew   Mexico

Trailing plants with leaves striped with silver and purple. The variety *quadricolor* has foliage striped with red and white. Small, three-petalled flowers, white, with pink tips, appear on old plants. Summer to autumn.

ZEPHYRANTES
(Amaryllidaceae)

Hardy and half-hardy bulbous plants with narrow grass-like foliage and flowers like those of a crocus.

Cultural requirements: Light sandy soil, rich in humus, and a position at the foot of a south or west wall.

Propagation: By offsets in late summer.

Z. candida 1 ft (30 cm)   S. America

The white, crocus-like flowers are green-tinged at the base of the petals. In a warm sheltered border they will freely naturalize themselves. Autumn.

ZINNIA
(Compositae)

Popular half-hardy annuals widely grown for summer bedding.

Cultural requirements: Deep rich soil with plenty of well-rotted manure or compost; a sunny situation.

Propagation: From seed in gentle heat under glass in spring or outdoors later where plants are to flower.

Z. elegans up to 3 ft (1 m)   Mexico

The flowers have a colour range that includes lilac, red, rose-pink, buff, and creamy-white. Summer to autumn.

Z. haageana 1 ft (30 cm)   Mexico

Small single golden-yellow or orange-scarlet flowers. There are many different strains and hybrids of the above-mentioned species. These include giant flowered, chrysanthemum-flowered, pompons, and dwarfs as well as some outstanding F_1 hybrids of which the 'Peter Pan' strains are a good example. 'Envy' is a large flowered zinnia, chartreuse-green in colour, that is a great favourite with flower arrangers. 'Lilliput' is compact and dwarf with a wide colour range of double flowers. Summer to autumn.

ZYGOCACTUS
(Cactaceae)

Succulent greenhouse plants that double as easy to grow room plants.

Cultural requirements: John Innes No. 2 or a proprietary cactus compost and a sunny greenhouse shelf or window-ledge. Minimum winter temperature 50 °F (10 °C).

Propagation: By cuttings of stem sections in sandy soil in spring or summer.

Z. truncatus up to 1 ft (30 cm)
Christmas Cactus   Brazil

The carmine-red flowers appear at the tips of the flattened leaf-like stems. Winter.

Carters
Book for Gardeners

A. G. L. Hellyer
M.B.E., F.L.S., V.M.H., A.H.R.H.S.

Published in collaboration with Carters Tested Seeds Ltd, here is a book of universal appeal. Beginners, as well as the more experienced; those with small, medium, or large gardens; people who enjoy growing house plants; in fact, all who garden as a hobby will gain a great deal from this wise and practical book.

The author, who has a string of best-sellers to his name, presents simply but thoroughly all the facts the gardener needs in dealing with:

Planning	Rock and water features
Lawns and pavings	Greenhouse and frame
Screens and hedges	Vegetables
Annuals and bedding plants	Herb beds
Bulbs, corms, and tubers	Fruit
Hardy plants	Feeding plants
Roses	Keeping plants healthy
Shrubs and climbers	Weed control
Trees	

Extensive colour illustrations enhance the text in every chapter, many of which have also quick-reference tables to guide the reader in successfully growing a great range of plants, shrubs, and trees.

Practical work in the garden is made clear with a series of drawings specially commissioned from Mike Taylor, all in full colour. Dimensions are given in metric units as well as the more familiar English ones so that the text is intelligible to the widest audience here and abroad.

A. G. L. Hellyer. It is no exaggeration to describe Arthur Hellyer as the doyen of writers on gardening. In addition to being the author of numerous books, he has edited *Amateur Gardening* (1946–67), *Gardening Illustrated* (1947–56), and he is the gardening correspondent of *The Financial Times*. He writes from extensive practical experience, being the owner of two gardens himself: one on heavy land in a frost pocket in Sussex and the other in a dry, sunny quarry in Jersey.

160 pp. 235 × 155 mm/186 colour photographs/104 line drawings/tables/index/SBN 434 90725 1

Carters
Book for the Casual Gardener

Jim Mather

Most of us can't spare as much time as we would like on our gardens. The author tells us not only how to make the best use of our limited time but also how to enjoy it. He shows us how to run a garden so that it is no longer a drudgery.

Jim Mather provides much helpful advice on the easiest way to start a garden from scratch, planning ahead and introducing additional features when time permits. He has useful suggestions to offer on planting and tending lawns and hedges; which bulbs, roses, annuals, and biennials involve the least work; how to construct and maintain garden pools and rock gardens; the simple cultivation of fruit and vegetables, indoor and greenhouse plants; and he gives advice on propagation, chemical aids, and equipment. All these aspects of gardening are lavishly illustrated.

In short, this book will help all those who feel that their gardens get the better of them and those who want a good show of colour and plenty of fresh vegetables for the least amount of effort.

Jim Mather has been Gardening Editor of *The Sunday Mirror* since 1960, and was also for a time Editor of *The Greenhouse*. He cultivates over 12 acres at his home in rural Surrey, where he maintains a large experimental garden, trial plots, and orchard. He was awarded the Emergency Reserve Decoration for military service in peace and war.

160 pp. 235 × 155 mm/157 colour and 19 black and white photographs/4 garden plans/index/ SBN 434 91237 9